THE
Expositor's Bible Commentary

with The New International Version

1, 2 CORINTHIANS

THE
Expositor's Bible Commentary

with The New International Version

1, 2 CORINTHIANS

W. Harold Mare
Murray J. Harris

ZondervanPublishingHouse
Grand Rapids, Michigan

A Division of HarperCollinsPublishers

General Editor:

FRANK E. GAEBELEIN
Former Headmaster, Stony Brook School
Former Coeditor, *Christianity Today*

Associate Editors:

J. D. DOUGLAS
Editor, *The New International
Dictionary of the Christian Church*

RICHARD P. POLCYN

---

1 and 2 Corinthians
Copyright © 1995 by W. Harold Mare and Murray J. Harris

Requests for information should be addressed to:
Zondervan Publishing House
Grand Rapids, Michigan 49530

Library of Congress Cataloging-in-Publication Data

The expositor's Bible commentary : with the New International Version of the Holy Bible /
   Frank E. Gaebelein, general editor of series.
      p.   cm.
   Includes bibliographical references and index.
      Contents: v. 1–2. Matthew / D. A. Carson —   Mark / Walter W. Wessel — Luke / Walter
   L. Liefeld — John / Merrill C. Tenney—Acts / Richard N. Longenecker — Romans / Everett
   F. Harrison — 1 and 2 Corinthians / W. Harold Mare and Murray J. Harris — Galatians and
   Ephesians / James Montgomery Boice and A. Skevington Wood
      ISBN: 0-310-20110-1(softcover)
      1. Bible N.T.—Commentaries. I. Gaebelein, Frank Ely, 1899–1983.
   BS2341.2.E96 1995
   220.7-dc 00   94-47450
                                                                                           CIP

Printed in the United States of America

95 96 97 98 99 00 / ❖ DH / 10 9 8 7 6 5 4 3 2 1

CONTENTS

PREFACE

The title of this work defines its purpose. Written primarily by expositors for expositors, it aims to provide preachers, teachers, and students of the Bible with a new and comprehensive commentary on the books of the Old and New Testaments. Its stance is that of a scholarly evangelicalism committed to the divine inspiration, complete trustworthiness, and full authority of the Bible. Its seventy-eight contributors come from the United States, Canada, England, Scotland, Australia, New Zealand, and Switzerland, and from various religious groups, including Anglican, Baptist, Brethren, Free, Independent, Methodist, Nazarene, Presbyterian, and Reformed churches. Most of them teach at colleges, universities, or theological seminaries.

No book has been more closely studied over a longer period of time than the Bible. From the Midrashic commentaries going back to the period of Ezra, through parts of the Dead Sea Scrolls and the Patristic literature, and on to the present, the Scriptures have been expounded. Indeed, there have been times when, as in the Reformation and on occasions since then, exposition has been at the cutting edge of Christian advance. Luther was a powerful exegete, and Calvin is still called "the prince of expositors."

Their successors have been many. And now, when the outburst of new translations and their unparalleled circulation have expanded the readership of the Bible, the need for exposition takes on fresh urgency.

Not that God's Word can ever become captive to its expositors. Among all other books, it stands first in its combination of perspicuity and profundity. Though a child can be made "wise for salvation" by believing its witness to Christ, the greatest mind cannot plumb the depths of its truth (2 Tim. 3:15; Rom. 11:33). As Gregory the Great said, "Holy Scripture is a stream of running water, where alike the elephant may swim, and the lamb walk." So, because of the inexhaustible nature of Scripture, the task of opening up its meaning is still a perennial obligation of biblical scholarship.

How that task is done inevitably reflects the outlook of those engaged in it. Every Bible scholar has presuppositions. To this neither the editors of these volumes nor the contributors to them are exceptions. They share a common commitment to the supernatural Christianity set forth in the inspired Word. Their purpose is not to supplant the many valuable commentaries that have preceded this work and from which both the editors and contributors have learned. It is rather to draw on the resources of contemporary evangelical scholarship in producing a new reference work for understanding the Scriptures.

A commentary that will continue to be useful through the years should handle contemporary trends in biblical studies in such a way as to avoid becoming outdated when critical fashions change. Biblical criticism is not in itself inadmissable, as some have mistakenly thought. When scholars investigate the authorship, date, literary characteristics, and purpose of a biblical document, they are practicing biblical criticism. So also when, in order to ascertain as nearly as possible the original form of the text, they deal with variant readings, scribal errors, emendations, and other phenomena in the manuscripts. To do these things is essential to responsible exegesis and exposition. And always there is the need to distinguish hypothesis from fact, conjecture from truth.

The chief principle of interpretation followed in this commentary is the grammatico-historical one—namely, that the primary aim of the exegete is to make clear the meaning of the text at the time and in the circumstances of its writing. This endeavor to understand what in the first instance the inspired writers actually said must not be confused with an inflexible literalism. Scripture makes lavish use of symbols and figures of speech; great portions of it are poetical. Yet when it speaks in this way, it speaks no less truly than it does in its historical and doctrinal portions. To understand its message requires attention to matters of grammar and syntax, word meanings, idioms, and literary forms—all in relation to the historical and cultural setting of the text.

The contributors to this work necessarily reflect varying convictions. In certain controversial matters the policy is that of clear statement of the contributors' own views followed by fair presentation of other ones. The treatment of eschatology, though it reflects differences of interpretation, is consistent with a general premillennial position. (Not all contributors, however, are premillennial.) But prophecy is more than prediction, and so this commentary gives due recognition to the major lode of godly social concern in the prophetic writings.

THE EXPOSITOR'S BIBLE COMMENTARY is presented as a scholarly work, though not primarily one of technical criticism. In its main portion, the Exposition, and in Volume 1 (General and Special Articles), all Semitic and Greek words are transliterated and the English equivalents given. As for the Notes, here Semitic and Greek characters are used but always with transliterations and English meanings, so that this portion of the commentary will be as accessible as possible to readers unacquainted with the original languages.

It is the conviction of the general editor, shared by his colleagues in the Zondervan editorial department, that in writing about the Bible, lucidity is not incompatible with scholarship. They are therefore endeavoring to make this a clear and understandable work.

The translation used in it is the New International Version (North American Edition). To the International Bible Society thanks are due for permission to use this most recent of the major Bible translations. It was chosen because of the clarity and beauty of its style and its faithfulness to the original texts.

To the associate editor, Richard P. Polcyn, and to the contributing editors—Dr. Walter C. Kaiser, Jr., Dr. Bruce K. Waltke, and Dr. Ralph H. Alexander for the Old Testament, and Dr. James Montgomery Boice and Dr. Merrill C. Tenney for the New Testament—the general editor expresses his gratitude for their unfailing cooperation and their generosity in advising him out of their expert scholarship. And to the many other contributors he is indebted for their invaluable part in this work. Finally, he owes a special debt of gratitude to Dr. Robert K. DeVries, publisher, The Zondervan Corporation, and Miss Elizabeth Brown, secretary, for their assistance and encouragement.

Whatever else it is—the greatest and most beautiful of books, the primary source of law and morality, the fountain of wisdom, and the infallible guide to life—the Bible is above all the inspired witness to Jesus Christ. May this work fulfill its function of expounding the Scriptures with grace and clarity, so that its users may find that both Old and New Testaments do indeed lead to our Lord Jesus Christ, who alone could say, "I have come that they may have life, and have it to the full" (John 10:10).

FRANK E. GAEBELEIN

ABBREVIATIONS

A. General Abbreviations

A	Codex Alexandrinus	Nestle	Nestle (ed.) *Novum Testamentum Graece*
Akkad.	Akkadian		
ℵ	Codex Sinaiticus	no.	number
Ap. Lit.	Apocalyptic Literature	NT	New Testament
Apoc.	Apocrypha	obs.	obsolete
Aq.	Aquila's Greek Translation of the Old Testament	OL	Old Latin
		OS	Old Syriac
Arab.	Arabic	OT	Old Testament
Aram.	Aramaic	p., pp.	page, pages
b	Babylonian Gemara	par.	paragraph
B	Codex Vaticanus	Pers.	Persian
C	Codex Ephraemi Syri	Pesh.	Peshitta
c.	*circa*, about	Phoen.	Phoenician
cf.	*confer*, compare	pl.	plural
ch., chs.	chapter, chapters	Pseudep.	Pseudepigrapha
cod., codd.	codex, codices	Q	Quelle ("Sayings" source in the Gospels)
D	Codex Bezae		
DSS	Dead Sea Scrolls (see E.)	qt.	quoted by
ed., edd.	edited, edition, editor; editions	q.v.	*quod vide*, which see
e.g.	*exempli gratia*, for example	R	Rabbah
Egyp.	Egyptian	rev.	revised, reviser, revision
et al.	*et alii*, and others	Rom.	Roman
EV	English Versions of the Bible	RVm	Revised Version margin
fem.	feminine	Samar.	Samaritan recension
ff.	following (verses, pages, etc.)	SCM	Student Christian Movement Press
fl.	flourished	Sem.	Semitic
ft.	foot, feet	sing.	singular
gen.	genitive	SPCK	Society for the Promotion of Christian Knowledge
Gr.	Greek		
Heb.	Hebrew	Sumer.	Sumerian
Hitt.	Hittite	s.v.	*sub verbo*, under the word
ibid.	*ibidem*, in the same place	Syr.	Syriac
id.	*idem*, the same	Symm.	Symmachus
i.e.	*id est*, that is	T	Talmud
impf.	imperfect	Targ.	Targum
infra.	below	Theod.	Theodotion
in loc.	*in loco*, in the place cited	TR	Textus Receptus
j	Jerusalem or Palestinian Gemara	tr.	translation, translator, translated
Lat.	Latin	UBS	Tha United Bible Societies' Greek Text
LL.	Late Latin		
LXX	Septuagint	Ugar.	Ugaritic
M	Mishnah	u.s.	*ut supra*, as above
masc.	masculine	v., vv.	verse, verses
mg.	margin	viz.	*videlicet*, namely
Mid	Midrash	vol.	volume
MS(S)	manuscript(s)	vs.	versus
MT	Masoretic text	Vul.	Vulgate
n.	note	WH	Westcott and Hort, *The New Testament in Greek*
n.d.	no date		

B. Abbreviations for Modern Translations and Paraphrases

AmT	Smith and Goodspeed, *The Complete Bible, An American Translation*	Mof	J. Moffatt, *A New Translation of the Bible*
ASV	American Standard Version, American Revised Version (1901)	NAB	The New American Bible
		NASB	New American Standard Bible
		NEB	The New English Bible
		NIV	The New International Version
Beck	Beck, *The New Testament in the Language of Today*	Ph	J. B. Phillips *The New Testament in Modern English*
BV	Berkeley Version (The Modern Language Bible)	RSV	Revised Standard Version
		RV	Revised Version — 1881–1885
JB	The Jerusalem Bible	TCNT	Twentieth Century New Testament
JPS	*Jewish Publication Society Version of the Old Testament*	TEV	Today's English Version
KJV	King James Version	Wey	*Weymouth's New Testament in Modern Speech*
Knox	R.G. Knox, *The Holy Bible: A Translation from the Latin Vulgate in the Light of the Hebrew and Greek Original*	Wms	C. B. Williams, *The New Testament: A Translation in the Language of the People*
LB	The Living Bible		

C. Abbreviations for Periodicals and Reference Works

AASOR	*Annual of the American Schools of Oriental Research*	BASOR	*Bulletin of the American Schools of Oriental Research*
AB	*Anchor Bible*	BC	Foakes-Jackson and Lake: *The Beginnings of Christianity*
AIs	de Vaux: *Ancient Israel*		
AJA	*American Journal of Archaeology*	BDB	Brown, Driver, and Briggs: *Hebrew-English Lexicon of the Old Testament*
AJSL	*American Journal of Semitic Languages and Literatures*	BDF	Blass, Debrunner, and Funk: *A Greek Grammar of the New Testament and Other Early Christian Literature*
AJT	*American Journal of Theology*		
Alf	Alford: *Greek Testament Commentary*	BDT	Harrison: *Baker's Dictionary of Theology*
ANEA	*Ancient Near Eastern Archaeology*	Beng.	Bengel's *Gnomon*
ANEP	Pritchard: *Ancient Near Eastern Pictures*	BETS	*Bulletin of the Evangelical Theological Society*
ANET	Pritchard· *Ancient Near Eastern Texts*	BH	*Biblia Hebraica*
		BHS	*Biblia Hebraica Stuttgartensia*
ANF	Roberts and Donaldson: *The Ante-Nicene Fathers*	BJRL	*Bulletin of the John Rylands Library*
A-S	Abbot-Smith: *Manual Greek Lexicon of the New Testament*	BS	*Bibliotheca Sacra*
		BT	*Babylonian Talmud*
AThR	*Anglican Theological Review*	BTh	*Biblical Theology*
BA	*Biblical Archaeologist*	BW	*Biblical World*
BAG	Bauer, Arndt, and Gingrich: *Greek-English Lexicon of the New Testament*	CAH	*Cambridge Ancient History*
		CanJTh	*Canadian Journal of Theology*
		CBQ	*Catholic Biblical Quarterly*
BAGD	Bauer, Arndt, Gingrich, and Danker: *Greek-English Lexicon of the New Testament* 2nd edition	CBSC	*Cambridge Bible for Schools and Colleges*
		CE	*Catholic Encyclopedia*
		CGT	*Cambridge Greek Testament*

CHS	Lange: *Commentary on the Holy Scriptures*	IDB	*The Interpreter's Dictionary of the Bible*
ChT	*Christianity Today*	IEJ	*Israel Exploration Journal*
DDB	*Davis' Dictionary of the Bible*	Int	*Interpretation*
Deiss BS	Deissmann: *Bible Studies*	INT	E. Harrison: *Introduction to the New Testament*
Deiss LAE	Deissmann: *Light From the Ancient East*	IOT	R. K. Harrison: *Introduction to the Old Testament*
DNTT	*Dictionary of New Testament Theology*	ISBE	*The International Standard Bible Encyclopedia*
EBC	*The Expositor's Bible Commentary*	ITQ	*Irish Theological Quarterly*
EBi	*Encyclopaedia Biblica*	JAAR	*Journal of American Academy of Religion*
EBr	*Encyclopaedia Britannica*		
EDB	*Encyclopedic Dictionary of the Bible*	JAOS	*Journal of American Oriental Society*
EGT	Nicoll: *Expositor's Greek Testament*	JBL	*Journal of Biblical Literature*
EQ	*Evangelical Quarterly*	JE	*Jewish Encyclopedia*
ET	*Evangelische Theologie*	JETS	*Journal of Evangelical Theological Society*
ExB	*The Expositor's Bible*		
Exp	*The Expositor*	JFB	Jamieson, Fausset, and Brown: *Commentary on the Old and New Testament*
ExpT	*The Expository Times*		
FLAP	Finegan: *Light From the Ancient Past*		
GKC	Gesenius, Kautzsch, Cowley, *Hebrew Grammar*, 2nd Eng. ed.	JNES	*Journal of Near Eastern Studies*
		Jos. Antiq.	Josephus: *The Antiquities of the Jews*
GR	*Gordon Review*	Jos. War	Josephus: *The Jewish War*
HBD	*Harper's Bible Dictionary*	JQR	*Jewish Quarterly Review*
HDAC	Hastings: *Dictionary of the Apostolic Church*	JR	*Journal of Religion*
		JSJ	*Journal for the Study of Judaism in the Persian, Hellenistic and Roman Periods*
HDB	Hastings: *Dictionary of the Bible*		
HDBrev.	Hastings: *Dictionary of the Bible*, one-vol. rev. by Grant and Rowley	JSOR	*Journal of the Society of Oriental Research*
		JSS	*Journal of Semitic Studies*
HDCG	Hastings: *Dictionary of Christ and the Gospels*	JT	*Jerusalem Talmud*
		JTS	*Journal of Theological Studies*
HERE	Hastings: *Encyclopedia of Religion and Ethics*	KAHL	Kenyon: *Archaeology in the Holy Land*
HGEOTP	Heidel: *The Gilgamesh Epic and Old Testament Parallels*	KB	Koehler-Baumgartner: *Lexicon in Veteris Testament Libros*
HJP	Schurer: *A History of the Jewish People in the Time of Christ*	KD	Keil and Delitzsch: *Commentary on the Old Testament*
		LSJ	Liddell, Scott, Jones: *Greek-English Lexicon*
HR	Hatch and Redpath: *Concordance to the Septuagint*	LTJM	Edersheim: *The Life and Times of Jesus the Messiah*
HTR	*Harvard Theological Review*	MM	Moulton and Milligan: *The Vocabulary of the Greek Testament*
HUCA	*Hebrew Union College Annual*		
IB	*The Interpreter's Bible*		
ICC	*International Critical Commentary*	MNT	Moffatt: *New Testament Commentary*

MST	McClintock and Strong: *Cyclopedia of Biblical, Theological, and Ecclesiastical Literature*	SJT	*Scottish Journal of Theology*
NBC	Davidson, Kevan, and Stibbs: *The New Bible Commentary,* 1st ed.	SOT	Girdlestone: *Synonyms of Old Testament*
NBCrev.	Guthrie and Motyer: *The New Bible Commentary,* rev. ed.	SOTI	Archer: *A Survey of Old Testament Introduction*
NBD	J. D. Douglas: *The New Bible Dictionary*	ST	*Studia Theologica*
		TCERK	Loetscher: *The Twentieth Century Encyclopedia of Religious Knowledge*
NCB	*New Century Bible*	TDNT	Kittel: *Theological Dictionary of the New Testament*
NCE	*New Catholic Encyclopedia*		
NIC	*New International Commentary*	TDOT	*Theological Dictionary of the Old Testament*
NIDCC	Douglas: *The New International Dictionary of the Christian Church*	THAT	*Theologisches Handbuch zum Alten Testament*
NovTest	*Novum Testamentum*	ThT	*Theology Today*
NSI	Cooke: *Handbook of North Semitic Inscriptions*	TNTC	*Tyndale New Testament Commentaries*
NTS	*New Testament Studies*	Trench	Trench: *Synonyms of the New Testament*
ODCC	*The Oxford Dictionary of the Christian Church,* rev. ed.	TWOT	*Theological Wordbook of the Old Testament*
Peake	Black and Rowley: *Peake's Commentary on the Bible*	UBD	*Unger's Bible Dictionary*
		UT	Gordon: *Ugaritic Textbook*
PEQ	*Palestine Exploration Quarterly*	VB	Allmen: *Vocabulary of the Bible*
PNFl	P. Schaff: *The Nicene and Post-Nicene Fathers* (1st series)	VetTest	*Vetus Testamentum*
		Vincent	Vincent: *Word-Pictures in the New Testament*
PNF2	P. Schaff and H. Wace: *The Nicene and Post-Nicene Fathers* (2nd series)	WBC	*Wycliffe Bible Commentary*
		WBE	*Wycliffe Bible Encyclopedia*
PTR	*Princeton Theological Review*	WC	*Westminster Commentaries*
RB	*Revue Biblique*	WesBC	*Wesleyan Bible Commentaries*
RHG	Robertson's *Grammar of the Greek New Testament in the Light of Historical Research*	WTJ	*Westminster Theological Journal*
		ZAW	*Zeitschrift für die alttestamentliche Wissenschaft*
RTWB	Richardson: *A Theological Wordbook of the Bible*	ZNW	*Zeitschrift für die neutestamentliche Wissenschaft*
SBK	Strack and Billerbeck: *Kommentar zum Neuen Testament aus Talmud und Midrash*	ZPBD	*The Zondervan Pictorial Bible Dictionary*
		ZPEB	*The Zondervan Pictorial Encyclopedia of the Bible*
SHERK	*The New Schaff-Herzog Encyclopedia of Religious Knowledge*	ZWT	*Zeitschrift für wissenschaftliche Theologie*

D. Abbreviations for Books of the Bible, the Apocrypha, and the Pseudepigrapha

OLD TESTAMENT

Gen	2 Chron	Dan
Exod	Ezra	Hos
Lev	Neh	Joel
Num	Esth	Amos
Deut	Job	Obad
Josh	Ps(Pss)	Jonah
Judg	Prov	Mic
Ruth	Eccl	Nah
1 Sam	S of Songs	Hab
2 Sam	Isa	Zeph
1 Kings	Jer	Hag
2 Kings	Lam	Zech
1 Chron	Ezek	Mal

NEW TESTAMENT

Matt	1 Tim
Mark	2 Tim
Luke	Titus
John	Philem
Acts	Heb
Rom	James
1 Cor	1 Peter
2 Cor	2 Peter
Gal	1 John
Eph	2 John
Phil	3 John
Col	Jude
1 Thess	Rev
2 Thess	

APOCRYPHA

1 Esd	1 Esdras	Ep Jer	Epistle of Jeremy
2 Esd	2 Esdras	S Th Ch	Song of the Three Child. (or Young Men)
Tobit	Tobit		
Jud	Judith	Sus	Susanna
Add Esth	Additions to Esther	Bel	Bel and the Dragon
Wisd Sol	Wisdom of Solomon	Pr Man	Prayer of Manasseh
Ecclus	Ecclesiasticus (Wisdom of Jesus the Son of Sirach)	1 Macc	1 Maccabees
		2 Macc	2 Maccabees
Baruch	Baruch		

PSEUDEPIGRAPHA

As Moses	Assumption of Moses	Pirke Aboth	Pirke Aboth
2 Baruch	Syriac Apocalypse of Baruch	Ps 151	Psalm 151
3 Baruch	Greek Apocalypse of Baruch	Pss Sol	Psalms of Solomon
1 Enoch	Ethiopic Book of Enoch	Sib Oracles	Sibylline Oracles
2 Enoch	Slavonic Book of Enoch	Story Ah	Story of Ahikar
3 Enoch	Hebrew Book of Enoch	T Abram	Testament of Abraham
4 Ezra	4 Ezra	T Adam	Testament of Adam
JA	Joseph and Asenath	T Benjamin	Testament of Benjamin
Jub	Book of Jubilees	T Dan	Testament of Dan
L Aristeas	Letter of Aristeas	T Gad	Testament of Gad
Life AE	Life of Adam and Eve	T Job	Testament of Job
Liv Proph	Lives of the Prophets	T Jos	Testament of Joseph
MA Isa	Martyrdom and Ascension of Isaiah	T Levi	Testament of Levi
		T Naph	Testament of Naphtali
3 Macc	3 Maccabees	T 12 Pat	Testaments of the Twe Patriarchs
4 Macc	4 Maccabees		
Odes Sol	Odes of Solomon	Zad Frag	Zadokite Fragments
P Jer	Paralipomena of Jeremiah		

E. Abbreviations of Names of Dead Sea Scrolls and Related Texts

CD	Cairo (Genizah text of the) Damascus (Document)	1QSa	Appendix A (Rule of the Congregation) to 1Qs
DSS	Dead Sea Scrolls	1QSb	Appendix B (Blessings) to 1QS
Hev	Nahal Hever texts	3Q15	Copper Scroll from Qumran Cave 3
Mas	Masada Texts		
Mird	Khirbet mird texts	4QExod a	Exodus Scroll, exemplar "a" from Qumran Cave 4
Mur	Wadi Murabba'at texts		
P	Pesher (commentary)	4QFlor	Florilegium (or Eschatological Midrashim) from Qumran Cave 4
Q	Qumran		
1Q, 2Q, etc.	Numbered caves of Qumran, yielding written material; followed by abbreviation of biblical or apocryphal book.		
		4Qmess ar	Aramaic "Messianic" text from Qumran Cave 4
QL	Qumran Literature	4QpNah	Pesher on portions of Nahum from Qumran Cave 4
1QapGen	Genesis Apocryphon of Qumran Cave 1	4QPrNab	Prayer of Nabonidus from Qumran Cave 4
1QH	*Hodayot* (Thanksgiving Hymns) from Qumran Cave 1	4QpPs37	Pesher on portions of Psalm 37 from Qumran Cave 4
1QIsa a,b	First or second copy of Isaiah from Qumran Cave 1	4QTest	Testimonia text from Qumran Cave 4
1QpHab	Pesher on Habakkuk from Qumran Cave 1	4QTLevi	Testament of Levi from Qumran Cave 4
1QM	*Milhamah* (War Scroll)	4QPhyl	Phylacteries from Qumran Cave 4
1QpMic	Pesher on portions of Micah from Qumran Cave 1	11QMelch	Melchizedek text from Qumran Cave 11
1QS	*Serek Hayyahad* (Rule of the Community, Manual of Discipline)	11QtgJob	Targum of Job from Qumran Cave 11

TRANSLITERATIONS

Hebrew

א = '		ד = $\underline{d}$		י = y		ס = s		ר = r
ב = b		ה = h		כ = k		ע = '		שׂ = $\acute{s}$
בּ = $\underline{b}$		ו = w		ך כ = $\underline{k}$		פ = p		שׁ = $\check{s}$
ג = g		ז = z		ל = l		ף פ = $\underline{p}$		תּ = t
גּ = $\underline{g}$		ח = ḥ		ם מ = m		ץ צ = ṣ		ת = $\underline{t}$
ד = d		ט = ṭ		ן נ = n		ק = q		

(ה) ָ = $\hat{a}$ (h)		ָ = $\bar{a}$		ַ = a		ֱ = ^{a}
ֵ ה = $\hat{e}$		ֵ = $\bar{e}$		ֲ = e		ֳ = ^{e}
ִ ֿ = $\hat{i}$		ֹ = $\bar{o}$		ִ = i		ְ = ^{e} (if vocal)
וֹ = $\hat{o}$				ֹ = o		ֳ = ^{o}
וּ = $\hat{u}$				ֻ = u		

Aramaic

' b g d h w z ḥ ṭ y k l m n s ' p ṣ q r $\acute{s}$ $\check{s}$ t

Arabic

' b t ṯ ǧ ḥ ḫ d ḏ r z s š ṣ ḍ ṭ ẓ ' ġ f q k l m n h w y

Ugaritic

' b g d $\underline{d}$ h w z ḥ ḫ ṭ ẓ y k l m n s ś ' ġ ṗ ṣ q r š t ṯ

xv

Greek

α	—	a	π	—	p	αι	—	ai
β	—	b	ρ	—	r	αὐ	—	au
γ	—	g	σ,ς	—	s	ει	—	ei
δ	—	d	τ	—	t	εὐ	—	eu
ε	—	e	υ	—	y	ηὐ	—	ēu
ζ	—	z	φ	—	ph	οι	—	oi
η	—	ē	χ	—	ch	οὐ	—	ou
θ	—	th	ψ	—	ps	υι	—	hui
ι	—	i	ω	—	ō			
κ	—	k				ῥ	—	rh
λ	—	l	γγ	—	ng	ʽ	—	h
μ	—	m	γκ	—	nk			
ν	—	n	γξ	—	nx	ᾳ	—	ā
ξ	—	x	γχ	—	nch	ῃ	—	ē
ο	—	o				ῳ	—	ō

1 CORINTHIANS

W. Harold Mare

1 CORINTHIANS

Introduction

1. Background, Including General Historical and Archaeological Data

The ancient city of Corinth was located on the isthmus between Attica to the northeast and the Greek Peloponnesus to the south and had controlling access to two seas—the Aegean, about five miles to the east and the Ionian on the west. Its eastern port was Cenchrea, located on the Saronic Gulf (Acts 18:18; Rom 16:1), its western harbor was at Lechaeum on the Corinthian Gulf. This proximity to the seas and its nearness to Athens, only forty-five miles to the northeast, gave Corinth a position of strategic commercial importance and military defense. It lay below the steep north side of the 1,800-foot high fortress rock, the Acrocorinth with its temple of Aphrodite (Strabo, *Geography*, 8.6.21). Thus located, the city received shipping from Italy, Sicily, and Spain, as well as from Asia Minor, Syria, Phoenicia, and Egypt. Instead of going "round the horn" at Cape Malea at the south end of the Peloponnesus, ships either docked at the Isthmus and transported their cargoes by land vehicles from one sea to another, or if the ships were small, they were dragged the five miles across the isthmus. Today there is a canal running through the narrowest part of the isthmus near Corinth.

Corinth was called "the bridge of the sea" (Pind. *Nem* VI. 40) and "the gate of the Peloponnesus" (Xen. *Ages*. 2.17). It was considered a "prosperous" (Pind. *Olym*. 13.4.; Herodotus 3.52) and "rich" (Thucydides, *Hist*. 1, 13, 5) city. For Strabo (8.6.23) Corinth was "always great and wealthy." At the peak of its power and influence the city probably had a free population of 200,000 in addition to half a million slaves in its navy and in its many colonies (HDAC, p. 249).

About the end of the third millennium B.C. Corinth and the rest of Greece were invaded in the Bronze Age by an alien people who may have been forerunners of the Greeks. From that time the site of Corinth itself was abandoned until about 1350 B.C., when a new settlement came into being. But for the next three hundred years material evidences for the city are scarce. It would seem that this resettled Corinth had by the time of the Trojan War (c. 1200 B.C.) prospered so greatly that Homer could speak of it as "wealthy Corinth" (Il. 2.570).

During the Iron Age, the city grew in size and wealth. By about 800 B.C. it had acquired considerable importance as a commercial and military center. The importance of Corinth continued with fluctuations that were due to the struggles among the Greek states and their subjugation under Philip II of Macedon and his son, Alexander the Great.

Still later, when the Greeks attempted to break the yoke of Macedon, the Romans became involved and so Corinth was destroyed by the Romans under Lucius Mummius in 146 B.C., only to be reestablished in 46 B.C. by Julius Caesar and called Colonia Laus Julia Corinthus. Caesar populated it with Roman war veterans and freedmen. In the reign of Augustus (27 B.C.–A.D. 14) and his successors, Corinth was built on the pattern of a Roman city, with all remaining buildings reclaimed and new ones added in and around the old market place (the *agora*), the place in which the *bema* (the judgment tribunal platform) stood, where Paul appeared before Gallio (Acts 18:12).[1] In this period Corinth became the capital of the Roman province of Achaia (cf. Acts 18:1, 2), which included all the Peloponnesus and most of the rest of Greece and Macedonia.

During the Roman period and in its position as a political center, Corinth again became prosperous, with vast income coming from its sea trade and from the development of its arts and industries. Its pottery and Corinthian brass (a mixture of gold, silver, and copper) were world famous (cf. Ovid [43 B.C.–17 A.D.] *Met.* 6:416).

The celebration of the Isthmian games at the temple of Poseidon (Strabo 8.6.22) made a considerable contribution to Hellenic life. This temple was located about seven miles east of Corinth, not far from the eastern end of the isthmus. But with the games there came an emphasis on luxury and profligacy, because the sanctuary of Poseidon was given over to the worship of the Corinthian Aphrodite, (probably a counterpart of the Syrian Astarte) whose temple on the Acrocorinth had more than 1,000 *hierodouloi* (female prostitutes). Strabo says (8.6.20) that many people came to Corinth on account of these priestesses, and the city grew rich. *Korinthiazomai* (meaning "to live like a Corinthian in the practice of sexual immorality") was the expression used at an earlier time by Aristophanes (*Fragmenta* 354) to describe a person of loose life.

Paul probably came to this important but immoral city in the fall of A.D. 50, after having preached the gospel to the highly intellectual Athenians. That this is the time of Paul's stay at the city is established by comparing the reference in Acts 18:12 to Gallio, the Roman procounsul (*anthupatos*) with that to a Gallio, procounsul of Achaia, mentioned on an inscription of the Emperor Claudius at Delphi to be dated between January and August, A.D. 52.

Now since the Gallio of the inscription is already mentioned as in office in the first half of A.D. 52, he must have begun his proconsulship July 1, A.D. 51, July 1 being the time each year when Roman proconsuls took office. Paul ministered a year and a half in Corinth (Acts 18:11) before he was brought by the Jews into court before Gallio (v.12). No mention is made of Gallio being in office as proconsul of Achaia when Paul first came to Corinth to work as a tentmaker and to preach (Acts 18:1–5). But some time later, after opposition to the gospel had had time to grow (vv.6–10), Gallio is mentioned as having a case against Paul brought before him (vv.12–17). So the conclusion is that Paul arrived

---

[1] *Cf.* Oscar Broneer, "Corinth," *Biblical Archaeologist,* vol. 14 (Dec., 1951), no. 4, 80–82.

in Corinth some time before Gallio, probably by the fall of A.D. 50, a period of about nine months before the proconsul took office on July 1, A.D. 51. Sometime after this official opposition Paul left Corinth for Syria, sailing from Cenchrea (v.18).

In the Corinthian church were both Jews and Gentiles, as inferred from Paul's reference to them in chapter 1. This is also attested by Latin names, such as Gaius, Fortunatus, Crispus, Justus, and Achaicus (1 Cor 1:14; 16:17) and by the mention of the Jews, Aquila and Priscilla (Acts 18:1-4) and of Crispus, the ruler of the synagogue (v.8). Sosthenes, another synagogue ruler there (v.17)—if he is the Sosthenes of 1 Corinthians 1:1—also became a member of the congregation. But no doubt the greater part of the church was composed of native Greeks; cf. Paul's reference to the Greeks who seek after wisdom (1 Cor 1:20-24) and also his reference to the congregation's being Gentiles (12:2).

The existence of a synagogue in Corinth (Acts 18:4-8) is pointed to by an inscribed lintel block with enough of the words remaining to make out the reading "Synagogue of the Hewbrews."[2] From the way the letters are formed, Broneer thinks that the inscription is of the fourth or fifth centuries A.D.[3] However, others think the inscription is to be dated between 100 B.C. and A.D. 200. Deissmann (quoted with approval by Finegan) says that "as extreme limits within which the inscription must have been made, the dates of 100 B.C. and 200 A.D. might with some reservation" be assumed. Deissmann also comments that the miserable nature of the inscription, which has no ornamentation, fits the social position of the Jewish people at Corinth with whom Paul was dealing.[4] This agrees with Paul's remarks to the Corinthians: "Not many of you were wise by human standards; not many were influential; not many were of noble birth" (1 Cor 1:26). But even if it is argued that the inscription is later than the time the Corinthian Church was founded, it is natural to assume, because of the Jews tenacity in remaining settled in religious communities where they were dispersed, as at Rome[5] and Alexandria, that the Jewish community in Corinth had an earlier synagogue building when Paul established the church there. Pausanias in his *Descriptions of Greece* describes the city following his visit to Corinth at about A.D. 170, but his interest is more in heathen cults.

Though it is not possible to identify the building in Corinth to which the synagogue inscription belonged, archaeological work can identify other buildings of the ancient city. An ornamented triumphal gateway, located at the south end of the Lechaeum Road, led into the marketplace (*i.e.*, the Greek *agora*, or Roman forum)—c. 600 feet long and c. 300 feet wide. Around the market were a good many shops, numbers of which had individual wells, suggesting that much wine was made and drunk in the city. (Cf. Paul's warning in 1 Cor 6:10 that drunkards will not "inherit" the kingdom of God.)

Located near the center of the marketplace was the *bema* (Gr.) or *rostra* (Latin), the judicial bench or tribunal platform (cf. 2 Cor 5:10, "the judgment seat of Christ"). This was a speakers' platform; officials addressed audiences assembled there. Originally, the *bema* was covered with carved marble, as extant fragments bear testimony. On either side of it were waiting rooms with mosaic floors and marble benches, and in these rooms

---

[2][ΣΥΝ] ΑΓΩΓΗΕΒΡ[ΑΙΩΝ], [*Sun*] *agōgē Ebr* [*aiōn*]. Cf. Merrill C. Tenney, *New Testament Times* (Grand Rapids: Eerdmans, 1965), p. 275.

[3]Broneer, "Corinth," p. 88, footnote.

[4]A. Deissmann, *Light from the Ancient East*, revised (New York: George H. Doran Co., 1927), p. 16. Cf. J. Finegan, *Light from the Ancient Past* (Princeton, N.J.: Princeton University Press, 1959), pp. 361, 362.

[5]Inscriptions indicate that at Rome there were a large number of synagogue communities as early as the Emperor Augustus's time, (cf. Philo, *The Embassy to Gaius*, 155, 156; cf. also Emil Schürer, *A History of the Jewish People in the Time of Jesus Christ*, 2nd rev. ed., DW 2, vol. 2 (New York: Charles Scribner's Sons, 1890, 1891) pp. 247, 283.

cases were heard by the magistrate. It was not, however, in one of these side rooms, but outside in front of the *bema* proper, that the antagonistic Jews brought Paul before the Roman proconsul Gallio (Acts 18:12–17), for such a mob action would not have been allowed in a Roman court room.

To the south of the *bema* toward the Acrocorinth (the rocky butte behind the city) at the south stoa (a colonnaded building) there came into the marketplace a paved road that probably connected with the road leading east to Cenchrea, the port from which Paul sailed to Ephesus and then to Syria (Acts 18:18–22).

Besides its many temples and shrines, including the temple of Apollo, the remains of which stand out on the landscape today, the city had two theaters to the north and west, one of which could seat 18,000 people. In a paved street at the east side of this theater was found a re-used paving block with this inscription: "Erastus, the aedile [commissioner of public works] bore the expense of this pavement" (Latin: ERASTUS PRO. AED. S. P. STRAVIT. Cf. Tenney, *New Testament Times*, p. 274). This Erastus may well have been the one who became Paul's fellow worker. See Acts 19:22 and Romans 16:23 (where he is called "the city's director of public works"). Erastus was evidently one of the few "influential" and "noble" persons Paul refers to in 1 Corinthians 1:26.[6]

Later on, by the tenth century A.D., a church existed on the ruins of the *bema*, but the superstructure of the *bema* had by this time fallen. Also in the Julian Basilica on the east side of the market a ninth-to-tenth-century A.D. inscription on a fragment of a white marble slab has been found. It includes the letters, "The —— Church of Saint Paul" and is probably from the church built on top of the *bema*.[7]

Besides his initial stay in Corinth as recorded in Acts 18, Paul's contact with the Corinthians can be outlined as follows: 'At Ephesus (Acts 19) he apparently wrote the "previous letter" (1 Cor 5:9—now lost to us). Besides hearing of the Corinthians' seeming misunderstanding of his "previous letter," Paul had reports from Chloe's household of disorders in the church there (1 Cor 1:11). He then may have received a delegation from Corinth (16:17) who presented him with questions from the congregation (cf. 7:1). As a result, he wrote 1 Corinthians. Paul may have heard other unfavorable reports from the church and paid them a "painful visit" (2 Cor 2:1), which evidently occurred following the writing of 1 Corinthians and its reception by the church. The painful visit was no doubt necessary because the church had failed to act on Paul's advice given in 1 Corinthians. Upon his return to Ephesus, he sent the church a "sorrowful letter" (2 Cor 2:4; 7:8, 9), probably carried by Titus.

Some have taken this letter to be 1 Corinthians but others feel that 1 Corinthians does not express the feeling of Paul's shedding "many tears" (2 Cor 2:4). That he repented of having written this "sorrowful letter" (2 Cor 7:8) is thought to be inappropriate for an inspired letter like 1 Corinthians. However, if this "sorrowful letter" is simply a lost epistle of Paul, the question is whether it, too, was inspired and, if so, how are we to understand his repenting of writing it? The question is answered, in part at least, by realizing that the word "repent" in 2 Corinthians 7:8 is not *metanoeō*, for repenting of sin, but *metamelomai*, "to be sorry," "to regret." Further, Paul means he regretted that they had been made sad, not that he regretted writing the letter under the guidance of

---

[6]Cf. Finegan, *Light from the Ancient Past*, pp. 359–362; and Broneer, "Corinth," pp. 90–94.

[7]R.L. Scranton, *Corinth: Results of Excavations*, vol. 1, part 3, *Monuments in the Lower Agora and North of the Archaic Temple* (Princeton: American School of Classical Studies at Athens, 1951), p. 132; and J.H. Kent, *Corinth: Results of Excavations*, vol. 8, part III, *The Inscriptions 1926–1950* (Princeton: The American School of Classical Studies at Athens, 1966), pp. 211, 212.

the Holy Spirit.[8] From Ephesus Paul went to Macedonia, where he received from Titus an encouraging report (2 Cor 7:5-7). So he wrote 2 Corinthians expressing his gratitude for the improvement. Later he spent the winter in Corinth (Acts 20:2, 3) before departing for Jerusalem with the contribution for the poor among the Christians of Palestine. On the basis of this analysis of the events, we may conclude that Paul wrote the Corinthians four letters (two of which have been lost) and that he paid the church three visits, including the one referred to in Acts 18. (See also Guthrie, pp. 424-438.)

2. Unity

1 Corinthians gives all indications of being a unity. The thought progresses in orderly fashion from the greetings and thanksgiving to the discussion about the rival cliques in the church and its internal problems of incest and lawsuits. Members of Chloe's household seem to have reported to Paul on all these matters. Next Paul discusses the questions brought by the Corinthian delegation (1 Cor 16:17)—questions of marriage, eating meat offered to heathen idols, disorderly public worship, spiritual gifts, and the resurrection. Then Paul naturally goes on to remark about the Corinthians' offering for the poor and his travel plans; he closes with greetings. Obviously the letter is a connected whole. Because of supposed contradictions, some scholars have thought 1 and 2 Corinthians to be a mixture of different sections of Pauline writing pieced together in their present form. But such theories do not afford Paul a natural latitude for developing his material in accord with the particular church problem or problems coming to his attention over a period of time (Guthrie, pp. 439-441).

3. Authorship

It is generally acknowledged that, whether the material we have in 1 Corinthians is as it came from Paul, he was the author. Early external evidence from the following confirms this conclusion: Clement of Rome, *To the Corinthians* (ch. 47), Polycarp, *To the Philippians* (ch. 11), Irenaeus, *Against Heresies*, 4, 27 (45), Clement of Alexandria (e.g., *Paedag.* 1, 6 [33]), and Tertullian, *de Praescript. adv. Haer.*, (Ch. 33, 11:46).[9]

4. Date and Place of Origin, and Destination

Quite obviously, the letter was written some time subsequent to Paul's first visit to Corinth. Following his departure from the city, he sailed from Cenchrea for Syria by way of Ephesus. Landing at the Palestinian port of Caesarea, he then visited the Jerusalem churches and journeyed on north to his home church at Antioch in Syria (Acts 18:18-23).

After some time in Antioch, Paul left on his third missionary journey and visited the churches of Galatia and Phrygia (Acts 18:23). He finally came to Ephesus (19:1), preaching and teaching there for almost three years (19:10; 20:31). According to Bruce, the two

---

[8]Cf. H.A.W. Meyer, *The Epistles to the Corinthians* (New York: Funk and Wagnalls, 1884), pp. 566, 567.
[9]Henry Alford, *Greek Testament*, vol. 2, 5th ed. (London: Revingtons, 1865), p. 46.

years was probably that and a few months more. With the three months of 19:8, this would make up the three years of 20:31; i.e., three years less a few months.[10]

While at Ephesus, Paul heard of the Corinthians' troubles and questions through reports from Chloe's house (1 Cor 1:11) and possibly through a delegation from Corinth (16:17). At this point he wrote the Epistle.

That 1 Corinthians was written on the third missionary journey and from Ephesus and in the spring of A.D. 55/56 is evident from the following reasons: (1) Paul says he is writing from Ephesus (1 Cor 16:8, 9, 19). (2) He wrote the letter several years after his initial departure from Corinth in the fall of A.D. 51, because it was written subsequent to Apollos's stay at the city (Acts 18:26, 27; 1 Cor 1:12) and after Timothy and Erastus had been sent by Paul from Ephesus to Macedonia (Acts 19:22) and Timothy had been sent on to Corinth (1 Cor 4:17). Further, it took some time for the Corinthian problems to develop and for news of them to reach Paul. (3) The letter was written before the beginning of summer, because in 1 Corinthians 16:8 Paul intimates that it is a relatively short time to Pentecost (i.e., late spring) after which he intends to leave Ephesus. The time of writing is certainly before winter, for Paul states that he wants to come and winter with them (1 Cor 16:6, cf. Acts 20:3). This all adds up to some four or five years after his initial departure from Corinth in the fall of A.D. 51, counting his journey to Jerusalem and extended stay in Syrian Antioch (Acts 18:18, 23) and his almost three-year ministry in Ephesus (19:8, 10; 20:31).

It is not fully clear who carried the letter to Corinth. But it seems likely that its bearers were Stephanas, Fortunatus, and Achaicus who according to 1 Corinthians 16:17 had arrived from Corinth and were with Paul. Since in 1 Corinthians 16:18 the apostle says that the Corinthian Christians should show respect for these men, it is logical to conclude that they were returning to Corinth and so it would have been natural for Paul to send the Epistle with them.

5. Occasion

First Corinthians is a source book of answers to church problems in the past and today. Findlay calls it "the doctrine of the cross in its social application."[11] After the introductory material, Paul begins to answer the theological and practical problems raised through a report (either oral or written) from members of the household of Chloe (1 Cor 1:11). Following this, a letter came from the church (7:1), possibly brought by a delegation (16:17) and posing a number of questions. These things, together with Paul's desire to send greetings to Corinth, was sufficient occasion for him to write the letter.

6. Purpose

In responding to the reports and answering the questions, it was Paul's purpose to rectify certain serious doctrinal and moral sins and irregularities of Christian living, including disorderly conduct in worship. These aberrations included false views of the resurrection of Christ and the resurrection of the body (1 Cor 15), incest, adultery, and

---

[10]F.F. Bruce, The Acts of the Apostles: *The Greek Text with Introduction and Commentary* (Grand Rapids: Eerdmans, 1965), p. 356.

[11]*Expositor's Greek Testament*, vol. 2 (Grand Rapids: Eerdmans, n.d.), p. 739.

other sexual immorality (1 Cor 5). They also included unchristian actions in taking fellow Christians to court (1 Cor 6), misuse of Christian liberty (1 Cor 8 and 10), disorders in observing the Lord's Supper (1 Cor 11:17–34), and other disorders in the worship service (1 Cor 14).

7. Literary Form

Modern critics have tried to divide up the Corinthian Epistles in an attempt to show how they were compiled. Among recent partition theories are those of J. Weiss, J. Hering, M. Goguel, and J.T. Dean (Guthrie, p. 439). For example, Weiss saw 1 Corinthians as composed of three parts representing a development in Paul's relationship with the Corinthians. Hering found the Epistle composed of two parts. Goguel, taking 1 and 2 Corinthians together, saw six parts. But such complex theories do not sufficiently account for the psychological factors and different subjects involved. These factors argue for the unity of 1 Corinthians, as Paul in writing it deliberately changed the subject matter and tone as he proceeded from section to section of the letter. Moreover, it may well be that he did not compose the whole letter at one time. He may have written the first part in response to reports that came through Chloe; then later, after receiving the letter from the Corinthians (1 Cor 7:1) he may have written the rest.

So though the expression and tone change in various parts of 1 Corinthians, we may take it that the letter is from Paul who wrote it within a relatively short period of time. The Greek is characteristically that of the apostle.

8. Theological Values

Several theological emphases stand out in 1 Corinthians and are related to the daily living of Christians as well as to the corporate testimony of the worshiping church. For example, in chapter 15 Paul sets forth valid reasons for believing in the bodily resurrection of Christ and relates this to Christ's second coming. And in chapter 11 the doctrine of the Lord's Supper is effectively taught, along with the admonition for Christians to take it seriously.

In chapters 5 and 6 Paul speaks forcefully against the incident of incest and adultery in the church and condemns all sexual immorality. The practical problem of whether a Christian should marry and how he should conduct himself in a married or unmarried state is adequately discussed in chapter 7. In the sixth chapter the thorny problem of believers' taking other believers into secular court is faced and Christian arbitration suggested. The believer's Christian liberty versus his responsibility to his Christian brother is clearly delineated and explained in chapters 8 and 10. In the area of ecclesiology, the subjects of Christian gifts and their use for the church, as well as orderly conduct in church services, are fully expounded in chapters 12 to 14.

9. Canonicity

There is no question of the canonicity of 1 Corinthians. Since the book was clearly written by Paul, an apostle, it was to be accepted immediately by the church as God's

Word.[12] Paul makes the strong statement: In 1 Corinthians 14:37 "If anybody thinks he is a prophet or spiritually gifted, let him acknowledge that what I am writing to you is the Lord's command."

Second, the early church bore witness that 1 Corinthians was considered authoritative and a part of the NT canon. Marcion ascribes (c. A.D. 140–150) to this corpus the term *apostolikon,* and undoubtedly 1 Corinthians was a part of that corpus.[13] Guthrie has noted that "of great significance is the fact that the earliest Canon of the New Testament writings of which we have any evidence consisted almost exclusively of Pauline writings" (Guthrie, p. 643). Some thirty to forty years after the period of Marcion's major activity as noted above, the Muratorian canon (c. A.D. 170) appeared and included 1 Corinthians as one of the thirteen Epistles of Paul, so implying its equal authority with the others.

Obviously, 1 Corinthians was considered from the beginning one of the NT canonical books.

10. Text

The Greek text of 1 Corinthians is in good order, with relatively few crucial problems. In one place (1 Cor 15:47–55), the textual variants suggest some changes in the emphases of these verses. The basic Greek ms text of 1 Corinthians is good; it is the same as that of other of the Pauline Epistles and includes early uncials such as ℵ A B C D (Paris, Claromontanus) and early papyri including P[46] (Chester Beatty, c. 200), P[51] (P Oxy 2157; c. 400) and P[65] (Florence, 3rd cent.).[14]

11. Bibliography

Alford, Henry. *Greek Testament,* vol. II, 5th ed. London: Revingtons, 1865.
Barrett, C.K. *The First Epistle to Corinthians* in "Black's New Testament Commentary." New York: Harper, 1968.
Calvin, John. *New Testament Commentaries.* Philadelphia: Westminster Press, 1958.
Craig, C.T. and Short, J. *1 Corinthians* in IB, vol. 10. New York: Abingdon-Cokesbury, 1953.
Dean, J.T. *St. Paul and Corinth.* London: Lutterworth, 1947.
Evans, Ernest. *The Epistles of Paul the Apostle to the Corinthians.* Oxford: Clarendon Press, 1944.
Glen, John Stanley. *Pastoral Problems in First Corinthians.* Philadelphia: Westminster Press, 1964.
Godet, F. *Commentary on St. Paul's First Epistle to the Corinthians,* n.d. Reprint, tr. A. Cusin, Grand Rapids: Zondervan, 1971.
Grosheide, F.W. *Commentary on the First Epistle to the Corinthians* in NIC. Grand Rapids, Eerdmans, 1968.
Guthrie, Donald. *New Testament Introduction,* 3rd ed. revised. Downers Grove, Ill.: Inter-Varsity Press, 1970, 421–449.

---

[12]Cf. R.L. Harris, *Inspiration and Canonicity* (Grand Rapids: Zondervan, 1957), pp. 234, 235.

[13]P. Schaff, *History of the Christian Church,* vol. 2 (New York: Charles Scribner's Sons, 1891), pp. 484–486; *The Cambridge History of the Bible,* vol. 1, ed. P.R. Ackroyd and C.F. Evans (Cambridge: Cambridge University Press, 1970), pp. 239, 240, 294.

[14]For more details, see Kurt Aland, et al., *The Greek New Testament,* 2nd ed. (New York: United Bible Societies, 1968), Introduction; Bruce M. Metzger, *A Textual Commentary on the Greek New Testament* (New York: United Bible Societies, 1971), Introduction.

Hering, J. *The First Epistle of St. Paul to the Corinthians* from the second French ed. by A.W. Heathcote and P.J. Allcock. London: Epworth Press, 1962.

Hodge, Charles. *I Corinthians.* New York: A.C. Armstrong, 1891.

Howard, W.F. *1 and 2 Corinthians* in "Abingdon Bible Commentary," Nashville: Abingdon, 1929.

Lenski, C.H. *The Interpretation of St. Paul's First and Second Epistles to the Corinthians.* Columbus, Ohio: Wartburg Press, 1946.

Metzger, Bruce M. *A Textual Commentary on the Greek New Testament,* A Companion Volume to the United Bible Societies' *Greek New Testament.* 3rd ed. New York: United Bible Societies, 1971.

Moffatt, J. *The First Epistle of Paul to the Corinthians* in "Moffatt's New Testament Commentary." New York: Harper, 1938.

Morris, Leon. *The First Epistle of Paul to the Corinthians* in "The Tyndale New Testament Commentary." Grand Rapids: Eerdmans, 1958.

Parry, John. *The First Epistle of Paul the Apostle to the Corinthians in the Revised Version* in "The Cambridge Bible for Schools and Colleges." Cambridge: Cambridge University Press, 1957.

Parry, R. St. John, ed. *The First Epistle of Paul the Apostle to the Corinthians,* in "Cambridge Greek Testament for Schools and Colleges." Cambridge: Cambridge University Press, 1916.

Reuf, J.S. *Paul's First Epistle to Corinth* in "Pelican's New Testament Commentaries." Baltimore: Hammondsworth, 1971.

Robertson, A. and Plummer, A. *A Critical and Exegetical Commentary on the First Epistle of St. Paul to the Corinthians,* 2nd ed., in ICC. Edinburgh: T. & T. Clark, 1929.

_____. *I Corinthians* in ICC. New York: Charles Scribner's Sons, 1916.

Scharlemann, Martin Henry. *Qumran and Corinth.* New York: Bookman Associates, 1962.

Schmidt, John. *Letters to Corinth.* Philadelphia: Muhlenberg Press, 1947.

Walter, Eugene. *The First Epistle to the Corinthians,* tr. Simon and Erika Young. New York: Herder and Herder, 1971.

Williams, C.S.C. *I and II Corinthians,* in "Peake's Commentary on the Bible." Edited by Matthew Black. London: Thomas Nelson, 1967.

12. Outline

I. Greetings (1:1–3)

II. Paul's Thanksgiving for God's Work in the Lives of the Saints (1:4–9)

III. The Problem of Divisions in the Church (1:10–17)

IV. The Wisdom of God—the Preaching of Christ Crucified (1:18–2:16)

    A. Christ, the Power and Wisdom of God (1:18–31)

    B. Paul Preaches Christ in the Power of God (2:1–5)

    C. Wisdom of Christ Revealed by the Holy Spirit (2:6–16)

V. Servants of Christ (3:1–4:21)

    A. Workers With God—False Estimate Corrected (3:1–23)

        1. Spiritual immaturity and divisiveness (3:1–9)

        2. Building on Christ, the foundation (3:10–17)

        3. Complete dependence on God, not men (3:18–23)

    B. Servants of Christ: The Ministry of the Apostles (4:1–21)

        1. Faithful servants (4:1–5)

        2. The proud Corinthians and the despised servants (4:6–13)

        3. The challenge to be God's humble servants also (4:14–21)

VI. Paul's Answer to Further Reported Problems in the Church (5:1–6:20)

    A. Paul's Condemnation of Sexual Immorality—Incest (5:1–13)

    B. Christian Morality Applied to Legal and Sexual Matters (6:1–20)

        1. Christian morality in legal matters (6:1–11)

        2. Christian morality in sexual matters (6:12–20)

VII. Paul's Answers to Questions Raised by the Church (7:1–14:40)

    A. Instructions Concerning Marriage (7:1–40)

        1. Christian obligations in marriage (7:1–16)

        2. Christian obligation to live according to God's call (7:17–24)

        3. Instructions concerning virgins (7:25–40)

    B. Instructions Concerning Christian Freedom: Its Privileges and Responsibilities (8:1–11:1)

        1. Eating meat sacrificed to idols (8:1–13)

            a. Knowledge and love contrasted (8:1–3)

            b. The meaning of eating meat sacrificed to idols (8:4–6)

            c. Freedom to be used with care (8:7–13)

        2. Paul: on giving up his rights as an apostle (9:1–18)

            a. Rights of an apostle (9:1–12a)

            b. Rights not used (9:12b–18)

        3. Paul: subjection of self for others and to meet God's approval (9:19–27)

        4. Warning: Israel's lack of self-restraint (10:1–13)

        5. Warning: attendance at pagan sacrifices means fellowship with idolatry (10:14–22)

PLAN OF THE CENTRAL AREA OF CORINTH

Courtesy of the American School of Classical Studies at Athens

PLAN OF THE CORINTHIA

Courtesy of the American School of Classical Studies at Athens

Text and Exposition

I. Greetings

1:1–3

[1]Paul, called to be an apostle of Christ Jesus by the will of God, and our brother Sosthenes,

[2]To the church of God in Corinth, to those sanctified in Christ Jesus and called to be holy, together with all those everywhere who call on the name of our Lord Jesus Christ—their Lord and ours:

[3]Grace and peace to you from God our Father and the Lord Jesus Christ.

1 Characteristically, the apostle begins by naming himself and also by identifying his position as an apostle of Jesus Christ. Only in Philippians, 1 and 2 Thessalonians, and Philemon does Paul begin without mentioning his apostleship. Here he refers to it because his authority has been challenged (cf. 1 Cor 1:12 and 9:1–27). Paul makes it clear that he is an apostle by divine calling through God's sovereign will (cf. his experience on the Damascus road, Acts 9:15). The word "apostle" (*apostolos*) means "a sent one" and connotes a commissioned envoy.

Sosthenes (the name was a common Greek one), whom Paul links to himself as a Christian brother, was evidently one of the apostle's special helpers and was presumably well known to the Corinthian church. Though his identity is not certain, it is possible that he was a leader of the Corinthian synagogue (Acts 18:17). If so, he must have been converted subsequently and gone off to help Paul in his Ephesian ministry.

2 The believers in Corinth are designated as the "church of God," a phrase that has OT associations as in the expression "assembly [or congregation] of the Lord" (Num 16:3; 20:4; Deut 23:1; 1 Chron 28:8) and the "assembly of Israel" (Lev 16:17; Deut 31:30). That Paul means that this church at Corinth is considered a part of the universal "church of God" is evident from his reference to Palestinian churches as also being a part of that body (1 Cor 15:9; cf. 10:31, 32). The phrase is used only by Paul in 1 Corinthians, 2 Corinthians 1:1, and Acts 20:28. (In the last reference there is a textual variant—"church of God" or "church of the Lord"; cf. UBS, in loc.) The apostle may have found it particularly useful in Corinth to distinguish the church from the secular *ekklēsiai* (assemblies) of mainland Greece and from the heathen religious organizations. The ancient *ekklēsiai* or assemblies of the secular world, in contrast to the Christian *ekklēsia* or church in its worship of God, were gatherings of the citizenry in a city-state to discuss and decide on matters of public interest (cf. Acts 19:39; Herodotus 3.142), as they certainly did in Corinth itself according to ancient inscriptions found there. For example, in two Corinthian inscriptions shown to be near the first half of the second century B.C., by the form of the letters, it is said, "The assembly decreed." (*Corinth: Results of the Excavations*, Vol. VIII, Part I, *Greek Inscriptions, 1896–1927*, ed. B.D. Meritt [Cambridge: Harvard University Press, 1931], numbers 2, 3.)

The Corinthian Christians are described as set apart and in a holy position before God because of their spiritual union with Jesus Christ. In speaking of them as "called to be holy"—i.e., set apart for God—Paul means that they are called to be God's holy people. So they are on an equal footing with the people of God everywhere, who also call on the name of Jesus Christ as Savior and Lord (cf. Acts 9:14, 21). The unity of believers in Christ is shown by Paul's emphatic words in v.2, "their Lord and ours."

3 This verse is identical to Romans 1:7b; 2 Corinthians 1:2; Galatians 1:3; Ephesians 1:2; and Philemon 1:3. Though carrying a sense of greeting, "grace and peace" also refer to the truth of redemption purchased by Christ. It was of God's grace that the Corinthian believers were saved (2 Cor 8:9; Eph 2:8, 9), just as all Christians are saved, and through this redemption Jesus Christ purchased peace with God for the sinner (Eph 2:14; cf. Rom 5:1).

Paul emphasizes that this grace and peace are of divine origin; they are from (*apo*) God our Father who planned redemption and from Christ who purchased it on the cross for the justification of his people and for blessing in their daily lives (cf. Rom 15:13, 33; Phil 4:6, 7).

Notes

1 Notice Paul's emphasis on κλητός (*klētos*, "called") in the phrase "called to be holy." Cf. v.9, "God through whom you were called into fellowship with His Son" (NASB). It was "through" (διά, *dia* with the genitive) the instrumentality of God's sovereign will that Paul was called. God is the efficient cause.

2 Εκκλησία (*ekklēsia*), is frequently LXX tr. for קהל (*kahal*, "assembly," "congregation," as in Deuteronomy 4:10; 9:10. Compare Acts 7:38, ἐν τῇ ἐκκλησίᾳ ἐν τῇ ἐρήμῳ (*en te ekklēsia en te erēmō*, "in the congregation in the desert"). The church of God is one church of which the church at Corinth was a part.

The participial form ἡγιασμένοις (*hēgiasmenois*) is in the perfect tense, indicating a position of holiness accomplished by God and continuing in force. The expression ἐν Χριστῷ Ἰησοῦ (*en Christō Iēsou*, "in Christ Jesus") speaks of the believer's spiritual location in Christ and so has the meaning "union with Christ." The term ὄνομα (*onoma*, "name") used here as in a number of other places (cf. Acts 4:12), signifies the person and the inherent character of the person designated by the name. Here the name, that is, the person Jesus Christ, is called on. The verb ἐπικαλέω (*epikaleō*, "called upon") is in the present middle participial form, indicating a continual earnest appeal and dependence on Christ, who alone can save.

II. Paul's Thanksgiving for God's Work in the Lives of the Saints

1:4-9

[4]I always thank God for you because of his grace given you in Christ Jesus. [5]For in him you have been enriched in every way—in all your speaking and in all your knowledge—[6]because our testimony about Christ was confirmed in you. [7]Therefore you do not lack any spiritual gift as you eagerly wait for our Lord Jesus Christ to be revealed. [8]He will keep you strong to the end, so that you will be blameless on the day of our Lord Jesus Christ. [9]God, who has called you into fellowship with his Son Jesus Christ our Lord, is faithful.

4-6 As is characteristic of Paul in other letters (cf. Rom 1:8; Phil 1:3-7; Col 1:3-8, et al.), he begins with thanksgiving to God for those he is addressing. He realizes that God has given them his grace through their union with Christ, enriching their lives by their ability to speak about God and by their knowledge of him (v.5). Paul is thankful that the testimony he gave them was confirmed or established in their lives.

The verb *eucharisteō*, in its present form here (a customary present) with the adverb *pantote*, ("I at all times give thanks"), indicates Paul's habitual prayer life in which he regularly interceded for the believers at Corinth as well as those at every place he preached the gospel (cf. Eph 1:16; Phil 1:3, et al.). Elsewhere Paul uses the concept of the grace of God to express his own call into the ministry as an apostle (Rom 12:3; 1 Cor 3:10; Gal 2:9; Eph 3:2, 3). But here he uses the expression to indicate aspects of God's work in the daily lives of the Christians at Corinth.

Greeks naturally put emphasis on knowledge and wisdom (cf. 1 Cor 1:18–25) and they certainly were good at expressing their thoughts. However, God had so enriched the lives of these people in spiritual perception and expression that they had been given increased ability in speaking. The extent of their enrichment is seen in the use of the adjective "all" with both concepts—"speaking" ("word," *logos*) and "knowledge" (v.5). Paul is convinced that this was a real work of God's grace because he saw his witness about Christ established in their lives at the time of their conversion and had heard about it since then.

The phrase "in every way" (*en panti*) is obviously limited to the qualities and experiences that were relevant to the Corinthians as exemplified by their ability in speaking and by their abundance of knowledge. "You have been enriched" (*eploutisthete*) certainly does not refer here to conversion or to baptism, but rather to God's blessing in knowing and speaking Christian things. The aorist tense of this verb here in a constative sense (*i.e.*, emphasizing a total definitive action), sums up God's work in the lives of the Corinthians—God did it, he made them rich! That their "speaking" and "knowledge" were interrelated is evidenced by the use in the Greek text of a single Greek preposition *en* ("in") to unite these two terms. Perhaps eloquent speaking was uppermost in their minds (cf. Apollos the orator, Acts 18:24–28). Or they may have tried to display vainly their wisdom, which Greeks were apt to do (cf. 1 Cor 1:22).

The reference to "knowledge" (*gnosis*) in v.5 should not be construed to mean that the Corinthians possessed some hidden mystical knowledge by which in itself and without the cross of Christ they could somehow reach God and be saved. As the heresy known as Gnosticism developed in later centuries, some thought they could do this. They were called Gnostics, from the Greek word *gnosis* (the word used in 1 Cor 1:5), which in Paul's day simply meant "knowledge." Cf. "*knowing* Christ Jesus my Lord" (Phil 3:8) and "I want to *know* Christ and the power of his resurrection and the fellowship in his sufferings, becoming like him in his death" (Phil 3:10). Paul is speaking of concrete knowledge based on the reality of Christ's person and his death on the cross. This is not Gnosticism's secret, mystical, and symbolic knowledge supposedly leading through self-effort to higher levels toward God.

7,8 Now Paul addresses himself to their needs for present and future Christian living. He introduces the thought by "therefore" followed by a present-tense verbal form: "Therefore you do not lack any spiritual gift." The verb *hystereō* has the basic meaning of "fail" or "lack." This potential lack does not necessarily refer to the lack of special gifts mentioned in 1 Corinthians 12–14, because there Paul indicates that each Christian is not to exercise every gift (1 Cor 12:27–31). Rather, he seems to be referring more generally to God's grace actively counteracting the sins and faults so prevalent in the Corinthian congregation. Paul expresses confidence that God will keep them strong and will present his people blameless before him at Christ's return, which they are eagerly waiting for (vv.7, 8).

The circumstantial participle *apekdechomenous*—translated "eagerly wait for" in NIV—is one of attendant circumstance. The word *apokalupsis* ("an unveiling," "a disclosure") can mean a revealing of truth, but here refers to the unveiling of Christ, his appearance at his second coming. Cf. "the day of our Lord Jesus Christ" in v.8. See also 1 Peter 1:7, 13.

It is not clear in v.8 who "he" refers to—the Father or Christ. Christ is the nearer antecedent (v.7), but in the light of the reference to God's faithfulness in v.9, it is best taken as referring to the Father. Through God's power and strengthening, Christians will certainly be blameless when Christ comes again.

9 Before concluding this section of thanksgiving, Paul assures the Corinthians of God's faithfulness. As God called them initially into fellowship with Christ, so he is faithful in completing the work, granting them every grace and gift for daily life (cf. Phil 1:6).

Observe the apostle's fivefold repetition of the name of Jesus Christ in this brief section. All of salvation—past, present, and future—is based on Christ's redemptive work. And he is coming again!

Some scholars, such as Schmiedels, have claimed that Paul's opponents were Jewish Christian Gnostics, on the theory that gnosticism was already fully developed in Paul's day or had been developed in pre-Christian times. (Cf. W. Schmithals, *Gnosticism in Corinth* [Nashville: Abingdon, 1971] and *Paul and the Gnostics* [Nashville: Abingdon, 1972].) Paul seems to have had foes with gnostic tendencies in mind when he wrote about "hollow and deceptive philosophy, which depends on human tradition and the basic principles of this world rather than on Christ" (Col. 2:8), calling them to depend on Christ himself "in whom are hidden all the treasures of wisdom and knowledge" (2:3). But this is far removed from a developed gnosticism of the second to the fifth centuries A.D., which depended on knowledge and wisdom themselves for rising higher to God. R.M. Wilson has shown that the parallels between NT terminology and thought, on the one hand, and that of later fully developed gnosticism and later Gnostic treatises of the second to fifth century A.D., on the other, are not sufficient to show a fully developed first-century gnosticism. (R.M. Wilson, *Gnosis and the New Testament* [Philadelphia: Fortress Press, 1968], pp.51ff. See also Donald Guthrie, *New Testament Introduction* [Downers Grove, Ill.: Inter-Varsity Press, 1970], pp.422, 423.)

III. The Problem of Divisions in the Church

1:10-17

¹⁰I appeal to you, brothers, in the name of our Lord Jesus Christ, that all of you agree with one another so that there may be no divisions among you and that you may be perfectly united in mind and thought. ¹¹My brothers, some from Chloe's household have informed me that there are quarrels among you. ¹²What I mean is this: One of you says, "I follow Paul"; another, "I follow Apollos"; another, "I follow Cephas"; still another, "I follow Christ."

¹³Is Christ divided? Was Paul crucified for you? Were you baptized into the name of Paul? ¹⁴I am thankful that I did not baptize any of you except Crispus and Gaius, ¹⁵so no one can say that you were baptized into my name. ¹⁶(Yes, I also baptized the household of Stephanas; beyond that, I don't remember if I baptized anyone else.) ¹⁷For Christ did not send me to baptize, but to preach the gospel—not with words of human wisdom, lest the cross of Christ be emptied of its power.

19

10 In the light of information given him about divisions in the church, Paul exhorts the Christians both positively and negatively. "I appeal" (*parakalo*) can have the note of appeal as in "exhort" or "encourage," or the stronger emphasis of "implore" or "entreat." It is this latter idea that best fits the context here. First he charges them to have a united testimony ("speak the same thing," KJV; "agree with one another," NIV, v.10). Then he adds his plea for inward harmony in mind and confession about Christ. Between these two positive exhortations Paul introduces the solemn purpose: "that there may be no divisions" in the Christian community. The word "divisions" (*schismata*, literally "tears" or "cracks") graphically conveys the idea of the dissensions that were rending the church. He makes this exhortation through (*dia*) the authority of Jesus Christ (10a), whose name they revere.

11 Paul, as this verse indicates, had received word about the divisions in the Corinthian church from members of a certain Chloe's house. Presumably, all of them were Christians and obviously had some vital connection with the church, doubtless being among its members. The genitive expression *tōn Chloēs* ("some from Chloe's household," literally "those of Chloe,") does not make clear what the exact relationship was, whether relatives, slaves, or friends. Paul speaks very specifically. He says that "those of Chloe" reported that there were "quarrels" in the church, quarrels of such a nature as to call for his reprimand.

12 The Corinthian church was divided into at least four factions, each having its own emphasis, following its own leader, and acting in antagonism to the other three. How frequently local church congregations today are likewise divided into cliques! At Corinth the four groups centered around four prominent leaders. First, there were those who claimed to be special adherents of Paul, possibly because of his emphasis on the ministry to the Gentiles, a ministry with which many of them were connected. Then there were those following Apollos, enamored of that learned and eloquent preacher from Alexandria (Acts 18:24; 19:1, Titus 3:13). The followers of Cephas (Peter's Aramaic name John 1:42) were no doubt impressed by this apostle's emphasis on the Jews. Possibly they connected him with the Judaizers. The mention of the "Christ" party suggests that some Corinthians claimed special relationship to Christ (2 Cor 10:7), or placed a special emphasis on him—an emphasis they felt the followers of Paul, Apollos, and Cephas had neglected or did not have.

13 Paul quickly destroys the validity of such distinctions. Christians are all one in Christ. He teaches this by asking, "Is Christ divided?" He shows the foolishness of even raising the question. This he does by asking two other questions by which he denies that Paul was crucified for them and that they were baptized in his name. The same could be said also of Apollos and Peter.

14-16 The mention of baptism leads Paul to comment that the Corinthian believers had no reason to depend on the efficacy of baptism by him as a sanctifying grace, because he had baptized so few—Crispus, Gaius, and the house of Stephanus, these being the only ones he could remember for the moment as having been baptized by him. Crispus probably was at one time the head of the Corinthian synagogue (Acts 18:8) and Gaius was probably the Gaius mentioned as Paul's host in Romans 16:23. Stephanas we know as the one Paul calls the "first fruits of Achaia" and he, with Fortunatus and Achaicus, was with Paul at Ephesus (1 Cor 16:15, 17). The whole house or household of this prominent man was baptized by Paul.

Oikos basically means "house." In some places (e.g., Luke 12:39) it means the dwelling itself, the physical building, but here it means the people who make up the household, the family. Presumably this included both his blood relations and their servants—an example of a household baptism.

17 Why Paul did not baptize more during his stay at Corinth we are not told. It could be that he counted the new Corinthian believers to be in a catechetical-instruction stage under his teaching and that he would depend on Apollos his successor at Corinth (Acts 19:1) to take care of this sacrament of Christian witness at the proper time. At any rate, in order to balance his rather prominent reference to baptism, the apostle now states that his essential work was preaching the gospel (Acts 26:17, 18). His baptizing people was, he teaches (v.17), an accompaniment of his preaching, and his mention of this gives him an opportunity to talk about the thrust of his preaching ministry. His method was to preach not "with words of human wisdom," by which he means, not with the cleverness of human argumentation. He states this lest, in dependence on human argument, the heart of the message of the cross should be emptied of its essential meaning.

The present tense of the verb *euangelizesthai* stresses the priority of Paul's continuing task of preaching the gospel; baptizing was a consequence of preaching and was of secondary importance.

The phrase *en sophia logou* can be translated "in cleverness of speaking," with dependence on philosophical arguments such as those of Plato and Aristotle and the clever sophistries of current Greek life.

Notes

13 The perfect tense verb form μεμέρισται (*memeristai*) conveys the thought "Has Christ already been divided and continues so in the congregation?" In this kind of a situation, each leader with his group could have claimed to have a special source through Christ for salvation. By bringing up himself as an example (second negative; see the μὴ [*mē*] negative that expects a "no" response to a question), Paul shows that no one of the human leaders has any vicarious power for salvation but that Christ is the savior who unites all.

R. St. John Parry (in loc.) suggests that *memeristai* can be taken passively (as we have done) and tr., "Has Christ been divided?" or in the middle voice: "Has Christ shared [you] with others?" But he notes that for this latter there is no expressed object (you) for the verb. He correctly favors the passive.

IV. The Wisdom of God—the Preaching of Christ Crucified (1:18–2:16)

A. *Christ, the Power and Wisdom of God*

1:18–25

> ¹⁸For the message of the cross is foolishness to those who are perishing, but to us who are being saved it is the power of God. ¹⁹For it is written:
>
> > "I will destroy the wisdom of the wise;
> > the intelligence of the intelligent I will frustrate."

²⁰Where is the wise man? Where is the scholar? Where is the philosopher of this age? Has not God made foolish the wisdom of the world? ²¹For since in the wisdom of God the world through its wisdom did not know him, God was pleased through the foolishness of what was preached to save those who believe. ²²Jews demand miraculous signs and Greeks look for wisdom, ²³but we preach Christ crucified: a stumbling block to Jews and foolishness to Gentiles, ²⁴but to those whom God has called, both Jews and Greeks, Christ the power of God and the wisdom of God. ²⁵For the foolishness of God is wiser than man's wisdom, and the weakness of God is stronger than man's strength.

In this section Paul emphasizes that salvation is in Christ and not in the wisdom of men. Because Christ, the power and wisdom of God, is the source of men's salvation, men have no basis for boasting.

18-25 These verses flow logically from the proposition of v.17 that Paul did not come preaching with human wisdom. As he avoids this human ostentation, he realizes that the straightforward presentation of the message of the cross produces two effects. It is foolishness to those who are lost, but the power of God to those who are being saved (Rom 1:16). In his emphasis that God's power for salvation is in the cross, Paul in v.19 introduces an OT quotation from Isaiah 29:14 to show that God dismisses the wisdom of men as a means of salvation. In the Isaiah context, the Lord deplores the man-made precepts and mouthing of words for salvation (Isa 29:13) and declares that he will set aside men's wisdom and understanding as a means of finding favor with him. This thought Paul now adapts to his argument.

Having established God's rejection of man's striving for salvation through wisdom, the apostle now asks just where in fact "the wise man" (v.20) can be found who is able to do what the message of the cross of Christ has done. By "wise man" Paul may already be alluding to the Greeks (v.22b). The "scholar" (*grammateus*, "scribe"—"teacher of the law," NIV elsewhere) was the Jewish professional who was skilled in the law and often emphasized its technicalities. "The philosopher of this age" (v.20) was the man who wanted to dispute every issue and solve it by human reason. The designation could fit both Greek and Jew.

The term *grammateus* (v.20), related to the verb "write," sometimes means merely "secretary" or "clerk" (Acts 19:13), but in first-century A.D. Jewish circles it was a technical term to indicate "a teacher of the law," "an expert in the Jewish law." For the saved Jews in the Corinthian congregation this idea would be relevant. *Suzētēs* ("philosopher," "disputer," "debater") is a more general term used here to cover any other human attempt by intellectual endeavor to insure salvation. The negative *ouchi*, the strengthened form of *ouk*, ("not") used at the beginning of a question anticipates a positive response whether obtained or not: "Has not God made foolish ... ?"

Paul goes on to explain in v.21 that in God's all-wise purpose men with all their philosophical and religious wisdom and searching "did not come to know God" as the definite aoristic effect of the verb shows. This is not to deny the truth that, as Paul says in Romans 1:18-20, men have had a certain knowledge of God through the natural creation. Rather, Paul says, it was God's good purpose (*eudokēsen*) to save those who believe by the seemingly foolish process of preaching the cross. The *kerygma* is the preached message, "the message of the cross" (v.18).

In explanation of the world's seeking God through wisdom, Paul states that the Jews seek for "miraculous signs," and the Greeks seek wisdom (v.22), and through these means they hope to find the answers to the questions about God and life. The Jews were seeking signs to identify the Messiah and the apocalyptic deliverance they hoped God would bring them (cf. Mark 8:11; John 6:30). But Jesus had said that the Jews would be given only "the sign of the prophet Jonah" (Matt. 12:39, 40) to point to his death as Messiah. Thinking of an eschatological Messiah, the disciples of Jesus also wondered about the restoration of the kingdom to Israel, which the Lord said would come later in God's time (Acts 1:6, 7). By the word Hellēnes ("Greeks") the apostle referred primarily to the native Greeks of Corinth, though in a broader sense that word also refers here to the whole non-Jewish world (cf. Col. 3:11). See in v.23 Paul's use of "Gentiles" instead of "Greeks."

Paul now says (v.23) that his task is to preach Christ crucified. The perfect-tense form of the participle (estaurōmenon) conveys the thought that Christ's death has a continuous vicarious effect (cf. Gal. 2:20). To the unsaved Jews, however, this message of a crucified Christ was a "stumbling block," an offense, (Gr. skandalon; cf. English "scandal") for they expected a political deliverer. To the non-Jewish world (ethnē) the cross was "foolishness"—criminals died on crosses, and they could not see how the cross provided any moral philosophical standard to help them toward salvation. Furthermore, the Greeks and Romans looked on one crucified as the lowest of criminals, so how could such a one be considered a savior? (Lucian, De morte Peregrini, 13, mocks at those who worship a crucified sophist.) From their viewpoint, the Greeks would have had difficulty in conceiving of how a god, being spirit, could become incarnate and thus provide a god-man atonement for sin. This was a philosophical problem for them, though they conceived of the Olympian gods—Zeus, Hera, Athena, etc.—as having human characteristics, including sin, and as somehow having the ability of begetting and of being begotten by humankind.

In contrast, Paul states that God has his chosen ones, "the called" (klētous) from both the Jews and Gentiles (v.24). Paul has preached to such people about God's effective power to save them and of his wise plan through Christ to bring this about. He next uses a kind of paradoxical hyperbole (v.25) to present the greatness of God's wisdom: God has foolishness, God has weakness! What Paul means is that God's smallest, least significant thought is more worthwhile than the wisest plans of mankind. And God's seemingly insignificant expression of his creative and providential power, as the coming of the dew or the unfolding of a leaf, is greater and more effective than the mightiest thoughts and acts of men. He has complete control and fully accomplishes his purposes, while the power, acts, and thoughts of men are in comparison as nothing.

Notes

18 The present tense used in both the participles τοῖς ἀπολλυμένοις (tois apollymenois, "those who are perishing") and τοῖς σωζομένοις (tois sōzomenois, "those who are being saved,") emphasizes the progressive state of those concerned: those who think the message foolish are now on the way to a final lostness in hell; those who respond are in the process of being saved by God's power—they are declared righteous by God and are in the process of being made holy, a process to be completed when Christ comes again. (Compare the use of these words in Luke 13:23; Acts 2:47; 2 Cor 2:15; 4:3; and 2 Thess 2:10). By μωρία (mōria, "foolishness") Paul means that the message does not make any sense to those who are perishing.

19 The meaning of the perfect tense form γέγραπται (gegraptai, "it is written") conveys the idea that the effect of what God promised in Isa 29:14 continues to be true. The passage as Paul cites it is practically identical with LXX. It differs from LXX only in the use of the verb ἀθετήσω

(atheteō, "I will set aside, "thwart") in the place of κρύψω (krypsō, "I will hide, conceal"). The idea, however, is the same: God will make ineffective the insight or understanding of man as a means of attaining salvation. The Heb. term סתר (satar) in Isa 29:14, in the Hithpael stem, carries a passive connotation with its intensive reciprocal meaning; "shall be hid completely from themselves." This idea Paul may have sought to convey from the Heb. by his use of atheteō.

24 In the Gr. text, before the word χριστόν (Christon) a verb is understood. The verb "preach" can be supplied from v.23 with the meaning "We preach Christ as the power of God and the wisdom of God."

25 The expression τῶν ἀνθρώπων (tōn anthrōpōn, "of the men") is inclusive of all mankind: God's "insignificant" thought and smallest act are greater than those of "the men"; i.e., the totality of men.

1:26-31

> 26Brothers, think of what you were when you were called. Not many of you were wise by human standards; not many were influential; not many were of noble birth. 27But God chose the foolish things of the world to shame the wise; God chose the weak things of the world to shame the strong. 28He chose the lowly things of this world and the despised things—and the things that are not—to nullify the things that are, 29so that no man may boast before him. 30It is because of him that you are in Christ Jesus, who has become for us wisdom from God—that is, our righteousness, holiness and redemption. 31Therefore, as it is written: "Let him who boasts boast in the Lord."

26 Having contrasted God's strength and man's weakness, Paul now speaks about the circumstances under which God has called his people. Not many of them were of the intellectual-philosopher class, nor of the politically powerful, nor of the upper level of society.

The present tense of the verb *blepete* (NIV, "think of") emphasizes the current attention to be paid to God's calling of his people. *Klēsis* ("calling"; NIV, "called") is a noun with an action ending (*-sis*) and stresses God's dynamic drawing of his people to himself (Rom 11:29; Eph 1:18). In the light of its use in 1:22, *sophoi* ("wise") here places the emphasis on the Greek intellectual or philosopher class, those wise "according to human standards" (*kata sarka*). By *dunatoi* ("influential") Paul means to include the politically powerful. *Eugeneis* ("those of noble birth") includes all the upper classes—the aristocracy. By these three terms, then, Paul has given the sweep of all that men count socially, politically, and intellectually important.

27 God has chosen from the world those who seem foolish and those who seem weak and helpless so that he might put to shame the wise and powerful by showing how temporary and insignificant as to salvation their achievements are. And in his grace he has showered his mercy on the foolish and weak of this world and made them strong and wise in Christ.

28 Paul continues by stating that God has chosen those of the lower levels of society. First he mentions the slave class (the *agenē*, "low born") and the despised (*ta exouthenē-mena*). These terms were particularly appropriate for the situation at Corinth because there were so many slaves there. Also among those God has called, Paul lists the *ta mē onta*, "the things that are not"—i.e., "the nonexistent," those who seem to the world to

be nonentities. God has done this, Paul says, that he might show those who seem to be important (*ta onta*, "the things that are") that they can accomplish nothing for their own salvation because their wisdom, power, and importance are ineffective for this.

29 God has worked this way—chosen men according to his grace and not according to their merits—to show that no man may boast in God's presence that he has gained his salvation by his own effort.

30,31 Instead of boasting, redeemed men must realize that salvation is all of God's grace: it is because of God's effective plan that they are in Christ Jesus, (i.e., in saving union with Christ; cf. John 15:1–7; Rom 5:12–21). This saving relationship is a true one because Christ has become or been made for us wisdom from God so that through him we have come to know God (John 1:18; 14:6–9) and are made "wise for salvation" (2 Tim 3:14–17). Paul shifts from "you" to "we" to make certain the readers understand that all Christians, including himself, have this vital union with Christ.

Paul adds other effects or results of our union with Christ: he is righteousness, sanctification, and redemption for us. These concepts may be taken (1) as separate truths in addition to God's wisdom in sending Christ to die or (2) as explanatory of the wise plan effective in the substitutionary atonement. The second interpretation is to be preferred because of the particles *te kai . . . kai*. The sentence, then, should read: "He has become for us wisdom from God, that is, righteousness and sanctification and redemption." Christ in God's wise plan has become our righteousness and has taken our sin on himself (2 Cor 5:21). Christ has become our sanctification and has made possible our growth in grace in the Christian life (Rom 8:9, 10; Eph 2:8–10; 2 Pet 3:18). He is our redemption (*apolutrōsis*)—the person by whom we have been delivered from sin (Rom 3:24), the devil, hell, and the grave (1 Cor 15:55–57).

Because of God's gracious provision of salvation in this way, all praise must go to the Lord. To strengthen this conclusion, he appeals (v.31) to the authority of an OT quotation (Jer 9:24), using it in a condensed form. In OT times as in NT times, it was the duty of saved persons to glory in the Lord for his great salvation.

So it is not through human wisdom, strength, or worldly position that one is saved, but only through God's wise plan and power accomplished through the cross.

Notes

27 By using the neuter pl. forms with μῶρα (*mōra*, "foolish things"), ἀσθενῆ *asthenē* ("weak things"), and ἀγενῆ (*agenē*, "lowly things"), Paul indicates that his emphasis is not on individuals as such but on the qualities and characteristics that make up those individuals. The present tense subjunctive form καταισχύνῃ (*kataischynē*) shows that God continually brings to shame all those who think themselves strong in these respects. The aorist form καταργήσῃ (*katargēsē*) emphasizes that God will totally nullify the efforts of those who make their influence felt in this world.

29 The term πᾶσα σάρξ (*pasa sarx*, lit. "all flesh") is a figure of speech (synecdoche, a part of a whole) meaning "all people"—they will have no right ever to "boast"—aorist, καυχήσηται (*kauchēsētai*)—in God's presence.

30 The ἐξ αὐτοῦ (*ex autou*, "of him") is Paul's way of expressing, like Aristotle, the efficient

cause—God is the ultimate efficient cause, through this sovereign plan, of his people being "in Christ Jesus" (cf. John 15:1–10).

31 The *hina* clause would naturally expect a subjunctive form of the verb, but the apostle does not complete the thought in this normal way because of the imperative καυχάσθω (*kauchasthō*), which he gets from the OT quotation of Jer 9:23, 24.

B. Paul Preaches Christ in the Power of God

2:1–5

> [1]When I came to you, brothers, I did not come with eloquence or superior wisdom as I proclaimed to you the testimony about God. [2]For I resolved to know nothing while I was with you except Jesus Christ and him crucified. [3]I came to you in weakness and fear, and with much trembling. [4]My message and my preaching were not with wise and persuasive words, but with a demonstration of the Spirit's power, [5]so that your faith might not rest on men's wisdom, but on God's power.

Paul now returns to the manner of his own preaching introduced in 1:17. He argues that since salvation is attained not through human wisdom or might but only through the cross, he came to Corinth in dependence on the Holy Spirit as he simply preached Christ and the efficacy of his death.

1 In alluding to his visit to Corinth, he is thinking of the initial trip recorded in Acts 18:1–18, when the Corinthians first heard the message and believed. He did not depend on overpowering oratory (*hyperochēn logou*) or philosophical argument (*sophia*). He rather came preaching the "mystery" (*mystērion*) of God—the message not fully understood by them before, but now explained by him and illuminated by the Holy Spirit (2:10–14). In this verse, however, NIV has "testimony" (*martyrion*). See note on v.1.

2 Paul says he came with the sole purpose of centering his attention on the truth concerning Jesus Christ—on the fact and meaning of his crucifixion. The "for" (*gar*) introducing this verse confirms the statement of v.1 about his simple proclamation of the cross. It was not sufficient for Paul to tell about Jesus and his life; he had also to tell about his death for sinners (Acts 10:37–43). Christ died on a Roman cross at Jerusalem and his death was effective then and is effective now to bring forgiveness to sinners (Gal 2:16).

3 Now Paul adds, in effect, "I came preaching, simply as a frail insufficient human being; I came with fear and a great deal of trembling as I realized the importance of preaching the eternal gospel." In writing somewhat later to the Christians at Philippi, he encourages them to live their lives in a similar humble attitude, but at the same time with complete reliance on God (Phil 2:12, 13).

4 So his message and preaching conform to his personal attitude—he does not present his message in a way that depends on overpowering them with wise and persuasive arguments. Though he came in this unostentatious way, yet (*alla*) he came in a display of spiritual power because of the work of the Spirit. In this Epistle it is here that Paul first mentions the Holy Spirit's ministry.

5 Paul's purpose (*hina*), accompanying his humble presentation, is that their Christian faith might not be a superficial, misdirected belief coming from human wisdom, but a real Christian faith generated by the power of God, who also worked in Paul as he

preached (v.4). "The faith" (*hē pistis*) spoken of here with the definite article is not to be taken just as the act of believing but as the substance of their belief based on the person and work of Christ. It might be paraphrased, "their Christian faith." We must have the word of God as well as the power of God through the Spirit.

Notes

1 The better combination of MSS favor the word μυστήριον (*mystērion*), though some good MSS have μαρτύριον (*martyrion*, "testimony," "witness"), the tr. given by KJV. In the Bible, *mystērion* does not mean something necessarily unknown, but something not as fully understood at one time as it was at another (See Dan 2:18ff.; 4:9; and Rom 16:25, 26; also see W.H. Mare, "Paul's Mystery in Ephesians 3," *ETS Bulletin*, vol. 8, no. 2 [Spring, 1965], pp. 77ff.)

By the phrase καθ᾽ ὑπεροχήν (*kath' hyperochēn*), Paul implies that he did not come depending on any superiority of speech. This term is used elsewhere in the NT only in 1 Tim 2:2 of rulers in a superior or prominent position. The verb καταγγέλλω (*katangellō*, "proclaim"), like its synonym κηρύσσω (*kērysso*), is sometimes used, as in 1 Cor 9:14, with εὐαγγέλιον (*euangelion*, "gospel," the "good news"; cf. also the use of *kēryssō* with *euangelion* in Matt 4:23; Mark 1:14; Gal 2:2).

2 By the use of the aorist form ἔκρινα (*ekrina*, "I resolved" or "decided"), Paul sets forth the total objective of his Corinthian ministry to preach the crucified Christ. The negative οὐ (*ou*) may be taken more properly with *ekrina* in nearer antecedent than with the infinitive εἰδέναι (*eidenai*), thus: "I did not resolve to know." In smoother English this may be tr., "I resolved not to know" or, "I resolved to know nothing" (NIV).

The perfect passive participal ἐσταυρωμένον (*estaurōmenon*) carries with it the definiteness of the past factualness of Christ's crucifixion, but also carries its effects into the present.

4 The words πειθοῖς σοφίας λόγοις (*peithois sophias logois*, "wise and persuasive words") have somewhat shaky MS support; almost of equal value is the reading πειθοῖ ... (*peithoi* ..., "with persuasiveness of wisdom expressed in words"). The basic meaning is the same. The insertion of the word ἀνθρωπίνης (*anthrōpinēs*, "human") found in some MSS seems to be an explanatory gloss inserted by copyists and is plainly secondary (Metzger, p.564).

5 The twin prepositional phrases ἐν σοφίᾳ ... ἐν δυνάμει (*en sophia ... en dynamei*) are both causal in force here and are in absolute contrast (ἀλλ᾽ *all'*, "but")—i.e., not men but God.

C. *Wisdom of Christ Revealed by the Holy Spirit* (2:1–16)

2:6–9

⁶We do, however, speak a message of wisdom among the mature, but not the wisdom of this age or of the rulers of this age, who are coming to nothing. ⁷No, we speak of God's secret wisdom, a wisdom that has been hidden and that God destined for our glory before time began. ⁸None of the rulers of this age understood it, for if they had, they would not have crucified the Lord of glory. ⁹However, as it is written:

> "No eye has seen,
>   no ear has heard,
> no mind has conceived
>   what God has prepared for those who love him"—

Paul now makes clear that his presentation of God's eternal plan of salvation (v.7) is based, through the Holy Spirit, on the wisdom of God revealed to Paul and to others, a wisdom to be understood by those who are God's people.

6 In case some think that the gospel is devoid of wisdom, Paul states that it involves a higher wisdom discernible by those who are mature (*teleioi*)—those who have attained the goal and are spiritually mature. Though some understand "the mature" as referring to those far advanced in spiritual understanding compared with infants in Christ (cf. 1 Cor 3:1), the context favors the conclusion that these spiritually mature were the saved—those enlightened by the Holy Spirit—in contrast to the unsaved. This latter view is supported by Paul's argument that it is the unsaved who think the gospel is foolish (1:21–23) and that the unsaved person does not receive the things of the Spirit of God (2:14). This wisdom, Paul says, does not come from this age of time and space and certainly not from the rulers of this age (those who are of highest importance in the world), because such people crucified the Lord of glory (v.8). Paul says these rulers with their wisdom will end up in futility (v.6b).

7 Describing God's wisdom further, Paul states that it is a wisdom that is contained in a mystery ("God's secret wisdom") not fully revealed, but which God had planned before the beginning of the ages. This plan originated in God's mind, and though outlined in the OT, is not as fully explained and understood there as it is in the NT. Moreover, God conceived of this plan of redemption in relation to the final glory of the Christian when he shares with Christ the glory of God (Rom 8:17, 18).

8 None of the earthly rulers understood such redemption relating to wisdom, Paul explains. Otherwise, they would not have crucified "the Lord of glory." (Compare elsewhere the titles "King of glory" [Ps. 24:7–10] and "God of glory" [Ps. 29:3; Acts 7:2].) Christ's divinity ("Lord of glory") and his human nature (he was crucified in a real body on a hard, real cross) are now brought together by the apostle, leading to the conclusion that God the Son as incarnate in man died on the cross (Acts 20:28, "... the church of God, which he bought with his own blood"). By "rulers" Paul means the leaders of the Sadducees, Pharisees, teachers of the Law, and Herod Antipas, as well as the Romans represented by Pilate and his soldiers (Acts 4:25–28).

9 However, Paul says, the "hidden" wisdom he has been preaching is the wisdom referred to in the OT. It was set forth in the promises God had prepared and laid up for his people—for those who love him. It is these promises that people like the rulers of this world do not see and have not obeyed. The thought of them has not even entered the natural man's mind. That God has prepared these things for us Christians implies that sometime we will know and share in these promised blessings (Rom 8:18–25), which, Paul hastens to say, have been revealed to God's people by the Spirit (v.10).

The expression "it is written" (*gegraptai*) (v.9), though often used to cite OT Scripture (cf. Matt 4:4; Mark 11:17; Rom 1:17, et al.), might merely mean "to use the language of Scripture," or "to speak generally from Scripture" (cf. John 1:45), without meaning that the passage is formally cited. The first two lines of the quotation and the last line are a loose reference to Isaiah 64:4, whereas the third line may be merely a thought from the OT generally as summarized by Paul. Verse 9 does not make a complete sentence in Greek (see the dash at the end of the verse in NIV), but Paul, in giving more than one OT thought, is not attempting strictly to weave them into his sentence structure.

Notes

6 The term τέλειοι (*teleioi*, "mature") can possibly be taken to mean "adults" in comparison with the νήπιοι ἐν Χριστῷ (*nēpioi en Christō*, "immature Christians") of 1 Cor 3:1. But the contrasting term in 3:1 is πνευματικοί (*pneumatikoi*, "spiritual"), not *teleioi*. Rather, the meaning of *teleioi* as "mature" here is more likely an expression for those with the "mature insight" of the saved in distinction from the unsaved, contrasting with the technical use of this term for the "initiates" inducted into the mystery religions (cf. *Hermetic Writings* 4, 4; BAG).

The present tense of the participle καταργουμένων (*katargoumenōn*), stresses the continual passing away of the stream of rulers of this age.

7 Δόξα (*doxa*, "glory," "splendor,") implies reminiscences of the glorious God dwelling with his people in the OT (Exod 24:17; 40:34; Num 14:10) and a foretaste of the future glory the Lord's people will share with the triune God (Rev 21:10, 11, 22, 23).

8 The ἥν (*hen*—fem. accusative relative pronoun) beginning this v. does not refer to the immediately preceding δόξαν (*doxan*, "glory"—also fem.) because it is not glory that the rulers did not understand. Rather, they did not grasp the ςοφία (sophia, "wisdom") of the plan of God. Also this *hen* clause is parallel to the similiar type of clause in v.7, which obviously refers to an expressed σοφίαν (*sophian*) at the beginning of that v.

The perfect form ἔγνωκεν (*egnōken*, "they did not understand"; NIV—"None ... understood it") conveys the totality of their ignorance of God's wisdom continued from the past.

9 It is not certain whether even the first two (and fourth) lines are to be taken as a formal quotation from the OT. If they are, Isa 64:4 is loosely quoted by Paul here from LXX. That Paul's use of the v. in this place does not fit with the context of the v. in Isa is no difficulty, because the apostle shows he is not trying to prove his argument about God's wisdom by Isa 64:4, or he would have begun with ὅτι (*hoti*, "because"). But he uses "as," in the sense of citing general truth from this Isa passage. The third line of the quote may possibly echo Isa 65:17, "come into mind."

2:10–16

¹⁰but God has revealed it to us by his Spirit.

The Spirit searches all things, even the deep things of God. ¹¹For who among men knows the thoughts of a man except the man's spirit within him? In the same way no one knows the thoughts of God except the Spirit of God. ¹²We have not received the spirit of the world but the Spirit who is from God, that we may understand what God has freely given us. ¹³This is what we speak, not in words taught us by human wisdom but in words taught by the Spirit, expressing spiritual truths in spiritual words. ¹⁴The man without the Spirit does not accept the things that come from the Spirit of God, for they are foolishness to him, and he cannot understand them, because they are spiritually discerned. ¹⁵The spiritual man makes judgments about all things, but he himself is not subject to any man's judgment:

¹⁶"For who has known the mind of the Lord
that he may instruct him?"

But we have the mind of Christ.

These verses stress the work of the Holy Spirit in revealing the wisdom of God.

10 "But" (*de*), Paul says, God has revealed "to us"; that is, to Paul, to the other apostles, and their associates, the spiritual wisdom that the unsaved rulers of this world did not understand. The verb Paul uses (*apokaluptō*, "reveal") is a strong term, usually used in the NT to indicate divine revelation of certain supernatural secrets (Matt 16:17; Luke

10:22) or used in an eschatological sense of the revelation connected with certain persons and events (Rom 8:18; 1 Cor 3:13). Note also that throughout vv.10–16 Paul speaks mostly in the first person plural, "we" (not "you"), strengthening the interpretation that he is referring primarily to divine revelation given to apostles. Later in 1 Corinthians 3:1–3 Paul returns to addressing the Corinthians as "you." But what is true primarily of Paul and the other apostles, is true secondarily for all Christians—the Spirit helps them to interpret Scripture. The phrase "by [or through] the Spirit" certainly refers to the Holy Spirit, as is shown by the presence of the definite article (*tou*) with Spirit— *the* Spirit. The interpretation "through the human spirit" would not make any sense here because the rulers of this age did not (through human spirit) understand the wisdom of God.

The latter part of v.10 amplifies the first part by showing the *extent* ("all things") and *depth* ("the deep things of God") of the Holy Spirit's revelation of God's wisdom and truth. The present tense of the verb (*eraunaō*, "searches") indicates the continual and effective ministry of the Spirit in his all-pervading infallible guidance of the writers of Scripture (2 Peter 1:21) and in his effective work in the lives of believers (Eph 1:17–19; 3:16–19).

11 The *gar* ("for") here points to an illustration that will show that the spiritual wisdom and truths of God can be understood only through the Holy Spirit, just as human wisdom needs the human spirit to understand it. The conclusion is that only the Holy Spirit can reveal God's wisdom and truth to man. The concept of "spirit" in this verse involves a real personality who thinks and acts—not a force. The expression "the man's spirit within him"—i.e., his human personality being in him—is not to be taken as suggesting that the Holy Spirit of God is in God in the same way—the grammar of v.11b does not suggest this. The only analogy made is that as the human spirit knows or understands human wisdom, so (*houtōs*), the Spirit of God, being God himself, understands the wisdom of God.

12 By way of application, Paul states that it is the Spirit of God they have received. This is in contrast to some other kind of spirit through which some might try to know God's wisdom and truth—whether the spirit of the wisdom of this world (1 Cor 1:20; 2:6; 3:19) or another kind of spirit (cf. 1 John 4:2–6). The purpose of the Holy Spirit's special work of revelation (v.10), Paul says, is that "we may understand what [i.e., the truths] God has freely given us" (v.12).

13 Here Paul reverts to the nature of his own ministry (cf. vv.4, 5). He wants it known that he speaks "not in words taught . . . by human wisdom but in words taught by the Spirit," as he and other associates express spiritual truths in words conveying the real spiritual truth. Again, the contrast is between human wisdom and wisdom from God.

14 In using the generic term "man" (*anthrōpos*), the apostle now shows he is speaking of unsaved man in general, governed as he is only by his "soulish-human" (*psychikos*) nature, not accepting the enlightenment and truths from the spirit of God. Therefore such a person considers those truths to be foolish. Paul makes it even stronger when he says that "the man without the Spirit" cannot understand because these truths can be discerned and understood only with the guidance of the Spirit.

Psychikos (the Greek word that begins this verse) basically means "that which pertains to the soul or life," a word used in NT and patristic literature to refer to the life of the

30

natural world and so contrasted with the supernatural world and the Spirit. So from this comes the translation "man without the Spirit."

It is possible that the words "of God," with the words "the Spirit," are a copyist's addition—a number of MSS omit the words. However, the vast majority of MSS favors their inclusion. Note that the sense is clear either way, that the Spirit of God is in view.

It is to be observed that the verb *anakrino*, translated "discern" in v.14, is the same verb translated "make judgments" and "subject to man's judgments" in v.15. The idea in each case is to make intelligent spiritual decisions. *Anakrino*, though meaning "examine," here includes the decision following the examination (cf. 4:3).

15 In contrast, the person who is guided by the Spirit draws discerning conclusions about all things, that is, about all kinds of spiritual things, but such a spiritual man is not subject to spiritual judgments by any man, i.e., by any man without the Spirit (v.14). This is undoubtedly what Paul means by v.15b, for he elsewhere teaches Christians to make judgments concerning the spiritual condition and actions of other Christians. (See 1 Cor 5:9-12; 12:3; Gal 1:8.)

16 This verse is confirmatory of v.15. In quoting the LXX of Isaiah 40:13, Paul establishes further that the Christian is not subject to man's judgment in spiritual things. The quotation in the form of a question casts doubt on man's knowing God's wisdom, but the statement (v.16b) gives reassurance that the Christian does know it. This explains v.15b—the person who has God's Spirit is not subject to judgments by one who does not have the Spirit.

Paul introduces the "mind of Christ" terminology in order to relate it to the OT expression he has just quoted—"the mind of the Lord." The verse implies that we and *all* God's people can understand spiritual truths and spiritual wisdom in a way similar to the way the Lord knows them. Verse 16 climaxes Paul's argument about his preaching God's "foolishness" (the cross of Christ) without ostentation. Let the philosophers of Greece (cf. Acts 17:18, 32) and the Jews in their sign-seeking jeer and mock. They cannot really judge the message of Paul, who has the mind of Christ, because they do not have the Spirit of God and cannot judge spiritual truths.

Notes

10 Some MSS represented by TR (and KJV) add the pronoun αὐτοῦ (*autou*, "his") to πνεύματος (*pneumatos*, "spirit") but this is clearly an explanatory addition not supported by the better MSS.

11 In v.11b there is no corresponding ἐν αὐτῷ (*en autō*, "in him") and the clause simply states that only the Spirit of God (an OT and NT designation of the third person of the Trinity; cf. 1 Sam 10:10; 2 Chron 15:1; Rom 8:9; 1 John 4:2) can understand the things of God.

12 A few MSS have added the demonstrative pronoun τούτου (*toutou*) after κόσμου (*kosmou*, "of this world") a copyist's addition probably to parallel the expression with the phrase "of this age" in 2:6. The shorter text without *toutou* is to be preferred and is supported by the best and the most MSS.

13 The phrase πνευματικοῖς . . . συγκρίνοντες (*pneumatikois . . . synkrinontes*) has evoked at least four different interpretations, depending on how the participle *synkrinontes* is tr.: (1) "bring together" or "give," (2) "compare," or (3) "explain" or "interpret," and depending also on how

the gender of the adjectives is taken. *Pneumatikois* can be either masc. or neuter dative pl.; *pneumatika* can in this context be only neuter accusative pl. The phrase can mean (1) "giving spiritual truth a spiritual form," (2) "comparing spiritual truths with spiritual truths," (3) "interpreting spiritual truths to spiritual men," and (4) "explaining or expressing spiritual truths in spiritual words." Though any of the four interpretations can be argued, view 4 best fits the context of the v. in which Paul has said that he speaks in spiritual words (i.e., words taught by the Spirit, who gives to Paul spiritual truths in spiritual words)—words filled with concrete but spiritual meaning.

15 The τα (*ta*, "the") before (*panta*, "all things") has some good MS evidence, though copyists could have added it, fearing that *panta* could otherwise be taken as masc. accusative sing., "every man."

16 Paul is evidently quoting from the LXX of Isa 40:13; he varies from Rahlfs' LXX text by adding a γάρ (*gar*) and using the verb συμβιβάσει (*symbibasei*) instead of its cognate noun. The meaning is the same.

V. Servants of Christ (3:1–4:21)

A. *Workers With God—False Estimate Corrected (3:1–23)*

1. *Spiritual immaturity and divisiveness*

3:1–9

> ¹Brothers, I could not address you as spiritual but as worldly—mere infants in Christ. ²I gave you milk, not solid food, for you were not yet ready for it. Indeed, you are still not ready. ³You are still worldly. For since there is jealousy and quarreling among you, are you not worldly? Are you not acting like mere men? ⁴For when one says, "I follow Paul," and another, "I follow Apollos," are you not mere men?
>
> ⁵What, after all, is Apollos? And what is Paul? Only servants, through whom you came to believe—as the Lord has assigned to each his task. ⁶I planted the seed, Apollos watered it, but God made it grow. ⁷So neither he who plants nor he who waters is anything, but only God, who makes things grow. ⁸The man who plants and the man who waters have one purpose, and each will be rewarded according to his own labor. ⁹For we are God's fellow workers; you are God's field, God's building.

In this passage Paul speaks to the Corinthians about the lack of spiritual discernment he has been discussing in chapter 2. This lack is seen in their misconceptions about those who are co-laborers with God. The corrective is given in his later statements about the importance of working correctly for the Lord (3:10–17) and not depending on man or on human wisdom (3:18–23).

1 As in 2:1, Paul calls the Corinthians "brothers" before reprimanding them for their spiritual immaturity. Not only had he not preached to them with persuasive words (2:1–5), but here he states he could not even speak to them as to those with spiritual maturity. They were acting immaturely as those motivated by the world's thoughts and actions. Part of what he means is shown by his reference in vv.4, 5 to the party contentions he had discussed in 1:10–17. The word *pneumatikos* ("pertaining to the spirit," "spiritual") must be interpreted differently in 3:1 from its meaning in 2:14, 15, where Paul uses it to denote the saved person in contrast to the unsaved (one who is without the Spirit). Here in combination with *sarkinos* ("fleshly") and *nēpios* ("infant;" cf. 1 Cor

2:6, *teleios*, "mature"), the adjective *pneumatikos* applies to believers who are spiritually mature Christians—i.e., those led into maturity by the Spirit in contrast with the immature ones still controlled by the fleshly prejudices and viewpoints dominating the unsaved of the world.

2 Paul now amplifies the reference in v.1 to infants, by explaining that when he first came, he fed the Corinthian Christians spiritual milk—i.e., the elementary salvation truths of the gospel. He could not teach them deeper doctrines (*brōma*, "solid food") because as infants in Christ they could not spiritually digest them. The *alla oude eti nyn*, ("Indeed you are still not ready," v.2), emphasizes their continuing immaturity.

3 The descriptive term *sarkikos* ("fleshly") further indicates that these Christians showed characteristics of spiritual immaturity. The *gar* ("for") prepares for Paul's illustrations of this worldliness—"jealousy" (*zēlos*) and quarreling (*eris*), which plague the Christian community. Also implied is allusion to their divisions (v.4).

The question in v.3 is stated in Greek in a way that expects a positive answer. This suggests that the Corinthians, if honest with themselves, should admit their failing here. To walk *kata anthrōpon* ("according to man"—NIV, "acting like mere men") means to live only the way the ordinary sinful man lives—in selfishness, pride, and envy.

4 Paul's example of himself and Apollos who shared in the ministry at Corinth (Acts 18: 1–28) was needed to show the Corinthians that they had a distorted view of the Lord's work. Whenever they thought of God's work in terms of belonging to or following a particular Christian worker, they were simply acting on the human level and taking sides just as the world does.

5 In using *oun* ("then"; "after all," NIV), Paul shows he is answering the question "How should Paul and Apollos be viewed?" Observe how, because Paul wants to impress the Christians with the fact that he and Apollos are simply servants, he avoids using the first person plural, "we are servants" but leaves out the verb, so that the implication is that he and Apollos and whatever other workers there might be are no more than servants. The point is that no Christian worker is ever to be idolized. Indeed, those who are idolized can become instruments for fragmenting the work of God. Believers are to realize that Christian workers are simply God's servants (*diakonoi*)—agents through whom people believe in Christ. By "believe" in v.5 Paul does not mean just the initial trust in Christ (Rom 3:22–24) but, as v.6 shows, the planting, watering, and God-given increase—the whole process of growth in the Christian life to maturity (2 Pet 3:18).

6–9 Paul bluntly states, "I planted the seed" and quickly adds, "Apollos watered it, but God made it grow." In vv.7–9 he draws some conclusions from his basic premise: First, since we are merely God's servants, we are really nothing in that we cannot ourselves produce any spiritual results. Rather (again *alla*, "but," is used), it is only God who can do that (v.7).

Second, Paul teaches that the servants with their various functions are really one, being united in God's work (v.8a). Third, though they are one in the work, yet (*de*) they are individually subordinate to God and responsible to him who will reward them according to their faithful labor (v.8b).

Finally, Paul concludes (v.9) that all is of God and that the church ("God's building") is his work. Yet he uses men of different talents and temperaments to help him cause the church to grow. They are, Paul says, the spiritual "field" (*georgion*) in which God's servants are working. In speaking of their being God's *georgion* (God's cultivated field) and of Paul and Apollos and others as God's workers in the field (1 Cor 3:6-9), the apostle brings to the minds of the Corinthians the farming going on in the plain below the city. There the land was plowed, the crops reaped, the grapevines tended, and the grapes gathered—a crop "for which Corinth has for centuries been famous (our word 'currant' is a medieval corruption for Corinth)" (Broneer, "Corinth," B A, Vol SIV 1951, p. 96). Note also the familiar figure of the church in Ephesians 2:20-22 and 1 Peter 2:5. And now, in what Paul has said in vv.6-9 there is a transition to his discussion that is to follow in vv.10-17.

Notes

1 Actually, πνευματικοῖς (*pneumatikois*), taken as masc., can be tr. "spirit-filled people" in contrast to σαρκίνοις (*sarkinois*, "fleshly," "those controlled by the flesh").

3 The word διχοστασία (*dichostasia*, "dissensions," "quarreling"—not in the Gr. text used as the basis for NIV), following ἔρις (*eris*), is early and has diversified MS witness (P[46] D, et al.). Yet its absence in such MSS as P[11] vid ℵ B, et al., speaks against it and favors the possibility of the additional word being a western gloss, possibly derived from the list of vices in Galatians 5:22 (cf. Rom 16:17). The phrase κατὰ ἄνθρωπον (*kata anthrōpon*) is an adverbial phrase: "humanly," "in a human way," in contrast to "in a godly way."

Whereas in v.1 σαρκίνοις (*sarkinois*) means "belonging to the flesh," "having the characteristics of the flesh," σαρκικοί (*sarkikoi*), used in v.3, means "composed of flesh" and stresses that the Corinthian Christians were full of fleshly activities.

The οὐχί (*ouchi*, "not"), a strengthened form of οὐκ (*ouk*), expects an affirmative response when beginning a question.

5 Here διάκονοι (*diakonoi*) is not used in a technical sense of those who serve as church officers (as in Phil 1:1; 1 Tim 3:8), but in the general sense of "servants," whether of a king (Matt 22:13) or otherwise.

The aorist form, ἐπιστεύσατε (*episteusate*, "you believed"), is to be taken as punctiliar action in the broadest circle of their Christian experience. They believed initially in Paul's ministry when they were born again, but that trust in the Savior deepened and broadened in their sanctification through the continued ministry of Paul and then of Apollos.

6 The three aorist verb forms in this verse ἐφύτευσα, ἐπότισεν, ηὔξανεν (*ephyteusa, epotisen, ēuxanen,* "planted, watered, gave the increase"), coming in quick succession, stress the accomplishment of work for Christ and the finality of God's blessing in spiritual fruit following upon it.

7 Though the participle αὐξάνων (*auxanōn*) means here "cause to grow," yet in the figure of the grain field it must include that spiritual germinating principle God alone initiates (cf. John 3:5), just as he does for the physical seed the farmer plants and waters.

8 Κόπον (*kopon*, "labor, toil") suggests that the Christian is to serve God intently and intensely to the best of his ability—i.e., to "toil" for the Lord. For this he will receive a reward.

2. Building on Christ the foundation

3:10-17

10By the grace God has given me, I laid a foundation as an expert builder, and others are building on it. But each one should be careful how he builds. 11For no one can lay any foundation other than the one already laid, which is Jesus Christ. ¹²If any man builds on this foundation using gold, silver, costly stones, wood, hay or straw, ¹³his work will be shown for what it is, because the Day will bring it to light. It will be revealed with fire, and the fire will test the quality of each man's work. ¹⁴If what he has built survives, he will receive his reward. ¹⁵If it is burned up, he will suffer loss; he himself will be saved, but only as one escaping through the flames.

¹⁶Don't you know that you yourselves are God's temple and that God's Spirit lives in you? ¹⁷If anyone destroys God's temple, God will destroy him; for God's temple is sacred, and you are that temple.

Paul now discusses how God's servants can build the church of Christ. The foundation laid down through the preaching of the cross of Christ (1:18) is always the same—Jesus Christ. The Christian workers bring to it their labor and the spiritual materials they use to build the church upon Jesus Christ. At the end is the payday, at the second coming of Christ, when the right kind of work will be rewarded and the wrong kind will be destroyed. The section ends with a declaration that Christians are the temple of God, and a warning that no man is to destroy this temple, for he will then be destroyed.

10,11 Paul views his skill as an expert builder as being possible only through the grace of God. As an expert builder (cf. Prov 8:30), one who knew God's plan for the building of his church (Eph 3:7-10), he had laid the doctrinal foundation of "Jesus Christ and him crucified" (2:2; cf. Isa 28:16; Acts 4:11; Eph 2:20; 1 Peter 2:6). He acknowledges that others, such as Apollos, also build on this foundation of Christ. Then he gives a warning: Every builder—Paul, Apollos, and whoever works for God—must be careful how he builds. The shift in thought is now from the worker to his work.

Verse 11 implies the reason for the warning: though the workers cannot lay a foundation other than Christ, they had better be careful how they build on him. Any defects in their work will be their own fault. Christ cannot be blamed for it.

12-15 Instead of talking about the details of the building itself, Paul turns his attention to the kind of materials Christian workers are using: the materials of preaching the cross for the salvation, building up believers (cf. 1:18), and living a Christian life that is commensurate with that preaching (2:2-4). The purity and depth of such Christian teaching and a life corresponding to it are crucial, for that kind of building material will stand the test of fire on the day of the Lord's judgment.

Since valuable metals and precious stones (cf. Rev 21:18-21) were used to adorn ancient temples, Paul could have taken his imagery from Herod's temple in Jerusalem (Matt 24:1, 2) or from the beautiful public and religious buildings in Athens (Acts 17:23) and Corinth (where the remains of the sixth century B.C. temple of Apollo still stands today). Such imagery would be sufficient to convey the thought of pure doctrine. The frames of ordinary houses and buildings were built of wood; hay or dried-grass, mixed with mud, was used for the walls; and roofs were thatched with straw or stalks. So the kind of insipid teaching and life represented by these lesser things will also have to face the test of the pure fire of God's justice and judgment, when it will be consumed.

The "day" is not a day of calamity or hardship brought by man, but rather "the day of the Lord" (1 Thess 5:2-9), the day of the second coming of Christ (cf. 2 Thess 2:2). The "quality" (v.13) is to be equated with the kinds of materials of doctrine and life that are used. The fire is the fire of God's judgment. Fire in the Scripture is used figuratively in two ways: as a purifying agent (Matt 3:11; Mark 9:49); and as that which consumes

(Matt 3:12; 2 Thess 1:7, 8; Heb 12:29). So it is a fitting symbol here for God's judgment, as he tests the quality of the Christian's work.

Those Christians whose works stand the test of fire (v.14; cf. 1 Peter 1:7) will be rewarded (cf. Matt 25:14-30; Luke 19:11-27). Those whose works are consumed by the fire will themselves escape the flames (as if they were to jump out of the burning wooden structure they had built) and will be saved alone, without any works of praise to present to Christ.

16,17 The temple is reminiscent of the OT tabernacle and temple as well as the holy sanctuary built by Herod. It is to be distinguished from *hieron*, the "temple area." As Jesus speaks of his earthly body as the "temple" (John 2:19-21), so his redeemed people, indwelt by the Spirit of God (1 Cor 6:19), can be called individually and collectively God's temple.

Paul challenges the church with the fact that they together (note the plural constructions) are the spiritual temple of God, because the Spirit of God dwells in them (Eph 2:22; 1 Peter 2:5). Therefore anyone who builds this temple in a shoddy way deserves the destruction of his doctrine and false testimony described in v.15. Implicit in this is a warning against any false teachers coming in among the believers.

More pointedly, Paul states (v.17) that anyone who actually destroys or tends to destroy (i.e., defile or damage) God's temple will be destroyed by God (cf. Lev 15:31). The reason is clear: God's temple is holy, sacred, set apart (Isa 28:16; Rev 3:12). God in his justice and holiness cannot allow part of his holy work to be damaged without bringing retribution. Here is a fitting warning to every Christian minister and worker.

Notes

10 The ἀρχιτέκτων (*architectōn*, "expert builder"; cf. "architect") in Gr. practice was the one who supervised the other workers. In a sense, this broad meaning applies here, for though Paul performed his task skillfully, leaving Apollos and others to do their own work, yet he felt responsible for the total work of the church (cf. 2 Cor 11:28). The present tense of the verb ἐποικοδομεῖ (*epoikodomei*, "[others are] building on it") allows for the inclusion of other Christian workers besides Apollos.

13 The article ἡ (*ē*, "the") with ἡμέρα (*hēmera*, "day") shows that Paul is talking about the specific time when judgment will come for Christians—that time referred to in 2 Cor 5:10, when all Christians will appear before Christ's judgment bench to give account of Christian service. NIV rightly capitalizes "Day."

The intensive pronoun αὐτό (*auto*) used with the word "fire," meaning "the fire itself," is supported by some of the best early MSS but omitted by others. NIV leaves it out.

14-17 The εἰ (*ei*) conditional sentences (first class, assumed as true), posit that some in fact will be faithful workers and some will not.

3. *Complete dependence on God, not men*

3:18-23

¹⁸Do not deceive yourselves. If any one of you thinks he is wise by the standards of this age, he should become a "fool" so that he may become wise. ¹⁹For the wisdom of this world is foolishness in God's sight. As it is written: "He catches the

wise in their craftiness" ²⁰and again, "The Lord knows that the thoughts of the wise are futile." ²¹So then, no more boasting about men! All things are yours, ²²whether Paul or Apollos or Cephas or the world or life or death or the present or the future—all are yours, ²³and you are of Christ, and Christ is of God.

18-20 Paul now returns to the subject of wisdom and warns the believers not to be deceived into thinking that the wisdom of this human age is sufficient for obtaining salvation and for building up the church of God. Rather, if some Christian thinks himself to be wise by this world's standards, he must renounce dependence on this wisdom so that he may really receive God's wisdom (v.18).

In proof of this, Paul again mentions the truth of 1:18-25—the seeming foolishness of the preaching of the cross is really God's true wisdom for salvation. Directly and forcefully he declares that the wisdom of this world is foolishness in God's sight (v.19). He uses two OT Scriptures to support this. The first, is a somewhat free rendering of Job 5:12, 13, which he applies in a special sense to God. The graphic word "catches" vividly portrays the idea that men in their craftiness are no match for God—they set up their schemes of salvation against God's but he catches them up short.

20 Here Paul's quotation of the LXX of Psalm 94:11 shows that the Lord knows all the futile thoughts of the so-called wise men—nothing that enters their minds is beyond his understanding. All that is not in tune with God's thoughts is vain.

21,22 The conclusion of the matter is that no Christian is to boast or glory in the wisdom and attainments of men—not even Paul or Apollos. We are not to put our trust in anything human. The reason is that all things—yes, all the blessings of God in the whole universe—belong to the redeemed church. So the ministry of Paul, Apollos, Cephas (Peter), and any other Christian worker belongs to God's people. Also the *kosmos* (the world itself), the processes of living and dying, the present and the future—all are to be viewed in relationship to God's purposes and plans for his redeemed people. So Paul can say, "All things are yours." Everything is for the believers' benefit, everything belongs to them.

23 "And you are of Christ, and Christ is of God." Though all things belong to the Christian, they are not centered in him, for all things actually and finally belong to God. They belong to the Christian, then, as he himself belongs to God through the mediatorship of Jesus Christ, the Son of God. Christ and the Father are one (John 1:1; 10:30), yet Christ was sent by the Father into the world (John 10:36; 17:18) to effect our redemption so that we may "inherit the kingdom" (James 2:5).

Notes

---

18 The present imperative ἐξαπατάτω (*exepatatō*) suggests that some in the congregation were already deceiving themselves and must stop doing so.

The first class conditional sentence with εἰ (*ei*) and the indicative suggests that a factual condition existed in that some were actually thinking they were wise according to the world's standards.

20 In the LXX quotation of Ps 94:11 Paul leaves out the broader term, ἀνθρώπων (*anthrōpōn,* "men") so that he may apply the passage to the narrower thought of "wise men." The rest of the statement is identical with LXX. The term διαλογισμούς (*dialogismous*) may include the reasoning processes of men's minds (cf. Matt 16:7; Luke 12:17).

21 The ὥστε (*hōste*, "so then") clause with the imperative introduces the climax of the argument: Since God knows the so-called wisdom of the world and makes it ineffectual and worthless in the light of his great plan of salvation, the Christian has no right to boast about men and their wisdom.

22 The perfect participle ἐνεστῶτα (*enestōta*) means that which exists in the present, "the present age," (cf. Gal 1:4) in contrast to the coming age, the second coming of Christ and beyond (cf. Eph 1:21).

B. Servants of Christ: the Ministry of the Apostles (4:1–21)

1. Faithful servants

4:1–5

> [1] So then, men ought to regard us as servants of Christ and as those entrusted with the secret things of God. [2] Now it is required that those who have been given a trust must prove faithful. [3] I care very little if I am judged by you or by any human court; indeed, I do not even judge myself. [4] My conscience is clear, but that does not make me innocent. It is the Lord who judges me. [5] Therefore, judge nothing before the appointed time; wait till the Lord comes. He will bring to light what is hidden in darkness and will expose the motives of men's hearts. At that time each will receive his praise from God.

The beginning of this chapter follows up the preceding discussion about Christian workers. Here Paul adds that these who are counted as servants of Christ are also to be considered stewards of God—those to whom a trust has been committed, a trust they are to prove faithful to.

1 The impersonal *anthrōpos* simply makes the command general: Let man after man count Paul and other Christian workers servants of Christ. The genitive, "of Christ," can be taken in the sense of possession—"servants belonging to Christ." Though *hyperetas* ("servants") may once have had a more etymological meaning relating to "a rower" on board ship, its more general meaning was "servant" or "attendant." Here it means a subordinate servant functioning as a free man, not as a slave (*doulos*). Thus, Paul and Apollos were free servants of Christ, fully responsible to him, and not to the Corinthians.

"Those entrusted with" (*oikonomous*, "house stewards") refers to a position often held by a slave (Joseph, Gen 39:2–19), who managed the affairs of the household entrusted to him. "The secret things of God" indicates those mysteries of salvation God has revealed in his Word (Rom 16:25; Eph 1:9; 3:3, 4; 1 Tim 3:16)—the things man cannot discover by his human wisdom. (See note on "mystery" under 1 Cor 2:1.) These truths of the cross have been entrusted to Christian workers to be carefully used and guarded. As subordinate servants of Christ, they have no right of authority over those truths, but minister them in Christ's name to God's people.

2 Here Paul turns to examine the character of those who are handling God's truth: they, including himself, must first of all show themselves faithful.

3,4 In these verses, the apostle expresses the truth that since he is the Lord's servant and steward, it is to the Lord that he owes responsibility and it is the Lord who judges him for the quality of his service. Human judgment has little value. Even self-evaluation is unreliable, Paul says. Christ is the Lord of the conscience and is the one who can evaluate it properly.

5 Now the apostle leaps forward to the return of Christ when all Christians will have their works examined at the judgment seat of Christ (2 Cor 5:10). Because of this, he charges the Corinthians not to judge his faithfulness. This can be done truthfully only by the Lord when he comes. The present tense of *krinō* ("judge") is graphic and implies that the Corinthians were already judging. Paul is saying to them, "Curb your habit of judging." *Kairos* ("time") is strictly the appointed or definite time when the Lord will come back.

Ta krypta tou skotous ("what is hidden in darkness") are the acts and motives concealed in the inner recesses of a person's mind and heart. In Hebrew poetic style (cf. Pss 18:10; 22:1), Paul says the Lord will "expose the motives of men's hearts" in explanation of his statement "He will bring to light what is hidden in darkness."

Thus, at the second coming of Christ those who have been faithful in their work for the Lord will receive praise from him. Paul has already spoken about the servant receiving "wages" from the Lord (3:8). Compare the parables of the talents and the pounds, in which there is praise and pay for faithful work (Matt 25:14-23; Luke 19:12-19). As the final judging must be done by God, so the final praise will come from him.

Notes

---

2 The aorist subjunctive form εὑρεθῇ (*heurethē*, with punctiliar action—"that he be found, be proved") looks at the person's ministry as a whole. The Lord looks at it as one picture, expecting to find the servant faithful in all his ministry.

3 The verb ἀνακρίνω (*anakrinō*) definitely conveys the idea of "examine" (Acts 12:19; 17:11), but it can also include, as here, the additional concept of the decision made following the examination (cf. 1 Cor 2:15).

Strictly speaking, the phrase ὑπὸ ἀθρωπίνης ἡμέρας (*hypo anthrōpinēs hēmeras*) means "by a human day." But just as the term "day of the Lord" (1 Cor 1:8; 5:5) involves God's judgment in that eschatological day, so in this context a "human day" means man's judgment in the day when his (man's) courts are in session. NIV well tr. the phrase "by any human court."

4 Paul's use of the δικαιόω (*dikaioō*), "justify" for "judges" does not involve the teaching of justification, which he presents elsewhere (Rom 3:24; 5:1; cf. also *Westminster Shorter Catechism*, Question 38). What he is now saying is that his conscience cannot declare his ministry to be perfectly faithful and therefore make him innocent of any wrongdoing in his service. Rather, God must make that judgment. The perfect tense form, δεδικαίωμαι (*dedikaiōmai*), gives this meaning: "I do not stand in a perfect state of justification or innocence just because my conscience is clear."

5 Paul uses here the simple form κρίνω (*krinō*, "judge") rather than the compound ἀνακρίνω (*anakrinō*, "examine and then judge"). In using *krinō*, Paul is saying that the Corinthians were actually making a final judgment regarding his faithfulness. If he had used *anakrinō*, he would have been stating that they were judging him in accordance with a full and proper investigation. At any rate, in using *krinō* and the accompanying phrase, "till the Lord comes," the apostle assumes a hasty and inappropriate judgment on their part.

Καιρός (*kairos*), which can indicate a point of time (Matt 24:45) as well as a period of time (Rom 3:26), is to be taken here in the context of the Lord's day of judgment as "an appointed time." At times *kairos* is to be contrasted with χρόνος (*chronos*), extended time (cf. Acts 1:7: χρόνους, "times"; καιρούς, "dates").

---

2. The proud Corinthians and the despised servants

4:6–13

> [6]Now, brothers, I have applied these things to myself and Apollos for your benefit, so that you may learn from us the meaning of the saying, "Do not go beyond what is written." Then you will not take pride in one man over against another. [7]For who makes you different from anyone else? What do you have that you did not receive? And if you did receive it, why do you boast as though you did not?
> [8]Already you have all you want! Already you have become rich! You have become kings—and that without us! How I wish that you really had become kings so that we might be kings with you! [9]For it seems to me that God has put us apostles on display at the end of the procession, like men condemned to die in the arena. We have been made a spectacle to the whole universe, to angels as well as to men. [10]We are fools for Christ, but you are so wise in Christ! We are weak, but you are strong! You are honored, we are dishonored! [11]To this very hour we go hungry and thirsty, we are in rags, we are brutally treated, we are homeless. [12]We work hard with our own hands. When we are cursed, we bless; when we are persecuted, we endure it; [13]when we are slandered, we answer kindly. Up to this moment we have become the scum of the earth, the refuse of the world.

Paul describes the difference between himself and Apollos and some of the other Christian leaders. The Corinthians, he says, were proud and claimed to be spiritually rich. On the other hand, Paul and Apollos were considered weak and were despised and persecuted.

6 What Paul has said about not judging or misjudging Apollos or himself he wants understood as applying to the Corinthians' attitude toward all of God's people; they should not take pride in some and despise others. In referring to this tension and misconception on their part, the apostle could be alluding to the real leaders of the factious parties for whom the other names—Paul, Apollos, Peter, and Christ—had been substituted. But then it seems strange that he does not name them. Or he may be simply referring to some who were responsible for stirring up this misconception about how God's ministers should be viewed.

In using the expression "I have applied these things to myself and Apollos" (v.6), Paul is saying that he is teaching them by personal illustration that ministers are only examples, and not merely teaching them abstract principles.

The saying "Do not go beyond what is written"—since it contains in it the familiar *gegraptai*, "it is written," used often to introduce OT quotations—seems to be a general statement advising the Corinthians not to go beyond any written doctrine in the OT. The last clause in v.6, like the preceding clause, is one of result and fits into the context as follows: If they learn not to go beyond the teaching of the Scripture about how they should treat God's teachers and all of God's people, then the result will be that they will not be conceited in taking a stand for one teacher or person over against another.

40

7 Some Christians evidently were boasting because of their talents and because of their positions and parties. So Paul puts the rhetorical question to them: "What do you have that you did not receive?" The obvious answer is that they received all from God and had no right to boast.

8 Paul derides their conceit. He does this with irony by a series of dramatic boasts of theirs: they, so they think, have all they need; they are rich and are reigning like kings, even without any help from Paul. The Corinthians evidently thought they had reached full maturity and were ruling and reigning rather than walking humbly with God.

9 Continuing the irony, Paul replies that in his opinion—he speaks mildly, using the expression "it seems to me"—God has not placed the apostles in a reigning position such as the Corinthians think they themselves are in. The irony is that the Corinthians were trying to "reign," while their spiritual fathers and examples were far from "reigning." Actually, Paul goes on to explain that God has publicly displayed the apostles as humble, despised men—men worthy of death. He seems to be using the term "us apostles" in the widest sense to include not only Peter and himself but also Apollos (1:12) and perhaps other prominent Christian workers who were associated with the apostles—e.g., Barnabas (Acts 14:14), Andronicus and Junius (Rom 16:7), and James, the Lord's half brother (Gal 1:19). He pictures those of the apostolic band as condemned to death and led forth by a conqueror. By his use of *theatron* ("spectacle") he seems to be alluding to the figure of condemned men tortured and exposed to the wild animals in the colosseum. They are also pictured as despised before the whole world (*kosmos*) and the angelic hosts.

10 Paul makes a series of contrasts between the proud Corinthians and the "dishonored" apostles—all from the warped viewpoint of the Corinthians. What a contrast: the apostles—foolish, weak, and dishonored; the Corinthians—wise, strong, and honored!

11-13 To set the record straight, Paul goes on to describe in detail the hardships he and his fellow Christian workers have suffered throughout their ministry (cf. the expressions "to this very hour" [v.11] and "up to this moment" [v.13]). He first emphasizes the physical deprivations they were suffering: hunger, thirst, lack of clothing, rough treatment, and homelessness. To remind the Corinthians again that he has no desire to be a physical burden to them, he injects the statement "We work hard with our own hands" (v.12).

Then he continues the list of his sufferings. This time he mentions mainly the verbal abuse Paul and his friends took and their response to it. They were frequently reviled, but they called on God to bless their revilers! He interjects, "When we are persecuted, we endure it." Then he goes back to the theme of verbal abuse (v.13a): "When we are slandered, we answer kindly." Climaxing this moving passage, Paul states that he and his fellow workers have become the scum of the earth, and the refuse of all men.

Notes

---

6 The word μετασχηματίζω (*metaschēmatizō*) literally means "to change the form of something,"

and as used here means "to say something in a different form," or "speak in a figure of speech or practical illustration."

7 The γάρ (gar, "for," "indeed") makes a vital connection with v.6: Why, Paul is asking, should you take pride in some men over others, for who really makes you different from others? The conclusion follows that all men receive what they have from God. The εἰ (ei, "if") is a condition assumed to be true—i.e., "if you received it, as in fact you did."

8 The perfect tense of the verb construction κεκορεσμένοι ἐστέ (kekoresmenoi este) stresses the present continuance of a fact that is already true as they view it: "You are already living in a state of having all the spiritual food you need." The next verbs in this sentence are in the aorist tense, indicating point of fact: "You have become rich! You have become kings. . . ."

9 Κόσμος (kosmos) is used here in the enlarged sense of "universe," introducing the dual concept of angels who inhabit the universe and men who live on earth.

10 The use of ἀσθενεῖς (astheneis, "weak") and ἰσχυροί (ischyroi, "strong") may be a reference to 1 Cor 1:27, to the weak and strong things of this world.

11,12 The tenses of these verbs are all present, emphasizing that these activities were experienced day by day by Paul and his companions. The verb γυμνιτεύω (gymniteuō), tr. "naked" in KJV actually means to be "poorly clothed." (Cf. "in rags," NIV.)

13 The term περικαθάρματα (perikatharmata), denotes the dirt or filth removed by thorough cleansing; περίψημα (peripsēma) also indicates dirt removed by scraping. The use of both terms strongly emphasizes how the world has despised and rejected Paul and his friends. Both words can be used ritually of filth that has been removed, and so some have tr. the words as "scapegoats" (BAG, s.v.).

---

3. The challenge to be God's humble servants also

4:14-21

14I am not writing this to shame you, but to warn you, as my dear children. 15Even though you have ten thousand guardians in Christ, you do not have many fathers, for in Christ Jesus I became your father through the gospel. 16Therefore I urge you to imitate me. 17For this reason I am sending to you Timothy, my son whom I love, who is faithful in the Lord. He will remind you of my way of life in Christ Jesus, which agrees with what I teach everywhere in every church.

18Some of you have become arrogant, as if I were not coming to you. 19But I will come to you very soon, if the Lord is willing, and then I will find out not only how these arrogant people are talking, but what power they have. 20For the kingdom of God is not a matter of talk but of power. 21What do you prefer? Shall I come to you with punishment, or in love and with a gentle spirit?

Paul concludes this section (4:1–21) with a challenge for the Corinthian Christians to be spiritually humble, and to this end he says that he has sent Timothy to help them and that he himself will come, too.

14-17 Paul now explains that his seeming harshness in writing this to the Corinthians was not to shame them but to warn them of the seriousness and perverseness of their actions and their pride. He grants that they have countless guides or guardians but denies that they have spiritual fathers to advise them. But since he has begotten (egennēsa) them in Christ (i.e., by Christ's atoning work) through the gospel and is therefore their spiritual father, he feels he has a right to advise them. In speaking of the leaders of the Corinthians as paidagōgoi ("guardians"), the apostle is calling attention to the distinction between himself, their spiritual father, and those leaders, many of whom could be called "guardians," or "guides." In the ancient Roman Empire, *paidagōgoi* indicated "slave-guides," who escorted the boys to and from school and were in charge of their general conduct. So, in a sense, they could be called instructors (cf. Gal 3:24). Hodge has well said that there are three agencies used by God for the conversion of men: "The efficiency is in Christ by his Spirit; the administrative agency is in preachers; the instrumental agency is in the word" (in loc.).

Since Paul could rightfully claim to be their spiritual father, he feels he can ask them to become imitators of him (cf. 1 Cor 11:1; Gal 4:12; Phil 3:17; 1 Thess 1:6; 2 Thess 3:9). In the light of this request, he says he has sent Timothy to them to help them in their progress. Timothy, too, was Paul's beloved child, "begotten" through the gospel, and faithful in the Lord—i.e., in his service for Christ.

Though Paul mentions having sent Timothy, the latter was evidently not the messenger who brought the 1 Corinthians letter. It is true that *epempsa* ("I have sent") can well be taken to mean, "I have sent [him and he has just arrived with 1 Corinthians]" (an epistolary aorist). But *epempsa* could just as well be interpreted, "I sent [him before I sent this letter to you]" (a common definitive past-tense use of the aorist). Supporting this latter interpretation is the fact that Timothy is not mentioned in the greetings either at the beginning or at the end of this letter, indicating he was not with Paul in Ephesus at the time Paul wrote 1 Corinthians. Further, Acts 19:22 states that Paul had sent Timothy from Ephesus to Macedonia, also the implication from 1 Corinthians 16:10 is that he was to continue on to Corinth and was still on his way there when this first letter to the Corinthians had reached the city. It is more likely that Stephanus, Fortunatus, and Achaicus, who are indicated as being from Corinth and who are said to be with Paul (1 Cor 16:17), were the bearers of the letter. In 1 Corinthians 16:18 they are commended and respect is asked for them. So Paul implies that these three were to return to Corinth. Paul expects that when Timothy arrives at Corinth he will cause the saints there to reflect on all Paul's work and actions, which correspond to his teaching in all the churches. As should be true of every Christian, Paul practiced what he preached.

18-21 Now concerning his own proposed trip to Corinth, Paul addresses some in the church who had acted arrogantly as though he were not going to come and did not dare to do so. These were the false teachers who were trying to undermine his authority (cf. 1 Cor 9:1-3; 2 Cor 12:12) by saying he was unstable (2 Cor 1:17) and weak and that his message was of no importance (2 Cor 10:10).

Paul replies that, the Lord willing, he will come without delay, and then will find out the real power of the arrogant persons who are doing all the talking against him (v.19). *Alla* ("but") emphasizes the contrast: Talk is cheap! What real power do these people have to promote their unscriptural and derogatory ideas? Paul uses the expression "kingdom of God" in v.20, not in its future eschatological sense, but, as the reference to the arrogant Corinthians here shows, in a present spiritual sense of God reigning over his people and demonstrating his power in their lives. The apostle is talking about the life that comes from Christ (2 Cor 5:17), the new birth and its power (cf. John 3:3-8).

Paul climaxes his thought with the question, "What do you prefer?" (v.21). He poses two alternatives: Do you want me to come "with punishment or in love and with a gentle spirit?" So Paul has answered their charge that he is afraid.

The expression "a spirit of gentleness" is certainly not to be taken as referring to the Holy Spirit, but to Paul's own spirit. Coupled as it is with "in love," it means that Paul wants to come in a manner expressing gentleness.

Notes

14 With ἀλλά (alla, "but"), the position of the participles ἐντρέπων (entrepōn, "shame") and νουθετῶν (nouthetōn, "warn") at opposite ends of the sentence emphasizes the contrast by putting stress on the second participle ("warn") as the result the apostle really desires.

15 The ἐάν (ean, "if") condition is to be taken here with ἀλλά (alla, "but") in the conclusion: "If you should have ... " to mean, "Even though you have ... you certainly do not have many fathers." The contrast is strong between πατέρας (pateras, "the many fathers") and ἐγέννησα (egennēsa, "I have fathered [you]").

16 Μιμηταί (mimētai), from which we get our word "mimic" simply means "imitators," a fitting description of the role of little children who naturally imitate the actions and attitudes of their fathers and mothers. The present form of the dynamic verb γίνεσθε (ginesthe, "become") here is graphic: "continue to become in practice [imitators]."

17 Grammatically, the expression "in the Lord" can go with both "beloved" and "faithful": "my child beloved and faithful in the Lord."

18 The relative adverb ὡς (hōs) here denotes the idea of "on the assumption that," the entire statement then reading, "some have been arrogant on the assumption that I am not going to visit you."

19 The verb γινώσκω (ginōskō) here conveys more than simply to know a fact. It means "ascertain, find out" the inner working of the arrogant Corinthians. The perfect participle πεφυσιωμένων (pephysiōmenōn) indicates that those who had become arrogant are still in that state.

VI. Paul's Answer to Further Reported Problems in the Church (5:1–6:20)

A. Paul's Condemnation of Sexual Immorality—Incest (5:1-13)

5:1-8

¹It is actually reported that there is sexual immorality among you, and of a kind that does not occur even among pagans: A man has his father's wife. ²And you are proud! Shouldn't you rather have been filled with grief and have put out of your fellowship the man who did this? ³Even though I am not physically present, I am with you in spirit. And I have already passed judgment on the one who did this, just as if I were present. ⁴When you are assembled in the name of our Lord Jesus and I am with you in spirit, and the power of our Lord Jesus is present, ⁵hand this man over to Satan, so that his sinful nature may be destroyed and his spirit saved on the day of the Lord.

⁶Your boasting is not good. Don't you know that a little yeast works through the whole batch of dough? ⁷Get rid of the old yeast that you may be a new batch without yeast—as you really are. For Christ, our Passover lamb, has been sacrificed. ⁸Therefore, let us keep the Festival, not with the old yeast, the yeast of malice and wickedness, but with bread without yeast, the bread of sincerity and truth.

The sin of sexual immorality and the church's indifference to it is the second major evil in the Corinthian congregation that Paul mentions. Corinth was noted for its loose and licentious living (cf. introduction, p. 180), a situation duplicated in the prevailing lack of moral standards in these latter years of the twentieth century.

In this chapter Paul condemns the sin of incest, which he calls *porneia* ("sexual immorality"). He rebukes the church for its arrogance in the matter and its failure to excommunicate the violator—something Paul insists on (vv.1-5). The purity he describes is symbolized in the removal of leaven in the celebration of the OT Passover, which is fulfilled in Christ, "our Passover lamb" (vv.6–8).

Later (vv.9–13) he gives instruction that the church should guard its own membership against sexually immoral persons, but that it should not try to Christianize unbelievers by forcing biblical standards on them.

1 "Fornication," used in KJV for *porneia*, does not communicate today. *Porneia* conveys the idea of extramarital sexual relations of any kind, so the NIV translation, "sexual immorality," is accurate. The word *holōs*, translated "commonly" in KJV, is better rendered "actually." This may mean, "generally speaking it is reported," or "it is really reported"; the present tense of the verb *akouetai* helps convey the idea that the report is continually spreading. The use of *gunaika*, literally "woman," graphically shows that it was the man's stepmother he had married. The NT expression "to have a woman" means to marry her (cf. Matt 14:4; 22:28 [Greek]; 1 Cor 7:2, 29). The sin of incest, Paul says, is not even practiced among the non-Christians. Cicero (*pro Cluent* 5, 6) states it was an incredible crime and practically unheard of. Such a marriage was strictly forbidden according to Leviticus 18:8 and Deuteronomy 22:30 and carried with it a curse (Deut 27:20). Rabbinic law in the main seems to have allowed such a marriage when a proselyte married his stepmother, since his becoming a proselyte broke all bonds of relationship. (See Strack-Billerbeck, *Kommentar zum N.T. aus Talmud und Midrasch* [Munich: Beck, 1922–1961], 3:343–358.) It is possible that some in the Corinthian church who may have come from the synagogue there could have known of this allowance. Part of an inscription indicating the presence of such a synagogue has been found. (See J. Finegan, *Light From the Ancient Past* [Princeton, N.J., Princeton University Press, 1959], pp. 361, 362; see also page 177 above in this commentary.) Though as a Pharisee (cf. Phil 3:5), Paul knew the system of Jewish law with its varying interpretations, he applies the OT law and the teaching on marriage quite strictly.

2,3 Paul again alludes to the pride of the Corinthians. This time it was a pride that, rather than cause them to mourn over the shocking sin, allowed them to tolerate such a sinner in the congregation. Paul presses his judgment of the case by saying that he is with them in spirit and has already passed judgment on the offending person.

4,5 Though the local congregation itself is to gather and discipline the offender, Paul reminds them of his apostolic authority over them by saying, "I am with you in spirit." However, he does not overassert his authority, because he recognizes that the decision is to be made "in the name of our Lord Jesus" (i.e., by the authority of the Lord Jesus; because of his person, his name carries authority—see also Acts 4:12) and that it is to be done with "the power of our Lord Jesus." These two expressions amplify each other: church discipline is to be exercised carefully on the authority of Jesus' name and the verdict given is accompanied by the spiritual power of the Lord Jesus. By saying, "Hand this man over to Satan, so that his sinful nature [or body] may be destroyed," Paul means to include the man's excommunication (at least by implication; cf. v.2) and his suffering physically in some way, even as far as death (cf. 1 Tim 1:20). The word *sarx* (flesh, v.5) can mean the "sinful nature" (NIV), but since "flesh" in this verse is in contrast to "spirit," the reference seems to be to the body. That Satan had power to afflict the body is evident from frequent NT references to the effects of demon possession (cf. Matt 9:32, 33; Luke 9:39–42) and to satanic activity in causing affliction or limitation (2 Cor 12:7; 1 Thess 2:18). This bodily punishment by Satan, Paul hoped, would have the effect of causing the man to repent so that his spirit (his person) might be saved in the day of the Lord—i.e., at the second coming of Christ. Though Paul teaches church excommunication here and a deliverance to Satan for physical punishment with a view to repentance, he does not say that the man should divorce his stepmother. This would be in accord with the scriptural teaching that marriage is an indissoluble bond (Gen 2:24). He does imply that the man should repent so that his spirit would be saved. Some have held the interpretation that 2 Corinthians 2:6, 7 and 7:9–12 refer to this man and that he repented. If true, such an interpretation implies that the man was to be allowed to come back into fellowship in spite of his incestuous marriage.

6–8 Paul illustrates Christian holiness and discipline by the OT teaching that no leaven was allowed in the bread eaten at the Passover feast. "Leaven," or "yeast," in Scripture generally conveys the idea of evil or sin (cf. Matt 16:6). That the church should allow such sin as that in the Corinthian church to go undisciplined would affect the attitude of the entire Christian community toward sin—"a little yeast works through the whole batch of dough." The church is to get rid of the old yeast—"the sin that so easily entangles" (Heb 12:1). So the command is to get rid of such sin individually and in the church, for the believing community is an unleavened batch of dough, a new creation in Christ, who has been sacrificed as our Passover lamb.

Christ, "our Passover lamb," died at the time of the Jewish Passover celebration. Actually he died on the next day following the sacrifice of the Passover lambs. This Passover day, which began the evening before when the lambs were sacrificed, is called rather generally the first day of the Feast of Unleavened Bread (Mark 14:12). This was the day of Preparation of Passover Week (John 19:14, NIV; cf. Matt 27:62; Mark 15:42; Luke 23:54), the "day of Preparation" being understood in the early Christian church to be Friday (cf. *Martyrdom of Polycarp* 7:1; it also means this in modern Greek).

So Paul concludes in v.8, "Let us keep the Festival"—that is, let us live the Christian life in holy consecration to God (cf. Rom 12:2; 1 Pet 2:5). This means, he says, that we are to live not with the old yeast of malice and wickedness, but on the basis of the unleavened principles of sincerity and truth. Therefore, such sins as incestuous marriage and the like cannot be tolerated or left undisciplined in the church.

Notes

1 Ὅλως (*holōs*) may go either with ἀκούεται (*akouetai*), meaning "it is actually reported," or with πορνεία (*porneia*), meaning "[it is reported that there is] actually sexual immorality...." The former interpretation (as in NIV) is better because, by grammatical position and as an adverb, *holōs* fits better with the verb *akouetai*. Probably because of Lev 18:8 ("father's wife") Paul uses the expression γυναῖκα ... ἔχειν (*gunaika ... echein*, "to have [his father's] wife") rather than the Gr. designation μητρυία (*mētryia* "stepmother").

2 The verb in the perfect passive form—i.e., "you exist in your arrogant pride," emphasizes again the general attitude Paul referred to in 4:18, 19. Οὐχὶ μᾶλλον (*ouchi mallon*, "not rather") strongly emphasizes the contrast between their arrogance and the grief they should have had. The expression ἀρθῇ ἐκ μέσου ὑμῶν, (*arthē ek mesou humōn*, literally, "he should be expelled from your company") is to be compared with ἀποσυνάγωγος γένηται (*aposynagōgos genētai*, "he should be put out of the synagogue," John 9:22). Both mean "to be excommunicated." The implication is that the church will perform this act (5:4, 7).

5 Ancient NT Gr. MSS favor somewhat the reading "the day of the Lord" (as in NIV) over the variants, "the day of the Lord Jesus," or ". . . of our Lord Jesus Christ." The meaning is the same.

7 The aorist verb ἐκκαθάρατε (ekkatharate, "get rid of completely") is very expressive here: "clear out of the house, get rid of any evidence of the old yeast." Cf. the first Passover with its unleavened bread (Exod 13:3-7). Generally in the NT and other related literature the verb θύω (thyō) indicates the sacrifice of animals. Christ is here clearly identified with the sacrificial lamb—Christ the Lamb of God (cf. John 1:29).

5:9-13

⁹I have written you in my letter not to associate with sexually immoral people— ¹⁰not at all meaning the people of this world who are immoral, or the greedy and swindlers, or idolaters. In that case you would have to leave this world. ¹¹But now I am writing you that you must not associate with anyone who calls himself a brother but is sexually immoral or greedy, an idolater or a slanderer, a drunkard or a swindler. With such a man do not even eat.

¹²What business is it of mine to judge those outside the church? Are you not to judge those inside? ¹³God will judge those outside. "Expel the wicked man from your number."

9 Though the letter here referred to could possibly be a reference to the preceding part of the present letter and the verb egrapsa could be taken to mean, "I write" (an epistolary aorist, taken from the reader's viewpoint; cf. Rom 16:22), it is more natural to conclude that this is a reference to a former letter that we do not possess. (That not all of an apostle's writings have been preserved presents no problem regarding the completeness of the canon. The church has all of the inspired writing God intended his people to have. [See Hodge, in loc.])

Paul now comments further on a subject referred to in the former letter—that of not associating with sexually immoral people (pornoi), a point the Corinthians had not fully understood. The social milieu in Corinth was notoriously immoral (cf. Introduction) and if the Corinthians took the command in the previous letter too literally, as they seem to have done, they would have had no contact with even some family members, business associates and social acquaintances. The word pornos ("the sexually immoral person") has reference to all types of sexual sins, including the sin of incest. The verb sunanamignysthai ("to associate with") could refer to church fellowship or more widely, as here, to any social contact.

10 Paul now proceeds to correct their misunderstanding. By referring to other categories of sinners besides the sexually immoral, he shows that in having referred to the pornoi in the previous letter, he meant only that they should not be a part of the church community. If Paul had meant that contact or even acquaintance with all sinners was to cease, then Christians could not live at all in human society.

By the words ou pantos ("not at all") Paul limits the extent of his command. The pornoi are the sexually immoral persons of all kinds. That they are called the sexually immoral "of this world" (the secular world system) establishes that they are not to be included as a part of the church community. The greedy persons here are literally the ones "who must have more." Compare the sin of greed (pleonexia) listed in Romans 1:29; Ephesians 4:19; Colossians 3:5. Greed is a serious sin and Paul touches on aspects of it in 6:7, 8. The harpax is one who steals by violence. "Extortioner" (KJV) does not convey this today and "swindler" (NIV) seems too weak.

11 The verb form *egrapsa* taken with *de nun* ("but now") is certainly here to be understood as an epistolary aorist and translated, "But now I am writing." Having explained that he did not mean Christians are to be totally dissociated from the world, Paul hastens to add that the church community is not to include such as the flagrant sinners he now enumerates, even if they carry the name "brother," a term that would identify them as part of the Christian fellowship. The kind of association not permitted with such false brothers is explained by the command "With such a man do not even eat." In sharing in a common meal Christians show their union with one another. This "eating" is not to be understood as the Lord's Supper, and probably indicates any meal, including the Christian *agape* (love) feast. The application then and now is that Christians are not to have this kind of association, for if a believer does so, he may raise a question concerning the validity of his own Christian profession. To the list of sinners in v.10 Paul now adds the slanderer (*loidoros*—probably referring to those who denigrated Paul) and the drunkard (*methusos*; cf. 1 Cor 6:10; 11:21; Eph 5:18; 1 Thess 5:7).

12,13 Here Paul teaches that though it is logical for the church to exercise spiritual discipline over members in its fellowship, it is not for the church to judge the present unsaved society.

By the Greek expression *tous exō* ("those without") the apostle means those outside the church's communion or fellowship. The words *tous esō* ("those within") means those within the church's fellowship. Paul now concludes (v.13) on the basis of the preceding argument that the wicked man who had married his stepmother must be put out of the church. This he commands by quoting somewhat loosely from Deuteronomy 22:24 (a context of adultery) and from Deuteronomy 24:7 (a context of stealing).

The strengthened form of the negative (*ouchi*, "not") used with the indicative verb in a question expects a positive response: "Are you not to judge those inside [the church]?" "Yes" is the expected reply.

Notes

13 There is a variation in the MSS as to whether κρινεῖ (*krinei*, "judge") is present or future (it is only a matter of the accent), and since the present tense of the verb can be interpreted as a futuristic present, there is no difference in meaning. The sense is "God will judge" as in NIV. The quotation from Deut 22:24 and 24:7 is exactly like the wording of LXX in those two passages, except that Paul has changed the LXX verb form ἐξαρεῖς (*exareis*) to the pl. ἐξάρατε (*exarate*) to fit his application to the Corinthians.

B. *Christian Morality Applied to Legal and Sexual Matters* (6:1-20)

1. *Christian morality in legal matters*

    6:1-11

    ¹If any of you has a dispute with another, dare he take it before the ungodly for judgment instead of before the saints? ²Do you not know that God's people will judge the world? And if you are to judge the world, are you not competent to judge trivial cases? ³Do you not know that we will judge angels? How much more the things of this life! ⁴Therefore, if you have disputes about such matters, appoint as judges even men of little account in the church! ⁵I say this to shame you. Is it

possible that there is nobody among you wise enough to judge a dispute between believers? [6]But instead, one brother goes to law against another—and this in front of unbelievers!

[7]The very fact that you have lawsuits among you means you have been completely defeated already. Why not rather be wronged? Why not rather be cheated? [8]Instead, you yourselves cheat and do wrong, and you do this to your brothers.

[9]Don't you know that the wicked will not inherit the kingdom of God? Do not be deceived: Neither the sexually immoral nor idolaters nor adulterers nor male prostitutes nor homosexual offenders [10]nor thieves nor the greedy nor drunkards nor slanderers nor swindlers will inherit the kingdom of God. [11]And that is what some of you were. But you were washed, you were sanctified, you were justified in the name of the Lord Jesus Christ and by the Spirit of our God.

Continuing in the area of moral and ethical practice, Paul now discusses the apparently common practice of the Corinthians of settling noncriminal property cases before non-Christian judges or arbitrators. He refers to the Roman law courts, such as those on either side of the *bema* (tribunal platform) where Roman law was strictly administered in accordance with Roman standards. "What about God's standards?" Paul asks. They as a Christian community should have been deciding such cases among themselves. In Christian love they should have "turned the other cheek" (Matt 5:39) and suffered wrong and loss of material goods (v.7) rather than go to court over such matters.

1,2 In speaking of Christians taking other Christians to court, Paul does not specify any criminal cases because he teaches elsewhere that these must be handled by the state (Rom 13:3, 4).

In the expression *pragma echōn* ("having a lawsuit or dispute"), Paul means to include different kinds of property cases (v.7). By "dare" (*tolmā*), he strongly admonishes rather than commands Christians to take their legal grievances for settlement before qualified Christians. In this way, he allows for the possibility that under some circumstances Christians might take cases to the secular civil court. Paul writes in the light of Roman law, which allowed Jews, for instance, to apply their own law in property matters; and Christians, who were not yet distinguished as a separate class, must have had the same privilege (Hodge, in loc.). According to rabbinic interpretation, it was unlawful to take cases before Gentile judges. Customarily, three judges were to handle cases among the Jews. (C.T. Craig, *The First Epistle to the Corinthians*, IB, vol.10 [New York: Abington-Cokesbury Press, 1953], p. 69; Strack and Billerbeck, *Kommentar zum N.T. aus Talmud und Midrasch*, 3:364, 365; Jean Juster, *Les Juifs dans l'Empire Romain*, 2 [Paris: P. Geuthner, 1914], pp. 93–126.) If appeal was made to Roman law for the right of Jewish and Christian communities to try their own property cases, certainly it would be right to take some cases before the civil court. By analogy, Paul who had received his Roman citizenship according to Roman law, appealed to the civil courts—to the Roman commander (Acts 22:25–29), to the governor (Acts 23:27; 24:10–21), and to the emperor (Acts 25:4–12)—to establish his right to a proper trial and proper treatment as a Roman citizen (Acts 16:37–39). In modern life this biblical principle allows for church cases to be brought into civil courts to determine the extent of the rights of the congregation, as for example, their right to own and retain their own church property. What concerned Paul was that the Corinthians were failing to exercise their prerogative in settling such cases themselves, a prerogative they would exercise at the Second Coming and in the eternal state (vv.2, 3).

The saints (*hoi hagioi*) are those who are holy—consecrated and set apart for God; thus the translation, "God's people" (v.2). They are in sharp contrast with the "ungodly" (*adikoi*, those who practice injustice—the unsaved). In saying that God's people will judge the world, Paul is writing eschatologically. At the second coming of Christ, God's people, who are joint heirs with Christ (Rom 8:17) will reign and judge the world with him in his millennial kingdom (2 Tim 2:12; Rev 20:4; cf. Dan 7:22 and Matt 19:28).

In cases now to be judged by Christians, decisions would be ministerial and declarative (Matt 16:18, 19; 18:18-20; John 20:19-23), and not punitive, penalties being reserved for the state (Rom 13:1-7).

3 To make his argument even stronger for the validity and competence of Christians to settle cases at Corinth, Paul teaches that Christians will even judge angels, but he does not specify any details (v.3). By using *angelous* without the article, Paul is not necessarily including all the angels. He must mean that Christians, when ruling in the future with Christ, will have a part in judging the devil and the fallen angels at the Second Coming (cf. Rev. 19:19, 20; 20:10). Or, the statement could mean, as Hodge suggests, that Christians will judge angels, even the good ones, in the sense of presiding with Christ over the angelic host (in loc.). Compare the statement of Matthew 19:28 about sitting "on twelve thrones, judging the twelve tribes," i.e., presiding over them.

4 It is uncertain whether the main verb *kathizete* ("appoint") should be taken as imperative with a sarcastic tone or as an indicative in a rhetorical question. In the first instance, the thought is this: "If you must have disputes about these mundane matters when you are destined to judge men and angels, well then go ahead and set the least esteemed members of the congregation to take care of these little matters!" On the second interpretation, the emphasis is on the apostle's surprise: "If you have such a case, do you set the least esteemed in the church in charge of it?" The answer then is "No," with the assumed concluding question as to why then they would turn these affairs over to the unsaved who know less about Christian affairs. The first option (cf. NIV) seems better, since it fits in with Paul's other ironic remarks to the Corinthians, such as in 4:8. For the second interpretation, the material is too elliptical and demands too much to be supplied. Some have tried to take the phrase "men of little account" as referring to the unsaved judges, but there is no evidence in the context that the Corinthians despised these judges.

5,6 Paul argues that if it is really necessary for such disputes to be handled, they should find a Christian wise enough to take care of them, rather than have Christian brothers opposed to each other in secular litigation. The apostle says they should be ashamed of themselves.

7,8 In climaxing his argument that though legal cases may have to be handled, Paul feels that their very existence among the Corinthians shows a malicious attitude and spiritual failure. Instead of being involved in all these disputes, they should be willing to suffer wrong rather than harm and cheat their fellow Christians.

9,10 Paul concludes that in practicing such acts of wickedness (*adikeo*) toward others they must realize that the wicked (*adikoi*) will not inherit the kingdom of God (cf. John 3:3-5). They are in a dangerous frame of mind—they need to clear their heads and realize that if they act wickedly in this way, they are no better than the wicked idolaters and others who will not inherit heaven. To the list of sinners already mentioned in 5:10,

11 Paul points out specific kinds of sexually immoral people: the adulterers (*moichoi*), the male prostitutes (*malakoi*) and homosexuals (*arsenokoitai*). (In Romans 1:26 Paul also mentions lesbians.) Also added to his list here are those who are thieves (*kleptai*). In the light of this comparison, the Corinthians should have seen how unchristian and sinful their actions were toward one another.

11 In describing their conversion, the apostle lists three transactions that occurred at the time when the Lord saved them: they were washed (*apolousasthe*), that is, they were spiritually cleansed by God, an act symbolized by baptism (cf. Matt 28:19); they were sanctified (*hēgiasthēte*), an expression either to be interpreted as an amplification of the concept "washed" (cf. Titus 3:5, 6) or meaning that they had been set apart as God's people (cf. 1 Pet 2:9); and they were justified (*edikaiōthēte*), showing God's act as judge in declaring the sinner righteous because of Christ (Rom 3:23-26; 5:1). This expression gives the legal basis for the cleansing mentioned above.

All this, Paul says, was done by God for them on the authority (in the name) of the Lord Jesus Christ and by the Spirit of our God—the regenerating power of the Holy Spirit.

Notes

2 Κριτηρίων (*kritērion*) is strictly the "law court," but is to be taken here as "the cases" that are tried in such courts.
4 The perfect passive participle ἐξουθενημένους (*exouthenēmenous*) means "those that stand despised or disdained" and so the tr. "men of little account." Καθίζω (*kathizō*, "cause to sit," or "seat") in this context means "install" or "appoint" judges for court (see Jos. *Ant* 13, 75).
7,8 The μὲν οὖν (*men oun*, "so," "then") denotes a continuation of the argument and so heightens the effect of the conclusion Paul is drawing from his previous discussion. There is a vivid contrast between the passive and the active uses of the two verbs ἀδικέω (*adikeō*, "suffer wrong" "do wrong") and ἀποστερέω (*apostereō*, "be cheated" "cheat"). The present tense in each case suggests that these injustices are currently in practice.
9 Μὴ πλανᾶσθε (*mē planasthe*), the present prohibition construction with the verb in the middle voice may be tr., "Stop deceiving yourselves."
11 The use of ταῦτα (*tauta*—neuter, "these things") with people is startling: "Some of you were these things." This expression points up the horrible condition they were in. The three aorist verb forms in v.11b emphasize the definiteness (point action) of the work of the Lord in their salvation. The verb ἀπελούσασθε (*apelousasthe*) is in the middle voice, meaning, "you washed yourselves" or "you got yourselves washed"; that is, they submitted themselves to the baptism sacrament (or ordinance) as the identifying sign for Christians and their covenant children (Acts 2:38, 39), indicating their belonging to Christ and his church. Others take this aorist middle as a passive, "you were washed," because the two following verbs are passive. This looser tr. is permissible under this interpretation: "You permitted yourselves to be washed." That baptism is likely referred to here as a sign of their spiritual cleansing and justification by God (cf. the sign of circumcision in Rom 4:9-12) is shown by the phrase "in the name [or 'authority' connected with the person] of the Lord Jesus Christ and by the Spirit of our God." Paul may well have in mind the words of Jesus in Matt 28:19.

2. Christian morality in sexual matters

6:12–20

> [12]"Everything is permissible for me"—but not everything is beneficial. "Everything is permissible for me"—but I will not be mastered by anything. [13]"Food for the stomach and the stomach for food"—but God will destroy them both. The body is not meant for sexual immorality, but for the Lord, and the Lord for the body. [14]By his power God raised the Lord from the dead, and he will raise us also. [15]Do you not know that your bodies are members of Christ himself? Shall I then take the members of Christ and unite them with a prostitute? Never! [16]Do you not know that he who unites himself with a prostitute is one with her in body? For it is said, "The two will become one flesh." [17]But he who unites himself with the Lord is one with him in spirit.
>
> [18]Flee from sexual immorality. All other sins a man commits are outside his body, but he who sins sexually sins against his own body. [19]Do you not know that your body is a temple of the Holy Spirit, who is in you, whom you have received from God? You are not your own; [20]you were bought at a price. Therefore honor God with your body.

Every action we contemplate should be tested by two questions: "Is it beneficial?" and "Will it overpower and enslave me and so have a detrimental effect on the church and my testimony for Christ?" Hodge (in loc.) entitles this section "Abuses of the Principle of Christian Liberty" but the passage includes far more than that. The main thrust of these verses argues against sexual immorality and for the glorifying of God in the Christian's body.

12,13 Undoubtedly there were some professing Christians in Corinth who, without examining the Scriptures and its implications, claimed that it was permissible for them to do anything they desired. In making such claims to unrestricted freedom, some evidently used the argument that since the physical activity of eating and digesting food ("food for the stomach and the stomach for food") did not have any bearing on Christian morals and one's inner spiritual life, so other physical activities such as promiscuous sex did not touch either on morals or spiritual life.

Paul grants that food and the stomach are temporal and transitory and, in God's providence, will disappear—but he denies that what affects the body is unimportant and this denial especially includes the undisciplined and unscriptural use of the body in sexual practices (v.13b). So he denies the argument of a parallel between eating and digesting food as a natural process and practicing sexual immorality as a natural process. Of course, he is not denying that sex in wedlock is natural and wholesome (7:3–5; cf. also Heb 13:4).

The apostle sets the stage for his discussion of the horrors of sexual immorality and in contrast the holy use of the Christian's body by stating that as the Christian evaluates his right to do "all things," he should face four questions: (1) Is the thing contemplated beneficial (*sumpherei*)? (2) Will the practice in question overpower and dominate (*exousiasthesomai*) him and will the result affect others? (3) Will the practice support the truth that the body is "for the Lord" who created it and intended it to be used for his glory? Also, (4) will it support the truth that "the Lord is for the body"—that is, the Lord has redeemed the body (vv.19, 20)? So the Christian must have no part with sexual immorality, because the body is not meant for sexual license (v.13b, cf. Gen 2:24) but for the Lord.

14 Now Paul states God's interest in the Christian's body. As God raised the body of Jesus from the tomb, so he will raise the bodies of his people from the grave through his power. Of interest is the difference in the verbs used: *ēgeiren*, "he raised" (the Lord); and *exegerei*, "he will raise [us] out of " (the grave)—the implication being that we, in contrast to the Lord, will be raised from corruption and from the group of corrupt sinners. The phrase "through the power of God" is probably to be taken with both parts of the sentence: the power of God that was used to raise the Lord is the same that will be used to raise his people.

15–17 A further argument that the Christian's body is for the Lord is that God's people are members of his mystical body (cf. 1 Cor 12:27). So Christians may not unite their bodies with that of a prostitute. For they should understand that sexual relations involve more than a physical act—they join the two persons together (v.16; quoting from Gen 2:24; cf. Matt 19:5). Since Christians have been joined in union to the Lord, they dare not form another union with a prostitute. Verse 17 states the case even more strongly: the one who cleaves (*kollōmenos*) to a prostitute is one body with her, but the one who cleaves (*kollōmenos*) to the Lord is united to him spiritually. In saying this, Paul is not making the union of normal marriage mutually exclusive of the union of God with his people. In Ephesians 5:21–32 Paul teaches that the human marriage union is valid and is to be viewed in the light of the Christian's higher union with the Lord—the wife to be subject to her husband "as to the Lord" (v.22) and the husband to love his wife "as Christ loved the church" (v.25). What Paul argues against in 1 Corinthians 6:15–17 is that the unholy union with a prostitute is a wicked perversion of the divinely established marriage union.

18 Paul goes on to say that the one who commits sexual immorality sins against his own body—that is, by weakening and perverting the very life process, as well as human character. In contrast, other sins are "outside the body."

19,20 Now Paul talks positively about how the Christian should view his body. First, he should consider that his body, including his whole personality, is the temple—the sacred dwelling place—of God, the Holy Spirit (cf. the Shekinah glory in the tabernacle, Exod 40:34). Second, the Christian has received the Spirit from God to help him against sin. Third, the Christian has no right to pervert and misuse his body, for he is not his own master but has been purchased by God for a price (v.20). That price, though not mentioned here, is the blood of Jesus Christ (Eph 1:7; 1 Pet 1:18, 19 et al.). The picture is of a slave of sin (Rom 6:17; cf. 1 Cor 7:23) being purchased from the horrible system of slavery.

The conclusion of the matter is that the Christian is to glorify God in his body. Because "body" and "temple" are both singular, some understand the teaching to be that not only each believer's body is a temple, but the whole body of believers is a temple (Grosheide, in loc.). However, since in the context Paul is writing about individuals and since the individual Christian is indwelt by the Holy Spirit, it is best to understand v.19 to mean that each individual Christian's body is a temple of the Holy Spirit. (*Naos* is the temple itself [cf. John 2:20, 21] in distinction from *hieron*, the entire temple area.)

"You were bought" is in the aorist tense, pointing back to Christ's redemptive work on the cross (Matt 20:28). There may be implications of the Christian's having been freed from becoming overpowered by sin (Rom 6:17, 18) and Satan (Col 1:13) and being benevolently enslaved to Christ (Rom 1:1) and to righteousness (Rom 6:18) in reflection of the Corinthian situation in which the "slave was from the time of his manumission the slave of the god" (Craig, in loc.)

Notes

12 There is a contrast between πάντα (panta, "all things") and τινός (tinos, "any one thing"). The emphasis is not on the "all things" that are permissible but on the "one thing" that may overpower.

13 Καταργέω (katargeō) is vivid. Literally, it means "make ineffective or powerless"; so here it indicates that God will do away with food and the need for the digestive processes of the stomach, evidently referring to the changed status of the resurrection body after the second coming of Christ.

15 The negative optative μὴ γένοιτο (mē genoito) indicates a strong wish—literally tr. "may it not be," more freely rendered, "Never!" "By no means!" "Perish the thought!" Robertson calls this use of the optative the volitive, which stresses the wish, the will (A.T. Robertson, *A Grammar of the Greek New Testament in the Light of Historical Research*, 5th ed. [New York: Harper and Brothers, 1923], pp. 936, 937).

16 The οἴδατε (oidate, "know") in vv.16, 19 goes beyond just knowing a fact. It implies recognition and understanding. The negative οὐκ (ouk) with a question implies in the argument a positive reply. The verb κολλάω (kollaō, "cleave") in this participial form, which can be taken as a middle as the context suggests, stresses the sexual offender's personal initiative and responsibility: "he joins himself to" the prostitute.

Whereas the Gen 2:24 quotation uses σαρξ (sarx, "flesh") in LXX, Paul uses the word σῶμα (sōma, "body"), but the same idea is in mind: the physico-spiritual life of the individuals is involved.

18 The present tense (durative action) of φεύγετε (pheugete), meaning "be fleeing from," suggests that constant vigilance against sexual immorality is called for.

20 The words "and in your spirit, which are God's," found in KJV, are not supported by many of the best ancient MSS and are not necessary nor central to Paul's argument regarding the Christian's use of his body. The words may have been added by scribes in later MSS, first in the margin and then in the text, to complete the thought on the nature of man as body and spirit and "to soften Paul's abruptness" (B.M. Metzger, *A Textual Commentary on the Greek New Testament* [New York: United Bible Societies, 1971], p. 553).

VII. Paul's Answers to Questions Raised by the Church (7:1–14:40)

In this section Paul begins to answer questions raised by the Corinthians in a letter they had written him (7:1). The material from 7:1 to 14:40 is devoted in a large part to answering questions raised in this communication. In his introductory expression "Now for the matters you wrote about," Paul shows he is answering this letter.

He uses the same introductory phrase (peri de) in other parts of 1 Corinthians in discussing other questions they had brought up: the unmarried (7:25), food sacrificed to idols (8:1), and spiritual gifts (12:1). It is not certain whether his instruction regarding giving for the need of the saints (16:1–4) was in answer to their written question, since it is separated by chapter 15 from the main section (7:1–14:40) dealing with these questions. But since the same introductory phrase occurs in 16:1, it is reasonable to conclude that 16:1–4 is a postscript answer to another of their questions. The subject of this "collection" (16:1) certainly was a matter on which the Corinthians needed enlightenment.

A. *Instructions Concerning Marriage* (7:1–40)

The Corinthians had written, asking at least two questions concerning this subject that is the topic of the entire chapter. The first was whether a Christian should get married at all (7:1) and the second was whether virgins should get married (7:25). Evidently there were those in Corinth who, as Jewish believers relying on Genesis 2:24, were advocating marriage. Others were no doubt arguing for the unmarried state.

Besides answering these questions, Paul deals with an additional point, that a Christian should live according to God's calling, whether married or single (7:17–24).

1. *Christian obligations in marriage*

7:1–16

> ¹Now for the matters you wrote about: It is good for a man not to marry. ²But since there is so much immorality, each man should have his own wife, and each woman her own husband. ³The husband should fulfill his marital duty to his wife, and likewise the wife to her husband. ⁴The wife's body does not belong to her alone but also to her husband. In the same way, the husband's body does not belong to him alone but also to his wife. ⁵Do not deprive each other except by mutual consent and for a time, so that you may devote yourselves to prayer. Then come together again so that Satan will not tempt you because of your lack of self-control. ⁶I say this as a concession, not as a command. ⁷I wish that all men were as I am. But each man has his own gift from God; one has this gift, another has that.
>
> ⁸Now to the unmarried and the widows I say: It is good for them to stay unmarried, as I am. ⁹But if they cannot control themselves, they should marry, for it is better to marry than to burn with passion.
>
> ¹⁰To the married I give this command (not I, but the Lord): A wife must not separate from her husband. ¹¹But if she does, she must remain unmarried or else be reconciled to her husband. And a husband must not divorce his wife.
>
> ¹²To the rest I say this (I, not the Lord): If any brother has a wife who is not a believer and she is willing to live with him, he must not divorce her. ¹³And if a woman has a husband who is not a believer and he is willing to live with her, she must not divorce him. ¹⁴For the unbelieving husband has been sanctified through his wife, and the unbelieving wife has been sanctified through her believing husband. Otherwise your children would be "unclean," but as it is, they are holy.
>
> ¹⁵But if the unbeliever leaves, let him do so. A believing man or woman is not bound in such circumstances; God has called us to live in peace. ¹⁶How do you know, wife, whether you will save your husband? Or, how do you know, husband, whether you will save your wife?

1 As to the question of the church on the pros and cons of being married, Paul may seem to agree completely with those who argued for a celibate life, and this in contrast to Genesis 2:18, "It is not good that the man should be alone" (RSV) and the usual Jewish view in favor of the married state. (The rabbis considered that marriage was an "unqualified duty for a man" [Craig, in loc.].) But Paul's statement of 7:1 is not to be taken absolutely; it is his suggestion specifically for Corinth because of some present crisis there that he refers to in 7:26 (cf. 7:29, 35). Part of this crisis may have been connected with possible times of persecution they might have to suffer for the Lord.

It is difficult to hold, as some do, that Paul here is teaching against marriage because he felt the second coming of Christ was necessarily near (Craig, in loc., and Parry, in loc.). If that were his position, he would naturally have argued against marriage in his other letters also. In Ephesians 5 and 1 Timothy 3 he speaks in favor of marriage. Further, in 1 Timothy 4:1-3 Paul states that "forbidding to marry" is one of the signs of the approaching end-time apostasy, and in Hebrews 13:4 it is said that "marriage should be honored." As Hodge has remarked, distresses and crises are connected with both the first and second comings of Christ and, we could add, in the time in between (*1 Corinthians*, in loc.; cf. Matt 24:3-14; 1 Peter 1:10-12). However, reference to "crises" (7:26) need not be pressed to mean that the Corinthian Christians should not get married because the Lord was to come shortly.

2-7 Having said that it would be good under the present circumstances not to get married, Paul hastens to add that the general rule for marriage should apply. The reason, especially true at Corinth, is the prevalence of sexual immorality—*porneias* is plural—and they also might be tempted to fall into this sin. Since the temptation might affect either sex, Paul specifies that each man is to have his own wife and each woman her own husband.

So that there will not be abnormal situations in the Christian marital status that may lead to sexual immorality (v.5), the apostle gives instruction as to the normal sexual behavior and attitude that the Christian man and wife should have (vv.3-6), and in doing so he argues against a forced asceticism. He argues that they should have normal sexual relations and he strengthens his argument by stating that the bodies of the marriage partners belong to each other. The verb *exousiazō* literally means "has rights over"; that is, "has exclusive claim to," which has already been shown in the teaching of 1 Corinthians 6:16, "the two will become one flesh." Having stated the principle in v.4, Paul adds the command that husbands and wives are not to withhold these normal marital rights from each other, except by mutual consent and agreement, and that only for a specified purpose and a specified period of time (v.5). This he says is so that they may spend time in prayer—i.e., that as those who are also united to Christ (6:17), they may exercise their rights and privileges in communing with God. But when this separate time of prayer is over, the married pair are to come together again, lest Satan tempt one or the other partner with sexual immorality because of their possible lack of sexual self-control. Paul recognizes the strong but normal sexual drive in the human being (cf. Gen 1:28, "be fruitful . . . fill the earth").

The present tense of the verb *apostereite* ("deprive") in the prohibition in v.5 indicates that some at Corinth were practicing a kind of celibacy within marriage. The construction may be translated, "Do not deprive one another (as you are doing)," or "Stop depriving one another." Through the word *kairon*, "time"—i.e., a specific period of time—the apostle impresses on Christians the limitation of time to apply for marriage partners to agree to be parted from one another.

Paul is quick to point out that Satan, the enemy of Christians (1 Peter 5:8), is present to motivate the people of God to use even good and normal human processes wrongly and so to displease God.

When Paul states (in v.6) that he says "this" not by direct command (from the Lord) but by permission or concession (*syngnōmēn*), it is not clear what the "this" refers to (cf. Hodge, in loc.). Some refer it to v.5, "come together again," but this thought is in a subordinate clause and does not fit the context that husband and wife were to be separated only for a limited time. Others refer it to the whole of v.5, with the inference that they could separate for other reasons than that given in v.5 and for unlimited periods, but this is against the commands of vv.3, 4. So it is better to understand "this" to refer to v.2, indicating that though marriage is desirable and is according to God's creation plan, it is not mandatory. That this is Paul's meaning is evident from v.7 where he says he really wishes all men were single like him. However, he recognizes that God gives each man his own gracious gift (v.7). Some are given the desire or the inclination to be married, and some have the power to refrain from marriage. *Charisma* ("gift of grace") seems to mean the wholesome inclination given by God either to pursue marriage or to refrain from it.

8,9 Paul gives advice to the single, whom he now classifies as the unmarried and the widows. It is, he states, good or advisable (*kalon;* cf. v.1) for them to remain in their single state for the reasons spelled out in 7:26, 32–35. (Observe that in another situation Paul counsels the younger widows to marry [1 Tim 5:14].) But now he hastens to add a postscript. If the situation is such that these persons cannot control their sexual desires, they should marry. The explanation (*gar,* "for") Paul gives is that it is better to get married than be inflamed with sexual desire, which is hard to control outside of marriage. *Pyrousthai,* related to *pyr* ("fire"), means "burn" or "be enflamed," and is here used figuratively of sexual desire.

10–16 Paul's next major concern relates to Christians and divorce. What he states in v.10 "to the married" (*gegamēkosin*) is by "command" (*parangellō*)—not his own, but the command of the Lord. For he has stated above that for the unmarried to remain so was a "good" thing if a person could control his sexual desires. But for a married couple to stay together is not just "good"—it is commanded by the Lord. How specifically Paul is citing the words of Jesus depends on whether at this time he had access to the notes of one of the gospel writers or to one of the Gospels themselves.

Paul could have had access to notes on the Gospels or to a Gospel itself, acquired from the apostles when Paul visited the Jerusalem area in the earlier part of his ministry (cf. Acts 9:26–28; 11:30; 15:1, 2). That such material, as well as any accurate oral tradition regarding Jesus, was available is seen from the statement given by Luke, Paul's close companion, that there were gospel accounts being drawn up and that he, Luke, had obtained accurate information from the eyewitnesses of the gospel events (Luke 1:1–4). Furthermore, the formula for the Lord's Supper in 1 Corinthians 11:23ff. certainly gives evidence that Paul acquired accurate information from an oral or written source concerning Jesus' teaching.

The burden of Christ's command was that the married were not to be divorced (Matt 5:32; 19:3–9; Luke 16:18)—a principle Paul summarizes from both sides of the marriage partnership—the woman is not to be separated from (or, possibly, separate herself from; cf. note on v.10) her husband, and the husband must not divorce his wife (v.11). There seems to have occurred at Corinth such a separation of a wife from her husband, for Paul says, "If she does [separate], she must remain unmarried, or else be reconciled to her husband." The change of verb tenses emphasizes the direction of Paul's thinking. She is to remain unmarried (present tense continuous action) like the other unmarried (v.8), or, better, she is to be "reconciled" to her husband (aorist, accomplished action). The stress of the passage on maintaining the marriage bond unbroken definitely strengthens the injunction for separated marriage partners to become reconciled.

In vv.12–16 Paul adds instructions beyond those given by the Lord Jesus—instructions having to do with mixed marriages, where one partner has, since marriage, become a Christian. Paul addresses himself to this problem and later to the subject of virgins

57

marrying (7:25–40) when he says, "To the rest [to the others with marital questions] I say this. . . ."

The factual indicative condition in v.12 (as in v.13), "If any brother has a wife who is not a believer [as some do] . . . ," shows that there were mixed marriages in the Christian community in this pagan city. Since Paul preached in Corinth for over a year and a half (Acts 18:11, 18), with many turning to the Lord, we may conclude that while he was still with them many marriages became mixed marriages. Had he at that time given them advice about this? Doubtless, he had. But the problem then was probably not so acute for the unbelieving partner when the other partner was a new Christian. The unbelieving one may have thought this stand for Christ was a passing fad or a superstition. As time went on, however, the condition in many Corinthian homes became more serious. In spite of Paul's teaching about Christian living and the sanctity of the home (cf. Eph 4–6), the unbelieving partners in some instances were threatening to leave their Christian husbands or wives. So Paul was confronted with the question, "What should the Christian marriage partners do?" We should note first, in the light of 2 Corinthians 6:14–7:1 (cf. Ezra 10:10), that Paul would not have allowed an already-professing Christian to marry an unbeliever. But on the question of what should be done by a husband or wife who has turned to the Lord after marriage, Paul is decisive (vv.12, 13). If the unbelieving partner is content or willing to live with the Christian, then the Christian must not divorce the partner—for the sake, Paul implies, of the marriage bond God has ordained. The present tense prohibition, *mē aphietō*, stresses that the marriage relationship is not to be broken at any time. The literal meaning is "He [she] is not to be attempting at one point or another to divorce her [him]."

Rather (v.14), the Christian partner should think of the truth that the Lord can use him as a godly, holy influence in such a mixed family relationship and in helping that family to be consecrated (set apart) to God. The word *hagiazō* ("to sanctify") does not refer to moral purity—Paul is certainly not teaching that the unbelieving partner is made morally pure. What the word emphasizes is a relationship to God, a claim of God on the person and family to be set apart for him (cf. Acts 20:32; 26:18). The perfect tense of the verb *hēgiastai* stresses that, being in a Christian family, the unbeliever has already become and continues to be a part of a family unit upon which God has his claim and which he will use for his service. The same is true of children born in such a family. That God has laid his hand on the Christian means that God has laid his hand on the children, and set them apart for himself. They are holy (*hagia*, "set apart for God") and not "unclean"— that is, not spiritually separated from God, as was and is the case in unbelieving families. The Bible's teaching elsewhere about the Christian parent and his covenant children set apart for God is also relevant to this passage. Consider Genesis 17:1-14, where the children of God's people of the OT are included among God's covenant people, and Acts 2:38, 39, where it is emphasized that God's promise applies to the children of believers, whether of those who are "near," the Jews, or those "afar off," the Gentiles (cf. Eph 2:12, 13). Covenant children are to be counted a part of God's people and should be nurtured in the Christian faith and in the fear of the Lord (Eph.6:4).

Dealing with the actual situation at Corinth, Paul realizes that in some instances the unbelieving marriage partner will not stay. So he teaches that in such an event (v.15) the believer must let the unbelieving partner go—"If [in fact—an actual condition] the unbeliever leaves, let him do so." At this point, Paul adds two reasons: First, in this case the believer is not "bound," for the unbeliever by willful desertion (the other legitimate reason for divorce besides sexual immorality [Matt 19:9]) has broken the marriage con-tract. The Greek perfect form of the verb is graphic—i.e., "the Christian brother or sister is not in a bound condition as a slave." A second reason for allowing an unwilling partner to leave is that God has called his people to live in peace, which would not be possible if the unbelieving partner were forced to live with the believer. Try to live with the unbelieving partner in the peace that God gives (Phil 4:6, 7), but do not attempt to force the unbeliever to stay.

The force of v.16 tempers any tendency to foster or encourage a rupture in the marriage. For Paul is teaching that the believer is to try to keep the mixed marriage together in the hope that the testimony of the believer will be used by God to bring the unbeliever to Christ. The factual condition of v.16 suggests there is a good hope that God in his providence will do just that.

Notes

1 Though the verb ἅπτομαι (haptomai), in the middle voice, literally means "to touch, take a hold of," in this context it means "to have sexual relations with." Since Paul has been arguing against illicit sexual relations in chapter 5, he obviously is referring here to legitimate marriage relations. This verbal expression is a euphemism for such relations (cf. Jos. Ant 1, 163; Gen 20:6; Prov 6:29).

3,4 The present tense imperative ἀποδιδότω (apodidotō) and present tense indicative, ἐξουσιά-ζει (exousiazei) are to be taken as gnomic presents, indicating that a general practice is advocated. Paul is not addressing a particular individual, but Christian men and women concerning the normal practice expected of them. Normal sexual relations are considered by Paul ὀφειλή (opheilē, an "obligation," a "duty,") to meet the normal emotional, spiritual, and physical needs of the human being.

5 The μήτι (mēti) "seems to add an element of uncertainty to the exception: 'unless perhaps;' ἄν (an) if genuine= 'in a particular case', further limiting the exception" (Parry, in loc.). Paul, as Findlay notes, considerably limits the exception of man and wife being separated from one another. First he adds τι (ti, "in some measure," "somehow"), then ἄν (an, "if the case should arise"), then ἐκ συμφώνου (ek symphōnou, "of consent"), assuring that the temporary separation is voluntary), and finally he adds πρὸς καιρόν (pros kairon, "for a time"). To safeguard any voluntary separation further from abuse, he adds the purpose for it: that they might spend time separately in prayer (G.G. Findlay, EGT [Grand Rapids: Eerdmans, n.d.], in loc.). Some later MSS have "and fasting," but this was no doubt added later by scribes because of the emphasis on asceticism. (Cf. Metzger, A Textual Commentary, p. 554.) Ἀκρασία (akrasia) means "lack of power," "indulgence," and certainly fits the thought of an overpowering sex drive to which Paul is alluding.

9 The condition here is a factual one ("If, as is sometimes true, . . .") and the change in the verb tenses is important—"For it is better to marry (γαμῆσαι, gamēsai, aorist) than to burn with passion" (πυροῦσθαι, purousthai, present).

10 The perfect tense γεγαμηκόσιν (gegamēkosin) means that "they have been married and are continuing in that state." The condition with the subjunctive (probability, possibility) in v.10 suggests that such separations were very possibly to happen.

Alford (in loc.) tr. Χωρισθῆναι (chōristhēnai) as passive: "be separated," adding, ". . . whether by formal divorce or otherwise; the χωρισθῇ below is, like this, an absolute passive; undefined whether by her own or her husband's doing." The succeeding ἀφιέναι (aphienai, "divorce," v.11), "the husband must not divorce his wife" seems to influence the passive form in v.10 to mean that the wife in v.10 is the offending party: "She must not separate herself."

14 Though the majority of ancient MSS have ἀδελφῷ (adelphō, "brother"), a few inferior witnesses, which TR follows, read "believing husband," evidently a scribal attempt to parallel the language to v.14a, "an unbelieving husband." (Cf. Metzger, A Textual Commentary, p. 555.)

59

15 The perfect tense form κέκληκεν (*keklēken*, "God has called") stresses the initial divine call of the believer with its continuing effect in daily living.

---

2. Christian obligation to live according to God's call

7:17-24

> [17]Nevertheless, each one should retain the place in life that the Lord assigned to him and to which God has called him. This is the rule I lay down in all the churches. [18]Was a man already circumcised when he was called? He should not become uncircumcised. Was a man uncircumcised when he was called? He should not be circumcised. [19]Circumcision is nothing and uncircumcision is nothing. Keeping God's commands is what counts. [20]Each one should remain in the situation which he was in when God called him. [21]Were you a slave when you were called? Don't let it trouble you—although if you can gain your freedom, do so. [22]For he who was a slave when he was called by the Lord is the Lord's freedman; similarly, he who was a free man when he was called is Christ's slave. [23]You were bought at a price; do not become slaves of men. [24]Brothers, each man, as responsible to God, should remain in the situation God called him to.

In extension of the principle that God has called his people to live in peace (v.15), Paul teaches that the Christian should live contentedly in any station of life in which God places him. The example is that of living obediently to God with full confidence in his sovereign purpose, whether one is a Jew or Gentile, slave or freedman. It is not that Paul is for the subjugation or elevation of certain segments of society, but he wants individual Christians to realize and accept God's sovereign purpose in saving and keeping them regardless of the level of society they are in. Paul is more afraid of the spirit of anarchy and rebellion, personal and national (cf. Rom 12:3; 13:1-7; 1 Cor 12:4-11; 2 Cor 10:13) than of social inequality.

It may well be that Paul's teaching that all Christians are equal (Gal 3:28), that all things material should be viewed as relatively insignificant in the light of eternal spiritual realities (2 Cor 4:18), and that the second coming of Christ will bring in a complete and new order of divine rule (1 Cor 15:23-28) had made the Christians restless and somewhat discontented with their lot in life. This place in life is what God has "assigned" and called (*keklēken* and *memeriken*) them to. God's people can and must live as Christians, whatever the social, economic, and religious level of society they are in. Their conditions do not affect their relationship and service to Jesus Christ,—whether they are married to a believer or, after having been saved, to an unbeliever; whether they are saved as Jews or Gentiles; or whether they are saved as slaves or freedmen.

17 The expression *ei me* ("nevertheless") at the beginning of this verse presents problems of interpretation. To take it as "unless," "except that," makes it difficult to relating the verse to what Paul has just said about the Christian who is married to an unbeliever, that he may possibly lead his partner to the Lord. It is best to translate the *ei mē* as "but" (KJV) or "nevertheless" (NIV), meaning that Paul is expanding his thought of the Christian's call to other areas besides that of marital status. The Christian should live for the Lord wherever he is. This, Paul says, is the principle that he orders to be followed in all the churches (cf. Eph 5:21-6:9; Col 3:18-4:1)—a principle that transcends all boundaries.

18,19 The apostle's first application of this principle is to the religio-national distinctions related to being Jews or Gentiles, being circumcised or uncircumcised. In a Gentile situation like that in Corinth, some Christian Jews may have tried to obliterate the OT covenant mark of circumcision (cf. 1 Macc 1:15). On the other hand, Judaizers tried to force circumcision on the Gentile Christians (cf. Acts 15:1-5; Gal 3:1-3; 5:1). Paul argues that this outward sign of circumcision with its stress on the Jew versus the non-Jew now has no significance. If a person was a circumcised Jew when he was saved, he should not become uncircumcised. If he was an uncircumcised Gentile, he should not be circumcised in order to become Jewish. Circumcision and uncircumcision now make no difference (Rom 2:25, 29; Gal 5:6), but keeping God's command is essential (v.19; cf. John 14:15).

20 By repetition, this verse emphasizes the principle in v.17. In the NT, *klēsis* is used of God's effectual call of his people to salvation (cf. Rom 11:29; Heb 3:1), but here it must be taken to include one's station in life.

21-23 Paul's other illustration relates to slavery. The key phrase in this passage is "Don't let it trouble you" (v.21). Paul is not speaking against human betterment or social service, but he is stressing that the Christian in Corinth is to live for the Lord *without anxiety* in his present situation. If he was a slave when he became a Christian, he should live on as a Christian even though he remains a slave. Some have interpreted Paul's use of *all' ei kai* (literally, "but if even") to mean that even if a slave had an opportunity to gain freedom, he should not follow it, in the light of his emphasis that the Christian is to remain in the social status in which he is called. (So H.A.W. Meyer in *The Epistles to the Corinthians* [New York: Funk and Wagnalls, 1884], pp. 166, 167.) But Paul's stress is on one's not being "troubled" as a Christian in his social situation, and the *all' ei kai* can just as well be translated "but if also" or "although also." So then the meaning would be "But if also you can gain your freedom, you had better take that opportunity," or, as NIV has it, "although if you can gain your freedom, do so." Observe, however, that the Bible teaches that Christianity does not guarantee material or social betterment but makes it a matter of individual responsibility (cf. Ps 73; Acts 11:29; 20:35).

Verse 22 refers to v.21a. Paul is saying, "If you were a slave when God called you, don't let it trouble you—you are the Lord's freedman. If you were free when called, remember you are Christ's slave." The spiritual antithesis is striking. The Lord has freed the Christian from the penalty of sin (2 Cor 5:21) and from Satan and his kingdom (Col 1:13) and bound us as "slaves" to himself (Rom 1:1).

Verse 23 points up the priority of Christ's authority over the Christian. In all earthly service he is to realize that his obedience and service is to Christ, not men. The reason is that God bought us with the price of Christ's blood (1 Cor 5:7; 1 Pet 1:18, 19). So because on this higher level we are slaves to Christ, we are not to become mere slaves of men. We serve faithfully in our earthly position, but we serve as slaves of Christ (cf. Eph 6:5-9, Col 3:24; 1 Tim 6:2).

In verse 24 Paul repeats the command of vv.17, 20 but adds the phrase *para theō* ("before God"), as though he is saying, "God is looking on and is there with you to help you."

Notes

17 The ἐι μή (*ei mē*) here is best taken with Blass-Debrunner as equivalent to ἀλλά (*alla*) or πλήν (*plēn*) and tr. "nevertheless" or "but." They observe that in the Gospels, at any rate, both *ei mē* and *alla* are a tr. for the Aramaic אלא (*illa*). The present tense (durative) imperative περιπατείτω (*peripateito*) here indicates literally that the person is to go on walking, and so stresses the continuous walk of the believer under God's sovereign direction.

23 The expression μὴ γίνεσθε (*mē ginesthe*, the present imperative of the verb "become") stresses the continual danger of becoming mere slaves of men. It might be tr. "Stop becoming...."

---

3. *Instructions concerning virgins* (7:25–40)

7:25–35

25Now about virgins: I have no command from the Lord, but I give a judgment as one who by the Lord's mercy is trustworthy. 26Because of the present crisis, I think that it is good for you to remain as you are. 27Are you married? Do not seek a divorce. Are you unmarried? Do not look for a wife. 28But if you do marry, you have not sinned; and if a virgin marries, she has not sinned. But those who marry will face many troubles in this life, and I want to spare you this.

29What I mean, brothers, is that the time is short. From now on those who have wives should live as if they had none; 30those who mourn, as if they did not; those who are happy, as if they were not; those who buy something, as if it were not theirs to keep; 31those who use the things of the world, as if not engrossed in them. For this world in its present form is passing away.

32I would like you to be free from concern. An unmarried man is concerned about the Lord's affairs—how he can please the Lord. 33But a married man is concerned about the affairs of this world—how he can please his wife— 34and his interests are divided. An unmarried woman or virgin is concerned about the Lord's affairs; Her aim is to be devoted to the Lord in both body and spirit. But a married woman is concerned about the affairs of this world—how she can please her husband. 35I am saying this for your own good, not to restrict you. I want you to live in a right way in undivided devotion to the Lord.

Now Paul answers the second main question: What about virgins and marriage? In this section he discusses the advisability in the present situation of remaining in an unmarried (virgin) state (vv.25–35). Then he advises that they do what they think is right for the virgin who is unmarried, whether it is by initiating marriage or by remaining single (vv.36–38). He concludes with a statement regarding the married woman's responsibilities to her husband and regarding her freedom to be married again in the Lord if her husband dies. However, Paul thinks she would be happier if she remained unmarried (vv.39, 40).

25–35 Paul argues that "because of the present crisis" it is better for a man or woman to remain in their present state, whether married or single (v.26). He advises this because there is such a short time to do the work of the Lord (v.29); and anyway the material conditions of this world are changing and disappearing—"this world in its present form is passing away" (v.31). Paul introduces certain corrective statements lest the Corinthians draw false conclusions from the main principle. In saying that they should stay married, he insists that marriage itself is not a matter of right or wrong (v.28). Paul also argues that the real problem they face in their present world situation is the proper expenditure of their time and energies. He is desirous that they devote their energies to the service of the Lord, and this they can do better if they are unmarried (vv.32–34). But he hastens to add that he does not mean to hamper them in such a way as to keep them from marrying—he only wants to help them. His advice, he implies, is not an argument for the superiority of celibacy or the obligatory nature of it (v.35).

25 Here the apostle makes it clear that he is not relying directly on a command from the Lord—i.e., from Jesus—as he was, for example, in Acts 20:35. Rather, he says that he is giving his own opinion on the matter, but that his opinion is to be taken seriously because by the Lord's mercy he is trustworthy and they should therefore listen to him. So he is not suggesting that his command is any less inspired but is only calling attention to the fact that what he is presenting is not derived from a direct teaching of Jesus himself.

26,27 Each person should remain as he now is "because of the present crisis." What this is he describes in v.27. In other words, remain married if you are married; single if you are single.

28 Here Paul hastens to make it plain that there is nothing sinful in marriage, whether entered into by a widow, a widower, or by a virgin. His main motive in dissuading the unmarried from marriage is to spare them the hardship and suffering in physical life ("in the flesh") that accompanies times of trouble and persecution.

29–31 The apostle explains that the time for doing the Lord's work is short and is coming to an end. This does not necessarily mean that he is speaking of the second coming of Christ, for Paul may have been anticipating severe persecutions and a resulting curtailment of freedom to witness. So for the time remaining Paul admonishes them not to be overwhelmed by the social and material problems of the world but to live as for the Lord. By "those who have wives should live as if they had none" (v.29) he means, "Live for the Lord in marriage." If life brings sadness, live beyond it, do not be bound by it. If things are joyous, do not be engrossed in them. Those who are blessed with material possessions are not to cling to them, as though they were to have them always. The reason for this challenge is that the *material things* (this is the meaning of *schēma*, v.31, "the present form") of this world are changing and disappearing (cf. Col 3:12–14).

32–35 Paul goes on to argue that if they want marriage, they must realize that it brings extra cares. And he wants them to be free from concern. They must observe that married persons, whether men or women, have their attentions centered on the desires and needs of their spouses (vv.33, 34). In saying that the unmarried woman or virgin is concerned with how she may please the Lord (v.34), Paul implies that the married person is apt to neglect this Christian duty. Since the apostle upholds the right and privilege of marriage even for himself (1 Cor 9:3–5), he must here be advising against marriage because of particular abuses and tensions at Corinth. He gives the advice, he says, for their own profit or benefit (*symphoron*), not to restrain them or put them in a noose (*brochos*). Rather, he wants them to live properly in complete and undivided devotion to the Lord (v.35).

Notes

25 It is possible that the gen. pl. τῶν παρθένων (*tōn parthenōn*) is to be taken as masc. (cf. Rev 14:4) including both masc. and fem. virgins, but the masc. form is used only infrequently in the literature of the early church period.

26 Ἄνθρωπος (*anthrōpos*) without the article means man generically—i.e., both men and women, as the illustrations of vv.27, 28 show.

27 The perfect tense of δέω (*deō*, "bind") and λύω (*luo*, "loose") stresses the permanent nature of the conditions described, whether of the married or the single.

29 The ἵνα (*hina*) with the subjunctive, expressed here and implied in succeeding vv., is to be taken as an imperative or volitive idea—they are to live this way (cf. Mark 5:23; Eph 5:33).

34 The MS witness is weak for v.34a: "and his interests . . . the Lord's affairs." But it is better than a few MS witnesses that say, "the woman and the unmarried virgin are divided. . . ." (See B.M. Metzger, *A Textual Commentary on the Greek New Testament* [New York: United Bible Societies, 1971], pp. 555, 556.)

35 The figure βρόχον ὑμῖν ἐπιβάλω (*brochon hymin epibalō*, "I may put a noose on you") is appropriate in the light of Paul's contention that in the special circumstances at Corinth marriage may be an encumbrance.

7:36-40

36If anyone thinks he is acting improperly toward the virgin he is engaged to, and if she is getting along in years and he feels he ought to marry, he should do as he wants. He is not sinning. They should get married. 37But the man who has settled the matter in his own mind, who is under no compulsion but has control over his own will, and who has made up his mind not to marry the virgin—this man also does the right thing. 38So then, he who marries the virgin does right, but he who does not marry her does even better.

39A woman is bound to her husband as long as he lives. But if her husband dies, she is free to marry anyone she wishes, but he must belong to the Lord. 40In my judgment, she is happier if she stays as she is—and I think that I have the Spirit of God.

36-40 Paul teaches that a virgin of marriageable age must be treated honorably, whether she becomes married or not. It may be right for her either to marry or remain single.

36 But who is meant by "he" is in v.36, the father of the virgin or the man who is engaged to her? Some have even interpreted the second view to mean that the virgin was a "spiritual" bride who lived with the man as a virgin. This latter view presents problems in the light of the Scriptures that teach that a man is to cleave to his wife and they are to be one flesh (Gen 2:24) and to "be fruitful" (Gen 1:28). The decision as to whether the "he" is father or fiancé turns on the meaning of *gamizō* ("marry") in v.36. Frequently, verbs ending in —*izō* are causative. If this is so here, then the translation "he who causes or gives his virgin to be married" would mean that "he" indicates the father, who in ancient times arranged for his daughter's marriage. But another viable view is that *gamizō* is not causative here, but is equivalent to *gameō* ("to marry"). If so, then "he" refers to the man who is considering the possibility of marrying his fiancée. Two arguments speak in favor of the second interpretation. First, v.38b has no object expressed for· the verb *gamizō* and so the verb can better be translated "marry," not

"cause to marry." Second, *gameō* ("marry") is used in the plural in v.36, "They should get married," where one might expect the singular form of *gamizō* if Paul meant to say, "Let *him* give her in marriage."

So the teaching is that if the situation in Corinth seems to be unfair to a particular virgin and especially if (*ean* with the subjunctive) she is passing her prime marriageable years, then the fiancé should go ahead and marry her. The word *hyperakmos* literally means "beyond the peak" of life, and so can be translated "if she should be getting along in years." Paul adds that there is no sin in their getting married (v.36).

37,38 In contrast, the man who feels no need to get married has done the right thing too. (The words "who is under no compulsion" refer to outward pressure to marry, such as some prior engagement contract or the pressure of a master on a slave.) However, Paul favors the man who does not marry (v.38).

39,40 In climaxing the discussion, Paul states that marriage is a life-long contract. If a woman marries, she is to cleave to her husband (Gen 2:24) till he dies. But when he dies, she is free to marry anyone she chooses, so long as he is a Christian. But, Paul says, the woman will be happier—freer from hardship and care—if she remains unmarried. This is his judgment for the Corinthian situation. When he says, rather modestly, "And I think that I have the Spirit of God," he means that in writing this also he is inspired by the Holy Spirit as were the other writers of Scripture. It is possible that some in Corinth were claiming inspiration; if so, Paul is contrasting himself with them in a veiled way.

"A woman is bound" (v.39, *dedetai*, perfect tense) is a strong expression for the unbroken ties of marriage. The passive *gamethēnai* ("to be married"; NIV, "to marry") indicates the women's consent to the new marriage relationship. The phrase *monon en kuriō* ("only in the Lord") means that the woman should marry only a Christian. The NIV translation "but he must belong to the Lord" brings this out.

Notes

36 The indicative condition of fact (v.36a) assumes that such a situation really exists. Ἀσχημονεῖν (*aschēmonein*, "to act improperly") in the light of what is implied by the clause "if she is getting past her prime of life" is best interpreted as meaning that the man could be treating his fiancée dishonorably by depriving her of the privilege of the marriage she desires. Paul seems to be making a play on words in using *aschēmonein*, "to act improperly" when he has just used εὐσχήμον (*euschēmon*, "live in a right way," v.35).

B. *Instructions Concerning Christian Freedom: Its Privileges and Responsibilities* (8:1–11:1)

This section focuses on the next question the delegation from Corinth put to Paul: "What about eating food offered in heathen sacrifices to idols?" Paul's answer leads to a discussion of the larger question of how a believer should use his Christian liberty. Paul lays down the principle that love for one's brother in Christ should be the motivating factor in contemplating one's Christian liberty (8:1–13). Then he gives a personal example of how he was ready to forego the exercise of his own rights as an apostle for the sake of God's people (9:1–18). He argues that though he was under obligation to no man, he showed his self-restraint and love by placing himself on the cultural and social level of all men so that he might reach some for Christ (9:19–27). By way of warning, he speaks of the lack of self-restraint of the OT Israelites, who actually embraced the idolatry they toyed with (10:1–13). So God's people must avoid participation in idol feasts and "flee from idolatry," because they belong to the Lord and have their own feast with him, the Lord's Supper (10:14–22). So Paul's conclusion is this: Live your testimony with loving concern for your brother, but, do not make an issue of meat sold in the market. Eat it as a gift from God. Do this, except when the point is explicitly made that the meat was offered in sacrifice to an idol. For you would in such a case seem to be participating in this religious heathen practice. Refrain, then, for your weaker brother's sake and for your own peace of mind. Above all, do everything for the glory of God (10:23–11:1).

1. *Eating meat sacrificed to idols* (8:1–13)

a. *Knowledge and love contrasted*

8:1–3

> [1]Now about meat sacrificed to idols: We know that we all possess knowledge. Knowledge puffs up, but love builds up. [2]The man who thinks he knows something does not yet know as he ought to know. [3]But the man who loves God is known by God.

1 By the *peri de* ("now about") Paul shows he is referring to another question asked by the Corinthian delegation (cf. 7:1, 25). The importance of the question of "foods offered in sacrifice to idols" (*eidōlothutōn*) becomes evident when one realizes how thoroughly idolatry and pagan sacrifices permeated all levels of Greek and Roman society. Indeed, people could hardly escape contact with the pagan practices and their influence. The meat offered on the pagan altars was usually divided into three portions: one portion was burned up, a second given to the priest, and the third given to the offerer. If the priest did not use his portion, it was taken to the meat market. Thus a considerable amount of sacrificed meat ending up in the public market, on the tables of pagan neighbors and friends, or at the pagan festivals. The problems Christians faced are obvious. Was the meat spiritually contaminated? Did the pagan god actually have an effect on the meat? Even if one did not think so, what would his participation do to his Christian brother who might have scruples about this? Though Christians today do not have to deal with this particular problem, they too must face questions of how to conduct themselves in a non-Christian society.

In v.1 Paul concedes that all Christians know—at least theoretically—the real meaning about the meat sacrificed to idols. But, he implies, there is something more—some may really feel that there is something wrong with that meat (v.7). So he adds that the mere knowledge that there is nothing wrong with it inflates one to a level of false security and indifference. Thus, love (*agapē*) is necessary. Love takes one beyond himself to aid another; it builds up. (It is possible to take v.1a, as some do, as a quotation from the Corinthians themselves: "We know that you say we all have knowledge.")

2 Paul now warns against dependence on simply knowing something, since a person never knows all he ought to know about a subject. Such an attitude exhibits a complete

dependence on one's own self-sufficient knowledge and illustrates what Paul means by saying, "Knowledge puffs up."

3 With the essential ingredient of love, knowledge is tempered and made the right kind of discerning and compassionate knowledge exhibited when one loves God. In loving God, a person shows that he is known by God—that God recognizes him as his own and as having the right kind of knowledge, because he is exercising it in love to his fellow-Christians and to God.

b. *The meaning of eating meat sacrificed to idols*

8:4–6

> [4]So then, about eating meat sacrificed to idols: We know that an idol is nothing at all in the world, and that there is no God but one. [5]For even if there are so-called gods, whether in heaven or on earth (as indeed there are many "gods" and many "lords"), [6]yet for us there is but one God, the Father, from whom all things came and for whom we live; and there is but one Lord, Jesus Christ, through whom all things came and through whom we live.

4 The word translated "meat" is really the broader word "food" (*brōsis*), but since the subject involves altar sacrifices and the meat market (*makellon*, 1 Cor 10:25; see commentary on this verse), the translation "meat" is proper. The main thing to remember in connection with such meat, Paul says, is that the idol before which it was sacrificed and the god it represents are actually nothing—that is, nothing as to personal reality and power. That he means this is clear from his statement "There is no God but one" (cf. Deut 6:4-9; 1 Kings 18:39; Isa 45:5). The phrase "in the world" means "in the universe."

5,6 Paul grants that there are "so-called gods" in heaven and earth such as those the pagans recognized in Greek and Roman mythology. In addition, he mentions the many "gods" and "lords" who are called such in Scripture (cf. Deut 10:17; Ps 136:2, 3) and who in the widest sense represent rulers in the universe who are subordinate to God (Col 1:16). So Paul is teaching that the "so-called gods" of the pagans are unreal and that the real "gods" and "lords," whatever they may be, are all subordinate to the only one supreme God whom alone we recognize. Actually, Paul declares the Christian's "one God, the Father ... one Lord, Jesus Christ, to be the source of all things and the One for whom Christians live" (v.6). Concerning the world, the Father is the source (*ex hou*) of all creation, and Jesus Christ is the dynamic One through whom (*di' hou*) creation came into existence. As for the Christian, he lives for God, the source of all, and has the power for so living through Jesus Christ. So why, implies Paul, should we be concerned with idols or meat sacrificed to idols?

c. *Freedom to be exercised with care*

8:7–13

> [7]But not everyone knows this. Some people are still so accustomed to idols that when they eat such meat, they think of it as having been sacrificed to an idol, and since their conscience is weak, it is defiled. [8]But food does not bring us near to God; we are no worse if we do not eat, and no better if we do.
> [9]Be careful, however, that the exercise of your freedom does not become a stumbling block to the weak. [10]For if anyone with a weak conscience sees you who

have this knowledge eating in an idol's temple, won't he be emboldened to eat what has been sacrificed to idols? ¹¹So this weak brother, for whom Christ died, is destroyed by your knowledge. ¹²When you sin against your brothers in this way and wound their weak conscience, you sin against Christ. ¹³Therefore, if what I eat causes my brother to fall into sin, I will never eat meat again, so that I will not cause him to fall.

7 The knowledge Paul now speaks of is the perceptive knowledge regarding an idol and the existence and position of the "so-called gods." But some may not fully realize the significance of these truths, because in their former unsaved state they had become so accustomed to idols and to the sacrificed meat that now when they eat such meat, they think of it only as something sacrificed to the idol, rather than as food provided by God. Their moral awareness—their conscience (*syneidēsis*)—is weak, being unable to discriminate in these matters and so is defiled. The verb *molunō* can mean "defile" as in Revelation 14:4, or can be used, as here, of being brought into a sense of guilt.

8 Paul's next statement can have a twofold thrust. First, as in 8:1, we should know that there is nothing inherently wrong with sacrificial meat and that in itself food neither enhances nor minimizes our standing before God. Second, since the eating of meat is of no spiritual importance and so is a matter of indifference, the Corinthians should realize that to eat sacrificial meat is not a practice to be insisted on for maintaining Christian liberty (Hodge, in loc.).

9–12 Though Christians have the *exousia* (the "authority") to act in such cases as the one mentioned, they must "be careful" (*blepete*), lest through the exercise of this authority to act in freedom they somehow cause the weak (in conscience) to stumble in living their Christian lives. By "stumbling block" is meant causing the weak brother not only to have a sense of guilt (v.7), but to go beyond this into sin (v.13) by compromising with pagan idolatry.

So Paul depicts for the Corinthians what may well have been an actual scene (v.10): Suppose, a brother who is weak in conscience sees you, who understand that an idol is nothing, reclining at table to eat (*katakeimenon*) in an idol temple; won't he also be encouraged to eat and so do what his conscience forbids him to do? When you do such a thing, he continues (v.11), you are using your freedom and knowledge to bring your weak brother down the path (*apollutai*, present tense of *apollumi*, "destroy") toward spiritual weakness and destruction. Paul does not mean ultimate spiritual destruction, for he calls this man a "brother, for whom Christ died." The stress is on weakening the faith and ruining the Christian life of the brother.

Speaking to the "strong" brother (v.12), Paul is saying, "If you cause the weak brother to stumble into sin, you yourselves are sinning in a twofold way: (1) against your brothers and (2) against Christ in that you are wounding the conscience of those who belong to Christ. The plurals in this verse imply that Paul has in mind a sizeable group at Corinth who were both the offenders and the offended.

13 In closing the discussion, the apostle includes himself. He may be indicating that when he was in Corinth, he had had to face this question and had, for the sake of the Christians there, refrained from eating meat that had been sacrificed to idols. So he ends with the personal declaration: Therefore, if what I eat causes my brother to fall into sin,

I will never eat meat again, so that I will not cause him to fall" (v.13)—a noble resolve that stands as an enduring principle for Christian living.

Notes

1 The article ἡ (hē, "the") used with γνῶσις (gnōsis, "knowledge") is demonstrative: "This kind of knowledge puffs up."
3 The perfect form here, ἔγνωσται (egnōstai) goes beyond the idea of "know" to that of "acknowledge," or "recognize," almost with the idea of "elect"—recognized by God as his own, (cf. Amos 3:2).
7 The textual problem in v.7a is whether the reading should be συνείδησις (suneidēsis, "conscience") instead of συνήθεια (sunētheia, "become accustomed to"). The latter, followed by NIV, is the witness of the better Gr. texts. If suneidēsis should be read as in KJV, then the idea is that their thought has been permeated with the consciousness or awareness that the idol is real.
11 The verb ἀπόλλυμι (apollumi) carries not only the meaning "destroy," in the sense of eternal destruction, but also the more qualified meaning of temporal "ruin" or "loss" (cf. Matt 9:17, of wineskins that are ruined; and James 1:11, of a blossom as it withers and its beauty fades, and in that sense is thought of as destroyed).
13 Here again Paul uses the first-class condition with εἰ (ei) and the indicative verb. By this construction he stresses the reality of the situation: "If food actually causes my brother to stumble. . . ."

2. Paul: on giving up his rights as an apostle (9:1–18)

a. Rights of an apostle

9:1–12a

> [1]Am I not free? Am I not an apostle? Have I not seen Jesus our Lord? Are you not the result of my work in the Lord? [2]Even though I may not be an apostle to others, surely I am to you! For you are the seal of my apostleship in the Lord.
> [3]This is my defense to those who sit in judgment on me. [4]Don't we have the right to food and drink? [5]Don't we have the right to take a believing wife along with us, as do the other apostles and the Lord's brothers and Cephas? [6]Or is it only I and Barnabas who must work for a living?
> [7]Who serves as a soldier at his own expense? Who plants a vineyard and does not eat of its grapes? Who tends a flock and does not drink of the milk? [8]Do I say this merely from a human point of view? Doesn't the Law say the same thing? [9]For it is written in the Law of Moses: "Do not muzzle an ox when it is treading out the grain." Is it about oxen that God is concerned? [10]Surely he says this for us, doesn't he? Yes, this was written for us, because when the plowman plows and the thresher threshes, they ought to do so in the hope of sharing in the harvest. [11]If we have sown spiritual seed among you, is it too much if we reap a material harvest from you? [12]If others have this right of support from you, shouldn't we have it all the more?

1,2 Paul's reference to the spiritual freedom we have in Christ, together with his claim of apostleship, leads him to expand the theme of Christian freedom and apply it in a wider context than that of sacrificial meat. The illustration is particularly pertinent because it involves himself and relates to his important rights as an apostle and Christian worker. The four rhetorical questions in v.1 relate to two themes: freedom and apostleship, the last three specifically relating to his apostleship. Paul contends that he is an apostle and then states one of the criteria for an apostle: he had seen the Lord (Acts 1:21, 22; 9:3–9). Another evidence of apostleship, as Hodge has pointed out (in loc.), is the working of signs and wonders (2 Cor 12:12), which Paul no doubt did in Corinth. This is followed by the contention that his apostleship had produced spiritual work "in the Lord"—the Corinthians were the fruit of his work. As v.2 shows, he expected them to accept him as an apostle—though others did not—because they were really the seal that stamped his apostleship in the Lord as genuine.

All four questions in v.1 are introduced by the Greek negative *ou*, which implies that the answer expected to each is yes. The "if" condition in v.2 is a factual one; he assumes the condition that some did not accept him as an apostle, but the Corinthians certainly (*ge*) did. *Sphragis* ("seal," "sign," or "stamp of approval") is used here in a figurative sense of that which authenticates: "You certify my apostleship."

3 Paul now begins to answer those who have criticized his apostleship on the ground that he had not exercised all the rights one might expect an apostle to use.

The word *apologia* is to be taken in the sense of a "defense" against a charge, a charge concerning which some men were judging him as it were in court. The verb *anakrinō* ("question, examine") has legal connotations, used in connection with judicial hearings. Here it is best taken figuratively of those who sat in judgment on Paul.

4–6 In these verses Paul brings up certain rights he and others, such as Barnabas, had the authority (*exousia*) to exercise. The first one, "the right to food and drink," must mean, in the context, at the expense of the church (cf. 1 Cor 9:9–11). Next he claims the right to have a wife join him in his missionary travels. To take this only spiritually, as some have done, and refer to rich women accompanying the apostles to meet their financial needs, is certainly out of keeping with the context—observe that Cephas (Peter) had a wife (Mark 1:30). In referring to the "rest of the apostles" (v.5), Paul is not saying that all were necessarily married, but that at least a larger part were. The phrase "brothers of the Lord" should be taken at face value—physical brothers, that is, half-brothers, children of both Joseph and Mary after Jesus was born (Matt 1:18–25; 12:46; 13:55; Acts 1:14; Gal 1:19). In v.6 Paul raises the practical question of his and Barnabas's right to be supported financially in the ministry. It was Paul's practice to support himself materially by tentmaking (Acts 18:2, 3; 1 Cor 4:12) in order not to be a burden to the church. Some apparently misunderstood this to mean that he was not on a par with other apostles and Christian workers who depended on the church to support them. In not denying that principle, Paul asserts, by way of a question, that he has a right to be supported.

7–10 These verses present illustrations supporting the proposition that God's servants have the right to be supported with food and drink and other necessities of life as they labor in the work. Verse 7 gives illustrations from common experiences in ancient life: the soldier supported at public or royal expense; the vineyard keeper, who eats of the grapes he gathers; the shepherd, who drinks milk from his flock. These illustrations are all obvious and might be added to from modern life. But as an additional argument (v.8), Paul adds the authority of Scripture, citing Deuteronomy 25:4, "Do not muzzle an ox when it is treading out the grain." This merciful command covered the practice in ancient times of oxen pulling the threshing sledge over the grain or treading it out with their feet (Isa 28:28; 41:15; Hos 10:11). The reason for the command, Paul says, is not just God's care for the cattle (cf. Matt 6:26–29), but because by it he wants to teach us a lesson about God's care for us (v.10). This is evident, too, in the provision for the farmer: When a plowman and thresher do their work, they do so expecting that through God's blessing they will share in the crop.

11,12 In these verses the same principles of the worker's sharing in the results of his crop are applied to God's spiritual work. Those who have sown the spiritual seed at Corinth with its resultant harvest can expect to have their material needs supplied from that harvest. Then Paul argues in v.12 that if the Corinthians have supported other Christian workers, should they not also support Paul and his companions, who have sown spiritual seed among them?

This basic principle is true today. The Christian worker who sows the spiritual seed of the gospel has a right to be supported materially by those who benefit from the gospel.

Notes

4,5 The double negative in this order, μὴ οὐ (*mē ou*), introduces the question with *mē*, here used as an interrogative indicator only, and negates the verb with *ou*, implying a qualified affirmative response, which can be translated here, "Do we fail to have the right to eat and drink?" This anticipates the answer "Of course not" (cf. Robertson, *A Grammar of the Greek New Testament*, pp. 1173, 1174; and Blass and Debrunner, *A Greek Grammar of the New Testament*, para. 427).

8 The question with μή (*mē*) gives the same negative turn: "I don't speak these things from a human viewpoint, do I?" The answer is "Of course not."

11 Σαρκικός (*sarkikos*, "fleshly") can refer to what is weak and sinful (1 Peter 2:11), but here it is to be taken as that which pertains to or satisfies the needs of the flesh, that is, "material things" (cf. also Rom 15:27).

---

b. *Rights not used*

9:12b–18

> But we did not use this right. On the contrary, we put up with anything rather than hinder the gospel of Christ. [13]Don't you know that those who work in the temple get their food from the temple, and those who serve at the altar share in what is offered on the altar? [14]In the same way, the Lord has commanded that those who preach the gospel should receive their living from the gospel.
> [15]But I have not used any of these rights. And I am not writing this in the hope that you will do such things for me. I would rather die than have anyone deprive me of this boast. [16]Yet when I preach the gospel, I cannot boast, for I am compelled to preach. Woe to me if I do not preach the gospel! [17]If I preach voluntarily, I have a reward; if not voluntarily, I am simply discharging the trust committed to me. [18]What then is my reward? Just this: that in preaching the gospel I may offer it free of charge, and so not make use of my rights in preaching it.

12b The apostle goes on to announce that he will not exercise these rights that are his and says that he and his companions do so that they may not hinder the advance of the gospel. The word *enkopē*, here with the more general meaning of "hindrance," has a basic idea of a "cutting" of some sort, such as that made in a road to hinder an enemy (Liddell-Scott).

13 To emphasize further the reason and importance for his self-restraint in exercising this right of support, Paul now turns to a religious illustration, applicable in biblical worship as well as in pagan temples. Observe that Paul does not quote Scripture here. His illustration is much broader. This argument has a particularly telling relation to the Corinthians with their former connections with pagan worship. Paul's language is pointed: When people serve in the temple, they are working (*ergazomai*), and this is true, too, of those who serve in performing sacrifices at the altar. Both eat of the temple offerings. Although Paul includes in his illustration worship-practices in general, it is noteworthy that he does not use the pagan word *bōmos* for altar, but *thysiastērion*. *Bōmos* does not occur anywhere in the NT except in Acts 17:23, where an Athenian altar is referred to, and carries too many heathen connotations to be used. (See W. Harold Mare, "The Greek Altar in The New Testament and Inter-Testamental Periods," *Grace Journal*, Vol. 10, No. 1, Winter, 1969.)

14 Now Paul applies the general religious principle (also practiced in the OT) to the NT, to the ministers of the gospel. The adverb "thus" shows that the principle of giving material support for those who serve in the temple is to be applied also to ministers of the gospel. That the Lord Jesus commanded (*diatassō*) that those who preach the gospel are to live (be supported) by the gospel—that is, by those who believe the gospel—is shown by Matthew 10:10 and Luke 10:8.

15,16 In spite of all this evidence, Paul again states that he has not used these privileges. He adds that he is not writing this to get them to give to his support, because he wants to be able to face those opposing him at Corinth with the boast that he is unselfishly serving them and the Lord in the gospel. For, he says, if it should be a matter only of his preaching, that gives him no cause to boast, because the Lord has laid on him the necessity of preaching (Acts 26:16–18). In further explanation, he cries out that woe would descend on him through God's judgment if he did not preach.

17,18 Now he explains that there is reward or pay (*misthos*) in preaching. He states the alternatives. If he preaches freely, voluntarily, he has a reward. If not, he is merely fulfilling the commission entrusted to him (Acts 26:16). His reward is the boasting he can make before them that he is preaching to them without charge and not making use of his rights as a gospel minister. Paul wants to prove to the Corinthians the genuineness of his ministry.

Notes

13 The question stated in this v. begins with the negative οὐκ (*ouk*) by which Paul expects an affirmative reply. The participle ἐργαζόμενοι (*ergazomenoi,* "working") is a general term used here to express temple service, but in the phrase παρεδρεύοντες τῷ θυσιαστηρίῳ (*paredreuontes tō thysiastēriō*) Paul emphasizes the heart of that service—serving at the altar.

14 The teaching then is that gospel ministers are also (οὔτως, *houtōs*) serving at the altar (cf. Rev. 1:6) in telling of Christ's sacrifice on the cross.

15 The perfect tense of χράομαι (*chraomai*, "to use") here conveys the idea that Paul had determined in the past not to use these rights and his resolve continues in the present. The aorist form ἔγραψα (*egrapsa*) could be taken as simple past—"I wrote" (that is, in some previous letter). It is better to take it as an epistolary aorist—present in idea as Paul writes it but past when it was read. So the tr. "I am not writing."

There is a grammatical break in v.15, a figure of speech called aposiopesis. Paul says, "I would rather die than—," a reading favored by the better MSS. If he had completed his statement in normal construction, it would have been something like the copyists' attempt at smoothing it out with ἵνα τις (*hina tis*); "I would rather die than have anyone deprive me of this boast" (NIV). But Paul's shortened expression is more dramatic.

16 The present tense form of εὐαγγελίζομαι (*euangelizomai*) suggests Paul's continual preaching all over (v.16a), but the aorist looks at his entire preaching activity as one total calling from God (v.16b).

17 The perfect passive form πεπίστευμαι (*pepisteumai*) carries with it the idea of a trust committed and carried on in the present.

---

3. *Paul: subjection of self for others and to meet God's approval*

9:19–27

> ¹⁹Though I am free and belong to no man, I make myself a slave to everyone, to win as many as possible. ²⁰To the Jews I became like a Jew, to win the Jews. To those under the law I became like one under the law (though I myself am not under the law), so as to win those under the law. ²¹To those not having the law I became like one not having the law (though I am not free from God's law but am under Christ's law), so as to win those not having the law. ²²To the weak I became weak, to win the weak. I have become all things to all men so that by all possible means I might save some. ²³I do all this for the sake of the gospel that I may share in its blessings.
>
> ²⁴Do you not know that in a race all the runners run, but only one gets the prize? Run in such a way as to get the prize. ²⁵Everyone who competes in the games goes into strict training. They do it to get a crown of laurel that will not last; but we do it to get a crown that will last forever. ²⁶Therefore, I do not run like a man running aimlessly; I do not fight like a man shadow boxing. ²⁷No, I beat my body and make it my slave so that after I have preached to others, I myself will not be disqualified for the prize.

19 Going beyond his right to financial support, the apostle now discusses other areas of life in which he had forfeited his right to freedom in order to win more to Christ. His statement is a strong one: "I am free from all men, but I have enslaved (*edoulōsa*, aorist) myself to all."

20 In discussing his self-sacrificing concern in vv.20–23, Paul mentions three groups— the Jews, the Gentiles, and those whose consciences are weak. For the Jews' sake Paul became like a Jew. That is, when necessary and regarding indifferent matters, he conformed to the practice of Jewish law (Acts 16:3; 18:18; 21:20–26) to win the Jews. "Those under the law" need not be taken as a separate group such as proselytes to Judaism, but as reference again to Jews—those to whom Paul accommodated himself. In the parenthetical phrase "though I myself am not under the law," Paul means that in his freedom he was not obligated to practice such Jewish laws as their rigorous ceremonial washings.

21 For the Gentiles "without the law," those who did not have any written revelation from God (Rom 2:12), Paul says he became like one not having the law and took his place in their culture in order to reach them (cf. Gal 2:11–21). But he hastens to correct any misunderstanding: he counts himself still under God's law, and even more, under Christ's law.

22 Those with a weak conscience (1 Cor 8:9–12) he also wants to be sure to win (v.22). He becomes "weak"—that is, he refrains from exercising his Christian freedom, and acts as they do respecting these indifferent things. He has forfeited his freedom for the sake of all, that by all these means some may be saved.

23 Paul does all this for the sake of the gospel that he might be a co-sharer (*synkoinōnos*, "communion," "fellowship") with the gospel, sharing in its blessings personally and in seeing others come to Christ.

24–27 By way of practical application, Paul now gives a strong exhortation for Christian self-denial, using himself as an example and employing athletic figures familiar to the Corinthians at their own Isthmian athletic games, which were hosted every other year by the people of Corinth. The particular events he refers to are running and boxing.

24,25 Paul assumes their common knowledge (*ouk oidate*, "don't you know") of the foot race in the stadium. Every one of them should run as these runners do, with all-out effort to get the prize. By the words "strict training," Paul refers to the athlete's self-control in diet and his rigorous bodily discipline. He observes that the athletes train vigorously for a "corruptible crown"—a laurel or celery wreath that would soon wither away. But the Christian's crown, eternal life and fellowship with God, will last forever (Rev 2:10).

26,27 Paul says of himself that he does not contend like an undisciplined runner or boxer. He states that he aims his blows against his own body, beating it black and blue (*hypōpiazō*; see the same word in Luke 18:5). The picture is graphic: the ancient boxers devastatingly punishing one another with knuckles bound with leather thongs. And so by pummeling his body, Paul enslaves it in order to gain the Christian prize. The ancient *kēryx* was the herald in the Greek games who announced the rules of the contest, but the Christian herald—*i.e.*, preacher—not only announces the rules but "plays" in the game as well. Paul had not only to preach the gospel but also to live the gospel. As Hodge has said (in loc.), Paul here acts on the principle that the righteous can scarcely be saved, though he also stresses that nothing can separate the Christian from God's love (Rom 8:38, 39). The Christian, confident of God's sovereign grace, is nevertheless conscious of his battle against sin.

Notes

20 The circumstantial participle ὤν (*ōn*) stresses Paul's present existent state; the phrase may be tr. "though I am not existing under the control of the law"; i.e., the Jewish ceremonies. The phrase μὴ ... νόμον (*mē ... nomon*) was not in TR and so was omitted from KJV. However, it is decisively supported by the best ancient MSS. It probably was accidentally omitted by some scribe(s) who overlooked one of the four occurrences of ὑπὸ νόμον in this verse.

21 There seems to be a play on the words ἄνομος (*anomos*, "without law"; i.e., outside the rules of Jewish ceremonies) and ἔννομος (*ennomos*, "within the law"; i.e., within the rules and control of Christ).

Excursus

In Paul's time many of the structures dedicated to the ancient gods had been restored and were in use again in worship of the gods and were no doubt evident to the visitor to Corinth. These included the archaic temple of Apollo, built about 550 B.C., seven of whose columns are still to be seen today. Nearby, on the north slope of the hill, was the shrine to Athena, the Bridler. It had been built to commemorate Bellerophon's harnessing of the winged horse, Pegasus, who was caught with Athena's help, when he was drinking at the fountain of Peirene at Corinth. Bellerophon (a local mythical hero) then used Pegasus in slaying the Chimaera (a she-monster with a lion's head, a goat's body, and a serpent's tail). This well-known story led to the winged horse's becoming the emblem used for hundreds of years on Corinthian coins. Poseidon, the sea-god, also had his shrine and fountain at Corinth, though his chief cultic place in this area was at Isthmia about seven miles to the east. (For location of places mentioned, see map, p. 187).

A short distance west of the archaic Apollo temple stands a stone-cut fountain house. Here, according to Greek myth, the Corinthian princess, Glauke, the bride of Jason, threw herself into the fountain waters at a time when her body was being destroyed by the poisoned robe given to her by Medea, the sorceress from the Black Sea area. In vengeance, Medea killed her own sons born of Jason. Close by was a statue of Terror, in the form of a woman, which was in existence in Paul's day, when images of baked clay were evidently thrown into the Fountain House of Glauke. This ceremony is believed to be a development from earlier human sacrifices made there by the Corinthians. The goddess Hera was worshiped in connection with this festival and a small temple of Roman times with colonnaded court near the Fountain of Glauke is identified as that of Hera.

Apollo was also worshiped at another place besides the archaic temple of Apollo. This shrine, located near the Fountain of Peirene in the northeast section of the excavated area of Corinth, was the Peribolos sanctuary of Apollo with its large paved court and colossal statue of the god in the center.

Other remains of the Roman period found in the Corinthian excavations include those of the temple of Aphrodite-Tyche (Venus-Fortune); a Pantheon, or "temple of all the gods"; a temple of Heracles (the Greek mythical hero famous for achieving "The Twelve Labors"); and a temple of Hermes (Mercury, the messenger of the gods). Besides these, there were the temple to Octavia, (the deified sister of the Emperor Augustus) and the temple of Jupiter Capitolinus (Zeus Koryphaios). Some distance from the marketplace, to the north, was the temple of Asklepios, the god of healing, to whom terra cotta likenesses of the diseased parts of the body were offered by those who were afflicted with these sicknesses. Some of these terra cotta likenesses are on display today in the Antiquities Museum at Ancient Corinth. Paul may have had in mind such sicknesses affecting the perishable human body as represented by the clay likenesses of these diseased parts when he declared to the Corinthians the truth of God's triumph over decay and death when at the resurrection the Christian dead "will be raised imperishable, and we shall be changed" (1 Cor 15:52; cf. also vv.53–55).

On the top of the Acrocorinth (the rocky pinnacle) behind ancient Corinth was the famous temple of Aphrodite (Venus) in whose service were one thousand prostitute slave priestesses. On the Acrocorinth's north slopes facing the city were other temples, such as that in honor of the Egyptian gods, Isis and Serapis. The worship of these gods probably started at Corinth either in the Hellenistic period (c.330 to 63 B.C.) or in the Roman period, after the city was founded as a Roman Colony in Caesar's time. (See Broneer, "Corinth," pp. 83–88.) On the Acrocorinth's north slopes was the temple of the goddess Demeter that had been in use from c.600 B.C. to A.D. 350. This structure contained a number of dining rooms, which may account for Paul's warning about not being a stumbling block by "eating in an idol's temple" (1 Cor 8:10; see Henry S. Robinson, "Excavations at Corinth, 1961–1962," in AJA, 67, [1963], pp. 216, 217; Miriam Ervin, "Newsletter from Greece," AJA, 74 [1970], pp. 267, 268; and Nancy Bookidis, *Hesperia*, 28 [1969], No. 3, pp. 297–310).

With such idolatry and other pagan practices dominating the life and culture of Corinth, no wonder Paul was so concerned for Christians not to be reckless in exercising their freedom to eat meat sold in butcher shops after it had been offered to some idol and consecrated in pagan worship in the city. Also, that is why Paul disciplined himself (1 Cor 9:19–27) in refraining from eating meat sacrificed to idols or in doing any other thing by which he would disappoint the Lord or offend his brothers in Christ.

4. *Warning: Israel's lack of self-restraint*

10:1–13

¹For I do not want you to be ignorant of the fact brothers, that our forefathers were all under the cloud and that they all passed through the sea. ²They were all baptized into Moses in the cloud and in the sea. ³They all ate the same spiritual food ⁴and drank the same spiritual drink; for they drank from the spiritual rock that accompanied them, and that rock was Christ. ⁵Nevertheless, God was not pleased with most of them, so their bodies were scattered over the desert.

⁶Now these things occurred as examples, to keep us from setting our hearts on evil things as they did. ⁷Do not be idolaters, as some of them were; as it is written: "The people sat down to eat and drink and got up to indulge in pagan revelry." ⁸We should not commit sexual immorality, as some of them did—and in one day twenty-three thousand of them died. ⁹We should not test the Lord, as some of them did—and were killed by snakes. ¹⁰And do not grumble, as some of them did—and were killed by the destroying angel.

¹¹These things happened to them as examples and were written down as warnings for us, on whom the fulfillment of the ages has come. ¹²So, if you think you are standing firm, be careful that you don't fall! ¹³No temptation has seized you except what is common to man. And God is faithful; he will not let you be tempted beyond what you can bear. But when you are tempted, he will also provide a way out so that you can stand up under it.

In this passage Paul takes the sins of Israel during the time of Moses as a basis for warning the Corinthians. Though the people of Israel had the covenant blessings and were miraculously delivered and sustained, yet most of them died in the wilderness because of disobedience and unbelief. Paul uses their experiences as examples, which he exhorts the Corinthians to heed.

1–5 The Greek word *gar* ("for") connects these verses with the argument in chapters 8 and 9. Having challenged the Christians in Corinth to self-discipline, Paul now looks back to Israel. First, he stresses their miraculous passage through the Red Sea. All the fathers shared in God's grace and all were in the race described in 9:24–27, but only

Caleb and Joshua entered Canaan and won the prize. Five times in vv.1–4 Paul says that all Israel shared in the blessings and the privileges of God's grace. But (*alla*, strong negative) God was not pleased with most of them, so he scattered their corpses over the desert (v.5).

"I do not want you to be ignorant," meaning "I want you to know," is elsewhere used by Paul in presenting important truth (Rom 1:13; 1 Thess 4:13). "Under the cloud" indicates that they were under God's guidance (Exod 13:21, 22; Num 9:15–23; 14:14; Deut 1:33; Ps 78:14)—a guidance that was sure, since they all passed through the Red Sea.

That "they were all baptized into Moses in the cloud and in the sea" simply means they were initiated and inaugurated under God into union with him and also with Moses and his leadership. Compare the expression "baptized into Christ" (Rom 6:3, 4; cf. Gal 3:27; and see Heb 3:1–6). The aorist middle form *ebaptisanto*, or the alternate passive MS reading *ebaptisthēsan*, means "they received baptism." Some have taken the expression to specify either sprinkling or immersion, but these ideas need not be pressed. The thought is a spiritual one (v.3). They were united to God and to his servant Moses. The cloud is a representation of God in his shekinah glory; the sea, of God's redemption and leadership.

That the food and drink in the wilderness are called spiritual (vv.3, 4) means that these physical objects were to be a means of grace to God's people. They were typical of Christ the true bread and drink to come (cf. John 6:30–65). That the terms are to be taken as typical is seen in the statement "that rock was Christ" (cf. 1 Cor 5:7), who was with them to save them.

But though they all shared these blessings, most of them were not pleasing to God (v.5; Heb 3:17–19). He saw in them a heart of unbelief (vv.6–10) and scattered their corpses in the desert.

6–10 Paul explains here that all these things were examples (*typoi*) for us to think about, lest we who also have received the covenant blessings should become displeasing to God by lusting after evil things as Israel did.

Then he describes (vv.7–10) what that lusting involved and warns against following their example. Many of Israel became idolaters. The illustration is that of Exodus 32:1–6, where it is said that Israel had Aaron make the golden calf. Exodus 32:6, quoted here, tells how Israel ate a sacrificial meal in dedication to the calf and then got up "to play" (KJV), that is, to dance in ceremonial revelry as the pagans danced before their gods. This may look back to Paul's discussion in 1 Corinthians 8 about meat sacrificed to idols.

As he continues his warning, he alludes to Israel's joining herself to Baalpeor (Num 25:1–9), an act involving both spiritual and sexual unfaithfulness. Hodge notes (in loc.), "This Baal-peor was the god of the Moabites who was worshiped by the prostitution of virgins. Idolatry and fornication were in that case inseparable." In v.8 Paul uses *porneuō*, the common NT word for "committing sexual immorality" that is a cognate of the words used in chapter 5. He softens its force, however, by including himself in the exhortation. The Greek text says 23,000 died, whereas the Hebrew and LXX texts of Numbers 25:9 says 24,000. Paul is speaking about how many died in that one day; he does not include others who were killed subsequently, among them being the leaders in the rebellion, whom God ordered Moses to hang (Num 25:4).

Verse 9 relates to the murmuring of Israel against the Lord for bringing them out of Egypt and tells of their drastic punishment (Num 21:6). Observe the plural pronoun "we," with which Paul includes himself in cautioning the Corinthians against complaining as Israel did. The verb *ekpeirazō* means "to put to the test—i.e., testing the Lord to see what he will do.

The next example (v.10) relates to Israel's grumbling against the Lord at Kadesh-barnea (Num 14:2) and their wishing they had died in Egypt or in the wilderness. The "destroyer" was the angel of God (cf. Exod 12:23), whom Paul indicates was sent to bring the plague spoken of in Numbers 14:37. The incident referred to may also be taken to be the destruction of Korah, Dathan, and Abiram (Num 16:30).

11-13 Paul now makes an application for the Corinthians. Paul sets forth the examples he uses as actually having occurred in history (notice the imperfect verb *sunebainen,* "they were happening") and as having been written down to warn us. The KJV translation "ends of the world" (v.11b) seems to suggest too much, as though Paul thought he and the Corinthians were in the time of the Second Coming. Actually, he is speaking of the stretch of time called "the fulfillment [or 'end'] of the ages, which was to continue from Paul's time into the indefinite future. The warning amounts to this: Do not be smug in your firm stand for Christ. Keep alert lest you fall.

Verse 13 is one of the most helpful verses in the NT and presents the great antidote to falling into sin through temptation. *Peirasmos,* "trial" or "temptation" is not itself sinful. God allows it as a way of purifying us (James 1:12), but the devil uses it to entice us into sin (cf. Matt 4:1). The temptations that come to the Christian are those all human beings face—they are unavoidable. But, says Paul, God is right there with us to keep us from being overwhelmed by the temptation. The words "with the temptation" could perhaps be taken to mean that God brings the temptation, but this is contrary to James 1:13. So it means, rather, that when we are tempted, God will help. He will provide a way out, not to avoid the temptation, but to meet it successfully and to stand firm under it.

Notes

2 Some MSS have the aorist middle of βαπτίζω (*baptizō*)—"they got themselves baptized." Other MSS have the passive—"they were baptized." The meaning is the same.
4 The article ἡ (*hē*) with both πέτρα (*petra,* "the rock") and Χριστός (*Christos,* "the Christ") shows that the rock typifies *the* Christ.
5 The verb κατεστρώθησαν (*katestrōthēsan*) is passive and vividly describes the scattering of the corpses (by the hand of God) all over the desert.
6 The term ἐπιθυμία (*epithymia,* "strong desire, longing") can be used in a good sense (Phil 1:23), but more often, as here, in a bad sense of lusting after what is forbidden (cf. 2 Tim 2:22).
10 The ὀλοθρευτής (*olothreutēs*) is the destroyer (cf. Exod 12:23; הַמַּשְׁחִית, *hammašḥit;* and Heb 11:28)—the angel of God designed to bring divine judgment.

5. *Warning: attendance at pagan sacrifices means fellowship with idolatry*

10:14-22

14Therefore, my dear friends, flee from idolatry. 15I speak to sensible people; judge for yourselves what I say. 16Is not the cup of thanksgiving for which we give thanks a participation in the blood of Christ? And is not the bread that we break

a participation in the body of Christ? [17]Because there is one loaf, we, who are many, are one body, for we all partake of the one loaf.

[18]Consider the people of Israel: Do not those who eat the sacrifices participate in the altar? [19]Do I mean then that a sacrifice offered to an idol is anything, or that an idol is anything? [20]No, but the sacrifices of pagans are offered to demons, not to God, and I do not want you to be participants with demons. [21]You cannot drink the cup of the Lord and the cup of demons too; you cannot have a part in both the Lord's table and the table of demons. [22]Are we trying to arouse the Lord's jealousy? Are we stronger than he?

Here Paul applies the example of Israel's idolatry to the problem of 1 Corinthians 8—eating meat sacrificed to idols. There is the danger of going a step beyond just eating sacrificed meat to that of joining the pagans in the sacrificial feasts in their pagan temples. To do this would be wrong and sinful. Paul illustrates this by showing that participation in the Lord's Supper signifies that the believer is in communion—in a sharing relationship (koinonia)—with the Savior. So participation in idol feasts in pagan temples means sharing in the pagan worship. Such participation is forbidden. This is the mistake Israel made. Christians today must discern how the illustration applies to their own lives.

14,15 The apostle's terse injunction, "Flee [present tense] from idolatry," applies not only to the weak who through eating might be led into idolatry but also to those with a strong conscience who in leading the weak into sin were guilty. Paul asks the Corinthians to use good sense and determine the truth of what he says.

16,17 Paul teaches that the cup of blessing or thanksgiving (eulogia) brings us spiritually into participation in the blood of Christ and into fellowship with him. The same is true of the bread. The "cup of blessing" was a technical term for the third cup drunk at the Jewish Passover, the time when the Lord's Supper was instituted (Matt 26:17-30 and parallel passages: Mark 14:12-26; Luke 22:7-23; John 13:21-30). That "participation in Christ's blood" is meant to be a memorial symbol of fellowship with Christ, and not a literal drinking of his blood, is clear from the fact that Christ had not yet died when he instituted this supper and that this participation is in remembering him, not in drinking him (1 Cor 11:25). So also we are one body because we partake of one bread.

18-20 Here Paul compares the OT sacrifices with pagan offerings. When the people of Israel sacrificed at the altar and ate part of the sacrifice (Lev 7:15; 8:31; Deut 12:17, 18), they participated in and became a part of the sacrificial system and worship of God. Paul says he does not mean that the meat sacrificed to an idol or the idol itself is anything, but he does mean that when the pagans sacrifice, they do so to demons and he doesn't want the Corinthians to share in worship having to do with demons. For one cannot be both—a participant in Christ and in demons also.

21 To make it clearer, Paul speaks of "The Lord's table"—a term that the Corinthian converts from paganism would readily associate with "tables" used for pagan idol meals. In the Oxyrhynchus Papyrus CX there is a revealing sentence that says, "Chairemon invites you to a meal at the table of the lord Serapis in the Serapeum, tomorrow the fifteenth from nine o'clock onwards." So Paul is teaching that a Christian cannot at the same time participate in the meal at the table of the pagan god and the table of the Lord.

22 The conclusion is that if we as Christians share in pagan idolatry, we will "arouse" (i.e., "stir up") the Lord's jealousy and thus incite him to action in his hatred of sin and for mixed allegiance (Deut 32:21; Ps 78:58). And surely, Paul says, we are not stronger than God and cannot overcome or subdue his jealousy and anger against sin if we share in pagan practices.

Notes

18 Κατὰ σάρκα (*kata sarka*, "according to the flesh") refers to Israel "physically, in the flesh"; hence the tr. "the people of Israel."

19 Φημί (*phēmi*, "I say") has the force of "I mean" (NIV, "Do I mean then . . . ?").

21 Note that μετέχω (*metechō*, "share, participate") is used here, rather than κοινωνία (*koinōnia* —used of a Christian's fellowship with Christ) because the same mutual fellowship could not exist in sharing both the table of the Lord and the table of demons.

6. *Freedom, but within limits: do all to the glory of God*

10:23–11:1

> ²³"Everything is permissible"—but not everything is beneficial. "Everything is permissible"—but not everything is constructive. ²⁴Nobody should seek his own good, but the good of others.
>
> ²⁵Eat anything sold in the meat market without raising questions of conscience, ²⁶for, "The earth is the Lord's, and everything in it."
>
> ²⁷If some unbeliever invites you to a meal and you want to go, eat whatever is put before you without raising questions of conscience. ²⁸But if anyone says to you, "This has been offered in sacrifice," then do not eat it, both for the sake of the man who told you and for conscience' sake—²⁹the other man's conscience, I mean, not yours. For why should my freedom be judged by another's conscience? ³⁰If I take part in the meal with thankfulness, why am I denounced because of something I thank God for?
>
> ³¹So whether you eat or drink or whatever you do, do it all for the glory of God. ³²Do not cause anyone to stumble, whether Jews, Greeks or the church of God—³³even as I try to please everybody in every way. For I am not seeking my own good but the good of many, so that they may be saved. ¹¹ᐟ¹Follow my example, as I follow the example of Christ.

Returning to the thought of 1 Corinthians 8 that eating meat sacrificed to idols is essentially a matter of indifference, Paul now adds that it can be harmful. He lays down three principles: First, though the Christian has the right to do all things, such as eating sacrificial meat, it may not be beneficial to themselves. Second, such practices of liberty may not in fact build up a fellow Christian. Third, in summary Paul teaches that Christians are not merely to seek their own good but to promote the good of their fellow Christians.

25–30 Specifically, Paul says, meat eaten at an idol feast is associated with pagan worship and is contaminated. Meat sold in the public meat market has lost its religious significance and is all right to eat.

The word *makellon* ("meat market," v.25) has interesting connections in Corinth. Near the Lechaeum Road, the paved footroad leading north from Corinth toward the western part of Lechaeum (see map of Corinthia, p. 187), a commercial building has been excavated. It has a paved court, which was surrounded by colonnades and small shops. Broneer ("Corinth," p. 89), relates that in the pavement of one shop a marble slab has been found, and claims it is inscribed with the Latin word for market and that this word has been transliterated in the Greek text of v.25. But J. Schneider, in TDNT, 4:370–372, says that the word *makellon* is of Greek origin, occurring on a building inscription in Epidauros about 400 B.C., though it appears in Roman inscriptions in Italy and in Latin-speaking colonies more than in Greek on Greek inscriptions. The word means "food market" as well as "meat market," which was a part of the *makellon*. Excavations have revealed the plan of such markets: a rectangular, columned court with a central fountain and a dome-shaped roof supported by columns and with booths on the sides and porticoes in front of them. According to Schneider (ibid.), the food market at Pompeii had on the east side an imperial cult area, embellished with statues, and in the southeast area there seems to have been a room for sacrificial meals.

Cadbury argues (in JBL, 53:134–141) that the *makellon*–meat market mentioned on the inscription found in Corinth was in existence in Paul's day, and so this establishment could be the very one Paul is referring to, where meat previously offered in sacrifice to idols was being sold. As has been said, this meat no longer retained its religious significance and was really all right to eat.

So, Paul teaches, eat this meat without raising questions, remembering that meat and all things come from the Lord (v.26). The OT quotation from Psalm 24:1 (cf. Pss 50:12; 89:11) was used as a Jewish blessing at mealtimes.

In approving of a believer joining an unbeliever at the latter's house for dinner (v.27), the apostle is thinking of the believer's giving the unbeliever a quiet, appreciative testimony. If, however, at the dinner someone (probably a fellow Christian; cf. v.29a) points out that the meat was offered to an idol, then the believer is to refrain from eating the meat. The reason for this is that he does not want his Christian freedom condemned through another man's conscience (v.29). Paul asks why he should be condemned for partaking of something in the meal he could really thank God for. The verb *blasphemeō* (v.30) means "to injure the reputation of," or actually "to revile" or "denounce" someone who has presumably done wrong. So the strong brother has the power to protect his "right" to eat by not eating meat in such a case.

31–33 These verses introduce a positive and more ultimate perspective. It is not just the other brother who should be in view, but God the creator and giver of all things. The *oun* ("therefore," "so") relates this ultimate concept to one's attitude toward the weak brother. The glory of God must be the Christian's objective in everything (1 Pet 4:11; Col 3:17; cf. *Westminster Shorter Catechism*, Question 1). But Paul says that doing all for the glory of God means thinking of the good of others, both Christians and non-Christians (v.32). The mention of Jews and Greeks may refer to the unsaved groups talked about in 1 Corinthians 1. By "the church of God" Paul means to include the brother with the weak conscience (cf. Rom 14:13, 21). So we find encompassed by these verses the two great commandments—love God and love your neighbor (Matt 22:37–39). Paul seeks to benefit others, not himself. His ultimate objective in all his conduct is that people might be saved—not superficially but fully and to the glory of God.

11:1 This verse really belongs to the previous discussion. The dynamic present imperative of *ginomai* gives the command a continual relevance then and now. "Ever become imitators (*mimētai*; cf. English "mimic") of me" is the literal translation. Paul is calling the Corinthians to the unity that had been disrupted (ch. 1). He can do this because he himself is an imitator of Christ (Gal 2:20)—the same Christ who had dealt gently with Paul in all his prejudices (Acts 26:12–18).

Notes

23 Συμφερεῖ (sympherei, "be useful," "beneficial") deals more with the basic principle, whereas οἰκοδομεῖ (oikodomei, "to build up," "edify") deals with the causative effect of Christian actions—they actually affect the spiritual growth of believers.

30 Χάρις (charis, "grace")—the grace of God (cf. Titus 2:13)—also often has the idea "be grateful for," and so means "thanks," "thankfulness" (e.g., 2 Cor 9:15).

32–11:1 Observe the occurrences of γίνεσθε (ginesthe): "become blameless" (v.32), "become imitators" (11:1). Christianity always presents the challenge of responsible Christian living.

33 The aorist (constative) subjunctive σωθῶσιν, (sōthōsin "that they might be saved") has the tota¹ view in mind—that they be shown to be totally saved with all the divine means of grace and through human agency, by God's plan to accomplish that salvation, which includes justification and sanctification (growth in grace) and finally glorification, when the believer gets to heaven (cf. 2 Tim 4:6–8).

C. Worship in the Church (11:2–14:40)

This entire section deals with problems connected with church worship—matters concerning the veiling of women (11:2–16), observing the Lord's Supper (11:17–34), and the granting and use of spiritual gifts (12:1–14:40).

1. Propriety in worship: covering of women's heads
11:2–16

²I praise you for remembering me in everything and for holding to the teachings, just as I passed them on to you.

³Now I want you to realize that the head of every man is Christ, and the head of the woman is man, and the head of Christ is God. ⁴Every man who prays or prophesies with his head covered dishonors his head. ⁵And every woman who prays or prophesies with her head uncovered dishonors her head—it is just as though her head were shaved. ⁶If a woman does not cover her head, she should have her hair cut off; and if it is a disgrace for a woman to have her hair cut or shaved off, she should cover her head. ⁷A man ought not to cover his head, since he is the image and glory of God; but the woman is the glory of man. ⁸For man did not come from woman, but woman from man; ⁹neither was man created for woman, but woman for man. ¹⁰For this reason, and because of the angels, the woman ought to have a sign of authority on her head.

¹¹In the Lord, however, woman is not independent of man, nor is man independent of woman. ¹²For as woman came from man, so also man is born of woman. But everything comes from God. ¹³Judge for yourselves: Is it proper for a woman to pray to God with her head uncovered? ¹⁴Does not the very nature of things teach you that if a man has long hair, it is a disgrace to him, ¹⁵but that if a woman has long hair, it is her glory? For long hair is given to her as a covering. ¹⁶If anyone wants to be contentious about this, we have no other practice—nor do the churches of God.

2,3 By his use of *de* ("now"; not *peri de,* "now about," as in 7:1 and 12:1) to begin this section, Paul shows he is taking up the subject on his own, not necessarily answering one of their questions.

3-16 These verses have evoked considerable difference of opinion about the nature of the head covering and the place of woman both in public worship and in her relationship to the man. The head covering has been taken to be either a veil or shawl, or else hair—either long or short. As to the use of veils, women in the ancient Orient were veiled in public, or when among strangers, but otherwise they were unveiled. Note that Rebecca was unveiled till she met Isaac (Gen 24:65). James B. Hurley notes that in contrast, ancient pottery shows Greek women in public without head coverings. ("Did Paul Require Veils or the Silence of Women? A Consideration of 1 Cor 11:2–16 and 1 Cor 14:33b–36," WTJ vol.35 [Winter, 1973], no. 2, p. 194). In Corinth the women may well have gone to public meetings without veils. But the question is whether Paul is talking about the use of veils in public worship (as Hodge, St. John Parry, and others hold) or about women letting their long hair hang loose (a sign of mourning or of the shame of an accused adultress [Hurley, ibid.; cf. Grosheide, in loc.]) rather than having their hair "put up."

4-6 Whichever view is held as to the nature of the head covering, the same basic principles emerge from the passage. In vv.3-10 Paul emphasizes the order of authority and administration in the divine structure of things. As every man is to be under Christ's authority and Christ is under God's authority, so the woman is under her husband's authority. (Paul does not mean by his analogy that subordination in each case is of the same completeness.) Therefore, the woman should not demonstrate her authority by having her head uncovered, as the man did when he was praying and prophesying. Evidently at Corinth women were coming to church with their heads improperly covered, thus causing disorder and disrespect in the services. Paul is not necessarily giving his opinion on the propriety of women praying or prophesying in the church, which he observes was being done, though he does so in 1 Corinthians 14:34 (Hodge). Some feel that since he mentions women praying and prophesying here, he approves of the practice (so Hurley). Paul does state here, however, that if a woman is in the public worship with her head uncovered, it is as if she had her head shaved (v.5). He concludes the argument by saying that if the woman in fact does have her head uncovered, she should have her hair cut; on the other hand, if it is shameful (and it is—note the condition of fact) for a woman to have her hair cut or her head shaved, then, of course, she should have her head properly covered (v.6).

7-9 In stating that a man should not have his head covered in church, Paul argues that this follows from the principle that man was prior to woman and is the image and glory of God—that, is he is to be subject to and represent God in authority. The woman, however, is the glory of the man—i.e., she is to be subject to man and to represent him in authority. Although God created Adam and Eve and gave them dominion over the creation (Gen 1:26), Paul argues for man's exercise of authority above woman's on the basis of man's prior creation to woman. The argument goes like this: Woman came from (*ex*) man (i.e., she was made from his body) and she was made for man's sake (*dia* with the accusative) and not the reverse (Gen 2:7).

Although it was not proper for a first-century Jewish man to cover his head for prayer (a custom, originally meant to indicate sorrow, that evidently really developed as a

83

practice in the fourth century A.D.), yet the act seems to have been innovatively tried in the Jewish synagogues of Paul's time. (See Strack and Billerbeck, *Kommentar Zum N.T.*, 3:423–426; Craig, in loc.)

10 The woman has a certain authority (*exousia*) in that in having her head properly covered in worship, she shows respect to the (good) angels who were in attendance. That these angels might be evil angels over whom women would have power certainly does not agree with the scriptural teaching that God's ministering angels (the good angels) serve God's people (Heb 1:14).

Perhaps angels are mentioned in this discussion about the place of women in the church to remind Christians that angels are present at the time of worship and that they are interested in the salvation of God's people (1 Peter 1:10–12; cf. Gal 3:10) and sensitive to the conduct of Christians at worship. So the angels would recognize the breach of decorum were Christian women not to have proper head coverings and the long hair distinguishing them as women—the "sign of authority on her head" (v.10), which symbolized her husband's authority over her.

11,12 But lest he be misunderstood as wanting to demote women, Paul now argues that man and woman are equal in the Lord and mutually dependent.

13–15 The final point in the passage is that man is to be distinguished from woman. Thus the Corinthians are to see that the woman should not pray with her head uncovered as the man does. They are reminded that in ordinary life man with his short hair is distinguished from woman with her long hair. If a man has long hair like a woman's, he is disgraced, but with long hair the woman gains glory in her position of subjection to man. Also long hair is actually given to her as a natural veil.

16 Finally, Paul states that the churches and he himself follow this principle that in worship men come with short hair and women with long, and that the man exercises the position of authority (v.16). This, he implies, should deter those who would want to be contentious about the matter. In using "we" (meaning the apostles), Paul teaches that the Corinthians are to take his statements given in the preceding verses (1 Cor 11:2–16) as having apostolic authority, and not as pious advice.

Summary

2–16 The instructions given by Paul relating to the place of women in the church were addressed to the cultural milieu of the Corinthian believers in the first century A.D. Corinth was a pagan Greek city out of which God was calling a church of his redeemed. That Greek women did appear in public without a head covering is evident from ancient Greek vase paintings, and women in the Corinthian church may have come to worship services in this way. Also some Christian women who were Greeks or Jews may have been going to church with hair disheveled and hanging loose. This might have given the impression that they were mourning or it might even imply that they had been accused of adultery. So disorder and unrest might have begun to mar the services.

The apostle Paul, of course, wanted to correct any such improprieties. But his teaching in 1 Corinthians 11:2–16 goes far beyond the cultural conditions affecting the Corinthian church. Indeed, it was applicable also to other first-century churches (1 Cor 11:16b) and to God's people at any time. The principles Paul presents here that are to govern the church and individual Christians in their life and conduct are as follows:

1. Christians should live as individuals and in corporate worship in the light of the perfect unity and interrelatedness of the persons of the Godhead. The Father and the Son are perfectly united (John 10:30) and yet there is a difference administratively: God is the head of Christ (1 Cor 11:3). So Christians are one, but they too have to be administratively subordinate to one another.

2. Christians are to remember that God first created man, then woman (Gen 2:21–23) and placed the man as administrative head over the woman and the woman as his helper-companion (Gen 2:18). So in the Christian community, the man is to conduct himself as a man (1 Cor 11:4) and as the head of the woman (v.3), while the woman is to conduct herself as woman with dignity without doing anything that would bring dishonor to her (v.5).

3. Since Christians live in the Christian community of the home and that of the church, they are to remember that God has established the man and the woman as equal human beings: "As woman came from man, so also man is born of woman" (v.12). So in the Christian community believers should treat one another with mutual respect and admiration as they realize each other's God-given special functions and positions.

4. Christian men and women should remember that, though God has made them equal human beings, yet he has made them distinct sexes. That distinction is not to be blurred in their realization that they are mutually dependent (v.11)—the man on the woman and the woman on the man. It is also to be observed in their physical appearance (vv.13–15), so that in worship the woman can be recognized as woman and the man as man.

5. God is a God of order. This means order in worship and peaceful decorum in the church (v.16). Therefore Christian men and women should conduct themselves in a respectful, orderly way not only in worship but also in daily life.

Notes

4 The phrase κατὰ κεφαλῆς ἔχων (kata kephalēs echōn) is to be interpreted as meaning "having something on the head" (literally, "having [something] down from [or over] one's head"), such as a veil (BAG, κατά, I, la).

5,6 Ξυράω (xyraō) in the middle voice means "to have oneself shaved" and is used here of the head, whereas κειρῶ (keirō) in the middle voice means "to have one's hair cut."

10 The use of ἐξουσία (exousia) in this context has been taken as pointing to "a means of exercising power or authority." Some have interpreted this to mean that by the veil the woman could avoid amorous glances of angels. But since angels do not marry (Matt 22:30), this view is unacceptable. On the contrary, by covering her head, a woman reverently shows her position as the angels look on.

15 Ἀντί (anti) here is to be taken to mean "as" or "for" in the sense that the Christian woman's hair is to be considered a *proper* substitute for a head covering for worship. This is perhaps preferable to the tr. "instead of," which might lead to the conclusion that the apostle is suggesting that the hair is a replacement for any kind of head covering, even that worn by the pagan women.

2. *The Lord's Supper*

11:17–34

17In the following directives I have no praise for you, for your meetings do more harm than good. 18In the first place, I hear that when you come together as a church, there are divisions among you, and to some extent I believe it. 19No doubt there have to be differences among you to show which of you have God's approval. 20When you come together, it is not the Lord's Supper you eat, 21for as you eat, each of you goes ahead without waiting for anybody else. One remains hungry, another gets drunk. 22Don't you have homes to eat and drink in? Or do you despise the church of God and humiliate those who have nothing? What shall I say to you? Shall I praise you for this? Certainly not!

23For I received from the Lord what I also passed on to you: The Lord Jesus, on the night he was betrayed, took bread, 24and when he had given thanks, he broke it and said, "This is my body, which is for you; do this in remembrance of me." 25In the same way, after supper he took the cup, saying, "This cup is the new covenant in my blood; do this, whenever you drink it, in remembrance of me." 26For whenever you eat this bread and drink this cup, you proclaim the Lord's death until he comes.

27Therefore, whoever eats the bread or drinks the cup of the Lord in an unworthy manner will be guilty of sinning against the body and blood of the Lord. 28A man ought to examine himself before he eats of the bread and drinks of the cup. 29For anyone who eats and drinks without recognizing the body of the Lord eats and drinks judgment on himself. 30That is why many among you are weak and sick, and a number of you have fallen asleep. 31But if we judged ourselves, we would not come under judgment. 32When we are judged by the Lord, we are being disciplined so that we will not be condemned with the world.

33So then, my brothers, when you come together to eat, wait for each other. 34If anyone is hungry, he should eat at home, so that when you meet together it may not result in judgment.

And when I come I will give further directions.

In dealing with the Lord's Supper, Paul discusses three matters: first, the problem of believers making a mockery of the Supper because of abuses practiced at the *agape*—the love feast or dinner accompanying the Supper (vv.17–22); second, the necessity of taking the Lord's Supper seriously through rehearsing its institution as given by the Lord (vv.23–26); and third, the warning about partaking of the Supper unworthily (vv.27–34).

17–19 Regarding the meal that evidently preceded the communion service, the apostle condemns the conduct of the believers as harmful (v.17) and degrading to the communion (see v.20). Their actions at the common *agape* meal were betraying the divisions, including class distinctions between the rich and the poor. Though he might discount part of what he heard, Paul felt he had to believe some of it (v.18). Knowing human nature, he assumes some such divisions are inevitable even among Christians, so that those who act worthy of God's approval might be evident (v.19). The word *haireseis* must mean "factions" here, not "heresies" or "heretical sects" as the word can also mean.

20 "It is not the Lord's Supper you eat" may be interpreted in two ways—either by supplying the word "it" as in NIV, or by taking the verb *estin* ("to be") followed by the infinitive to mean "can." Thus the rendering may be, "You cannot eat [or celebrate] the Lord's Supper" (Hodge). Either translation fits the context. What Paul means is that in acting the way he is about to describe, they were not approaching the Lord's Supper in the right manner but were nullifying its spiritual meaning.

21,22 The Christian common meal or *agape* feast apparently followed the pattern of public sacred feasting among the Jews and Greeks. Following Greek custom, the food was brought together for all to share (cf. the modern church's "potluck" or "bring-and-share" supper), with the rich bringing more and the poor less. As Paul described it, however, cliques were established and the food was divided inequitably. The rich took their "lion's" share and became gluttons and the poor remained empty. So they were despising or bringing contempt on the church of God and humiliating the poor.

23,24 The chief reason why Paul cannot commend their actions is that they do not agree with the spirit of the Lord's Supper as he had received it. Using technical words relating to "receiving" and "passing on" the tradition, he says he "received" (*parelabon*) the ceremony of the Lord's Supper from (*apo*) the Lord. Some (e.g., Hodge) have felt that he received it from Christ directly. But the preposition *apo* ("from") does not prove that Paul means he received the message directly from the Lord; in that case the preposition *para* ("from," "from beside") would have been appropriate (G.G. Findlay, EGT, in loc.). Yet some have thought that when Jesus appeared to Paul (Acts 9:4–6 et al.), he could have given him this message also. The preferred interpretation, however, is probably that Paul received (*parelabon*) the words of the institution of the Supper through its being passed on through others just as he then passed them on (*paredōka*) to the Corinthians—i.e., through a process of repetition. (Observe the similarity of Paul's words about the Supper with Matt 26:26–29; Mark 14:22–25; Luke 22:14–20.)

Since the Supper was celebrated in connection with the Passover (according to Matt 26:17–29; Luke 22:7–20), we assume that the bread that was available was unleavened. Jesus gave thanks (*eucharistēsas*—cf. Eucharist). This was the Jewish practice at a meal. The breaking of the bread (also in the Synoptics) was symbolic of Christ's bruised and broken body (Isa 53:5). The better MSS, reflected in NIV and other newer versions, read, "This is my body which is for you" without the addition "broken" (KJV), which, however, is implied from the context. The word "this" most naturally means in the context "this bread" that Christ held in his hand as a symbol to represent his body, not Christ's body itself, as some hold (cf. somewhat similar figures in John 10:7; 1 Cor 10:4). The command (cf. Luke 22:19) "Do this in remembrance of me," which, along with Luke 22:20, some versions omit (RSV, NEB) or print in brackets (TEV, BV), though others (NIV, JB) retain them (cf. note on 1 Cor 11:24), is implied in the words "Take, eat."

25,26 That the Lord's Supper was connected with the Passover meal is cléar in the phrase "after the supper," meaning, as the synoptic Gospels show, "after the Passover Supper." This cup was the third of the Passover cups, as C.E.B. Cranfield, shows in "St. Mark" in *The Cambridge Greek Testament Commentary*, C.F.D. Moule, ed. (Cambridge: Cambridge University Press, 1966), p. 426. The word "cup," used metonymously for its contents, symbolizes the covenant in Jesus' blood (Luke 22:20). The covenant (*diathekē*) idea is that of God's sealing his agreement of salvation with his people through Christ's blood. It is a new covenant in being the fulfillment of the covenant promises of God in the OT exemplified in the sacrificial system (cf. Eph 2:12). In the ceremony Jesus does not say how often the communion was to be held but indicates that it is to be periodic—"whenever you eat ... and drink"—and it is to be continued to the Second Advent—"until he comes" (v.26). The statement "you proclaim" involves the personal application of the meaning of the Lord's death in the believer's testimony.

27 Participating "in an unworthy manner" entails coming to the table in an irreverent and sinful way and so sinning against the body and blood of Christ. This is what some of the Corinthians had been doing (vv.20–22). (Of course, any other sinful approach to the table would be unworthy also.) The apostle does not teach that in eating and drinking the elements Christians are physically eating of Christ. The supper is a memorial feast (v.24) and a means of grace.

28–30 Now Paul shows how to guard against unworthy partaking of the Lord's Supper. "To examine [oneself]" is to put oneself to the test as to the attitude of his heart, his outward conduct, and his understanding of the true nature and purpose of the Supper. This is making the Supper a means of spiritual grace. By self-examination the believer guards against eating and drinking to his own judgment through not recognizing the importance of this Supper that commemorates the death of Christ. That Paul is not speaking about God's eternal judgment is seen by the lack of the article with *krima*. It is "judgment," not "the judgment." Examples of such judgment are in sickness and death.

31,32 The purpose of self-examination is to come to the table prepared in heart. Paul's teaching justifies the wholesome practice of some churches in having a communion preparatory service that affords opportunity for such self-examination. Here he quickly adds that even when a Christian is judged by the Lord, this judgment is not punitive to destruction, but a form of fatherly discipline (Heb 12:5) to bring God's child to repentance, so that he will not be finally and totally judged with the unsaved world (Rev 20:12–15).

33,34 Paul now deals positively with the *agape* meal. In eating it, the Corinthians should show respect for their brothers' physical as well as spiritual needs by waiting for each other and eating together. If they come only to satisfy their physical craving and not for communion with the Lord and his people, then they should eat their meal at home, for otherwise God will judge them in some way.

Verse 34b suggests that there were other irregularities regarding worship and the Lord's Supper but they were not sufficiently urgent for the apostle to deal with them here.

Notes

20 Κυριακός (*kyriakos*) strictly meaning "belonging to the Lord," is here used of the Lord's Supper. Compare Rev 1:10, ἐν τῇ κυριακῇ ἡμέρᾳ (*en tē kyriakē hēmera*, "on the Lord's day"); i.e., the day belonging to Jesus and his resurrection—the first day of the week.
23 The impf. verb form παρεδίδετο (*paredideto*) stresses that the betraying process was in motion when Jesus instituted the Supper. There is no evidence that the Supper was derived from Hellenistic pagan cult meals as some have argued (see Craig, in loc.).
24 Some MSS, mostly koine-Byzantine, add the word "broken." But the best reading (P[46] א A B C, et al.) does not have it. This statement of Jesus in v.24 is practically equivalent to Jesus' words given in Luke 22:19, as tr. in NIV. Some scholars have suggested that most of the statement in Luke was originally not in this Lucan passage because a few MSS witnesses (the Western-type texts) omit it. But the vast majority of the ancient MS evidence favors its inclusion in Luke 22:19

and so points to its authenticity there. And that Paul cites these words suggests that it was an original saying of Jesus currently available for Luke also to put into his Gospel.

30 The verb κοιμάω (koimaō, only passive in NT) means "fall asleep," sometimes of physical sleep (Luke 22:45), but often is a euphemistic figure for dying (cf. John 11:11-14; Acts 7:60).

31 Διακρίνω (diakrinō, "judge [correctly]") adds a legal aspect to the thought that δοκιμάζω (dokimazō, "examine [v.28]," "test" [as of gold, 1 Peter 1:7]) does not include.

32 The tenses of the verbs παιδευόμεθα (paideuometha, present) and κατακριθῶμεν (katakrithō-men, aorist) contrast the present continuing experience of discipline with the final reality of the future judgment.

---

3. The use of spiritual gifts

12:1-14:40

This long section on spiritual gifts may be divided into several sections. The first emphasizes the source of the gifts, the Holy Spirit (12:1-11); the second the diversity of the gifts in their unity (12:12-31a); the third, the necessary ingredient of love in the exercise of all gifts (12:31b-13:13); the fourth, a discussion of the priority of prophecy over tongues with rules for the exercise of each (14:1-25); and finally, Paul teaches that all church worship must be done decently and in order (14:26-40).

a. The Holy Spirit, the source of spiritual gifts

12:1-11

1Now about spiritual gifts, brothers, I do not want you to be ignorant. 2You know that when you were pagans, somehow or other you were influenced and led astray to dumb idols. 3Therefore I tell you that no one who is speaking by the Spirit of God says, "Jesus be cursed," and no one can say, "Jesus is Lord," except by the Holy Spirit.

4There are different kinds of spiritual gifts, but the same Spirit. 5There are different kinds of service, but the same Lord. 6There are different kinds of working, but the same God works all of them in all men.

7Now to each man the manifestation of the Spirit is given for the common good. 8To one there is given through the Spirit the ability to speak with wisdom, to another the ability to speak with knowledge by means of the same Spirit, 9to another faith by the same Spirit, to another gifts of healing by that one Spirit, 10to another miraculous powers, to another prophecy, to another the ability to distinguish between spirits, to another the ability to speak in different kinds of tongues, and to still another the interpretation of tongues. 11All these are the work of one and the same Spirit, and he gives them to each man, just as he determines.

1 This section presents a new subject and an answer to another question asked by the Corinthian delegation (cf. peri de, "now about," 1 Cor 7:1, 25; 8:1; 16:1).

2-6 In saying that they had been "led astray to dumb idols," Paul implies that the Corinthians had experienced the effects of evil spirits in their former pagan worship. In contrast, he now stresses the twofold test of the presence of the Holy Spirit in a believer's life. Negatively, no person by the Spirit can curse Jesus; and positively, only by the Spirit can a person openly testify that Jesus is Lord (v.3). The term kyrios ("Lord") is used by LXX to translate Jehovah in the OT (cf. Matt 16:16; John 4:2, 3, 15). In this context Paul recognizes the deity of Jesus and of the Holy Spirit in the use of the phrases "Jesus is Lord" and "Spirit of God." Anathema (translated "be cursed") was, strictly speaking, something that was devoted to God and that could be thought of as given over to him with a view to its destruction. So it could be thought of as being "accursed" (cf. Josh 6:17, 18)—the meaning consistently used in the NT. (See Hodge and Grosheide, in loc.).

By using the words *diakoniai* ("servings") and *energemata* ("workings"), Paul indicates that such gifts were useful in serving the Christian community (vv.5, 6). In vv.4-6 he teaches that the Trinity is involved in administration of these gifts: the Spirit; the Lord; God (cf. 2 Cor 13:13 and Eph 4:3-6).

For a full discussion of the Holy Spirit in the NT see Frederick Dale Bruner, *A Theology of the Holy Spirit* (Grand Rapids: Eerdmans, 1970).

7-11 Paul goes on to declare that many spiritual gifts are given by the spirit for the total good or profit (*sympheron*) of his church. Different gifts are given different people—not all have the same gift (cf. 12:29, 30). The gifts given to each person are clearly intended to be used for the common good.

The gifts listed begin with the most important one—the ability to express the message of God's wisdom in the gospel of Christ. The second is the ability to communicate with knowledge by the Spirit. "Knowledge" (*gnōsis*) in the biblical sense is to be taken as the knowledge of God's way of salvation through the cross, not the secret heretical gnostic teaching about working one's way to heaven. Compare the esoteric use of "know" in the Gnostic *Gospel According to Thomas*, tr. A. Guillaumont et al. (Leiden: E.J. Brill, 1959).

The gift of "faith" does not refer to the initial trust in Christ for salvation but to deeper expressions of faith, such as undergoing hardships, martyrdom, etc., and so *pistis* ("faith") can in this case be rendered "faithfulness." Others view faith here as exemplified in gifts of healing, tongues, etc. But this does not seem to be in view, since Paul speaks of these gifts in vv.9, 10.

The next two gifts—the outwardly demonstrable ones of healings and miracles—belong together and were particularly applicable to the ministry of Paul and the other apostles (Acts 19:11, 12; 28:7-9; 2 Cor 12:12). *Dynameis* means literally "acts of power" (cf. Acts 1:8), which here and in 12:28, 29 specifically means miracles. The mention of the gift of prophecy anticipates 1 Corinthians 14 and seems to include an ability to give insights into, and to convey the deeper meanings of, God's redemptive program in his Word. It is to be distinguished from the inspiration of the Holy Spirit (2 Tim 3:16) given the apostles and their associates to prophesy in setting forth God's truth. Paul separates the apostles' office from that of prophets in 12:28, where the prophetic office is listed between that of the apostles and the teachers and did not include in it, in this period of church development, the miracle-working function listed separately in 12:29. The latter function was often included in the earlier practice of the prophetic office (cf. John the Baptist, Christ, and his apostles). See a specific treatment of this point in W. Harold Mare, "Prophet and Teacher in the New Testament Period," JETS, vol.9, no.3 (Summer 1966), pp. 146-148.

By the gift of distinguishing between spirits (v.10b), Paul must be indicating a distinct ability beyond that which the apostle John calls on Christians in general to exercise (1 John 4:1). The ability to speak in different kinds of tongues has been taken to mean speaking in ecstatic, humanly unintelligible utterances, possibly similar to the ecstatic speech exhibited in pagan Greek Dionysiac expressions. In the light of Acts 2:4ff., where it is said that the Holy Spirit gave them ability to speak with different kinds of language, i.e., known foreign languages (Acts 2:7-11), we are safe to say that the ability mentioned here in 1 Cor 12:10 is the ability to speak unlearned languages. LSJ does not list under *glōssa* any meaning under the category of ecstatic speech. Rather, the emphasis of the word is "language," "dialect," "foreign" language.

There have been differences adduced, differences that can be shown not to be basic, between the tongues-speaking at Pentecost in Acts 2 and that in 1 Corinthians 12-14. The following supposed differences were proposed by J. Oswald Sanders (quoted by David M. Howard in *By the Power of the Holy Spirit* [Downers Grove, Illinois: Inter-Varsity Press, 1973], pp 115, 116):

1. At Pentecost the disciples spoke to men (Acts 2:6) but at Corinth the speaking was to God (1 Cor. 14:2, 9). Reply: In Corinth, though the speaking in tongues was to God, it was also a speaking to men when there was speaking in the church service with someone to interpret (1 Cor 14:26, 27).

2. At Pentecost tongues were a sign or credential to believers but at Corinth to unbelievers (1 Cor 14:22). Reply: At Pentecost at the time when the people heard the tongues they were unbelievers (Acts 2:12, 13); it was only when they heard the message in Peter's sermon that many of them believed (Acts 2:41).

3. At Pentecost the unbelievers were filled with awe and marvelled (Acts 2:7, 8), but at Corinth the unbelievers thought the Christians were mad (1 Cor 14:23). Reply: In Acts 2 the unbelievers also were bewildered (v.6); they were amazed and *perplexed* (v.12), and some even thought the believers were intoxicated and they made fun of them (v.13).

4. At Pentecost there was harmony (Acts 2:1), at Corinth confusion (1 Cor 14:23). Reply: This contrast must not be pressed to imply a difference in the nature of the tongues spoken; it only reveals the generally disorderly conduct of the Corinthian congregation seen in their party spirit (1:10-17) and in their reprehensible conduct at the Lord's Supper (11:17-34).

The foregoing points of Sanders do not prove a genuine difference in the nature of tongues between Acts 2 and 1 Corinthians 12-14. The only concrete evidence we have as to the nature of the tongues-speaking in the early church is to be found in the only clear scriptural example we have—that given in Acts 2 where the speaking is a speaking in foreign languages that were to be understood, and were understood. Since in this initial instance in Acts 2 the speaking in foreign tongues was done by the apostles and their close companions, it is logical to conclude that as the apostles were involved in the subsequent scriptural examples of tongues-speaking (Acts 10:44-46; 19:1-7; 1 Cor. 12-14), in these situations also speaking in tongues is to be understood as speaking in a foreign language.

In 1 Cor 12:10d Paul hastens to add that such speaking in tongues should be accompanied by interpretation or translation by someone with that ability. This subject is expanded in 1 Corinthians 14. (Also see my article "Guiding Principles for Historical Grammatical Exegesis," in *Grace Journal*, vol.14, no. 3 [Fall, 1973], p. 14.) That Paul is simply giving a sampling of gifts is evident from his expansion of the list in 12:27-30 and Romans 12:3-8.

Paul concludes that regardless of what spiritual gift each person has, the Holy Spirit has sovereignly distributed them to produce his own spiritual results (v.11). Therefore, no one should despise another person's gift, a gift given by the Spirit for the good of all (v.7). This theme the apostle develops in vv.12-26. The Spirit mentioned here is set forth as one who is sovereignly God (he wills to give the gifts) and personally active (he "works" all these gifts in the lives of his people).

Notes

8-10 Some have tried to classify the gifts by using ἕτερος (*heteros*) to indicate main divisions in the enumeration and ἄλλος (*allos*) to show subordinate divisions (Hodge; cf. also Meyer). However, such a classification does not always put similar gifts together. Compare v.10, where miracles and tongues go together, but one has *allos* and the other *heteros*. Here the words are to be taken as synonyms. Compare also the variety of prepositions used to indicate the same vital working of the Spirit: διά (*dia*, "through") and κατά (*kata*, "according to") in v.8, and ἐν (*en*, "by") in v.9.

10 Ἐνέργημα (*energema*; cf. the English word "energy") is an action word: "activities" that bring forth miracles.

b. *Unity in the diversity of gifts in the body of Christ*

12:12-26

> [12]The body is a unit, though it is made up of many parts; and though all its parts are many, they form one body. So it is with Christ. [13]For we were all baptized by one Spirit into one body—whether Jews or Greeks, slave or free—and we were all given the one Spirit to drink.
>
> [14]Now the body is not made up of one part but of many. [15]If the foot should say, "Because I am not a hand, I do not belong to the body," it would not for that reason cease to be part of the body. [16]And if the ear should say, "Because I am not an eye, I do not belong to the body," it would not for that reason cease to be part of the body. [17]If the whole body were an eye, where would the sense of hearing be? If the whole body were an ear, where would the sense of smell be? [18]But in fact, God has arranged the parts in the body, every one of them, just as he wanted them to be. [19]If they were all one part, where would the body be? [20]As it is, there are many parts, but one body.
>
> [21]The eye cannot say to the hand, "I don't need you!" And the head cannot say to the feet, "I don't need you!" [22]On the contrary, those parts of the body that seem to be weaker are indispensable, [23]and the parts that we think are less honorable we treat with special honor. And the parts that are unpresentable are treated with special modesty, [24]while our presentable parts need no special treatment. But God has combined the members of the body and has given greater honor to the parts that lacked it, [25]so that there should be no division in the body, but that its parts should have equal concern for each other. [26]If one part suffers, every part suffers with it; if one part is honored, every part rejoices with it.

12,13 Paul now illustrates the diversity and unity of the spiritual gifts by the example of the human body. It is made up of many parts, all of them of importance, and yet the whole body functions as a unit. By the words "So it is with Christ," he means so it is with Christ's body, the church. That the church, the invisible church, is an organic whole is seen in that every believer, regardless of racial and religious connection (Jew or Greek) or social standing (slave or freeman), has been united by the one Spirit into one spiritual body in baptism. The figure is now reversed—all the believers have drunk one Spirit; that is, each one has received the same Holy Spirit (cf. 1 Cor 6:19; Eph 5:18-20). Some have taken these thoughts as references to the Christian sacraments—water baptism and Holy Communion. But since there is no imagery of the cup, as in 1 Corinthians 11:25, it is doubtful that this is Paul's primary intent. Rather, he is emphasizing spiritual baptism, and the communion of spiritual food and drink (cf. Rom 6:4; 1 Cor 10:3, 4). It is not the local church alone Paul is speaking of here, but the church universal. This drinking of the Spirit is seen in Jesus' invitation in John 7:37–39.

14–20 Paul now emphasizes the necessity of having diversity in a body for it to operate as one. Each part (such as the eye or the ear) must be willing to perform its own function and not seek to function in a role for which it was not made. The whole body cannot be a single part, or it would not be a functioning body. So it is with the church. Members with one gift should not repudiate that gift and complain that they do not have some other gift. The apostles were to function as apostles, the elders as elders (1 Pet 5:5), the deacons as deacons (Acts 6:1–6), etc.

The logic of v.17 is compelling: no body can function as all eye, all hearing, or all smelling. So for the church to function properly, it must have different gifts and offices.

In vv.18–20 Paul brings the believers back to the sovereign purposes of God. It is God who has organized the body in the way he wants it. The implication is that it is the same with the church; according to God's will, it is composed of many parts, so that it may function as one body—the body of Christ.

21–26 Here the emphasis is on the mutual dependence and concern of the various members of the body. As the organs of the human body—such as the eye, hand, head, and feet—need each other, so the members of the church with their various functions need each other. Moreover, the least attractive and inconspicuous parts of the body are important and should be treated with respect (vv.22, 23). So also the inconspicuous members of the church are essential—those who pray, those who work with their hands and bring their meager tithes into the church, etc. As the humbler parts of the body are given special attention by covering them with appropriate clothing and, as in the case of the digestive organs, providing them with food, so the inconspicuous members of the church—the poor, the despised, the less prominent—are to be cherished and nurtured.

The *alla* ("but") in the middle of v.24 brings the argument back to God's sovereign purposes. He has brought the members of the body together in perfect harmony. By saying that God "has given greater honor to the parts that lacked it," Paul means that through implanting modesty and self-respect in our hearts, God has caused us to protect our unpresentable parts (as the sex organs) from exploitation by properly covering them. All this concern for the body is for the purpose of enabling it to operate in unity, so all its parts will mutually respond to each other's needs—e.g., the brain sending nerve signals to the hand. In using the word *schisma* ("schism," "division") in v.25 Paul reminds the Corinthians of the discussion in 1:10–17. As it is with the body, so with the church (v.26). What happens to one part affects the well-being of the whole.

Notes

---

13 The aorist forms ἐβαπτίσθημεν (*ebaptisthēmen*) and ἐποτίσθημεν (*epotisthēmen*) argue against the view that this verse refers to the ongoing practice of water baptism and Communion, as though the physical acts would somehow make the Christians one body. If the physical rites were in view, present tense verbs would be expected, giving the meaning "Members of your church are being baptized and you are sharing in the elements of Communion." Rather, the aorist tense of both verbs helps place the emphasis on the spiritual nature of baptism and regeneration: the total group, the church, was viewed collectively by Paul and seen by him in a spiritual way as one body in Christ partaking of regeneration through the Holy Spirit (cf. Titus 3:5).

23 Εὐσχημοσύνη (euschēmosynē) meaning "presentability" as with clothing, in this context becomes related to "modesty." (So NIV; cf. BAG.)

24 Συγκεράννυμι (synkerannymi, "mix together" or "unite") means that God has united or blended the members effectively into one body.

---

c. Offices and gifts in the one body of Christ, his church

12:27-31

> [27]Now you are the body of Christ, and each one of you is a part of it. [28]And in the church God has appointed first of all apostles, second prophets, third teachers, then workers of miracles, also those having gifts of healing, those able to help others, those with gifts of administration, and finally those speaking in different kinds of tongues. [29]Are all apostles? Are all prophets? Are all teachers? Do all work miracles? [30]Do all have gifts of healing? Do all speak in tongues? Do all interpret? [31]But eagerly desire the greater gifts.
>
> And now I will show you the most excellent way.

As he speaks about that spiritual unity of the body of Christ, Paul declares that each Christian has his function as a part of that body. He illustrates this by a selective list of church offices and spiritual gifts (cf. Rom 12:3–8; Eph 4:11).

27 Some have thought that *sōma* without the article *to* ("the") refers to the local congregation and is to be translated "a body [of Christ]" (Grosheide). But the genitive form "of Christ" (without the article) used with the word "body" (also without the article) makes the whole phrase specific: "the body of Christ." Therefore, the entire Christian church is in mind. Observe also the plural "apostles," indicating a wider reference than to Corinth alone.

28 Paul is saying that it is the sovereign God who dispenses (*etheto*; cf. Acts 20:28; 1 Tim 1:12; 2:7; 2 Tim 1:11) offices and gifts to his church. The order of the gifts is instructive. The first three—apostles, prophets, and teachers—are in the same order as in Ephesians 4:11 (cf. Rom 12:6, 7) and, as placed first, are to be considered of greatest importance. The next gifts are set off from the first three by *epeita* ("then") and range in order from miracles to the ability to speak in different kinds of tongues, which, being mentioned last, seem to be of least importance. The office of apostle was all-encompassing, including the gifts of prophecy, teaching, miracles, and the rest. But the prophetic gift (cf. Acts 11:24; 13:1; 15:32; 21:10) did not include apostolicity, though it did include teaching. The teacher class did not compare, per se, with that of apostles or prophets. Paul speaks of the first three—apostles, prophets, and teachers—as classes of persons ruling in the church. The rest of the list includes gifts given various members of the church—gifts that, while of lesser significance, are yet of importance.

Those having the gift of *antilēmpsis* ("those able to help others," NIV) are persons gifted in helping the church officers deal with the poor and sick. Those with *kybernēsis* ("administration") have ability to govern and manage affairs in the church.

29,30 By these rhetorical questions, all of which imply "no" for an answer, Paul stresses the principle of divine selectivity. He is saying that not all believers function in each of the ways listed. God selects individuals and gives them their specific gifts (v.28). Paul ends v.30 with the gift of interpretation of tongues, because he is to comment on this in chapter 14. As in v.28, so in v.30, "tongues" comes last in his list.

31 Having mentioned tongues and their interpretation, Paul urges Christians to seek the better gifts—not that of speaking in tongues, which the Corinthians apparently wanted to have more fully. The possession of specific gifts, says Paul, is not so important as the way in which the gifts are exercised. Verse 31b serves to introduce chapter 13.

Notes

28 The aorist form ἔθετο (etheto, "he placed" or "appointed") emphasizes the sovereign act of God in determining who will exercise which gifts in his church.

d. *The supreme position of love in the ministry of the church*

12:31b–13:13

¹²:³¹ᵇAnd now I will show you the most excellent way. ¹³:¹If I speak in the tongues of men and of angels, but have not love, I am only a resounding gong or a clanging cymbal. ²If I have the gift of prophecy, and can fathom all mysteries and all knowledge, and if I have a faith that can move mountains, but have not love, I am nothing. ³If I give all I possess to the poor and surrender my body to the flames, but have not love, I gain nothing.
⁴Love is patient, love is kind. It does not envy, it does not boast, it is not proud. ⁵It is not rude, it is not self-seeking, it is not easily angered, it keeps no record of wrongs. ⁶Love does not delight in evil but rejoices in the truth. ⁷It always protects, always trusts, always hopes, always perseveres.
⁸Love never fails. But where there are prophecies, they will cease; where there are tongues, they will be stilled; where there is knowledge, it will pass away. ⁹For we know in part and we prophesy in part, ¹⁰but when perfection comes, the imperfect disappears. ¹¹When I was a child, I talked like a child, I thought like a child, I reasoned like a child. When I became a man, I put childish ways behind me. ¹²Now we see but a poor reflection; then we shall see face to face. Now I know in part; then I shall know fully, even as I am fully known.
¹³And now these three remain: faith, hope and love. But the greatest of these is love.

This supremely beautiful chapter speaks first of the superiority and necessity of love—gifts are nothing without love (12:31b–13:1–3). It then describes the essential character of Christian love (4–7) and tells of the enduring nature of love (8–12). Finally, it proclaims love to be greater even than faith and hope (v.13).

12:31b–13:1–3 Love is the most excellent way for a Christian to use his spiritual gifts. (12:31b is repeated here, since it is an important transition.) The word *agapē* ("love") is used in the NT of the deep and abiding affection of God and Christ for each other (John 15:10; 17:26) and for us (1 John 4:9). It is also used of Christians in their relationship with one another (e.g., John 13:34, 35). Often more intense and deeper in meaning than *philos* ("having affection for," Matt 10:37; Luke 7:5, et al.), it is quite distinct from *eros*, sensual or sexual love. Christians are to love, because they belong to God, and "God is love" (1 John 4:8).

In referring to tongues and prophecy (vv.1–3), Paul is apparently trying to counteract the excessive emphasis the Corinthians were evidently placing on these gifts to the detriment of love for Christ and to their fellowmen. Tongues of men and angels are obviously the languages men and angels use. (On occasion, angels spoke to men in human language; e.g., Luke 1:13–20, 26–38). The mention of tongues in v.1 shows that Paul is referring in these chapters to human foreign languages as well as intelligent angelic communication. It was in the temple worship that the "resounding gong" and "clanging cymbal" were struck (2 Sam 6:5; 1 Chron 13:8; Ps 150:5). Also prophecy, understanding mysteries and knowledge, and possessing dynamic faith are all nothing apart from love. Both "mysteries" (*mysteria*) and "knowledge" (*gnōsis*) are governed by the same verb *eido* ("know," "fathom") and must mean the deep, secret things to be discovered about God's redemptive works. "Faith" (*pistis*) is not saving faith (as in Rom 5:1), but special acts of faith as in performing miracles, as the reference to the moving of mountains shows (cf. Matt 21:21). Moreover, Paul says that giving all one's material wealth to the poor can be done without love and that one can even be martyred or submit voluntarily to torture without a sense of love for others. To take "surrender my body to the flames" as referring to an extreme form of martyrdom is preferable to taking it as some form of branding connected with slavery (cf. Hodge, in loc.).

4–7 Christian love is now described positively and negatively. Its positive characteristics are patience and kindness (v.4a), delight in the truth, and a protective, trusting, hopeful, and persevering attitude (vv.6b, 7). That love is patient (v.4) means that it is slow to become resentful (Hodge, in loc.). Verses 4b–6a state love's characteristics negatively. To be "rude" or "behave disgracefully" (v.5) may refer obliquely to the disorderly conduct at worship referred to in 11:2–16 and in chapter 14). KJV's "thinks no evil" (v.5b) gives an incorrect idea. The verb *logizomai* means "to reckon or take account of." So NIV says, "It keeps no record of wrongs." Indeed, for love to keep a record of wrongs would violate its nature. In v.6 the verbs *chairō* and *syngchairō* are basically the same; yet there is a difference. Love does not "delight" or "rejoice" (*chairō*) in evil in which it has no part; but it does "rejoice in" (*syngchairō*) the truth with which it does have a part.

Furthermore, love covers the faults of others rather than delighting in them (v.7). It is trusting, optimistic, and willing to endure persecution (cf. Rom 5:3, 4). In short, it "perseveres."

8–12 Love is permanent, in contrast with prophecies, tongues, and knowledge—all of which will cease to exist because they will cease to be needed. In v.8, Paul uses the verb (*katargeō*, "abolish"; hence "cease," "pass away") to describe the cessation of prophecies and of knowledge; of tongues, he says "they will be stilled" (NIV). Here the verb is *pauō*, which also means "cease." The reason these three will cease is that they are imperfect and partial (vv.9, 10) compared to perfect knowledge and prophetic understanding in heaven. He does not say when they will cease. Some think he meant that the need for miraculous gifts would cease to exist at the end of the apostolic period. This view is based in part on the implications of the meaning of the term *teleion* ("perfection") v.10, which is taken to refer here to the completion of the canon at the end of the first century A.D. With this view, the term "prophecies" in v.8 is taken narrowly as referring to direct, inspired revelatory communication from the Holy Spirit or possibly to some special aid given by the Spirit to understand and present truth already revealed, as given in the written Scriptures (cf. Hodge, in loc.). All this, then, was done away when the canon was completed about A.D.100. This cessation would apply also to tongues and to the special gift of knowledge (vv.8, 9)—the "gift correctly to understand and properly exhibit the truths revealed by the apostles and prophets" (Hodge, in loc.).

There is something to commend this view as an argument against the position that the gifts mentioned in vv. 8–10 continued, beyond the apostolic period, especially prophetic revelation. For if such revelation is held to continue, then might not the Koran, *The Book of Mormon,* and *Science and Health* be considered inspired revelations from God?

Nevertheless, it is difficult to prove the cessation of these gifts at the end of the first century A.D. by taking *teleion* to refer to a completion of the canon at that time, since that idea is completely extraneous to the context. While *teleion* can and does refer to something completed at some time in the future, the time of that future completion is not suggested in v.10 as being close.

On the other hand, in a number of contexts the related words *telos* ("end," "termination;" "last part") and *teleō* ("bring to an end") are used in relation to the second coming of Christ. This is true in both non-Pauline writing (cf. James 5:11; Rev 20:5, 7; 21:6; 22:13) and 1 Corinthians 1:8; 15:24. Since in the contexts of the Second Coming these related words are used and since Paul himself used *telos* in talking about the Second Coming elsewhere in 1 Corinthians, it seems more normal to understand *teleion* in v.10 to mean that "perfection" is to come about at the Second Coming, or, if before, when the Christian dies and is taken to be with the Lord (2 Cor 5:1–10).

There are other problems regarding the completion-of-the-canon view of *teleion* here. The conditional temporal *hotan* with the subjunctive form of the verb, "[whenever the end] should come" (v.10), suggests that Paul felt an indefiniteness about when the end he has in mind would come. But he shows no such indefiniteness in regard to the written Scriptures or the special position of the apostles (9:1, 2), whose work would be assumed to be coming to an end shortly upon their death. Similarly, the *hotan* with the subjunctive clauses and *telos* used of the Second Coming in 15:24, are also indefinite and open-ended: "then . . . when [or, whenever] he hands over the kingdom. . . ." Here again, Paul does not know exactly when this will occur. In contrast, the *hote* with the indicative clauses in 13:11 are quite definite as to the time of their occurrences: "When I was a child . . . when I became a man."

One more problem with taking *teleion* to refer to the completion of the canon is found in the *tote*, ("then," "at that time") clauses in v.12. Did Paul really expect to live to the time of the completion of the canon and then expect to "know" or "know completely," when other apostles (e.g., John) might (and actually did) live longer than he and it would be they who at that time would "know completely"?

All things considered, it is better to argue for the cessation of the gifts of prophecy, tongues, and the special gift of knowledge on the basis of the larger context of Paul's writings and on the basis of the grammar of vv.9, 13: prophecies, tongues, and knowledge will pass away soon. Paul's viewpoint seems to be that it would be when the important office of apostle with its requirement of men having seen the Lord and having been a witness to his resurrection (Gal 1:14–24) is no longer exercised. But "now" (*nyni*) faith, hope, and love continue to remain (*menei*, present continuous sense).

Paul's illustration of a child's thoughts and speech, real but inadequately conceived and expressed in comparison with those of mature person (v.11) aptly conveys the difference between the Christian's present understanding and expression of spiritual things and the perfect understanding and expression he will have in heaven (v.12). The metaphor is that of the imperfect reflection seen in one of the polished metal mirrors (cf. James 1:23) of the ancient world in contrast with seeing the Lord face to face (cf. Gen 32:30; Num 12:8; 2 Cor 3:18). Paul's thought in 12b may be expanded as follows: Now through the Word of God, I know in part; then, in the presence of the Lord I will know fully, to the full extent that a redeemed finite human being can know and in a way similar in kind to the way the Lord in his infinite wisdom fully and infinitely knows me. The Corinthians, Paul implies, must not boast now of their gifts (cf. 13:4), for those gifts are nothing compared to what is in store for the Christians in heaven.

13 In a temporal sense, the words "and now" can mean that faith, hope, and love continue "now, at this moment," to be succeeded later by something else. This, however, is out of context with the preceding verses. Rather, "and now" introduces a conclusion; namely, "and now, there are faith, hope, and love—they, to be sure, remain now and forever." By faith and hope remaining in eternity Paul means that trust (*pistis*) in the Lord begun in this life will continue forever and that hope in the Lord begun now (Rom 8:24, 25) will expand and issue into an eternal expectation of his perfect plan for our eternal existence with him (cf. Rev 22:3-5). Paul has alluded to a special faith in v.2; now he expands it into an ongoing eternal faith and hope in an eternal God. Love is the greatest of these three graces because through faith love unites the Christian personally to God (1 John 4:10, 19) and through God's love (Rom 5:5) we are enabled to love one another (John 13:34, 35). Love is communicating grace and identifies us as children of God (John 13:34, 35; 1 John 4:8, et al.).

Notes

3 The textual reading κανθήσομαι or κανθήσωμαι (*kauthēsomai, kauthēsōmai*, "burn") is supported by somewhat inferior MS evidence, but agrees with the OT events of Dan 3:15ff. The better-supported καυχήσωμαι (*kauchēsōmai*, "that I may glory" or "boast") does fit Paul's usage of the word elsewhere (9:15; 2 Cor 12:1; see Metzger, *A Textual Commentary*, pp. 563, 564) but does not fit well with Paul's other illustrations of good deeds. The concept of "boasting" in this list of good works is awkward. Therefore, the first reading is better. Later scribes must have changed the verb "burn" to "boast" to avoid any suggestion of ridiculing martyrdom by fire. (Cf. C. T. Craig, IB, 10:171.)

4-7 All the verbs are in the present tense and should be taken as gnomic presents, expressing characteristics of love that are true in all times.

12 It is better to take δι' ἐσόπτρου (*di' esoptrou*) as instrumental, giving the reading "by means of a mirror" (cf. James 1:23) rather than "through a window," referring to opaque mica used for windows in ancient times (cf. Hodge, in loc.). The repeated verb ἐπιγνώσκω (*epignōskō*), tr. "know fully" in NIV, refers in its first occurrence in 12b to the limited horizon of a perfect but finite human being; in its second occurrence it shifts to the boundless horizon of the infinite Lord, the difference being accentuated by the aorist passive form ἐπεγνώσθην (*epegnōsthēn*, "I am known"); i.e., "I am known [by a greater one—the Lord]."

e. The priority of prophecy over tongues and rules for the exercise of both

14:1-25

Follow the way of love and eagerly desire spiritual gifts, especially the gift of prophecy. [2]For anyone who speaks in a tongue does not speak to men but to God. Indeed, no one understands him; he utters mysteries with his spirit. [3]But everyone who prophesies speaks to men for their strengthening, encouragement and comfort. [4]He who speaks in a tongue edifies himself, but he who prophesies edifies the church. [5]I would like every one of you to speak in tongues, but I would rather have you prophesy. He who prophesies is greater than one who speaks in tongues, unless he interprets, so that the church may be edified.

[6]Now, brothers, if I come to you and speak in tongues, what good will I be to you, unless I bring you some revelation or knowledge or prophecy or teaching? Even in the case of lifeless things that make sounds, such as the flute or harp, how will anyone know what tune is being played unless there is a distinction in the notes? [8]Again, if the trumpet does not sound a clear call, who will get ready for battle? [9]So it is with you. Unless you speak intelligible words with your tongue, how will anyone know what you are saying? You will just be speaking into the air. [10]Undoubtedly there are all sorts of languages in the world, yet none of them is without meaning. [11]If then I do not grasp the meaning of what someone is saying, I am a foreigner to the speaker, and he is a foreigner to me. [12]So it is with you. Since you are eager to have spiritual gifts, try to excel in gifts that build up the church.

[13]For this reason the man who speaks in a tongue should pray that he may interpret what he says. [14]For if I pray in a tongue, my spirit prays, but my mind is unfruitful. [15]So what shall I do? I will pray with my spirit, but I will also pray with my mind; I will sing with my spirit, but I will also sing with my mind. [16]If you are praising God with your spirit, how can one who finds himself among those who do not understand say "Amen" to your thanksgiving, since he does not know what you are saying? [17]You may be giving thanks well enough, but the other man is not edified.

[18]I thank God that I speak in tongues more than all of you. [19]But in the church I would rather speak five intelligible words to instruct others than ten thousand words in a tongue.

[20]Brothers, stop thinking like children. In regard to evil be infants, but in your thinking be adults. [21]In the Law it is written:

"Through men of strange tongues
and through the lips of foreigners
I will speak to this people,
but even then they will not listen to me,"
says the Lord.

[22]Tongues, then, are a sign, not for believers but for unbelievers; prophecy, however, is for believers, not for unbelievers. [23]So if the whole church comes together and everyone speaks in tongues, and some who do not understand or some unbelievers come in, will they not say that you are out of your mind? [24]But if an unbeliever or someone who does not understand comes in while everybody is prophesying, he will be convinced by all that he is a sinner and will be judged by all, [25]and the secrets of his heart will be laid bare. So he will fall down and worship God, exclaiming, "God is really among you!"

This significant chapter deals with two important subjects: (1) the relative value and use of prophecy and speaking in tongues (vv.1–25) and (2) orderly conduct in public worship (vv.26–40).

1-15 Having established in 1 Corinthians 13 that prophecy, tongues, and all spiritual gifts must be exercised in love, Paul now argues that prophesying is to be preferred over speaking in tongues because the former, since it is understood, edifies the church; whereas, without an interpreter, the latter does not. Because of Paul's stress on the need for interpretation (vv.5, 13), the implication is that the Corinthians, in their desire to speak in tongues and their pride in it alone, had neglected this essential matter.

1 In making the transition from the beautiful thirteenth chapter (14:1a), Paul uses a strong verb—"pursue" ("follow the way of," NIV; cf. Phil 3:12, 14)—as he charges them to seek love. This is a stronger verb than the following one—"eagerly desire"—which he applies to seeking spiritual gifts. So love must have the priority, and after that the gift of prophecy must particularly be sought.

2 Paul shows why tongues are not to be preferred. In speaking in tongues, the speaker is talking only to God (cf. Rom 8:26) in a "tongue" (note the singular noun)—i.e., in a language unknown to other people, who cannot understand what is said. "Mysteries" refers to the deep truths of God's salvation (cf. Acts 2:11). "By [or, with] the spirit" (*pneumati*) is not to be understood as referring to the Holy Spirit, who is not mentioned in the context, but to the person's own spirit (vv.14, 15; cf. John 4:24).

3,4 Paul now describes the advantage of prophesying. In prophesying, one edifies the church, whereas in speaking in tongues, he builds himself up in his seeking spiritual fellowship with God. There is no mention here that the speaker understood the tongues; not till later does Paul discuss the problem of understanding and insist that the gift of interpretation should be sought by speakers in tongues (vv.13-15). The verb *oikodomeō* ("edify") used in v.4 has the primary meaning of "build." Here Paul uses it in the nonliteral sense of "edify" or "strengthen." The related noun *oikodomē* ("the process of building," "a building" or "edifice") has, as in Paul's thought, the figurative meaning of "edifying" or "building up." "Encouragement" (*parakelēsis*) and "comfort" (*paramythia*) are aspects of that edifying.

5 Here is an emphatic restatement of v.1b. Speak in tongues, you Corinthians, yes; but more than that, I want you to prophesy, because this gift brings understanding and strengthening to the church. However, if there is an interpretation of the tongue, then speaking in tongues can strengthen the church.

6 At this point Paul draws a conclusion (*nyni de*, "but now"). Since tongues without interpretation do not edify, what good would it do the Corinthians if Paul came speaking in tongues unless the message he brought were understandable? The four kinds of messages he lists may be put into two categories: (1) supernatural revelation (cf. Gal 2:2) and prophecy and (2) natural tools of communication—knowledge and teaching (cf. 1 Cor 12: 8-10). It is possible, however, to take "prophecy" in this verse as nonsupernatural, in the sense of the ability to search out the deep things of God. Note also that the conditions are stated as possible, not factual. Paul is not saying that he will come to them speaking in tongues, but only that if he were to do so, it would be futile unless he brought an understandable message.

7-9 Paul now gives some vivid illustrations. The flute and the harp were well-known and valued musical instruments in Greece (cf. Apollo and his harp), and the Jews there would be acquainted with the music of temple worship. But music is nothing more than senseless sounds without systematic differences in pitch, tone, and time. All, both Greeks and Jews, would understand the necessity of the trumpet's call to battle. Compare the use of the *salpinx* (the "war trumpet") in Homer's *Iliad* (18.219) and the ram's horn trumpet of the OT (Num 10:9; Josh 6:4, 9). Applying the illustrations, Paul says that it is not the mere sound of speaking that is important, but whether the sounds can be understood by the hearers.

10–12 Paul's speaking of the languages of the world along with his reference to the "foreigner" (*barbaros*, "barbarian"; see note on v.11) substantiates the conclusion that in his discussion of tongues he has in mind known foreign languages. *Phōnai* ("languages") can at times mean "voices," "sounds" (cf. v.7; Rev. 5:2), but here in connection with *aphōnos* ("without meaning"), it indicates languages that can convey meaning by their systematic distinction of sounds. The "meaning" (*dynamin*, literally "power") of the language refers to its "power" to convey meaning. In v.12 Paul applies these things to the Corinthians—"so it is with you." They are, in short, to major in gifts that will strengthen the church.

13,14 With the possibility of a non-understood tongue before them, Paul now argues that its interpretation be sought. He urges this not only so that those who hear but do not understand may know the meaning, but also that the speaker himself may be benefited by getting an intellectual as well as a spiritual blessing from the exercise. The expression "my mind is unfruitful" means that the mind does not intelligently share in the blessing of the man's spirit. The mind (the *nous*) is that faculty involved in conscious, meaningful reasoning and understanding of a thinking, reasoning person (cf. Grosheide, in loc.). Paul desires the Corinthians to have a complete blessing here, both in their spirits *and* in their minds.

15–17 Praying and singing in the spirit and mind (v.15) are involved in praising and giving thanks to God (v.16), all of which are to be a coherent part of Christian worship (Eph 5:18, 19). The *idiōtēs* (the "unlearned") the one who does not understand, is the Christian who is a church member but does not understand the tongue without an interpretation, or, the "inquirer" about Christianity who does not understand the language. He, too, is important, Paul implies, for he also was to be able to say "amen" to the thanksgiving conveyed in the strange language. But how can he say "amen" and mean it, when he does not understand what he has heard? Paul grants that the tongue may in itself be conveying thanksgiving to God, but it was important for the Christian without that gift to understand it (v.17). (The "Amen," meaning "it is true," comes out of OT worship as in 1 Chronicles 16:36 and Nehemiah 5:13; 8:6, where it is connected with praise to the Lord. It was also used in the synagogue and then in the early church; cf. Galatians 1:5; Ephesians 3:21.)

18,19 Having said that he has the ability to speak in foreign tongues more than all of them (an ability he could properly use), Paul hastens to add he would rather speak a few words in a language the church knows so that they might grow spiritually (*katēcheō*, the word for catechize, Luke 1:4), than to speak volumes in a tongue that does not communicate.

20–25 In this section Paul implies that prophecy is superior to speaking in tongues because though tongues, as in Acts 2, can be impressive to the unbelievers in showing

101

that God is present and can lead them to face the claims of Christ, yet prophecy can be more effectively used to bring the unbeliever to the place of conviction of sin. This was true of Peter's sermon following the speaking in tongues at Pentecost (Acts 2:14–37).

First Paul calls on the Corinthians to think maturely, as "adults" in Christ, and not to be controlled by evil dispositions and motives in their appraisal of tongues (v.20). To illustrate his point that tongues can impress the unbeliever, but that there is no special mark of divine blessing to have people in the congregation who can speak in a language not understood, Paul cites a prophecy from Isaiah 28:11, 12 (cf. Deut 28:49). The point of the quotation is that if Israel would not hear the Lord through the prophets, they would not hear even when he spoke in foreign languages to them through foreign people. So, Paul is saying, why put so much stress on tongues?

He concludes (*hōste*, "then," v.22) that tongues can be and really are a sign of something miraculous (*sēmeion*), an indication of God's presence to the unbeliever (cf. Acts 2). The believer does not need that sign. He already has the indwelling Holy Spirit (Rom 8:9–11; 1 Cor 6:19). But this is not all. Too much emphasis should not be placed on tongues even for unbelievers, for excessive use of this gift will have an adverse effect on them and they will think that the Christians are out of their minds (v.23). Furthermore, all—the whole church as well as the unbelievers—need the blessing of prophecy that can bring unbelievers who come into the church meeting under conviction of sin (vv.24, 25). The one who "does not understand," the *idiōtēs*, seems to be an unbeliever who has already begun to show interest in the Gospel—an inquirer. The effect of Christian prophecy on the unbeliever is threefold: He will be convicted of sin (cf. John 16:8); he will be called to take account of his sins and examine his sinful condition; and will have his sinful heart and past laid open to inspection (cf. John 4:16–19). The triple use of "all" in the Greek (v.24) emphasizes that all the church through its prophetic message has, in God's providence, a part in bringing the unbeliever to this place of conviction. For the unbeliever in the church service will recognize that God really is present and dealing with him.

Notes

1 The present-tense verbs are graphically descriptive: διώκετε (*diōkete*, "be pursuing"), ζηλοῦτε (*zēloute*, "be desiring"), and προφητεύητε (*prophēteuēte*, "that you may be practicing the gift of prophecy").

11 The βάρβαρος (*barbaros*, the "barbarian") was one who was not a Gr. and did not speak Gr. (Aeschylus, *Persians* 255; Herodotus 1:58, et al.).

19 The better-attested τῷ νοΐ μου (*tō noi mou*, "with my mind") was later changed, probably as an attempt at clarification, to διὰ τοῦ νοός μου (*dia tou noos mou*, "through my mind"), which was then mistaken by a few MSS to be διὰ τοῦ νόμου (*dia tou nomou*) "through the law," or διὰ τὸν νόμον (*dia ton nomon*), "on account of the law."

22 The interpretation of this v. is difficult in the light of vv.23, 24, where unbelievers are repelled by tongues and blessed by prophecy. We reject, however, the view expressed by R. St. John Parry (in loc.) that v.22, therefore, possibly be considered a gloss. Rather, we feel an answer is to be found in seeing a difference in emphasis in the vv., as suggested in the commentary. Verse 22 suggests that tongues were an initial blessing for unbelievers as a miraculous sign of God's presence. Verses 23, 24 argue against too heavy an emphasis on "tongues" even with unbelievers, for they too need the meaningful instruction of prophecy. Compare the tongues and prophesying in Acts 2:1–37.

24 The ἄπιστος (*apistos*, "unbeliever") and ἰδιώτης (*idiōtēs*, "one without understanding," the "inquirer") are both in the unbeliever class in contrast to the saved of the Christian church.

---

f. Orderly conduct in Christian worship

14:26-40

26What then shall we say, brothers? When you come together, everyone has a hymn, or a word of instruction, a revelation, a tongue, or an interpretation. All of these must be done for the strengthening of the church. 27If anyone speaks in a tongue, two—or at the most three—should speak, one at a time, and someone must interpret. 28If there is no interpreter, the speaker should keep quiet in the church and speak to himself and God.

29Two or three prophets should speak, and the others should weigh carefully what is said. 30And if a revelation comes to someone who is sitting down, the first speaker should stop. 31For you can all prophesy in turn so that everyone may be instructed and encouraged. 32The spirits of prophets are subject to the control of prophets. 33For God is not a God of disorder but of peace.

As in all the congregations of the saints, 34women should remain silent in the churches. They are not allowed to speak, but must be in submission, as the Law says. 35If they want to inquire about something, they should ask their own husbands at home; for it is disgraceful for a woman to speak in the church. 36Did the word of God originate with you? Or are you the only people it has reached?

37If anybody thinks he is a prophet or spiritually gifted, let him acknowledge that what I am writing to you is the Lord's command. 38If he ignores this, he himself will be ignored.

39Therefore, my brothers, be eager to prophesy, and do not forbid speaking in tongues. 40But everything should be done in a fitting and orderly way.

In this section on conduct in church worship, Paul insists that all the parts of worship should be conducive to instruction and edification. Tongues, prophecy, and other gifts were to be practiced under strict regulation (26-33a). Also, for the sake of decorum in the churches, women were not to speak in public worship (33b-36). Paul declares that what he is writing is the Lord's instruction (37, 38). He concludes by encouraging the Corinthian Christians to seek to prophesy and not to prohibit people from speaking in tongues, provided that the whole of the worship service is decorous and orderly (39, 40).

26-30 The third person imperatives "it must be done" in these verses show that Paul is not so much addressing his remarks to particular individuals as to the corporate entity, the church, which itself should maintain this decorum. All these imperatives are in the present tense, indicating that the church was to keep a constant supervision over all these aspects of its service.

26-28 Verse 26 gives us a short outline of the elements of worship in Corinth: a hymn, instruction, revelation, a tongue, an interpretation. Some of this is reminiscent of Jewish worship (cf. Matt 26:30; Luke 4:16-30). All is for strengthening the church. The one occurrence of *hekastos* used with each of the following five occurrences of the verb form *echei* ("each one has ... each one has ...") suggests again the unity and diversification of gifts in the church. One peron has this ability, another that one; but all (*panta*) together are to be used to build up the church. As for tongues, they must be regulated, with only two or three speaking, one at a time and with someone interpreting (v.27). The phrase *ana meros* ("in turn"), though used elsewhere in Greek literature, occurs only here in the NT. Though v.13 suggests that the speaker in tongues might do the interpreting himself, the inference here is that it would probably be someone else. Without an interpreter, there was to be no public tongues-speaking in the church. This apparently placed on the one speaking in tongues the responsibility of finding out first if an interpreter was present. If there were none, the speaker must be silent in the church service and speak only to himself and God (v.28). Perhaps this means that if no interpreter was on hand, one should do his tongues-speaking at home.

29–33a As for regulations for prophesying in church, only a limited number—not over three—should speak, lest so much be said as to cause confusion. The mention of revelation (v.30) suggests that the prophecy in mind involved a revelation, a special deep teaching, which, however, was distinct from the kind of revelation that Scripture is (2 Tim 3:14–17). Such teaching should be heard even from one who had not been on his feet to speak. In some way the person with this revelation was a spokesman for God in giving some edifying message to the church. The "spirits of the prophets" (v.32) are the spirits of the prophets themselves who were guided by the Holy Spirit in using this special gift. And these prophetic utterances are subject to being checked (*hypotassō*) by other prophets for accuracy and orthodoxy. All this leads to the peace and order of which God is the author (v.33). The word *akatastasia* is a strong one, indicating great disturbance, disorder, or even insurrection or revolution (Luke 21:9). Paul is afraid of unregulated worship that might lead to disorderly conduct and belie the God of peace who has called them to be orderly.

33b–36 Paul now turns to the role of women in public worship, the implication being that men were to lead in worship. Paul's instruction for Corinth is that followed in all the churches. The phrase *tais ekklesiais tōn hagiōn* ("the congregations [or, the churches] of the saints") is distinctive, occurring only here in the NT. The expression emphasizes the universality of the Christian community. All the churches are composed of saints (those set apart for God), and should be governed by the same principle of orderly conduct.

The command seems absolute: Women are not to do any public speaking in the church. This restriction is not to be construed as demoting woman, since the expressions "be in submission" (*hypotassō*, cf. v.32) and "their own husbands" are to be interpreted as simply consistent with God's order of administration (cf. 1 Cor 11:7, 8; Eph 5:21–33). "The law says" must refer to the law as set forth in such places as Genesis 3:16; 1 Corinthians 11:3; Ephesians 5:22; 1 Timothy 1:12, and Titus 2:5. Some have explained the apostle's use of the word "speaking" (v.34) as connoting only general speaking and not forbidding a public address. But this is incompatible with Paul's other uses of "speaking" in the chapter (vv.5, 6, 9, et al.), which imply public utterances as in prophesying (v.5). A woman's request for knowledge is not to be denied, since she is a human being equal to the man. Her questions can be answered at home, and not by asking her husband in the public service and so possibly interrupting the sermon.

The word *gyne* used in vv.34, 35 has the general meaning of "woman," an adult female (cf. Matt 13:33; 27:55). But the same word is used to indicate a married woman (cf. Matt 14:3; Luke 1:5). Here in vv.34, 35 Paul uses the word in the general sense when he declares as a broad principle that "women should remain silent in the churches." That he assumes there were many married women in the congregation is evident from his reference to "their husbands" (v.35). He does not address himself to the question of where the unmarried women, such as those mentioned in 7:8, 36ff., were to get their questions answered. We may assume, however, that they were to talk in private (just as the married women were to inquire at home) with other qualified persons, such as Christian widows (7:8), their pastor (cf. Timothy as a pastor-counselor, 1 Tim 5:1, 2), or with elders who were "able to teach" (1 Tim. 3:2). At any rate, a woman's femininity must not be disgraced by her trying to take a man's role in the church.

But what about the seeming contradiction between these verses and 11:5ff., where Paul speaks of women praying and prophesying? The explanation may be that in chapter 11 Paul does not say that women were doing these things in public worship as discussed in chapter 14. (See B.B. Warfield, "Women Speaking in the Church" in *The Presbyterian*, Oct. 30, 1919, pp. 8, 9.)

Paul's rhetorical questions (v.36) are ironical and suggest that the Corinthians had their own separate customs regarding the role of women in public worship and were tending to act independently of the other churches who also had received these commands. They were presuming to act as though they had originated the Word of God (i.e., the gospel) and as if they could depart from Paul's commands and do as they pleased in these matters of church order.

37–40 Now, Paul steps delicately. He had given strict commands but wants to soften their impact. He asks for those who have the gift of prophecy and are spiritually gifted to authenticate the fact that his commands are from the Lord (v.37). But immediately Paul returns to his strict injunction (v.38). The tone is abrupt, the meaning is clear: anyone who ignores it will be ignored by Paul and the churches, or possibly even the Lord, and so be considered an unbeliever (1:18). (So Grosheide, in loc.)

The closing verses of the chapter (39, 40) revert to prophecy and tongues. Paul urges the Corinthians to keep on desiring to prophecy and not to prohibit people from speaking in tongues. But Christian worship must be marked by good order.

Notes

34,35 The Bezan codex (D) and related Western MSS put these vv. at the end of the chapter. Some suggest that this evidences a marginal gloss that got into the text at various places (Craig, in loc.) but there is no good evidence for this. The better MSS have the vv. as we read them.

37 Some MSS read the pl. ἐντολαί (entolai "commands"), obviously a scribe's assimilation to the previous plural relative pronoun ἅ (ha). The singular ἐντολή (entolē), is supported by a sufficiently widespread number of witnesses, including several early ones, as P[46] ℵ c A and B (cf. Metzger, *A Textual Commentary*).

38 Important representatives from the Alexandrian, Western, and Palestinian texts support the reading of the indicative passive form (probably futuristic in force) ἀγνοεῖται (agnoeitai, "he will be ignored"). This is against the imperative, active ἀγνοείτω (agnoeitō, "let him ignore it," as followed by KJV. It is better to take the reading agnoeitai, as NIV does, and observe that the alternative in the two occurrences of the word in this verse, one active and other passive, agrees with Paul's usage in 1 Corinthians 8:2, 3 (cf. Metzger, *A Textual Commentary*).

Summary

At this point a summary of the place of speaking in tongues in the apostolic community of the first century A.D. and also a discussion of tongues in the post-apostolic period and the relevance of tongues in the twentieth-century church is in order. First, in Paul's discussion of this and other gifts in chapters 12 to 14, he emphasizes priority of love over "tongues" and the other gifts (1 Cor 13).

Second, in the list of offices (those of apostles, prophets and teachers) and gifts for the church 12:27-31a), the office-gifts are listed first, with other gifts following, the last being "tongues." This implies that Paul gives priority to office-gifts over "tongues." Furthermore, among the office-gifts, that of apostles, who were unique in having seen the Lord, ceased to exist in the first century A.D.

Third, in his treatment of tongues and prophecy in chapter 14, Paul again shows his preference for prophecy over tongues, since the former was the gift that brought edification to the church (vv.1-5). He minimizes the importance of the gift of tongues when he says, "In the church I would rather speak five intelligible words to instruct others than ten thousands words in a tongue" (v.19).

Fourth, in his discussion in chapter 12 regarding the diversity of gifts and their functions in the church, the body of Christ, Paul uses the analogy of the human body with its various parts functioning in unique and distinct ways without each one trying to usurp the function of another part. So he shows that the gifts, including tongues, were not to be sought for the sake of the gifts nor was everyone to seek to have the same gift, such as tongues.

Fifth, God does not have to work by miraculous means to accomplish his purposes; he usually uses ordinary natural means—e.g., in the production of crops, he uses the sun, the rain, and the nutrients of the ground, as well as the hard work of men in farming the land. In connection with *charismata* (the Greek word from which we get the current term "charismatic"), which is translated "spiritual gifts" in NIV (1 Cor 12:4), it is significant that in 1 Corinthians 12:5-11 not all of the *charismata* mentioned are miraculous, as, e.g., the gifts of wisdom and knowledge (v.8), which are mentioned before the miraculous ones, including tongues. It is not essential that everyone have a miraculous gift; see 12:29, 30, where Paul uses rhetorical questions to show that not all Christians had, or were to have, one particular gift in common. The questions in the Greek sentences that comprise 12:29, 30 begin with *mē* negative, which expects a negative response.

Sixth, on the basis of the phenomenon of foreign languages spoken of in Acts 2:5-12, we have argued that the tongues referred to in 1 Corinthians 14:13-15, 20-25 were also foreign-language tongues—not ecstatic utterances, gibberish, or nonunderstandable erratic variations of consonants and vowels with indiscriminate modulation of pitch, speed, and volume.

Seventh, the essential offices for building up the body of Christ, the church, are, according to Paul (Eph 4:11-16), those of apostles, prophets, evangelists, and pastors-teachers (the one Greek article unites the pastor-teacher gift and office). He says nothing there about the necessity of miraculous gifts either in evangelism (Eph 4:11) or in the teaching-edifying ministry of the church (vv.12-16).

Eighth, the other NT passages in which Christian worship patterns are set forth do not include, or as in the exceptional case of the Corinthian church, do not emphasize, miraculous gifts and functions. This is true not only for worship in the developing church under Paul's ministry as portrayed in the last half of Acts and in the epistles, but also in the worship of the OT and early NT periods involving predominantly Jewish Christians—worship patterns taken over largely by the developing Jewish-Gentile Church. These important elements of worship were: the reading of Scripture and expounding it with understanding (Neh 8:1-8; Luke 4:16-30; Acts 2 and other sermons in Acts); prayer (1 Kings 8:10-61; Acts 14:23; 16:25); singing (1 Chron 25; Acts 16:25; Eph 5:19); Christian *koinonia* or fellowship (2 Kings 23:1-3; Acts 2:42); Christian ceremonies or sacraments (as the Passover [Exod 12] and the Lord's Supper [Acts 2:42; 20:7; 1 Cor 11:17-32]); and fasting (Acts 14:23). Miraculous gifts, including tongues, are (apart from the unique situation at Corinth—1 Cor 14:26), absent from these contexts, the conclusion being that they were not to be a necessary part of the general worship patterns of the church.

Ninth, miraculous activity, including speaking in a tongue, did come in biblical times from other sources than the Lord. Witness such activity induced by evil spirits and satanic forces—the Gerasene demon-possessed man (Luke 8:26-39), the spirit-possessed girl (Acts 16:16-18), the image of the evil beast that is given the power to speak by the other satanic beast (Rev 13:15). Psychological factors were involved in the superhuman strength and tongue-speaking activity of the Gerasene demon-possessed man, for upon his deliverance from the demons, he was found to be in his "right mind" (Luke 8:35). Therefore caution and balance are needed in relation to such miraculous activities as speaking in tongues.

Having pointed this out, we must also recognize that the Bible shows that other gifts were also perverted by Satan. The OT speaks more than once of false prophets, as does the NT. The Bible speaks of false pastors (e.g., "worthless shepherd," Zech. 11:17; "hirelings," John 10:12, 13) and frequently warns against false teachers. Yet no one would insist that either prophecy in its valid sense of speaking out for God to the people or the pastoral-teaching ministry is no longer valid. Misuse of a gift does not invalidate the gift itself. However, because of their intimate psychological nature, "tongues" must be viewed with special caution and not be overstressed.

Tenth, it is to be noted that directly after the first-century-A.D. apostolic period legitimate miraculous gifts, such as tongues, practically ceased. According to Warfield,

> There is little or no evidence at all for miracle-working during the first fifty years of the post-Apostolic Church; it is slight and unimportant for the next fifty years; it grows more abundant during the next century (the third); and it becomes abundant and precise only in the fourth century, to increase still further in the fifth and beyond. (*Miracles: Yesterday and Today* [Grand Rapids: Eerdmans, 1953], p. 10.)

In discussing the witness of the apostolic fathers (the early Christian writers of the late first century A.D. and the first half of the second century) Warfield goes on to say,

> The writings of the so-called Apostolic Fathers contain no clear and certain allusions to miracle-working or to the exercise of the charismatic gifts, contemporaneous with themselves. (Ibid.)

In the place of these authentic apostolic miraculous gifts, including tongues, there arose in later centuries reports of many preposterous miracles. One such story is told in *Los Evangelios Apocrifos* (ed. Aurelio de Santos Otero, 2nd ed. [Madrid, 1963], p. 219). According to the story, the infant Jesus, on the trip to Egypt, caused a palm tree "to bow down" so that a coconut might be picked for his mother. Such so-called miracles occur in the writings of the NT Apocrypha, both in the apocryphal gospels and the apocryphal apostolic and early church writings (E. Hennecke, *New Testament Apocrypha*, ed. W. Schneemelcher, Engl. trans. R.McL. Wilson, vols. 1, 2 [London: Lutterworth Press, 1963, 1965]). The questions to be asked are these: Why did the authentic miraculous gifts cease? Are such miraculous gifts to be sought today?

The first question leads us to ask why there was a preponderance of miraculous gifts, including tongues, at the time of the ministries of Jesus Christ and his apostles. Certainly, miraculous gifts do not appear as a part of God's working among the believers in all parts of the biblical record. Abraham, Isaac, Jacob, and the twelve patriarchs did not possess or use miraculous gifts (apart from receiving the Word of God in visions and dreams in a day when the Scriptures were being given). The same is true of David, Isaiah, Jeremiah, and others. However, when certain prophets of God needed particular support and verification, then God performed great miracles through them, as with Moses and Joshua (Exod 12–40; Joshua 1–7, et al.) and Elijah and Elisha (1 Kings 17–2 Kings 13).

Likewise, in the time of Jesus' ministry and that of his apostles, God verified the message and work of Jesus and the apostles, who had witnessed to God's work in Jesus' life, death, and resurrection, by performing mighty miracles through the apostles, including speaking in tongues. Then miracles ceased when the need for the particular witness was ended and the writing of the Scriptures was complete. Thus Warfield argues when, in speaking about the charismatic gifts, he says,

> It is required of all of them [the gifts, such as tongues] that they be exercised for the edification of the church; and a distinction is drawn between them in value, in proportion as they were for edification. But the immediate end for which they were given is not left doubtful, and that proves to be not directly the extension of the church, but the authentication of the Apostles as messengers from God. This does not mean, of course, that only the Apostles appear in the New Testament as working miracles, or that they alone are represented as recipients of the charismata. But it does mean that the charismata belonged in a true sense, to the Apostles, and constituted one of the signs of an Apostle. (*Miracles*, p. 21.)

Now as to the relevance of tongues-speaking in the church today, we may observe, in addition to the foregoing discussion, first, that the requirements Paul gives for the important offices of elder and deacon (1 Tim 3:1–13; Titus 1:5–9) say nothing about the necessity that the bearers of these offices have such gifts (cf. also Eph 4:11–13).

Second, the instructions given Christians as to how they are to live together in the various units of society (Eph 5:21–6:9; Col 3:18–4:1; 1 Peter 2:13–3:7; 5:1–7, et al.) say nothing about the exercise of these kinds of gifts.

In conclusion, the writer believes that the best answer to the question of the relevance of the gift of tongues today is found in the principle that God used this and other miraculous gifts in OT and apostolic times to authenticate the messengers of his Word, and that the present-day Christian is not to seek such gifts. This is not to say, however, that the churches collectively and individually should not pray that if it is God's will, the sick may be healed by his power, or that the church should not pray for deeper illumination in understanding God's inerrant written Word.

Having said this, the writer realizes that there are many Christians of orthodox and evangelical commitment who hold that the gift of tongues as set forth in Acts and 1 Corinthians 12–14 is relevant today. Some of them would no doubt recognize that speaking in tongues is the least of the gifts, as suggested in 1 Corinthians 12:28–30, where Paul placed it last in the list, or in 14:5, 18–20, 22–24, where he subordinates it to prophecy. But they would insist that the gift is not completely ruled out for this modern era, since Paul declares, "Do not forbid speaking in tongues" (14:39).

Moreover, some Christians who accept the present validity of tongues would doubtless say that contemporary conditions seem to point to the end time and are the reason for a resurgence of tongues. For corroboration, they point to actual instances of tongues-speaking, especially on the mission field. (For examples of the latter, see David Howard,

By the Power of the Holy Spirit [Downers Grove, Illinois: Inter-Varsity Press, 1973], pp. 29, 30, 107–110.) Also, they would emphasize that any practice of tongues-speaking today must be done in accordance with the guidelines laid down by Paul (14:26–40). Perhaps most would say that tongues-speaking may best be practiced in private (especially when there is no interpreter) where one can speak in a tongue to God alone (14:2, 8).

These present-day advocates of tongues would undoubtedly agree that this gift, as well as any of the other gifts, is not to be considered an end in itself but must be exercised in love (1 Cor 13:1–3)—not as a spiritual ornament to be seen or as a test of spiritual attainment. Rather, they would say, it is to be used as an instrument for the service and glorification of God.

VIII. The Resurrection of Christ and of the Christian (15:1–58)

This is the classic chapter on the resurrection. In it Paul argues the whole subject of the resurrection from the dead—a teaching that some in the church at Corinth had been questioning (see v.12).

How he had heard about this denial he does not say. But the question gives him an opportunity to bring again before the church the doctrine of the bodily resurrection of Christ, which, along with the death of Christ, he had faithfully communicated to them (vv.1–3). He validates the historical reality of Christ's resurrection by citing eyewitnesses, including himself (vv.4–11). He argues the validity of the resurrection of believers from the fact of the resurrection of Christ (vv.12–19) and then shows that Christ's having been raised and being the first-fruits of the believing dead, guarantees the sequence of events at the second coming of Christ (vv.20–28). He refers to the futility of certain practices of baptism for the dead (vv.29, 30) if the dead are not actually raised. He also asks why Christians should suffer for Christ if there is no resurrection and calls on the Corinthians to give up these doubts and witness to their faith in a risen Christ (vv.29–34). Finally, in a passage of great eloquence, Paul discusses the nature of the resurrection body and the victory over death that God will give us through our Lord Jesus Christ (vv.35–58).

A. *The Resurrection of Christ*

15:1–11

¹Now, brothers, I want to remind you of the gospel I preached to you, which you received and on which you have taken your stand. ²By this gospel you are saved, if you hold firmly to the word I preached to you. Otherwise, you have believed in vain.

³For what I received I passed on to you as of first importance: that Christ died for our sins according to the Scriptures, ⁴that he was buried, that he was raised on the third day according to the Scriptures, ⁵and that he appeared to Peter, and then to the Twelve. ⁶After that, he appeared to more than five hundred of the brothers at the same time, most of whom are still living, though some have fallen asleep. ⁷Then he appeared to James, then to all the apostles, ⁸and last of all he appeared to me also, as to one abnormally born.

⁹For I am the least of the apostles and do not even deserve to be called an apostle, because I persecuted the church of God. ¹⁰But by the grace of God I am what I am, and his grace to me was not without effect. No, I worked harder than all of them—yet not I, but the grace of God that was with me. ¹¹Whether, then, it was I or they, this is what we preach, and this is what you believed.

1,2 In the beginning of his masterly discussion of the resurrection, Paul reminds the Corinthian Christians that it is an integral part of the gospel he had preached and they had received and believed. The "if" clause in v.2 implies that Paul believes they are really holding firmly to the Word of God and are therefore saved. So the sentence "Otherwise you have believed in vain" means that the gospel assures salvation unless the supposed faith they had was actually empty and worthless and therefore unenduring.

3-8 Some have understood the words translated "of first importance" in the temporal sense of "at the first." But that seems redundant because at all times Paul's preaching identified the death and resurrection of Christ with the gospel. The stress is on the centrality of these doctrines to the gospel message.

Paul cites two kinds of witness to the historic events of Christ's death and resurrection (vv.3-8): the OT Scriptures and the testimony of eyewitnesses. He does not quote specific OT passages but must have had in mind such texts as Isaiah 53:5, 6 and Psalm 16:8-11. He mentions Christ's burial to show the genuineness of his death and resurrection; he actually died and actually was raised. Paul feels no compulsion to cite any eyewitnesses of Christ's death, because its factuality was commonly accepted. The resurrection was a different matter. If supernatural Christianity was to be believed, valid eyewitnesses must be cited to attest this historical event and set to rest doubt about the resurrection of the dead.

That "Christ died for our sins" (v.3) implies that Christ was sinless. That he was raised forever (the perfect tense is used here) agrees with the Scripture in Psalm 16:10; so also does Paul's statement about the third day, which may be based on Jesus' words in Matthew 12:40 that relate his three days in the tomb to Jonah's three days inside the fish (Jonah 1:17). According to Jewish reckoning, "three days" would include parts of Friday afternoon, all of Saturday, and Sunday morning. Compare the parts of two Sundays implied in the phrase "after eight days" (John 20:26).

Part of the gospel message Paul passed on to the Corinthians was eyewitness reports of the resurrection of Christ. Observe the close-knit series of "that" clauses in vv.3-6, extending from, "that Christ died" (v.3) through "that he appeared" (v.6) to eyewitnesses, some of whom Paul names. It is natural for him to include Cephas (Peter) and the apostles (possibly referring to the meeting recorded in Luke 24:36ff. and John 20:19ff.). "The Twelve" is a designation of the apostles as a group and is not to be pressed numerically, since Judas was no longer there and on one occasion Thomas (John 20:24) was not with them. The apostolic witness was of vital importance for the Corinthians and Paul doubtless included the witness of the 500 especially to impress doubting believers with the sheer number of eyewitnesses of the event. Some of the 500 may have been known to the Corinthians. This appearance of Christ to so many at once may have taken place in Galilee, where the eleven and possibly many more, went to meet the risen Lord (Matt 28:10, 16). "Fall asleep" is an early Christian expression for dying (cf. Acts 7:60).

The James mentioned in v.7 certainly is not one of the two apostles of that name— James the son of Zebedee and James the son of Alphaeus (Matt 10:2-4), since the whole group of apostles is mentioned next and would include these two. Instead, it must be the Lord's half-brother (Matt 13:55), who had, with his brothers, joined the apostolic band (Acts 1:14) and had become prominent in the Jerusalem church (Acts 15:13). We do not know when this appearance took place. Since Paul had mentioned "the Twelve" in v.5, "all the apostles" (v.7) must be used more loosely to include others who met with the apostolic band (cf. Acts 1:13-15). All this evidence (vv.5-8) was received by Paul from eyewitnesses (cf. Gal. 1:18, 19) and very possibly from some of the gospel writers. Paul includes himself as the last witness (v.8). He describes himself as one born of a miscarriage, thus he conveys his feeling that he was not a "normal" member of the apostolic group, but one who had been "snatched" out of his sin and rebellion by the glorified Christ (Acts 9:3–6).

9-11 In these verses Paul reflects on his own unworthiness and on God's matchless redeeming grace. Though he taught that all are unworthy before God (Rom 3:10–18)—a fact to which the Twelve were no exception—he felt himself particularly unworthy because he had persecuted the church. He calls it the church of God; therefore, in persecuting it, he felt he had persecuted God. With true humility, he attributes all his hard work for the cause of Christ solely to God's grace (v.10)—grace that had saved him and enabled him to serve. Then with great emphasis he declares that all—both he and the other apostles—preached the same gospel with the same stress on the resurrection, and this is the message the Corinthians believed.

B. *The Validity of the Resurrection of the Dead*

15:12-19

> [12]But if it is preached that Christ has been raised from the dead, how can some of you say that there is no resurrection of the dead? [13]If there is no resurrection of the dead, then not even Christ has been raised. [14]And if Christ has not been raised, our preaching is useless and so is your faith. [15]More than that, we are then found to be false witnesses about God, for we have testified about God that he raised Christ from the dead. But he did not raise him if in fact the dead are not raised. [16]For if the dead are not raised, then Christ has not been raised either. [17]And if Christ has not been raised, your faith is futile; you are still in your sins. [18]Then those also who have fallen asleep in Christ are lost. [19]If only for this life we have hope in Christ, we are to be pitied more than all men.

12-16 Here Paul presents his major proposition. Some at Corinth had argued that there was no resurrection of the dead. He replies that this is absolutely contrary to the proclamation that Christ has been raised. The perfect tense *egēgertai* ("has been raised"), with its emphasis on the present reality of the historic fact is important to Paul (cf. Gal 2:20). In the present context he uses the same verb form seven times, in each case in reference to Christ (vv.4, 12, 13, 14, 16, 17, 20). When speaking of "the resurrection of the dead," he uses the present tense of the same verb (vv.15, 16). The conditional sentences throughout this section begin with *ei de,* the condition being an assumed fact: "If it is preached [as it is] that Christ has been raised ..." (v.12). The same is true of vv.13, 14, 16, 17, and 19.

Having questioned the contention of some that the dead do not rise (v.12), the apostle states a series of conclusions flowing from the contention that the dead do not rise: (1) There is no resurrection of Christ (v.13); (2) preaching that he has been raised is then empty and meaningless (v.14a); (3) their resultant faith (in Christ who was supposed to have risen from the dead) is also meaningless (v.14b); and (4) his own testimony about Christ's resurrection is false, because it claims God did something he really did not do (v.15). Verse 16 closes this set of conclusions by reiterating the statement in v.13.

17-19 Once more Paul begins with *ei de* as he draws additional conclusions from the hypothesis that Christ has not risen from the dead: (1) Faith is not only vain or meaningless (*kenos*) (v.14), it is also fruitless (*mataios,* v.17); (2) believers still carry the guilt of their sins and are not justified (v.17b; cf. the converse in Rom 5:1); (3) there is no hope for those who have died in Christ—they have perished (v.18); and (4) therefore putting up with persecutions and hardships is futile; we are most to be pitied among men (v.19). The perfect tense of the verb *elpizō* ("we have hope") implies a continual hope in Christ throughout life.

Notes

1–3 That the gospel was a corpus of doctrine including the resurrection of Christ is clear from the neuter pronoun ὅ (*ho*, "that which"), the pronoun being repeated throughout vv.1–3. This "*ho* corpus" of the gospel is referred to in several ways: the Corinthians had received it (accusative case, vv.1b, 3b); they had taken their stand on it (dative case, v.1c); and they had been saved through it (genitive case, v.2a).

3 The phrase ὑπὲρ τῶν ἁμαρτιῶν ἡμῶν (*hyper tōn hamartiōn hēmōn*) is theologically strong, referring to the substitutionary atonement: Christ died *on behalf of our sins* or *in order to atone for* (or, *remove*) *our sins* (cf. Gal 1:4).

3,4 Γραφή (*graphē*), generally meaning "writing" of various sorts, has only a sacred significance in the NT, referring to the holy Scriptures.

5 The passive form ὤφθη (*ōphthē*), from ὁράω (*horaō*) is used deponently as "appeared" (cf. Luke 24:34; Heb 9:28) rather than passively, "was seen."

15 The phrase κατὰ θεοῦ (*kata theou*) strictly means "against God"; that is, accusing God of doing what he did not do (cf. St. John Parry, in loc.).

17 There is a shade of difference between μάταιος (*mataios*) and κενός (*kenos*) in v.14, the former meaning "fruitless," which augments the latter meaning of "empty."

18 The aorist (past-punctiliar) form ἀπωλόντο (*apōlonto*, "they have perished," "they are lost forever") is quite final. κοιμάω (*koimaō*) used for natural sleep (Luke 22:45), is used of the death of the body in such contexts as this one.

The comparative form ἐλεεινότεροι (*eleeinoteroi*) need not be taken as equivalent to a superlative, "most miserable," as in KJV. This is possible, but it makes best sense taken as a true comparative in meaning—"more pitied" or, as in NIV, "pitied more than all men." This agrees better with the order of the Gr. words, in which the comparative for *eleeinoteroi* is followed immediately by the genitive of comparison: τῶν πάντων (*tōn pantōn*). (Cf. 1 Cor 13:13, where μείζων [*meizōn*] is used to compare three things: "the greatest of these." But in 1 Cor 12:23, the comparative form ἀτιμότερα [*atimotera*] is to be taken with its usual comparative force: "less honorable." See Robertson, *A Grammar*, pp. 667, 668.)

19 The adverb μόνον (*monon*, "only"), though placed after the perfect periphrastic construction (i.e., a participle with the verb "to be") ἠλπικότες ἐσμέν (*ēlpikotes esmen*), is best taken with the entire clause to mean, "If all our hopes in Christ are confined to this life . . ." (Hodge).

C. *Christ the Guarantee of the Resurrection From the Dead*

15:20–28

²⁰But Christ has indeed been raised from the dead, the firstfruits of those who have fallen asleep. ²¹For since death came through a man, the resurrection of the dead comes also through a man. ²²For as in Adam all die, so in Christ all will be made alive. ²³But each in his own turn: Christ, the firstfruits; then, when he comes, those who belong to him. ²⁴Then the end will come, when he hands over the kingdom to God the Father after he has destroyed all dominion, authority and power. ²⁵For he must reign until God has put all his enemies under his feet. ²⁶The

last enemy to be destroyed is death. [27]For God "has put everything under his feet." Now when it says that "everything" has been put under him, it is clear that this does not include God himself, who put everything under Christ. [28]When he has done this, then the Son himself will be made subject to him who put everything under him, so that God may be all in all.

The "but ... indeed" (*nyni de*) is Paul's emphatic and conclusive way of introducing some vitally important affirmations (cf. *nyni de* in 13:13; Rom 3:21; 6:22; 7:6; Col 1:22, et al.). Certainly, Paul implies, none of the Corinthian believers would deny that an integral part of the gospel message is the resurrection of Christ (15:1–4). Therefore, they must now accept the sequel—Christ guarantees the resurrection of the Christian dead, as the word "firstfruits" teaches. By "firstfruits" Paul brings to bear the rich imagery of the OT. The "firstfruits"—the first sheaf of the harvest offered to the Lord (Lev 23:10–11, 17, 20)—was not only prior to the main harvest but was also an assurance that the rest of the harvest was coming. So with Christ. He preceded his people in his bodily resurrection and he is also the guarantee of their resurrection at his second coming.

21,22 These verses sound like Paul's two-category contrast in Rom 5:12–21. The man who brought death is Adam, and the one who will bring about the resurrection of the dead is Christ (cf. also 1 Cor 15:45). All who are represented in Adam—i.e., the whole human race—died. All who are in Christ—i.e., God's redeemed people—will be made alive at the resurrection (cf. John 5:25).

23 The expression, *hekastos en toi idioi tagmati* ("each in his own group") stresses the different times involved: Christ the "firstfruits" was made alive three days after his death; the other group, those who belong to Christ, will be made alive at the Parousia—his second coming. The term Parousia can simply mean a person's presence (Phil. 2:12), but when used of Christ, it refers especially to his second coming (cf. Matt 24:27).

Having recognized that Paul has time-sequences in mind (v.23), we assume that in vv.24ff. he continues with further time-sequences, as shown by the particle *eita* ("then"). That is, at the time of Christ's second coming and the resurrection of the blessed dead (cf. Rev 20:4–6), next ("then") in order will come the process of his handing over (*paradidoi* is *present* subjunctive) the kingdom to God. This will include his conquest of all earthly and all spiritual powers and enemies (cf. "things in heaven and on earth, visible and invisible ... thrones ... powers ... rulers ... authorities," Col 1:16). The picture is total, including the physical kingdoms of this world. This future total conquest of the rulers of this world is further suggested in the sentence beginning with "for" (*gar*, v.25). Christ must at that time (*eita*, "then," v.24) continue his reign—i.e., his millennial reign (Rev 20:4–6) till all his enemies are conquered. The expression "under his feet" is an OT figure for total conquest. Verse 25 is an allusion to Psalm 110:1 (cf. Matt 22:44). The mention of Zion in Psalm 110:2 suggests further that his enemies include those who attack Palestine (Rev 16:12–16) and Jerusalem (Rev 20:7–10) at the time of the millennial reign of Christ (Rev 20:4–6). Finally, the last enemy to be destroyed is death (v.26) at the close of the second-coming events at the great judgment (Rev 20:2–15). This will bring the consummation of Christ's conquest of his enemies and all other things, as implied by the prophetic statement about man and particularly about the incarnate Christ in Psalm 8:6, quoted in v.27.

Some think the reference to "the end" in vv.24–27 refers to the absolute end of this world, at which time believers will be raised. They hold that what follows "then" in v.24

is different from what follows "then" in v.23. According to this view, "There it [the 'then' of v.23] was the resurrection, but after 'the end' [v.24] there is no resurrection" (Grosheide, in loc.) preceded by a literal thousand-year reign in which Christ puts his enemies under his feet. But this interpretation changes quite radically Paul's idea of events following each other in temporal sequence, to an abrupt "then comes the end" where there is no more sequence. This seems arbitrary. Furthermore, it does not take adequate account of the fuller teaching on this subject in Rev 20:4-10—a passage that posits a reign of Christ and a time when this earth will have peace and rejuvenation before its final destruction (Rev 21:1). In Romans 8:18-25 it is stated that the whole creation (including the earth) will be delivered from "its bondage to decay" [NIV] and will be "brought into the glorious freedom" (that is, deliverance from decay) at the time of the "glorious freedom" of the children of God. All of this occurs, according to Revelation 20 and 21 *before* the destruction of the present heavens and earth. God's dealings with this present heaven and earth are described in Revelation 21:1, not as a rejuvenation, but as a total destruction of what is called the "first" heaven and earth; a "new" heaven and a "new" earth, an earth in which there is "no longer any sea," take the place of the old ones, we are told (cf. 2 Peter 3:10-13).

Verse 27 makes clear that in the "all things" God the Father is not made subject to Christ. On the other hand, v.28 suggests that the Son in a certain sense will be made subject to God the Father. That this does not mean inferiority of person or nature is shown by the future tense of the verb: "the Son himself will be made subject." If there were inherent inferiority, the present tense would be expected—i.e., "he is ever subjected to the Father." But the future aspect of Christ's subjection to the Father must rather be viewed in the light of the administrative process in which the world is brought from its sin and disorder into order by the power of the Son, who died and was raised and who then, in the economy of the Godhead, turns it all over to God the Father, the supreme administrative head. All this is to be done so that God will be recognized by all as sovereign, and he—the triune God—will be supreme (cf. Rev 22:3-5).

Notes

23 Ἔπειτα (*epeita*, "then" or "next") denotes succession in enumerations often with indications of chronological sequence (cf. 1 Thess 4:17) as well as here. Εἶτα (*eita*, "then" or "next") when following closely, indicates further chronological sequence (John 13:5; 19:27; 1 Tim 2:13, et al.), though sometimes, as in logical argumentation, it may not entail time sequence (Heb 12:9).

25 Though βασιλεύειν (*basileuein*) is a present infinitive with continuous action, it does not at this point in 1 Cor mean that Christ is reigning now. The context is "the end" (v.24) and the infinitive (a futuristic use of the present tense) is governed by the impersonal verb *dei*, meaning "It is necessary that he is to be reigning"—NIV, "For he must reign . . . ."

26 The present form καταργεῖται (*katargeitai*) is to be read as a futuristic present—"is going to be destroyed." Present spiritual death is not in view, for Paul speaks of death in an eschatological sense as the last enemy to be destroyed (see also vv.50-56).

D. *Implications of Denying the Resurrection From the Dead*

15:29–34

29Now if there is no resurrection, what will those do who are baptized for the dead? If the dead are not raised at all, why are people baptized for them? 30And as for us, why do we endanger ourselves every hour? 31I die every day—I mean that, brothers—just as surely as I glory over you in Christ Jesus our Lord. 32If I fought wild beasts in Ephesus for merely human reasons, what have I gained? If the dead are not raised,

"Let us eat and drink,
for tomorrow we die."

33Do not be misled: "Bad company corrupts good character." 34Come back to your senses as you ought, and stop sinning; for there are some who are ignorant of God—I say this to your shame.

29 Here Paul returns to his argument for the resurrection of the dead. There is a special difficulty in understanding v.29 because we do not know the background of the words "baptized for the dead." There are many interpretations, but it is difficult to find a satisfactory one. The present tense of "baptize" suggests that the practice of baptizing for the dead was current and evidently well known to the Corinthians.

Among the numerous explanations of the custom is that of Epiphanius (*Haer.* 28) who understood it to be a baptism of catechumens (i.e., those being instructed in Christian doctrine) on their death beds. But there is no evidence that this was practiced in Paul's day.

Other views center around the idea that Paul is referring to the practice of living believers being baptized for deceased believers. The reasons given for such a supposed practice are manifold. Chrysostom and others understood Paul to be referring to the statement in the baptismal creed "I believe in the resurrection of the dead," meaning that there was a baptism for the bodies of the dead in the hope of the resurrection. But the text does not support this complex thought, and such a creed came later than Paul's time. Craig (IB, in loc.) suggests that the custom may have been a reference to a superstitious baptism being practiced for those who had died as "outsiders" to the church. Or that believers may have baptized the graves above relatives who had died in Christ (Grosheide). But such a locative meaning as "above" or "over" for the preposition *hyper* with the genitive is not found elsewhere in the NT, and there is no historical evidence for any such custom. (H.A.W. Meyer, *The Epistles to the Corinthians* [New York: Funk and Wagnalls, 1884], p. 366.)

In another strange and complex view, Olshausen takes the passage to mean that the living believers had themselves baptized in place of the deceased believers, who thus had ceased to be members of the church, this custom being practiced so that the church membership would not be depleted. But new converts would fill up the ranks of the church, so that there would be no need for such a practice. Koster sees the practice as referring to living Christians who had got themselves baptized for the sake of deceased believers, to show their yearning for them and assuring their connection with them and participation with them in the resurrection. But not all this is implied in the text. (Ibid. pp. 364–368.)

In still another view, the concept of "baptize" in v.29 is interpreted not in relation to the actual sacrament or ordinance of baptism but is understood metaphorically and spiritually as meaning "identify." Thus, the idea would be "If there is no resurrection of the dead, why are believers identified as dead men? Why should they be crucified with Christ?" According to this view, Paul is saying, "I die daily," meaning "I am identified daily with Christ in his death." But a major problem with this interpretation is that it makes the preposition *hyper* mean "as," whereas its basic meaning with the genitive is "for," "in behalf of," or "in the place of." (See further D.G. Barnhouse, *God's Freedom: Exposition on Romans* [Grand Rapids: Eerdmans 1958], 6:32-35.)

According to Meyer, this verse means that believers already baptized were rebaptized for the benefit of believers who had died unbaptized. This was done on the assumption that it would count for the unbaptized dead and thereby assure their resurrection along with the baptized, living believers. As Meyer put it, "This custom propagated and maintained itself afterwards only among heretical sects, in particular among the Corinthians (Epiphanius, *Haer.* 28:7) and among the Marcionites (Chrysostom; cf. moreover, generally Tertullian, *de resurr. 48; Adv. Marc.* v.10)" (*The Epistles to the Corinthians*, pp. 364, 365).

At any rate, Paul simply mentions the superstitious custom without approving it and uses it to fortify his argument that there is a resurrection from the dead.

30-32 Another argument for the resurrection is that if it is not true, then suffering and hardship for the sake of Christ are useless. By "endangering ourselves every hour," Paul seems to be alluding to peril looming up in his ministry in Ephesus (cf. Acts 19), where he was when he wrote 1 Corinthians. He is in danger of death every day (v.31). He seals this assertion with the oath (Greek, *nē*, "I mean that, brothers") that this is as true as the fact that he glories over them and over their union with Christ. Paul's reference to fighting with wild beasts in Ephesus (v.32) may be taken literally or figuratively. But since from Acts 19 we see no evidence of such punishment and since it was questionable whether a Roman citizen would be subjected to such treatment, it is best to take the words metaphorically—the human enemies he fought with at Ephesus were like wild beasts. But, Paul says, why go through all this suffering if there is no hope of resurrection? To prove his point, he first quotes Isaiah 22:13, (possibly for the benefit of the Jewish believers at Corinth) from a context of reckless living that the Lord condemns. So without eternal hope through the resurrection, men have nothing to turn to but gratification of their appetites.

33 Turning now to Greek literature, Paul supports his position by quoting a piece of practical worldly wisdom from Menander's comedy, *Thais*, relevant to the situation in the Corinthian church. The "bad company" points to those who were teaching that there is no resurrection and so were a threat to the testimony of the church.

34 The call in v.34 is for the Corinthians to stop sinning in denying the resurrection of the dead and, so by implication, the resurrection of Christ—a denial leading to loose living. There were some in the church who did not know God or the precious doctrine of the resurrection. They were in a shameful condition, Paul says, because they had espoused such a denial of the truth.

Notes

31 The particle νή (nē) is one of strong affirmation and is used with an accusative of person or thing by which one swears or affirms.

32 The first-class Gr. condition of fact εἰ (ei) with the indicative, assumes the reality of Paul's encounter with danger in Ephesus—it had occurred. The second ei indicative condition assumes, for the sake of argument, that if it is in fact granted that the dead do not rise, then the pragmatic consequences are that one might as well live recklessly now. The aorist subjunctive forms Φάγωμεν (phagōmen) and πίωμεν (piōmen) relate to the total decision regarding living as if there were no resurrection: "Let us give ourselves over completely to eat and drink"—i.e., to total materialism.

34 The contrast in the kind of action in the two imperative verbs ἐκνήψατε (eknēpsate, aorist) and μὴ ἁμαρτάνετε (mē harmartanete, present) is graphic: "Come to your senses, fully and completely; and do not continue to sin."

E. *The Resurrection Body: Its Nature and Change*

15:35–58

35But someone may ask, "How are the dead raised? With what kind of body will they come?" 36How foolish! What you sow does not come to life unless it dies. 37When you sow, you do not plant the body that will be, but just a seed, perhaps of wheat or of something else. 38But God gives it a body as he has determined, and to each kind of seed he gives its own body. 39All flesh is not the same: Men have one kind of flesh, animals have another, birds another and fish another. 40There are also heavenly bodies and there are earthly bodies; but the splendor of the heavenly bodies is one kind, and the splendor of the earthly bodies is another. 41The sun has one kind of splendor, the moon another and the stars another; and star differs from star in splendor.

42So it will be with the resurrection of the dead. The body that is sown is perishable, it is raised imperishable; 43it is sown in dishonor, it is raised in glory; it is sown in weakness, it is raised in power; 44it is sown a natural body, it is raised a spiritual body.

If there is a natural body, there is also a spiritual body. 45So it is written: "The first man Adam became a living being"; the last Adam, a life-giving spirit. 46The spiritual did not come first, but the natural, and after that the spiritual. 47The first man was of the dust of the earth, the second man from heaven. 48As was the earthly man, so are those who are of the earth; and as is the man from heaven, so also are those who are of heaven. 49And just as we have borne the likeness of the earthly man, so we shall bear the likeness of the man from heaven.

50I declare to you, brothers, that flesh and blood cannot inherit the kingdom of God, nor does the perishable inherit the imperishable. 51Listen, I tell you a mystery: We shall not all sleep, but we shall all be changed—52in a flash, in the twinkling of an eye, at the last trumpet. For the trumpet will sound, the dead will be raised imperishable, and we shall be changed. 53For the perishable must clothe itself with the imperishable, and the mortal with immortality. 54When the perishable has been clothed with the imperishable, and the mortal with immortality, then the saying that is written will come true: "Death has been swallowed up in victory."

55"Where, O death, is your victory?
Where, O death, is your sting?"

56The sting of death is sin, and the power of sin is the law. 57But thanks be to God! He gives us the victory through our Lord Jesus Christ.

58Therefore, my dear brothers, stand firm. Let nothing move you. Always give yourselves fully to the work of the Lord, because you know that your labor in the Lord is not in vain.

With imcomparable logic, Paul's argument mounts toward its magnificent climax. First, he discusses the nature of the resurrection body (vv.35–49). Then he describes the transformation the body must undergo before death is conquered and the believer lives with God eternally (vv.50–58).

35–49 Paul answers the question some believers were asking—viz., since a resurrection body was like the sinful mortal body we now have (Hodge, Craig), how could the resurrection of such a body occur? (Grosheide). Paul raises questions as a means of answering some of the proposed objections. He calls the questions foolish and in replying to them uses an analogy to the organizational structure of the physical life and world. Different beings, while organized alike in their own order, differ from other orders. The seed analogy (v.37—cf. John 12:24) teaches that through "dying" (decaying in the ground) the seed gives birth by God's power to a new and different "body," yet one related to the seed it came from (vv.36b–38).

A second analogy involves the body of flesh various forms of animal life have—the differing kinds of flesh for men, animals, birds, and fish (v.39). A third analogy relates to inanimate objects of creation (vv.40, 41), in connection with which Paul again uses *sōma* ("body"). These, too, differ. The "heavenly bodies"—sun, moon, and stars—differ from "the earthly bodies," and their "splendor" differs from "the splendor of the earthly bodies." (Paul does not specify what he means by the latter—perhaps he had in mind the great mountains, canyons, and the like.) Moreover, he adds that the heavenly bodies themselves differ from one another in splendor and brilliance. So, Paul is arguing, God is able to take similar physical material and organize it differently to accomplish his purposes.

In vv.42–44a the apostle applies this to the truth of the resurrection of the body. God can take the mortal body, perishable (Gal. 6:8), dishonored, humiliated because of sin (Phil 3:20, 21), and weak (Mark 14:38)—a natural body like those of the animal world—and bring that body that "is sown" in death (cf. John 12:24) into a different order of life in a spiritual body. Such a body will indeed have immortality (2 Tim 1:10), glory (Phil 3:21), and power. It will have a spiritual way of functioning similar to the way heavenly bodies function in contradistinction to earthly bodies (St. John Parry). That by "spiritual" here (v.44) Paul means completely nonmaterial is incompatible with the whole context, which discusses the differing organizations of material substance. The spiritual body is an imperishable yet utterly real body—one of a different order and having different functions from the earthly body; it is a body given by God himself—a body glorified with eternal life.

Verses 44b–49 develop the distinction between the natural body and the spiritual body, by bringing in two categories—one of Adam and his descendants and the other of Christ, the last Adam, and his redeemed ones. By "natural body" Paul means one such as Adam had (v.45) when he was made of the dust of the ground and given the breath of life (cf. Gen 2:7). By "spiritual body" the apostle means that an imperishable body that has received eternal life from Christ, the life-giving Spirit (cf. John 5:26), including a metamorphosis of the physical body to adapt it spiritually (without either corruption or mortality) for living with God (Phil 3:21), just as Christ in his resurrected and glorified human body (Luke 24:36–43) went to heaven to be with the Father (cf. Acts 1:11, 2:33). There is, indeed, a real sense in which the accounts of the post-resurrection appearances of Christ in Luke 24; John 20 and 21; and Acts 1:1–9 shed light on the nature of the resurrection body. (See also 2 Cor 5:1–10.)

Paul asserts that the natural life came first and then the spiritual life was added to it, v.46. He illustrates this in vv.47–49 from Adam, who was made of the dust of the earth, and whose descendants (the whole human race) have natural, earthly bodies. In contrast, "the last Adam," Christ, came from heaven into a human body (the incarnation), a body that was glorified following his resurrection (Phil 3:21). He is the God-Man (John 3:13). Those who belong to him, Paul says, are also "of heaven" and will ultimately be like him (cf. 1 John 3:2).

50–58 Paul now comes to the conclusion of his argument for the resurrection. God's people must have more than the natural body to inherit the eternal kingdom of God. "Flesh and blood" refers to the mortal body—our present humanity, which Christ fully shared through his incarnation (Heb 2:14). This mortal body is perishable and cannot inherit that which is imperishable. So the unsaved cannot be in heaven at all, and the saved must have their bodies changed.

By using "mystery" in reference to the resurrection body, Paul implies that there are things about that body that the Corinthians did not understand, and about which he wants to inform them. First, not all Christians will "fall asleep." Some will be alive when Christ returns (1 Thess 4:15). Second, all Christians will receive changed bodies when Christ comes back and summons his people at the sound of the last trumpet (cf. Rev 11:15). This is called "the rapture" (1 Thess 4:13–17). Third, the change will occur instantaneously and completely for all Christians, whether living or dead. Fourth, the change will occur from one kind of body to another. Paul does not use the term "imperishable" in speaking of those living when Jesus comes, but the word "changed" (v.52). The meaning is clarified by v.53: The "perishable," those in Christ whose bodies are decaying in the grave, must be given "imperishable" bodies. The mortal, those in Christ living in mortal bodies at the time of Christ's return, must be given "changed" immortal bodies—bodies that will not die. When all this occurs (v.54), the triumphant words in Isaiah 25:8 and Hosea 13:14 will become a reality for God's people. With powerful effect, Paul quotes Hosea's striking rhetorical questions.

Then, with strong emphasis on the words "victory" and "sting," Paul reaches the climax of this song of triumph in vv.56, 57. If it were not for sin, death would have no sting. It is the law of God with its stringent moral demands that strengthens the power of sin by showing us how sinful we are, and thus condemns us. But death does not have the final victory! Hear the glorious closing exclamation (v.57): "Thanks be to God! He gives us the victory through our Lord Jesus Christ." Yes, victory, even over death and the grave, has been won through our Lord, who died and rose and is coming again.

Following this glorious outburst of eloquence, Paul concludes with a practical, down-to-earth exhortation. It is almost as if he is saying to the Corinthian Christians and indeed to all of us: "Now, my brothers and sisters, in the light of these sublime truths, be steadfast in doing the Lord's work, knowing that he will reward you at his coming."

Notes

40,41 The use of ἕτερος (heteros) suggests a difference in kind between heavenly and earthly bodies. The ἄλλος (allos) indicates a comparison of things of like kind—the sun, moon, etc. The same is true of its use in v.39.

44-46 The ψυχικός (*psychikos*) body is the physical body in contrast to the πνευματικός (*pneumatikos*) body, that body imbued with additional life from the Spirit of God.

47 Some ancient MSS read ἄνθρωπος ὁ κύριος (*anthrōpos ho kurios*) "the man, the Lord" (which KJV follows). But the best MSS omit *ho kurios*.

49 Though the MS evidence somewhat favors the subjunctive φορέσωμεν (*phoresōmen*, "let us bear"—a form that has some good MS evidence), the context favors the future indicative φορέσομεν (*phoresomen*, "we shall bear"—a form that also has some good MS evidence). Εἰκον (*eikon*) is an "image," like that of an emperor's head on a coin, an exact likeness of someone.

51 The best MS witnesses read ἀλλαγησόμεθα (*allagēsometha*, "we shall be changed"). Other readings, such as "we shall not all be changed" or "we shall sleep, but not all of us shall be changed," suggest muddled theological thinking and must be scribal interpolations. The first and best reading agrees with the like statement in v.52.

54 There is a shortened reading of this v. that leaves out the words "this mortal shall be clothed with immortality" (NIV, "the mortal with immortality"). This omission, though supported by several important MSS, probably arose through an oversight in copying, especially since these words appeared before in v.53.

55 Two sets of variants developed in this v., because the LXX of Hos 13:14 differs in part from the Heb. The variant in which νῖκος (*nikos*, "victory") appears before κέντρον (*kentron*, "sting") is to be preferred to the reverse (which KJV has) because of the word order in LXX, which has *kentron* last. The repetition of θάνατε (*thanate*, "death") is to be preferred as Paul's synonym for ᾅδη (*hadē*, "Hades" or "the grave"), which he never uses. (Cf. Metzger, *A Textual Commentary*, p. 570.) Paul adapts LXX δίκη (*dikē*, "judgment") for Heb. "plagues" to his word νῖκος (*nikos*, "victory")—i.e., victory over plagues.

58 The present imperative γίνεσθε (*ginesthe*) stresses constant Christian stability, as does πάντοτε (*pantote*) also: "Continue to stand firm ... always abound." The addition of the word κόπος (*kopos*, "toil") to ἔργον (*ergon*), the ordinary word for work, suggests that work for the Lord is to be hard work and that it involves hardship and suffering.

IX. The Collection for God's People, Requests, and Final Greetings (16:1-24)

A. *The Collection for God's People*

16:1-4

> ¹Now about the collection for God's people: Do what I told the Galatian churches to do. ²On the first day of every week, each one of you should set aside a sum of money in keeping with his income, saving it up, so that when I come no collections will have to be made. ³Then, when I arrive, I will give letters of introduction to the men you approve and send them with your gift to Jerusalem. ⁴If it seems advisable for me to go also, they will accompany me.

1-4 This section begins with the same formula, "Now about ..." (*peri de*), that was used in 7:1 and 12:1. The Corinthians had evidently asked about the collection to be taken up for God's people at Jerusalem (v.3). Paul must have spoken to them earlier about it, as he also did later (cf. 2 Cor 8-9). This offering for these poor in Jerusalem was much on his mind during his third missionary journey (cf. Rom 15:26). That he mentions the Galatian churches here, though not in 2 Corinthians 8-9 or Romans 15:26, implies that this collection was to be a widespread and extensive effort with the Corinthian Christians contributing along with those from other lands. Why some of the Christians in Jerusalem were poor (Rom 15:26) at this time (c. A.D. 55, 56) he does not say. It may have been in part because of the famine referred to in Acts 11:29 (c. A.D. 49). Some have thought that the poverty resulted from the Jerusalem Christians' being overgenerous in giving away their property and goods (cf. Acts 2:44, 45; 4:34, 35).

Verse 2 teaches that the collection was to be set aside by each individual (and family) on the first day of the week ("the first day from the Sabbath"—i.e., Sunday), but we are not told specifically that it was to be collected at church. Some have interpreted the words *par heautō* (literally "by himself") to mean "at home." But then why mention doing it on Sunday, when they could just as well do it regularly at home at other times? The meaning must rather be that the Christians were to bring their offerings to church on Sunday, since that was the day they assembled for worship (Acts 20:7; cf. Rev 1:10). It is significant that the early church father, Justin Martyr (second century A.D.) testified that contributions to the church were received on that day (Apology I, 67.6). Giving is to be proportionate; all were to participate, whether rich or poor; and the money was to be regularly set aside ("every week"). The offering was to be planned for and saved up ahead of time instead of being hurriedly and ineffectively collected when Paul visited them. It was to be properly handled by messengers approved by the Corinthians themselves (v.3)—i.e., those who, bearing letters of recommendation to the church at Jerusalem, carried the gift. Paul makes provision for approved messengers to avoid any suspicion of wrongdoing in connection with the funds (cf. 2 Cor 8:16-21).

In v.4 Paul does not explain why he is going to Jerusalem, but he probably is thinking that the pressure of missionary business to be conducted there (cf. Acts 21:17-19) might compel him to do so. Or, he may be thinking that it would be best for him to be in Jerusalem when the gift is delivered. At any rate, he says that if he should go, the approved messengers would go along with him.

Notes

---

2 Μίαν σαββάτου (*mian sabbatou*), literally "the first day of the sabbath," means first day from (i.e., after) the sabbath. The genitive *sabbatou* is ablatival in function here.

B. *Personal Requests*

16:5-18

5After I go through Macedonia, I will come to you—for I will be going through Macedonia. Perhaps I will stay with you awhile, or even spend the winter, so that you can help me on my journey, wherever I go. 7I do not want to see you now and make only a passing visit; I hope to spend some time with you, if the Lord permits. 8But I will stay on at Ephesus until Pentecost, 9because a great door for effective work has opened to me, and there are many who oppose me.

10If Timothy comes, see to it that he has nothing to fear while he is with you, for he is carrying on the work of the Lord, just as I am. 11No one, then, should refuse to accept him. Send him on his way in peace so that he may return to me. I am expecting him along with the brothers.

12Now about our brother Apollos: I strongly urged him to go to you with the brothers. He was quite unwilling to go now, but he will go when he has the opportunity.

13Be on your guard; stand firm in the faith; be men of courage; be strong. 14Do everything in love.

> ¹⁵You know that the household of Stephanas were the first converts in Achaia, and they have devoted themselves to the service of the saints. I urge you brothers, ¹⁶to submit to such as these and to everyone who joins in the work and labors at it. ¹⁷I was glad when Stephanas, Fortunatus and Achaicus arrived, because they have supplied what was lacking from you. ¹⁸For they refreshed my spirit and yours also. Such men deserve recognition.

These requests revolve around Paul's travel plans (as he expects to leave Ephesus) and around his friends—Timothy, Apollos and others who have helped the apostle, and the Corinthians.

5-9 The projected journey through Macedonia fits the record of Paul's travel in Acts 19:21 and 20:1, 2, which shows how in following that route he ended by spending three months in Greece—a period evidently involving his stay at Corinth. This intention of spending the winter with them (v.6) apparently relates to the "three months" mentioned in Acts 20:3. "To help him on his journey" must mean endorsing Paul's intended trip and encouraging him perhaps with fresh supplies and equipment. Paul did not seem to want to burden them by asking directly for money (cf. 1 Cor 9:7–12).

His work, Paul feels, is not yet finished at Ephesus (vv.8, 9), because there is a great door (cf. "door" in Acts 14:27; 2 Cor. 2:12; Col 4:3) of opportunity open there for him. The perfect tense *aneogen*, sets forth a completed state: "A great door for effective work *stands open*"—the Lord had opened it and the Lord in his providence was keeping it open. We are not told just who the opponents at Ephesus were, but according to Acts 19:23–27 they must have included the pagan craftsmen engaged in making miniature silver shrines of Artemis. The reference to Pentecost (the Jewish festival held on the fiftieth day after Passover) means that Paul expected to stay at Ephesus till well on into spring, then go during the summer to Macedonia (including Philippi), and finally spend the winter in Corinth. The following spring, by Pentecost time, the apostle was at Jerusalem. Compare Acts 20:6, which says they sailed from Philippi after the Feast of Unleavened Bread. This would mean that they left at least a week after Passover, which began the celebration of the week of the Feast of Unleavened Bread. Thus, Paul would have had time to reach Jerusalem by Pentecost (Acts 20:16), which occurred fifty days after Passover.

10,11 The reference to Timothy's coming is to be connected with Acts 19:22, where Paul sent Timothy (and Erastus) into Macedonia. Therefore, at the time Paul wrote this, Timothy was traveling and was expected to arrive in Corinth (1 Cor 4:17). Because Paul remembered that the Corinthians had acted so harshly toward himself (4:1, 8–13), he was afraid they would treat the timid Timothy (1 Tim 4:12) coldly (v.10).

Paul's young helper, Timothy, had been with him for several years (Acts 16:1–3) and (as the Corinthians must have known) was doing effective work. When Timothy's work for the Lord was finished at Corinth, Paul expected the Corinthians to send him back with all his needs supplied and with their blessing—"Send him on his way in peace," he wrote (v.11). The brothers coming back with Timothy may have included Erastus (Acts 19:22), who was a Corinthian believer (Rom. 16:23).

12 The way Paul brings up the matter of Apollos—"now about" (*peri de*, cf. 7:1; 12:1; 16:1)—suggests that the Corinthians had asked about him and had perhaps suggested that he visit them. The text implies that Apollos was working independently of Paul, for

Paul could only strongly urge him to go. Apollos was apparently with Paul when the Corinthians made their inquiry, but because of the past tense of the verb ("he was quite unwilling to go"), we gather that when Paul actually wrote 1 Corinthians Apollos probably was no longer with him.

13,14 Now Paul includes several apt exhortations, as he generally does at the end of his letters (Rom 16:17-19; 1 Thess 5:12-22, et al.). His reference to "the faith" reminds one of the discussion of the faith in 15:14, 17. *Andrizesthe* (v.13) is a dramatic verb, stressing masculinity. NIV renders it, "Be men of courage," or it might be translated, "Be men and women of courage."

15-18 The reference to "the household of Stephanas" was evidently prompted by the Corinthians lack of respect for them; by personal experience the apostle knew full well that the Corinthians were capable of disrespect. There is no conflict with Acts 17:34 in the statement in v.15 that those "in the household of Stephanas" were the first converts in Achaia, for in Acts 17:34 only individuals like Dionysius, Damaris, and "a number of others" at Athens are mentioned; here, however, a whole household (including the family and slaves; cf. Latin *familia*) is in view. He urges the Corinthians to submit to the household of Stephanas and others like them because they were totally committed to serving God's people. That the service performed (*diakonia*, from which we get our word "deacon") was not an official one is evidenced by the plural subject of the verb: "they have devoted themselves to the service" (v.15). It was the entire family that did this.

Fortunatus and Achaicus—mentioned here for the first time (v.17)—were, along with Stephanas, probably the ones who brought the letter referred to in 1 Corinthians 7:1 to the apostle. That this delegation had "supplied what was lacking" may be taken to mean that their coming had encouraged Paul by showing him that the Corinthians were at least willing to ask his advice. So they "refreshed his spirit" and the spirit of the Corinthians also (v.18) in that they were willing to go to Paul. Or perhaps Paul means that the Corinthians will be refreshed when the three men get back home and tell of their visit to him.

Notes

7 The ἐάν (*ean*) subjunctive condition here, "If the Lord should permit," emphasizes Paul's complete dependence on God's will for his life. The apostle's plan for a future stay with the Corinthians is completely in the Lord's hands.

10 The ἐάν (*ean*) subjunctive condition of possibility does not deny that Timothy would come, for Paul had sent him (4:17). Timothy is on the way, but when or if he actually gets there is in God's providence.

14 The third person present imperative γινέσθω (*ginesthō*) is important here in contrast to the second person imperatives in v.13. It is as if Paul is writing to the Christian community as a whole, saying that their society should be seen to be permeated with love: "Let all you do continue to be done in love."

18 The verb ἐπιγνώσκετε (*epignōskete*, with its prefexed preposition ἐπί [*epi*], indicating thoroughness, as in 1 Cor 13:12 and Luke 1:4: "know through and through") is here (and possibly also in Matt 17:12) used in a distinctive sense of "acknowledge," "give recognition to." It should

be noted, however, that in some contexts the preposition prefixed to this verb carries no emphasis and the verb is equivalent in meaning to the simple γινώσκω (ginōskō, "know"), as in Acts 27:39.

C. Final Greetings

16:19-24

> [19]The churches in the province of Asia send you greetings. Aquila and Priscilla greet you warmly in the Lord, and so does the church that meets at their house. [20]All the brothers here send you greetings. Greet one another with a holy kiss.
>
> [21]I, Paul, write this greeting in my own hand.
>
> [22]If anyone does not love the Lord—a curse be on him. Come, O Lord!
>
> [23]The grace of the Lord Jesus be with you.
>
> [24]My love to all of you in Christ Jesus.

Characteristically Paul concludes with a series of final greetings.

19,20 First, he wants the Corinthians to know that the churches of Asia are interested in them and send greetings. The term "Asia" is used by Paul for the Roman province of Asia located in what is now western Turkey. By "churches" Paul may be implying the existence of more than one church group in Ephesus and the existence of other churches in the area, such as at Colossae, Laodicea, and Hierapolis (Col. 4:13–16; also Rev 2, 3). The Word of the Lord had spread all over the province (Acts 19:10). It was natural for Aquila and Priscilla (Greek: "Prisca") to send greetings, since they had been of such help in founding the Corinthian church (Acts 18:2). They had left Corinth with Paul (Acts 18:18) and evidently were with him at Ephesus. While they were there, a church met in their house, which was also true at Rome (v.19; cf. Rom 16:3–5). To greet one "in the Lord" was to greet him as a professed believer. The holy kiss, mentioned also in Romans 16:16; 2 Corinthians 13:12; and 1 Thessalonians 5:26, was apparently a public practice among early believers to show their Christian affection and unity in the faith. The kiss of respect and friendship was customary in the ancient East. When the Corinthians receive this letter and read it in church, Paul encourages them to give one another this kiss of affection as a pledge of their spirit of unity and forgiveness. Such a greeting may have been practiced in the synagogue by first-century A.D. Jews—a practice in which men would have kissed men and women would have kissed women. (Cf. Archibald Robertson and Alfred Plummer, "The First Epistle of St. Paul to the Corinthians" in ICC [New York: Charles Scribner's Sons, 1916], p. 399.) If this custom was taken over by the early Christian church (which would be expected, since the church was at first composed basically of Christian Jews), it is unlikely that in the worship services the church would have practiced kissing between the sexes. Later, Tertullian seems to indicate that such kissing could be mixed (Ad Uxor II.4), but, in contrast, the Apostolic Constitutions (II.57.12) and the Clementine Liturgy, in instructions for Christian worship (cf. also Justine Martyr's Apology I.65) give the injunction that laymen should kiss laymen and the women should kiss women. (See H.L. Goudge, "The First Epistle to the Corinthians," in the *Westminster Commentaries*, 4th ed. [London: Methuen, 1915], p. 171.)

21-24 Paul is now ready to take the pen to append a greeting and sign the letter, as was his practice (Col 4:18; Philem 19). This was a mark of the letter's authenticity (2 Thess 3:17). Up to this point he had dictated the letter to an amanuensis (secretary).

Then, in view of the problems existing at Corinth, Paul felt the need of adding a strong warning: "a curse be on him" (v.22). A curse (Gr. *anathema*; cf. 12:3; Rom 9:3; Gal 1:8) meant that the person involved was to be delivered over or "devoted to the divine displeasure"; he was under the wrath and curse of God (cf. John 3:36).

Paul's use of this curse is not at variance with Jesus' words in Matthew 5:34, because there Jesus qualifies what he means, by saying in effect: "Do not take oaths on the basis of any of God's created things—the heavens, the earth, or Jerusalem." But here Paul is bringing God himself to witness and is saying he who does not love and obey God is under God's wrath. Having spoken so strongly, Paul then turns to the future hope and cries out, "Marana tha"—Aramaic words that came to be used in the early church (Grosheide) and that can best be translated "Our Lord, Come." This is better than translating it as Chrysostom does: "The Lord has come" (cf. Craig, in loc.).

Paul ends with his usual shorter benediction (Gal 6:18; Eph 6:24; Phil 4:23, et al.; cf. 2 Cor 13:14 for its enlarged trinitarian form). In concluding with an expression of his own love for all the believers (v.24), Paul wants the whole Corinthian church to know that, in spite of the stern way in which he has had to rebuke them, he really loves them.

Notes

19 Πολλά (*polla*, "many") is used here adverbially to intensify the verb "greet." So the meaning is "greet warmly."

20 Φίλημα (*philema*, "kiss") is related in word formation to φιλέω (*phileo*, "love," "regard with affection"). So the meaning could be "show affection outwardly, especially kiss."

22 The εἰ (*ei*) condition with the indicative is assumed to be true: "If in fact someone does not love the Lord." The use here of the verb φιλέω (*phileō*, "show affection for") helps this idea of the factual condition along. Real Christians would show in the Christian community and in society some outward indications of their affection for and commitment to, the Lord. If some, as seemed to be the case, did not, they were showing by that that they did not belong to the Lord. In this v. Paul did not use the word ἀγαπάω (*agapaō*), which is used in the NT many times more than *phileō* and which frequently expresses the idea "love deeply with purpose and understanding" (cf. John 3:16; 17:23, 24; Eph 5:2). The word *agapaō* would not have brought out so well for Paul an additional emphasis on the necessity of the outward affectionate expression of an inward love for the Lord which he could stress by using *phileō*. True as the above distinction between *phileō* and *agapaō* may frequently be, observe that in some cases there seems to be an overlapping of meaning between the two words (cf. John 3:35 and 5:20; but see Godet's comment, in his *Commentary on the Gospel of John*, 3rd. ed., vol. 2, p. 165).

The Aramaic words Μαρανα θα (*Marana tha*) have been thought to mean (1) "The Lord has come"; (2) "Our Lord is a sign"; (3) "Thou art Lord"; and (4) "Come, O Lord," as in NIV. The last is to be preferred because of the parallel prayer in Gr. in Rev 22:20.

2 CORINTHIANS

Murray J. Harris

2 CORINTHIANS

Introduction

1. Historical Background

    a. Paul's Ephesian ministry
    b. Events between 1 and 2 Corinthians

2. Unity

    a. 2 Corinthians 2:14–7:4
    b. 2 Corinthians 6:14–7:1
    c. 2 Corinthians 8–9
    d. 2 Corinthians 10–13

3. Authorship
4. Date
5. Place of Composition
6. Occasion and Purpose
7. Special Problems

    a. The "painful (or intermediate) visit"
       1) Its historicity
       2) Its time
       3) Its occasion, purpose, and outcome
    b. The "severe letter"
       1) Its purpose
       2) Its effect
       3) Its identification
    c. The collection for the poor at Jerusalem
       1) The contributors
       2) The recipients
       3) Its significance for Paul
       4) Its acceptance
    d. Paul's opponents at Corinth
       1) Their identity
       2) Their relation to Jerusalem
       3) Their teaching

8. Theological Values
9. Structure and Themes

    a. Structure
    b. Themes

10. Bibliography
11. Outline

1. Historical Background[1]

a. *Paul's Ephesian ministry*

There is probably no part of Paul's life more difficult to reconstruct accurately than the period of thirty or so months he spent in and around Ephesus (perhaps from the fall of A.D. 53 to the spring of A.D. 56). It was a stormy period, particularly toward its close. There were plentiful evangelistic opportunities (Acts 19:8–10; 20:20, 21, 31; 1 Cor 16:9) and many healings and conversions (Acts 19:11, 18–20). There was also widespread opposition owing to Paul's conspicuous success (Acts 19:9, 13–16; 1 Cor 4:9–13; 15:30–32; 2 Cor 4:8, 9; 6:4, 5, 8–10). Whether or not the Demetrius riot (Acts 19:23–41) actually precipitated his withdrawal from Ephesus, it must have climaxed the hostility directed against him by the devotees of Artemis, not to speak of the Jewish opposition he encountered in the city (Acts 20:19).

b. *Events between 1 and 2 Corinthians*

A chronological list of the events that took place between the writing of the two Corinthian Epistles will be helpful. Many of the details will be more fully discussed in the commentary or below under "Special problems" (7.). No such reconstruction of events, however, would command universal agreement.

1. After they received 1 Corinthians, the Christians at Corinth probably rectified most of the practical abuses for which Paul had censured them in his letter. For example, he says nothing further in 2 Corinthians about abuse of the Lord's Supper (1 Cor 11:17–34) or about litigation among Christians (1 Cor 6:1–8).

2. In spite of this and because of the arrival of Judaizing intruders from Palestine (2 Cor 11:4, 22), conditions in the church at Corinth deteriorated, necessitating Paul's "painful visit" (Ephesus–Corinth–Ephesus; see 7.a. below) (see 2 Cor 2:1; 12:14, 21; 13:1, 2).

3. At some time after this visit, Paul (or his representative) was openly insulted at Corinth by a spokesman of the anti-Pauline clique (2 Cor 2:5–8, 10; 7:12).

4. Titus was sent from Ephesus to Corinth with the "severe letter" (see 7.b. below), in which Paul called for the punishment of the wrongdoer (2 Cor 2:3, 4, 6, 9; 7:8, 12). In addition, Paul instructed Titus to organize the collection for the saints at Jerusalem (2 Cor 8:6a), which had gone by default since the Palestinian interlopers had arrived and had begun to derive their support from the church (cf. 2 Cor 11:7–12, 20; 12:14). Titus was to meet Paul in Troas, or, failing that, in Macedonia (= Philippi ?) (2 Cor 2:12, 13; 7:5, 6).

5. Paul left Ephesus shortly after the Demetrius riot (Acts 19:23–20:1), began evangelism in Troas (or the Troad) (2 Cor 2:12, 13), and then suffered his "affliction in Asia" (2 Cor 1:8–11).

6. Paul crossed to Macedonia (2 Cor 2:13; 7:5) and engaged in pastoral activity (Acts 20:1, 2) while organizing the collection in the Macedonian churches (2 Cor 8:1–4; 9:2).

7. Titus arrived in Macedonia with his welcome report of the Corinthians' responsiveness to the "severe letter" (2 Cor 7:5–16).

---

[1]For information about the city of Corinth and Paul's founding of the church there, see the Introduction to 1 Corinthians.

8. Paul's pastoral work in Macedonia continued and then gave place to pioneer evangelism along the Egnatian Road and probably in Illyricum (Rom 15:19–21).

9. On returning to Macedonia and hearing of fresh problems at Corinth, Paul wrote 2 Corinthians.

10. Paul spent three months in Greece (= primarily Corinth) (Acts 20:2, 3), during which time he wrote Romans.

2. Unity

In any consideration of the integrity of 2 Corinthians, four problem areas call for discussion.

a. *2 Corinthians 2:14–7:4*

Some scholars (e.g., W. Schmithals, G. Bornkamm, W. Marxsen) find in these chapters (without 6:14–7:1) a separate letter Paul wrote to Corinth before his "severe letter" (2 Cor 10–13). Now it is true that 7:5 naturally follows 2:13 in that it resumes the narrative of Paul's movements after leaving Troas. But it is not necessary to conclude that what intervenes forms a distinct letter. Indeed, 7:5 ("For when we came into Macedonia . . .") repeats what was said in 2:13 ("I . . . went on to Macedonia"), as though Paul recognized that he had digressed. And certain terms used in 7:4 (*paraklēsis*, "comfort"; *chara*, "joy"; *thlipsis*, "affliction") reappear in comparable forms in 7:5–7.

b. *2 Corinthians 6:14–7:1*

Within "the great digression" (2:14–7:4) there is found this pericope of six verses whose authenticity has been questioned on several grounds: (1) The passage forms a self-contained unit and lacks any specific references to the Corinthian situation. (2) It seems to interrupt the flow of thought from 6:13 to 7:2. (3) It contains six NT *hapax legomena* (words that occur only once in the specified text; i.e., here, the entire NT) and the allegedly un-Pauline expression "everything that contaminates body and spirit" (7:1, NIV). (4) It is said to betray a pharisaic exclusivism inappropriate to the apostle of liberty. (5) It contains striking affinities with the theology of the Qumran sect.

To accommodate these data, some have suggested that the passage is a non-Pauline interpolation (J.A. Fitzmyer, D. Georgi, J. Gnilka) or even an anti-Pauline fragment reflecting a viewpoint similar to that of Paul's Galatian opponents (H.D. Betz). Others believe it is Pauline, but an interpolation, perhaps a fragment of the "previous letter" (1 Cor 5:9) misplaced within the Corinthian correspondence (J.C. Hurd) or a fragment fortuitously inserted at this point in 2 Corinthians (R.P.C. Hanson). K.G. Kuhn suggests that Paul has remodeled an Essene text in a Christian mold.

All these proposals seem less convincing than the suggestion that Paul may be quoting an existing ethical homily of his own composition or simply digressing in typically Pauline fashion, possibly after a dictation pause at 6:13. At least, "make room for us in your hearts" in 7:2 seems to be intentionally resumptive of "open wide your hearts" in 6:13. Whether a Pauline quotation or a brief digression, these six verses may point to the reason for that element of uneasiness and embarrassed restraint (2 Cor 6:12, 13; 7:2) that marred the Corinthians' reconciliation with Paul, viz., an unwillingness to renounce all compromise with pagan idolatry.

c. 2 Corinthians 8–9

Two hundred years ago J.S. Semler proposed that 2 Corinthians 9 was a separate epistle addressed to Christian communities in Achaia other than Corinth. In this way Semler sought to account for the apparent repetition of material in the two chapters; the seemingly independent self-contained character of each chapter; the introductory statement in 9:1, which seems to imply no earlier discussion; and Paul's appeal to the Macedonian example in 8:1–7 and to the Corinthian example in 9:1–5.

A few scholars (e.g., E. Dinkler, J. Héring, H.D. Wendland, K.F. Nickle) still argue for the separation of these two chapters, but the majority of commentators rightly claim that they belong together to the same letter as 2 Corinthians 1–7. The marked change of tone between chapters 7 and 8 is explicable by Paul's transition from relieved and almost excessive exuberance over the recent past to somewhat embarrassed and diffident admonition concerning the immediate future. Other alleged problems will be discussed during the exegesis of the text.

d. 2 Corinthians 10–13

The relationship between 2 Corinthians 10–13 and 2 Corinthians 1–9 is the principal critical problem in this Epistle. Three major positions have been taken, the first two being called "the four-chapter hypothesis": (1) 2 Corinthians 10–13 was written earlier than 2 Corinthians 1–9 and forms part of the "severe letter"; (2) 2 Corinthians 10–13 was penned later than 2 Corinthians 1–9 and forms a separate fifth letter Paul wrote to Corinth (thus "previous letter" [1 Cor 5:9], "severe letter," 2 Cor 1–9; 2 Cor 10–13); and (3) 2 Corinthians is a unity; the first nine chapters and the last four belong to the same period of Paul's ministry.

Views (1) and (2) share a common foundation, though each builds a different superstructure on it. They have in common the conviction that the change of tone at 2 Corinthians 10:1, which is announced, unexpected, pronounced, and sustained, supports the dissection of the Epistle. Patent relief, unbridled joy, and gentle appeal are succeeded, it is said, by scathing remonstrance, biting irony, and impetuous self-defense. Such a sudden change to what is almost unalleviated remonstrance would merely have served (it is thought) to renew Paul's earlier suspense concerning the Corinthians' response to harsh words and to jeopardize both his cordial relations with the Corinthians and the progress of the collection. Again, proponents of both these views observe that 2 Corinthians 1–9 gives no intimation of an imminent visit such as that promised or threatened in 2 Corinthians 12:14; 13:1.

1. *2 Corinthians 10–13 earlier than 2 Corinthians 1–9.* On this first view, the superstructure consists of two basic claims. First, several passages in 2 Corinthians 1–9, it is alleged, contain intentional allusions to previous statements in 2 Corinthians 10–13. For example, 2 Corinthians 7:16 ("I ... have complete confidence in you") is said to allude to 2 Corinthians 10:1 ("I have confidence against you"); 2:3 to 13:10; 1:23 to 13:2; 2:9 to 10:6; 1:15 and 8:22 to 10:2; 4:2 to 12:16; 7:2 to 12:17; 1:12 to 11:10. But C.H. Buck has argued that 2 Corinthians 1:23; 2:3; 2:9 might just as appropriately allude to 1 Corinthians 4:18, 19; 4:21; 4:14 respectively. And R. Batey believes that in several passages in 2 Corinthians 10–13 Paul is intentionally retracting or modifying earlier expressions of confidence (cf. 2 Cor 10:8; 11:16–18, 30 with 2 Cor 1:12; 7:4, 16; and 2 Cor 10:1, 2 with 2 Cor 1:15; 7:16). The second claim relates to the phrase "the regions beyond you" in 2 Corinthians 10:16, that refers to Italy and Spain (see Rom 15:22–32). This expression is said to be geographically accurate only if Paul is writing from Ephesus

—the city where the "severe letter" was composed! But against this we may observe that, should a third point of reference in addition to Corinth and Italy-Spain actually be required by the phrase "the regions beyond you," Paul's missionary work began in Damascus—which would give an even straighter geographical line.

This version of "the four-chapter hypothesis" was first set forth systematically by A. Hausrath in 1870. It is probably still the dominant view, claiming such proponents as P.W. Schmiedel (1892), J.H. Kennedy (1897, the classic defense), A. Plummer (1903), K. Lake (1911), M. Goguel (1926), R.H. Strachan (1935), and R.P.C. Hanson (1954).

2. *2 Corinthians 10–13 later than 2 Corinthians 1–9.* This rival form of "the four-chapter hypothesis" was first proposed in a modified form by J.S. Semler in 1776, and as the twentieth century proceeds, it seems to be gaining increasing recognition among scholars as a viable alternative to Hausrath's theory. Its supporters in this century include C. Bruston (1917), H. Windisch (1924, the classic defense), L.P. Pherigo (1949), C.H. Buck (1950), J. Munck (1954), E. Osty (1959), C.K. Barrett (1964), R. Batey (1965), and F.F. Bruce (1968).

To continue the metaphor used above, the framework of this superstructure consists of two major arguments. First, 2 Corinthians 1–9 appears to bear testimony to a less critical stage of anti-Paulinism than that reflected in 2 Corinthians 10–13, and the opposition to Paul portrayed in 2 Corinthians 1–9 is more naturally interpreted as a foreshadowing rather than as the aftermath of the anti-Paulinism that led to 2 Corinthians 10–13. Second, what may be an identical visit of Titus to Corinth is mentioned in 2 Corinthians 8:17, 18, 22 as a future event but in 2 Corinthians 12:18 as a past event.

3. *2 Corinthians a unity.* The defenders of the integrity of 2 Corinthians have not been slow in highlighting the difficulties of the two hypotheses discussed above. Concerning Hausrath's theory they ask, Why is 2 Corinthians 10–13 silent about Paul's demand for the punishment of the offender (cf. 2 Cor 2:5, 6; 7:12) when this is the one incontestable feature of the "severe letter"? Would Paul have described the irony and invective of 2 Corinthians 10–13 as stemming from "great distress and anguish of heart" and as written "with many tears" (2 Cor 2:4)? Why does 2 Corinthians 10–13 promise an imminent visit (12:14; 13:1) when the "severe letter" replaced a painful visit (2 Cor 1:23; 2:1)? Why does 2 Corinthians 1–9 not describe the church's reaction to the invective of 2 Corinthians 10–13? And why does 2 Corinthians 1–9 betray no knowledge of a previous encounter between Paul and the group of intruders at Corinth, but refer only to a single erring member of the church? How could Paul have boasted to Titus about the Corinthians (2 Cor 7:14) if he had just composed 2 Corinthians 10–13?

Semler's theory raises the following questions, among others: What accounts for the relapse of the Corinthians into a state worse than that they had recently repented of? Why does 2 Corinthians 10–13 give no indication of Paul's having received news of the deterioration of conditions at Corinth?

Regarding both theories, some ask, What historical circumstances gave rise to the combination of two originally separate letters? How may the unambiguous textual tradition witnessing to the integrity of the Epistle be explained?

In further defense of the unity of 2 Corinthians, scholars have proposed numerous explanations of the sudden change of tone at 2 Corinthians 10:1. (See the commentary at the beginning of chapter 10.) Those who have defended the unity of the Epistle include J.H. Bernard (1903), H. Lietzmann (1909), A. Menzies (1912), H.L. Goudge (1927), E.B. Allo (1936, the classic defense), R.V.G. Tasker (1945), D. Guthrie (1961), P.E. Hughes (1961), W.G. Kümmel (1963), A.M.G. Stephenson (1964), and W.H. Bates (1965).

The choice seems to lie between views 2 and 3. In this commentary the unity of 2 Corinthians is tentatively assumed.

3. Authorship

Unlike some other Pauline Epistles, 2 Corinthians has rarely been called into question with regard to its authenticity. Even the founder of the so-called "Tübingen school," F.C. Baur, acknowledged it as genuinely Pauline, along with 1 Corinthians, Galatians, and Romans. As far as internal evidence is concerned, the author twice identifies himself as Paul (2 Cor 1:1; 10:1). A pious imitator would be unlikely to portray Paul as an apostle in danger of losing his authority at Corinth or an apostle struggling to preserve the Corinthians from apostasy.

With regard to the external evidence, the Epistle was unknown to Clement of Rome (c. A.D. 96), but is quoted by Polycarp (c. A.D. 105), Irenaeus (c. A.D. 185), Clement of Alexandria (c. A.D. 210), and Tertullian (c. A.D. 210). Also it is listed in Marcion's *Apostolicon* (c. A.D. 140) and in the Muratorian canon (late second century A.D.).

4. Date

By a brief examination of the data, we may reach a tentative conclusion regarding this complex question.

1. 1 Corinthians was probably written and sent in the spring, perhaps shortly before Passover. There may be allusions to an imminent paschal celebration in 1 Corinthians 5:7, 8 and to the presentation of the firstfruits in 1 Corinthians 15:20. And in 1 Corinthians 16:8 Paul indicates his intention to "stay on at Ephesus until Pentecost." This Pentecost must have been at least one or two months away, to allow time for Paul to take advantage of the opportunities for evangelism (1 Cor 16:9).

2. 2 Corinthians was probably written in the fall (autumn). Acts 20:6 relates that Paul left Philippi for Jerusalem in the spring ("after the Feast of Unleavened Bread"). Previously, three winter months had been spent in Corinth (Acts 20:3) where Paul arrived from Macedonia. Intimations of a forthcoming visit to Corinth found in 2 Corinthians 12:14; 13:1 suggest the Epistle was written shortly before that winter.

3. Possibly as much as eighteen or more months intervened between the writing of the two Epistles. Of course, if they were written in the spring and the fall, they could be dated in the same year, but the "winter" mentioned in 1 Corinthians 16:6 need not correspond to the winter alluded to in Acts 20:3, since Paul is simply stating tentative plans that were in fact superseded by those recorded in 2 Corinthians 1:15, 16. Nor does the phrase "last year" in 2 Corinthians 8:10; 9:2 necessarily point to a six-month interval. Which calendar Paul was using is uncertain. Thus the new year may have arrived on January 1 (Roman year), in the spring (Jewish ecclesiastical year), in midsummer (Athenian Olympiads), or in the fall (Jewish civil and Macedonian year). There are two positive pointers to a possible eighteen-month interval. In the first place, adequate time must be allowed for Paul to engage in pioneer evangelism along the Egnatian Way and in Illyricum of which he speaks in Romans 15:19. All agree that if Paul did evangelize the Roman province of Illyricum ("all the way around to Illyricum" may be inclusive or exclusive), it must have occurred between his Ephesian residence (Acts 19) and his arrival in Greece (Acts 20:2). Again, it is difficult, though not impossible, to fit into a

six-month period all the travel between Ephesus and Corinth and all the events at Corinth that took place between the writing of 1 Corinthians and 2 Corinthians (see 1.b. above).

4. The suggestion may therefore be made that 1 Corinthians was sent in the spring of A.D. 55 (Passover probably fell on April 2 and Pentecost on May 22 that year—so F.J. Badcock), while the sending of 2 Corinthians (assuming its unity) may be placed in the fall of A.D. 56. On the other hand, if 2 Corinthians 10–13 belongs to a later period than 2 Corinthians 1–9 (see 2.d.2 above), these last four chapters will date from the fall of A.D. 56, while the first nine chapters may have been sent at any time between the fall of A.D. 55 and early fall A.D. 56.

5. A tentative chronology of the major events occurring between 1 and 2 Corinthians (see 1.b. above) may now be suggested.

1 Corinthians	Spring A.D. 55
Painful visit	Summer or Fall 55
Severe letter	Spring 56
Paul leaves Ephesus	Spring 56
Paul in Macedonia	Summer 56
Titus arrives in Macedonia	Summer 56
2 Corinthians	Fall 56

5. Place of Composition

Several references within 2 Corinthians suggest that Paul was in the province of Macedonia when writing (see 7:5; 8:1; 9:2–4). Of special significance is the present tense (*kauchōmai*) in 9:2, "I have been boasting about it [viz., your eagerness to help] to the Macedonians" (NIV).

This is confirmed by those MSS (e.g., B^c K L P) that note in the subscription to the Epistle that it was written "from Philippi." Also, in 2 Corinthians 11:9 "Macedonia" means Philippi (see Phil 4:15). But of course it is not impossible that Paul was at Thessalonica or Berea (also Macedonian cities), since 2 Corinthians 8:1 and 9:2 speak of the churches and people of Macedonia and not simply of the Philippians.

6. Occasion and Purpose

The outline of events given above (1.b.) suggests that the circumstances prompting Paul to send 2 Corinthians were twofold: the arrival of his pastoral assistant Titus, who brought welcome news of the favorable response of the majority of the Corinthians to the "severe letter" (see 2 Cor 7:6–16), and the arrival of fresh, disturbing news concerning Corinth. An interval between the arrival of Titus and the sending of 2 Corinthians seems indicated by 2 Corinthians 7:8 (see the commentary).

Paul had several overriding purposes in writing. He wished (1) to express his great relief and delight at the Corinthians' positive response to his "severe letter" that had been delivered and reinforced by Titus (2 Cor 2:6, 9, 12–14; 7:5–16); (2) to exhort the Corinthians to complete their promised collection for the saints at Jerusalem before his arrival on the next visit (2 Cor 8:6, 7, 10, 11; 9:3–5); (3) to prepare them for his forthcoming visit by having them engage in self-examination and self-judgment (12:14; 13:1, 5,

11), so that they could discover the proper criteria for distinguishing between rival apostles (chapters 10 to 13); and so that Paul could be spared the pain of having to exercise discipline (2 Cor 10:2, 5, 6, 11; 11:3; 12:19–21; 13:10).

There were, of course, other subsidiary aims, such as his desire to inform them of the intensity of his trouble in Asia and solicit their prayer for future deliverance (1:8–11), to explain his changes of itinerary (1:12–2:4), to encourage the reaffirmation of their love for the penitent wrongdoer (2:5–11), to insist on their separation from all idolatrous associations (6:14–7:1), and to describe the true nature and high calling of the Christian ministry (2:14–7:4).

Was 2 Corinthians successful where 1 Corinthians had been only partially so? Apparently it was, because Paul made the promised visit (Acts 20:2, 3) and during this three-month stay in "Greece" (primarily Corinth, in the winter of A.D. 56–57) he wrote or completed his letter to the Romans, which gives no hint of trouble at Corinth. Also Romans 15:26 shows that the Corinthians did complete their collection for their fellow-believers at Jerusalem.

On the other hand, when Clement of Rome wrote to the church at Corinth in A.D. 96 he had to rebuke the same internal strife and rebellion against authority that had plagued the church forty years earlier.

7. Special Problems

a. The "painful (or intermediate) visit"

1) Its historicity

Although Luke makes no reference to the visit in Acts, there are several passages in 2 Corinthians showing that Paul had already visited Corinth twice, the second visit being "painful." First, 2 Corinthians 12:14 and 13:1, 2 refer to two prior actual visits. Second, 2 Corinthians 2:1 and 12:21 indicate that one of the two earlier visits was painful (en lypē, 2 Cor 2:1). It is inconceivable that Paul would describe his founding visit as "painful," in spite of the opposition he encountered at that time (Acts 18:6, 9, 10, 12–17).

2) Its time

Some scholars have argued that the visit occurred either before or after the "previous letter" (1 Cor 5:9) was written, i.e., before 1 Corinthians. But the silence of 1 Corinthians about a painful visit damages this hypothesis. Only one previous visit is presupposed in 1 Corinthians (2:1–5; 3:1–3, 6, 10; 11:2, 23), though a second visit is announced (1 Cor 4:18, 19, 21; 11:34; 16:2, 3, 5–7). And why would painful memories be revived in 2 Corinthians after being ignored or forgotten in 1 Corinthians?

The silence of 1 Corinthians and the allusions in 2 Corinthians concerning this distressing visit point to the same conclusion—the visit took place between 1 and 2 Corinthians. More precisely, it occurred after 1 Corinthians and before the "severe letter," because in writing 2 Corinthians Paul is dependent on Titus for his information about the outcome of the "severe letter"; he had not himself visited the church after the sending of the "severe letter."

3) Its occasion, purpose, and outcome

At some stage after the receipt of 1 Corinthians at Corinth, conditions within the church there deteriorated. Possibly there was a cleavage over the implementing of Paul's injunction of 1 Corinthians 5:2, 5, 13 about the incestuous man. Perhaps an ultra-loyal group of Paulinists (cf. 1 Cor 1:12; 2 Cor 2:6, 7) confronted the influential anti-Pauline clique of intruders from Palestine and their Corinthian adherents in a bid for control of the uncommitted and vacillating majority who were acquiescing in the *status quo* and were unwilling to follow either minority in making an issue of a matter of private morals. In any case, Paul received adverse news, perhaps from Timothy, that induced him to hurry to Corinth to reinforce the effect of 1 Corinthians and prevent any further undermining of his authority at Corinth through the activities of the Judaizing pseudo-apostles.

Little is known about what happened during the visit. Certainly Paul would have explained the reasons for the change in his travel plans (see the commentary on 1:15-17), for the Corinthians were expecting him to arrive from Macedonia (cf. 1 Cor 16:5, 6), not from Ephesus. Apparently he rebuked those guilty of immorality ("those who sinned earlier," 2 Cor 12:21; 13:2), but refrained from exercising summary discipline, choosing rather to issue a warning: "If I come again, I will not spare you" (cf. 2 Cor 13:2). Also he seems to have been humiliated by the Corinthians' failure to champion his cause against the false apostles (cf. 2 Cor 12:21). It is unlikely that the visit became "painful" because Paul was affronted by an intruder or a native Corinthian (cf. 2 Cor 2:5-11; 7:12). He was not a man who would retreat before an enemy only to resort to a letter and the intervention of his delegate Titus to gain what he himself had failed to achieve.

The sequel of this brief visit was that Paul or his representative was personally insulted by some individual at Corinth in an open act of defiance by which all the Corinthians were to some extent pained—if not at the actual time, at least later on (2 Cor 2:5-11; 7:12). So Paul sent Titus to Corinth after considerable persuasion (2 Cor 7:14) as his personal envoy to deliver the "severe letter" and organize the collection (2 Cor 8:6a).

b. The "severe letter"

"I wrote you out of great distress and anguish of heart and with many tears, not to grieve you but to let you know the depth of my love for you" (2 Cor 2:4). Such is Paul's own description of what has come to be known as the "severe letter," the "sorrowful letter," or the "letter of tears." (The preceding account of the "painful visit" and its aftermath [7.a.] includes a sketch of the circumstances that led to Paul's writing this letter.)

1) Its purpose

Clearly the general aim of the "severe letter" was to arouse the church to discipline "the one who did the wrong" (2 Cor 2:6, 9; 7:12). But 2 Corinthians contains four additional statements of Paul's purpose in writing: (1) to spare the Corinthians and himself another painful visit (1:23-2:4), (2) to demonstrate his affection for the Corinthians (2:4), (3) to put to the test the Corinthians' obedience to apostolic authority (2:9), and (4) to make them aware before God of their genuine concern and affection for him as their spiritual father (7:12; cf. 1 Cor 4:15)—in retrospect, Paul states this last as his principal objective.

2) *Its effect*

It was Titus who related to Paul the outcome of this "sorrowful letter" (2 Cor 7:6–16). The Corinthians as a whole had felt concern, remorse, and even apprehension over their behavior during the "painful visit." They now longed to see Paul again to assure him of their change of attitude. They had been zealous to punish the offender whose scandalous action had now provoked their indignation. Some Corinthians were in danger of being merciless in their punishment; so Paul needed to stay their hand and encourage them to forgive the offender now that he had repented (2 Cor 2:6–8).

When Titus gave his report, Paul's initial reaction was to regret (*metemelomēn*) that he had caused such pain, though that pain had been only temporary (2 Cor 7:8). Upon reflection, however, his opinion had altered: *ou metamelomai*, "I do not regret it" (2 Cor 7:8). The infliction of pain, though unavoidable, had proved remedial; in fact, God had inspired their grief and had prevented the letter from causing them any permanent injury (2 Cor 7:9–11a).

3) *Its identification*

With respect to the identity of the "severe letter," we have three alternatives. It may be identified with (1) 1 Corinthians; (2) a letter, partially preserved in 2 Corinthians 10–13, that preceded 2 Corinthians 1–9; or (3) a letter, no longer extant, written between 1 and 2 Corinthians.

a) *1 Corinthians*

This time-honored identification rests chiefly on the similarity between 1 Corinthians 5 and 2 Corinthians 2:5–11; 7:12. The incestuous man is "the one who did the wrong"; this man's father is "the one who suffered the wrong." After being handed over to Satan (= excommunication?) "so that his sinful nature may be destroyed" (1 Cor 5:5), the wrongdoer repented. In 2 Corinthians 2:7, 8 Paul urges that he be received back into church fellowship.

In spite of the impressive array of scholars who endorse this view, there are several compelling reasons for questioning it. First, 2 Corinthians 2:6, 9 suggests that the "letter of tears" dealt primarily with the wrongdoer and the need for his punishment. This is not true of 1 Corinthians. Second, why would Paul personally offer to forgive a man guilty of incest (2 Cor 2:10)? Third, if these references in the two Corinthian Epistles are to be equated, the incestuous man was not simply living with his *widowed* stepmother, but with his stepmother while his father ("the injured party") was still living. Surely such an offense, more precisely described as adultery (*moicheia*) than as sexual immorality (*porneia*, 1 Cor 5:1), would have scandalized even the Corinthians and impelled them to seek some form of redress for the father, if not punishment for the son. Fourth, 1 Corinthians does not seem to have been written in the place of another painful visit (see 1 Cor 4:18, 19; 11:34; 16:2, 3, 5–7) as is demanded by 2 Corinthians 1:23; 2:1, 3.

b) *A letter embodying 2 Corinthians 10–13*

Many commentators who believe that 2 Corinthians combines two originally separate letters place 2 Corinthians 10–13 before 2 Corinthians 1–9 and affirm that these four chapters form the principal part of the "letter of tears" (A. Hausrath's theory). The difficulties of this proposal have been discussed above (2.d.3).

c) A lost "intermediate letter"

Scholars who reject the two identifications of the "sorrowful letter" mentioned above are compelled to assume that the letter is no longer extant. They believe that it was probably an intensely personal letter, quite brief, and addressed to a specific unedifying situation, so that its nonpreservation is not a matter of surprise (cf. the "previous letter" of 1 Cor 5:9, 11).

This is the view adopted in this commentary.

c. The collection for the poor at Jerusalem

From A.D. 52 to 57 a considerable proportion of Paul's time and energies was devoted to organizing a collection among his Gentile churches for "the poor among the saints in Jerusalem" (Rom 15:26).

1) The contributors

There is general agreement that Acts 20:4 contains a list of the appointed delegates from certain Gentile churches who were Paul's traveling companions on his final visit to Jerusalem when he was delivering the collection. Sopater, Aristarchus, and Secundus represented the Macedonian Christians (see Acts 19:22; 2 Cor 8:1–5; 9:2, 4); Gaius and perhaps Timothy were delegates from Galatia (see Acts 18:23; 1 Cor 16:1); Tychicus and Trophimus traveled on behalf of the churches of Asia (see Acts 20:35). It is not known who represented Achaia, though believers in that province contributed to the offering (see Rom 15:26; 1 Cor 16:1–4; 2 Cor 8–9).

2) The recipients

The offering was destined for the Hebrew Christians at Jerusalem, who may have referred to themselves as "the poor" (hoi ptōchoi, Rom 15:26; Gal 2:10; = Heb. hā'ebyô-nîm, cf. Ebionites)—those who were completely dependent on God's provision (cf. Matt 5:3). Several factors account for their continuing poverty: (1) After their conversion to Christianity many Jews in Jerusalem would have been ostracized socially and economically. (2) The "experiment in community sharing" described in Acts 2:44, 45 and 4:32, 34, 35 undoubtedly would have aggravated, though it did not cause, their poverty. (3) Persistent food shortages in Palestine because of overpopulation culminated in the famine of A.D. 46 in the time of Emperor Claudius (Acts 11:27–30). (4) As the mother-church of Christendom, the Jerusalem church was obliged to support a proportionately large number of teachers and probably to provide hospitality for frequent Christian visitors to the holy city. (5) Jews in Palestine were subject to a crippling twofold taxation —Jewish and Roman.

3) Its significance for Paul

Some of the many motives that impelled Paul to organize the offering may be mentioned here. First and foremost among them was brotherly love (Rom 12:13; 13:8; Gal 6:10), making the offering a tangible expression of the interdependence of the members of the body of Christ (1 Cor 12:25, 26) that would honor Christ (2 Cor 8:19) and help effect equality of provision (2 Cor 8:13–15). Moreover, it effectively symbolized the unity of Jew and Gentile in Christ (Eph 2:11–22) and may have been designed to win over those jewish Christians who were still suspicious of Paul's Gentile mission (cf. Acts

11:2, 3). Also, the collection dramatized in material terms the spiritual indebtedness of Gentile believers to the church at Jerusalem (Rom 15:19, 27; cf. 1 Cor 9:11). Again, it marked the culmination of Paul's ministry in the eastern Mediterranean as he planned to turn westward after visiting Rome (Rom 15:24, 28). And finally, it was a visible sign of Paul's fulfillment of a promise (2 Cor 8:19; Gal 2:10) and perhaps a way of partially compensating for his earlier systematic persecution of the Jerusalem saints (Acts 8:3; 9:1; 26:10, 11; 1 Cor 15:9; Gal 1:13; 1 Tim 1:13).

4) *Its acceptance*

In spite of Paul's misgivings about the success of the enterprise (Rom 15:31), the offering was evidently gratefully received on his arrival in Jerusalem. Acts 21:17 suggests this. It is unlikely, however, that the collection accomplished all that Paul had hoped for regarding Jewish-Gentile relations within the Church. For example, Acts contains no record of Paul's receiving help from the Jerusalem church during his imprisonment in Jerusalem and Caesarea.

For an illuminating comparison between Paul's collection and the half-shekel temple tax paid annually by Jews, see K.F. Nickle, *The Collection* (Naperville: Allenson, 1966), pp. 87–93.

At the beginning of chapter 8 (p. 365 below) the progress of the collection at Corinth prior to the writing of 2 Corinthians is briefly summarized. For the outcome of the collection at Corinth, see the commentary at 9:15.

d. *Paul's opponents at Corinth*

Regarding the problem of Paul's opponents at Corinth, two basic questions clamor for solution: (1) their identity, and (2) their relation to the Twelve. Were they Jews or Judaizers or Gnostics? Were they in some sense delegates sent by the Jerusalem church, or were they wandering Hellenistic preachers with no relation to Judea?

In recent years these problems have prompted numerous articles, the more important being by E. Käsemann (1942), G. Friedrich (1963), and C.K. Barrett (1971) and several full-scale studies, including W. Schmithals, *Die Gnosis in Korinth* (1956, 1965[2])[2] (= *Gnosticism in Corinth*, 1971); D. Georgi, *Die Gegner des Paulus im 2. Korintherbrief* (1964); D.W. Oostendorp, *Another Jesus: A Gospel of Jewish-Christian Superiority* (1967).

1) *Their identity*

Although some scholars (e.g., F. Godet and W. Schmithals) have equated Paul's opponents in 2 Corinthians with those in 1 Corinthians, it is necessary to distinguish between certain native Corinthians who fostered the dissension described in 1 Corinthians and certain adversaries from outside Corinth (2 Cor 10:14; 11:4) who had a malevolent influence on the Corinthian believers. The link, if any, between these two groups may be found in the Christ "pɛ ·ty" (thus E.B. Allo) or the Peter "party" (thus C.K. Barrett).

That Paul's adversaries were Jews is acknowledged on all hands (cf. 2 Cor 11:22). But were they Judaizers? If a Judaizer is defined as one who insists on circumcision as a prerequisite for salvation (cf. Acts 15:1), they were not Judaizers, for 2 Corinthians lacks

---

[2]The superscript number immediately following the date refers to the edition of the book; i.e., here, the second edition.

any trace of a dispute over circumcision. But if a Judaizer is a person who tries to impose Jewish practices upon Gentiles as conditions either for salvation or for the enjoyment of Christian fellowship, then the opposition to Paul may appropriately be labeled Judaizing. Evidently his opponents did not insist on circumcision, as occurred at Galatia (Gal 6:12, 13), or on calendrical observances, as did the opposition at Colossae (Col 2:16). Perhaps as part of their general strategy to reproduce Jerusalem in Corinth or to claim Corinth for Jerusalem, they sought to impose on the Corinthians the provisions of the codicil of the Apostolic Decree, especially its food regulations (Acts 15:20, 29).[3] This is the suggestion of F.F. Bruce and C.K. Barrett and the view adopted in this commentary.

The fact that in 2 Corinthians Paul is less concerned with wisdom, knowledge, and *charismata* than he was in 1 Corinthians makes it unlikely that his adversaries were simply gnostic, far less Gnostics, who, in any case, would not be likely to carry commendatory letters. Some scholars (notably D. Georgi and G. Friedrich) have therefore proposed that Paul's rivals in 2 Corinthians were Hellenistic-Jewish itinerant preachers who professed to be servants of Christ and *theioi andres* ("divine men"). But again, letters of commendation would hardly be necessary for such wonder-workers whose deeds were their credentials.

2) Their relation to Jerusalem

What was the relation between Paul's antagonists at Corinth and the church of Jerusalem, particularly the three "pillars" (Gal 2:9) or the Twelve? Three views are possible. His antagonists might have been (1) an official delegation; (2) a semi-official delegation that left Jerusalem with the cognizance and tacit approval of the Twelve but which misrepresented them; or (3) self-appointed agents from Judea who appealed to the authority of the Twelve, especially Peter, in defense of their Judaizing program. Each position has had its proponents.

In support of the third view, several points may be made. First of all, that these persons were from Palestine may be inferred from the term *Hebraioi* (2 Cor 11:22; cf. Phil 3:5), which refers to Jews of Palestinian descent, especially those whose linguistic and cultural heritage was Palestinian, and perhaps from a claim they may have made to have known Christ personally (cf. 2 Cor 5:16). Moreover, we should probably draw a distinction between the "super-apostles" of 2 Corinthians 11:5; 12:11 and the "false apostles" of 11:13. The former expression may be Paul's ironical description of the exalted view of the Twelve held by the "false apostles" who appealed to them. Paul uses the term "false apostles" (*pseudapostoloi*) to describe the Palestinian intruders who falsely laid claim to apostleship and preached "another gospel" (2 Cor 11:4). Again, some persons from Judea had already invoked the authority of the Twelve without their authorization (Acts 15:24; cf. Gal 2:4), while others (prophets) had left Jerusalem apparently without specific commission (Acts 11:27). Whether or not the "false apostles" carried letters of commendation from Jerusalem is discussed at 3:1. Finally, one clique at Corinth had already set a precedent for appealing to Jerusalem by using the name of Peter (1 Cor 1:12).

We now turn to the message of these Jewish missionaries.

---

[3]There is no evidence in the Corinthian Epistles of Paul's own effort to enforce at Corinth the supplementary addition to the Decree (cf. Acts 15:41; 16:4) or that he regarded it as permanently and universally binding on Christians.

3) *Their teaching*

There can be no doubt that the primary aim of Paul's adversaries was to undermine and so destroy Paul's apostolic authority. What they taught was calculated to bring about Paul's downfall, at least in Corinth, and to establish their own credentials as authentic servants of Christ.

Paul, they alleged, was a double-minded worldling who acted capriciously (2 Cor 1:17, 18; 10:2–4) and lorded it over his converts (1:24; 7:2), so restricting their spiritual development (6:12). He carried no letters of commendation (3:1; 10:13, 14) because he commended himself (4:2, 5; 5:12; 6:4; 10:12, 18; 12:11; cf. 1 Cor 9:1–3; 14:18; 15:10b) as would a madman (5:13; 11:1, 16–19; 12:6, 11) or imposter (6:8). Just as his gospel was obscure (4:3; 6:2, 3), so also the letters he wrote were unintelligible or devious (1:13) and written with the perverse aim of condemning and destroying (7:2, 3; 10:8; 13:10) and causing pain (2:2, 4, 5; 7:8). He was impressive at a distance but weak and contemptible when he deigned to make a personal appearance (10:1, 2, 9–11; 11:6; 13:3, 4, 9). His refusal to accept remuneration from the Corinthians proved that he cared little for them and that he was aware of being a counterfeit apostle, not the mouthpiece of Christ (11:5, 7–11, 13; 12:11–15; 13:3a, 6). Yet he exploited the willingness of a church to support him by having his agents organize a collection, ostensibly for the saints at Jerusalem but in reality for himself (12:16–18). Such were some of the charges made by Paul's calumniators.

They seem to have made many claims about themselves, as may be inferred from Paul's reply (4:5). Proof of their genuine apostolicity could be found, they claimed, in their polished eloquence and erudite knowledge (11:6), their visions and revelations (5:13; 12:1, 7), their healing miracles (12:12), their possession of commendatory letters (3:1), their willingness to accept remuneration (11:12; cf. 1 Cor 9:5–7, 11, 12), their pure Palestinian origin (11:22), their being disciples of Jesus (5:16; 10:7), their high estimate of Moses (3:7–16) and Abraham (11:22), and their preaching of the true gospel of Jesus (11:4). Little wonder that the impressionable Corinthians were swayed by the vaunted self-sufficiency (3:5) of these rival claimants to apostleship!

8. Theological Values

Traditionally, Paul's two letters to Timothy and one to Titus are called "the Pastorals." But 2 Corinthians has a strong claim to be recognized as the Pastoral Epistle *par excellence*, because it contains not "pure" but "applied" *pastoralia*. Paul the pastor ha unconsciously penned a profound, though brief, autobiography. In this Epistle we can see beautiful examples of the tenderness of a spiritual shepherd sensitive to the needs of his flock (1:24; 2:6, 7; 6:1; 10:2; 13:5, 10) and also the pleading of a spiritual father jealous of his children's affection, purity, and unity (6:11–13; 11:2, 3; 13:11). To investigate Paul's pastoral techniques evident in both Corinthian Epistles is a rewarding study.

The Epistle also contains the classic discussions of the theology of Christian suffering (1:3–11; 4:7–18; 6:3–10; 12:1–10), the role of a minister of the new covenant (2:14–17; 4:1–5; 5:16–21; 11:28, 29; 12:14, 15), the relation between the old and new covenants (3:7–18), the theology of death and resurrection (4:7–5:10), and the principles and practice of Christian stewardship (2 Cor 8–9).

9. Structure and Themes

a. *Structure*

Second Corinthians falls into three clearly discernible sections: (1) chapters 1 to 7, which contain Paul's explanation of his conduct and apostolic ministry, are primarily apologetic; (2) chapters 8 and 9, which deal with the collection for the saints at Jerusalem, are hortatory; and (3) chapters 10 to 13, which form Paul's vindication of his apostolic authority, are polemical.

b. *Themes*

The distinctive tone of 2 Corinthians 1–7 (or 1–9) may be summed up in the phrase *chairein dei* ("I must rejoice"; see 2:3; 6:10; 7:4, 7, 9, 13, 16) while the expression *paraklēsis en thlipsei* ("comfort in the midst of affliction"; see 1:3–7; 7:4, 7, 13) epitomizes its major theme. On the other hand, *kauchasthai dei* (12:1, "I must boast") sums up the spirit of 2 Corinthians 10–13, and *dynamis en astheneia* (12:9, "strength in the midst of weakness") reveals its chief emphasis.

It is in establishing the principal themes of 2 Corinthians, rather than in illustrating its integrity or partition, that linguistic arguments are most potent. In 2 Corinthians 1–9 *paraklēsis* (as "comfort") occurs nine times and its verbal form (*parakaleō*, "comfort") eight times; *thlipsis* ("affliction") is found nine times and *thlibō* ("afflict") three times; *chara* ("joy") occurs twice and *chairō* ("rejoice") four times with reference to the joy of Paul or Titus at the Corinthian reconciliation. However, none of these words (except for two uses of *chairō* in 13:9, 11) is found in 2 Corinthians 10–13. Again, while *astheneia* ("weakness") is found six times and *astheneō* ("be weak") seven times in 2 Corinthians 10–13, neither word occurs in chapters 1 to 9. Finally, in chapters 10 to 13 the *kauchasthai* ("boast") concept appears nineteen times, always in an apologetic or vindicative sense, as opposed to the ten uses of the root in chapters 1 to 9 always in a complimentary sense.

10. Bibliography

Commentaries

Allo, E.B. *Saint Paul. Seconde Épître aux Corinthiens.* Paris: J. Gabalda, 1956, second edition.
Barrett, C.K. *A Commentary on the Second Epistle to the Corinthians.* London: A. and C. Black, 1973.
Bernard, J.H. "The Second Epistle to the Corinthians" in *The Expositor's Greek Testament.* Edited by W. Robertson Nicoll. Grand Rapids: Eerdmans, 1970 reprint of 1903 work, 3:1–119.
Bruce, F.F. *1 and 2 Corinthians.* London: Oliphants, 1971.
Denney, J. *The Second Epistle to the Corinthians.* London: Hodder and Stoughton, 1894.
Héring, J. *The Second Epistle of Saint Paul to the Corinthians.* London: Epworth, 1967.
Hodge, C. *A Commentary on the Second Epistle to the Corinthians.* London: Banner of Truth, 1959 reprint of 1857 work.
Hughes, P.E. *Paul's Second Epistle to the Corinthians.* Grand Rapids: Eerdmans, 1962.
Lietzmann, H. *An die Korinther. I. II.* Enlarged by W.G. Kümmel. Tübingen: J.C.B. Mohr, 1949, fourth edition.
Meyer, H.A.W. *Critical and Exegetical Handbook to the Epistles to the Corinthians.* New York: Funk and Wagnalls, 1884.

Plummer, A. *A Critical and Exegetical Commentary on the Second Epistle of St. Paul to the Corinthians.* Edinburgh: T. and T. Clark, 1915.
———. *The Second Epistle of Paul the Apostle to the Corinthians.* Cambridge: Cambridge University Press, 1903.
Tasker, R.V.G. *The Second Epistle of Paul to the Corinthians.* Grand Rapids: Eerdmans, 1958.

General Works

Barrett, C.K. *The Signs of an Apostle.* Philadelphia: Fortress, 1972.
Collange, J.F. *Énigmes de la Deuxième Épître de Paul aux Corinthiens.* Cambridge: Cambridge University Press, 1972.
Kennedy, J.H. *The Second and Third Epistles of St. Paul to the Corinthians.* London: Methuen, 1900.
Metzger, B.M. *A Textual Commentary on the Greek New Testament.* New York: United Bible Societies, 1971.
Nickle, K.F. *The Collection.* Naperville: Allenson, 1966.
Robertson, A.T. *The Glory of the Ministry.* New York: Revell, 1911.
Schmithals, W. *Gnosticism in Corinth.* New York: Abingdon, 1971.

Articles

Barrett, C.K. "Christianity at Corinth" in *Bulletin of the John Rylands Library*, XLVI (2, 1964), pp. 269–297.
———. "Paul's Opponents in II Corinthians" in *New Testament Studies*, XVII (3, 1971), pp. 233–254.
Bates, W.H. "The Integrity of II Corinthians" in *New Testament Studies*, XII (1, 1965), pp. 56–69.
Berry, R. "Death and Life in Christ. The Meaning of 2 Corinthians 5. 1–10" in *Scottish Journal of Theology*, XIV (1, 1961), pp. 60–76.
Bruce, F.F. "Paul and Jerusalem" in *Tyndale Bulletin*, XIX (1968), pp. 3–25.
Dunn, J.D.G. "2 Corinthians III. 17—'The Lord is the Spirit'" in *Journal of Theological Studies*, XXI (2, 1970), pp. 309–320.
Harris, M.J. "Paul's View of Death in 2 Corinthians 5:1–10" in *New Dimensions in New Testament Study*. Edited by R.N. Longenecker and M.C. Tenney. Grand Rapids: Zondervan, 1974, pp. 317–328.
Moule, C.F.D. "St. Paul and Dualism: The Pauline Concept of Resurrection" in *New Testament Studies*, XII (2, 1966), pp. 106–123.
Proudfoot, C.M. "Imitation of Realistic Participation? A Study of Paul's Concept of 'Suffering with Christ'" in *Interpretation*, XVII (2, 1963), pp. 140–160.
Stephenson, A.M.G. "A Defence of the Integrity of 2 Corinthians" in *The Authorship and Integrity of the New Testament*. London: SPCK, 1965, pp. 82–97.

11. Outline

Text and Exposition

I. Paul's Explanation of His Conduct and Apostolic Ministry (2 Corinthians 1–7)

A. *Introduction* (1:1–11)

1. *Salutation*

1:1, 2

> ¹Paul, an apostle of Christ Jesus by the will of God, and Timothy our brother,
> To the church of God in Corinth, together with all the saints throughout Achaia:
> ²Grace and peace to you from God our Father and the Lord Jesus Christ.

1 In all his Epistles except 1 and 2 Thessalonians, Philippians, and Philemon, Paul begins with a reference to his being "an apostle" of Christ Jesus. Although he was not one of the twelve chosen by Christ (Mark 3:14–19), Paul claimed equality with them (see 11:5; 12:11; Gal 2:6) on the basis of the special revelation of Christ God gave him at the time of his conversion (1 Cor 9:1; Gal 1:15, 16). Like them, he had been commissioned "by the will of God" to be a "chosen instrument" (Acts 9:15).

Paul's delight in speaking of a fellow Christian as "our brother" (*ho adelphos*) may be traced to Ananias's generous and reassuring use of that term ("Brother Saul," Acts 9:17) at a time when Damascene believers had every reason to regard Saul as the archenemy of the church (Acts 9:1, 2, 13, 14). The mention of Timothy (not Sosthenes, cf. 1 Cor 1:1) as a cosender of the letter may be intended to reinstate this timid young man (1 Tim 4:12; 2 Tim 1:7; 2:1) in the eyes of the Corinthians, possibly after his failure or limited success as Paul's representative at Corinth (see 1 Cor 4:17; 16:10, 11). But it is not certain that Timothy reached Corinth from Macedonia (Acts 19:22). At any rate, Titus had replaced Timothy as Paul's chief envoy to Corinth by the time this letter was written.

Paul refers to the principal addressees not as "the church of Corinth" but as "the church of God in Corinth," the local representatives of God's universal church. Linked with the Corinthians are "the saints"—God's people (*hoi hagioi*)—at such places as Athens (cf. Acts 17:34) and Cenchrea (cf. Rom 16:1). Perhaps this joint address explains the absence of personal greetings at the end of chapter thirteen.

2 This characteristically Pauline (and also Petrine) salutation combines and elevates the traditional Greek and Hebrew greetings. *Chairein* ("greetings," Acts 15:23; 23:26; James 1:1) becomes *charis* ("grace," God's unsought and unmerited favor), to which Paul makes reference at the beginning and end of every Epistle. And the Hebrew *šālôm* ("peace") is replaced by *eirēnē* ("peace"), the latter term referring to the peace that comes to man from God (cf. Phil 4:7) as a result of his having peace with God (Rom 5:1).

2. *Gratitude for divine comfort*

1:3–7

> ³Praise be to the God and Father of our Lord Jesus Christ, the Father of compassion and the God of all comfort, ⁴who comforts us in all our troubles, so that we can comfort those in any trouble with the comfort we ourselves have received from God. ⁵For just as the sufferings of Christ flow over into our lives, so also through Christ our comfort overflows. ⁶If we are distressed, it is for your

> comfort and salvation; if we are comforted, it is for your comfort, which produces in you patient endurance of the same sufferings we suffer. [7]And our hope for you is firm, because we know that just as you share in our sufferings, so also you share in our comfort.

The paragraph embodies the chief emphasis of chapters 1-7: "comfort in the midst of affliction" (see Introduction, 9). The *paraklēsis* ("comfort") root occurs no fewer than ten times in vv.3-7, the *thlipsis* ("trouble," "affliction") root three times, and the *pathēma* ("suffering") root four times.

3,4 Paul generally follows his salutation with thanksgiving for the divine grace evident in the lives of his converts (e.g., 1 Cor 1:4-9) and a summary of his prayer requests for them (e.g., Phil 1:3-11; Col 1:3-12). Here, however, he offers praise to God for consoling and encouraging him (see note), while later (v.11) he solicits his converts' prayer for himself. This untypical preoccupation with his own circumstances shows the distressing nature of the experience in Asia he had so recently been delivered from (vv.8-10). He highlights the aspects of God's character he had come to value in deeper measure as a result of personal need and divine response, viz., God's limitless compassion (cf. Ps 145:9; Mic 7:19) and never-failing comfort (cf. Isa 40:1; 51:3, 12; 66:13).

Paul sees his suffering (note Acts 9:15, 16; 20:22, 23) not merely as personally beneficial, driving him to trust God alone (v.9, and 12:7), but also as directly benefiting those he ministered to: "God ... comforts us ... so that we can comfort...." To experience God's "comfort" (i.e., help, consolation, and encouragement) in the midst of all one's affliction is to become indebted and equipped to communicate the divine comfort and sympathy to others who are in any kind of affliction or distress.

5 This verse supplies the reason (*hoti*, "for") why suffering equips the Christian to mediate God's comfort. Whenever Christ's sufferings were multiplied in Paul's life, God's comfort was also multiplied through the ministry of Christ. The greater the suffering, the greater the comfort and the greater the ability to share with others the divine sympathy. "The sufferings of Christ" (cf. Gal 6:17) cannot refer to the atoning passion of Christ that Paul regarded as a historical fact, a completed event (Rom 5:8-10; 6:10). They probably included all the sufferings that befall the "man in Christ" (12:2) engaged in the service of Christ (cf. 4:11, 12). They are *Christ's* sufferings not simply because they are similar to his but because they contribute to the fulfillment of the suffering destined for the Body of Christ (Acts 14:22; Col 1:24) or because Christ continues to identify himself with his afflicted Church (cf. Acts 9:4, 5).

6,7 Verse 6a restates and applies v.4b. Paul's suffering of affliction and endurance of trial ultimately benefited the Corinthians in that he was thereby equipped to administer divine encouragement to them when they were afflicted and to ensure their preservation when they underwent trial (cf. Eph 3:13; 2 Tim 2:10). The apostle then makes explicit what he has assumed (in v.6a) in arguing from *his* experience of suffering to *their* experience of comfort and deliverance, viz., his own receipt of divine comfort in the midst of affliction ("if we are comforted"). Whether he suffered affliction or whether he received comfort, the advantage remained the same for the Corinthians (cf. 4:8-12, 15). They too would know an inner revitalization, an infusion of divine strength that would enable them to endure patiently the same type of trial that confronted Paul (cf. 1 Peter 5:9).

Since Paul realized that to share Christ's sufferings always involved the experience of God's comfort through that suffering, his hope that the Corinthians would be triumphant in their time of trial was securely grounded (v.7).

Notes

3 Whenever Paul uses a first-person plural pronoun or verb (e.g., ἡμῶν [hēmōn, "our"] in v.3; παρακαλούμεθα [parakaloumetha, "the comfort we . . . received"] in v.4), the referent(s) may be (1) a plural subject made clear in the context, (2) Paul himself ("epistolary plural"), (3) Paul and his co-workers mentioned in the salutation or his amanuensis (exclusive "we"), (4) Paul and his addressees (inclusive "we"), (5) Jews, (6) all Christians, or (7) men in general. That Paul can on occasion oscillate from singular to plural, apparently without intending a distinction to be drawn, is shown by the γράφομεν (graphomen, "we write"), ἐλπίζω (elpizō, "I hope"), and ἡμᾶς (hēmas, "us") of vv.13, 14 and the singulars of vv.15-17.

4 A distinction may be drawn between πᾶς (pas) with the articular θλίψις (thlipsis), "in all trouble" (v.4a; cf. 7:4) and πᾶς with the anarthrous θλίψις, "in any trouble" (v.4b)—see BDF, par. 275 (3); RHG, p. 772.

6,7 Textual variants arose here through the accidental omission of καὶ σωτηρίας. . .παρακλήσεως (kai sōtērias. . .paraklēseōs, "and salvation. . .comfort") due to homoeoteleuton (παρακλήσεως. . .παρακλήσεως) and subsequent efforts to reintroduce the words.

3. Deliverance from a deadly peril

1:8-11

8We do not want you to be uninformed, brothers, about the hardships we suffered in the province of Asia. We were under great pressure, far beyond our ability to endure, so that we despaired even of life. 9Indeed, in our hearts we felt the sentence of death. But this happened that we might not rely on ourselves but on God, who raises the dead. 10He has delivered us from such a deadly peril, and he will deliver us. On him we have set our hope that he will continue to deliver us, 11as you help us by your prayers. Then many will give thanks on our behalf for the gracious favor granted us in answer to the prayers of many.

8 Paul proceeds to describe the particular affliction (thlipsis, rendered "hardships" in NIV) in which he received divine comfort and empowering. It overtook Paul "in the province of Asia," which, as in Acts 19:22, probably refers to some part of the province other than the leading city, Ephesus. (Otherwise "in Ephesus" would have been used, as in 1 Cor 15:32; 16:8), possibly the Lycus valley (so G.S. Duncan), or Troas (2:12, 13). That it had occurred recently—certainly after 1 Corinthians was written—seems indicated by the vividness of Paul's description of the divine deliverance.

Evidently the Corinthians were already aware of Paul's trial—hence the vague reference to "the affliction. . .in Asia" (RSV). He now informs his converts of its overwhelming and unique character. He had been so "utterly, unbearably crushed" (RSV) that he was forced to renounce all hope of survival. The rare word exaporēthēnai ("despaired") implies the total unavailability of an exit (poros, "passage") from oppressive circumstances.

149

9 In his estimation Paul had received at that time a death sentence from which there was no reprieve (see notes). But in the wake of this trying experience that was tantamount to death there followed a further experience that was tantamount to resurrection. Only divine intervention enabled him to retreat from the portals of death to the realm of the living. All this undermined Paul's self-confidence (see 1 Cor 15:31; 2 Cor 12:9, 10) and compelled his utter dependence on a God who raises the dead (cf. Rom 4:17) and therefore can rescue the dying from the grip of death (cf. Phil 2:27, 30).

10,11 "The Father of compassion" had delivered Paul from a deadly peril (cf. vv.3, 4). But since such perils were likely to recur, continuing divine intervention on his behalf was necessary if death was to be robbed of its prey. Immediately Paul qualifies his bold assertion, "and he will deliver us" (cf. 2 Tim 4:18), by adding, ". . . on him we have set our hope that he will continue to deliver us." He could not presume on "the gracious favor" of protection or deliverance from danger and death. This came from "the God of all comfort" (v.3) "in answer to the prayers of many" and it would prompt still further thanksgiving.

Of the various proposed identifications of Paul's affliction in Asia, five deserve mention: (1) his "fighting with wild beasts in Ephesus" (1 Cor 15:32; so Tertullian); (2) his suffering the "thirty-nine stripes" (11:24) after being arraigned before a local Jewish ecclesiastical court (so G.S. Duncan); (3) the riot at Ephesus instigated by Demetrius, the silversmith (Acts 19:23–41; so W.M. Ramsay), or an unsuccessful attempt by the populace, after the Ephesian uproar, to lynch the apostle (so H. Windisch); (4) a particular persecution encountered in Ephesus or elsewhere (cf. Acts 20:19; 1 Cor 16:9) shortly before his departure for Troas (so A. Plummer); and (5) a prostrating attack of a recurrent malady (so E.B. Allo). The last-mentioned view seems favored by the allusion in v.10 to Job 33:30 (LXX); the fact that a Jew could regard sickness as death and healing or recovery as a return to life (see, e.g., Hos 6:1, 2); the present tenses of vv.4–6; the perfective implications of *eschēkamen* ("we feel we received") in v.9 (see note there); and the twice-repeated *rhysetai* ("he will deliver") in v.10.

Notes

9 Ἀπόκριμα (*apokrima*) could signify a judicial sentence (here, "the sentence of death") or an official verdict (here the divine reply to Paul's desperate appeal for deliverance; see MM, p. 64; Deiss BS, p. 257). Ἐσχήκαμεν (*eschēkamen*, cf. Rom 5:2) implies both ἔσχομεν (*eschomen*, "we received") and ἔχομεν (*echomen*, "we [still] possess"); thus "we feel we received"—the sentence or verdict had not been reversed. But in 2:13 and 7:5 this perfect is probably aoristic.

10 Καὶ ῥύσεται (*kai rhysetai*, "and he will deliver," future), which is to be preferred over καὶ ῥύεται (*kai rhyetai*, present) as the more difficult reading, implies that Paul expected comparable "deadly perils" in the future.

11 The genitive absolute συνυπουργούντων καὶ ὑμῶν (*synypourgountōn kai hymōn*) may be conditional in sense: "provided you too work together with us." The bestowal of divine favor is intimately related to the offering of human prayer (Phil 1:19; Philem 22). And the verb implies that prayer is cooperative work (Rom 15:30), expressive of the interdependence of the members of Christ's body (1 Cor 12:25, 26).

B. *Paul's Conduct Explained* (1:12–2:13)

1. *Characteristics of his conduct*

1:12–14

> ¹²Now this is our boast: Our conscience testifies that we have conducted our-
> selves in the world, and especially in our relations with you, in the holiness and
> sincerity that are from God. We have done so not according to worldly wisdom but
> according to God's grace. ¹³For we do not write you anything you cannot read or
> understand. And I hope that, ¹⁴as you have understood us in part, you will come
> to understand fully that you can boast of us just as we will boast of you in the day
> of the Lord Jesus.

12–14 Before defending himself against the specific charges of vacillation and domineering leveled against him by his opponents (1:15–2:4), Paul deals with two more
general accusations: that he had acted shamelessly (or deviously, if *haplotēti*, "integrity,"
be the correct reading in v.12; see notes) and insincerely in his relations with the
Corinthians (cf. v.12a), and that in his letters he had shown worldly shrewdness and had
been evasive by writing one thing but meaning or intending another (cf. vv.12b, 13a).

These baseless charges Paul answers in the only way possible for him—by appealing
to the testimony of his own conscience and the Corinthians' knowledge of his conduct.
So, he claims that in both church and world his conduct had been characterized by
God-given purity of intention and openness and had been governed by the grace of God
(v.12). Then he asserts that in none of his correspondence—the Corinthians had already
received at least three letters from him—did his meaning become apparent only by
"reading between the lines." Rather, his meaning, which lay on the surface, could be
understood simply by reading (v.13a). Paul concludes by reminding his converts at
Corinth that they had already begun to appreciate his motives and intentions, especially
through the recent visit of Titus (see 7:6–16). He expresses the hope that they would
reach the full assurance that he could give them as much cause for pride now (cf. 5:12)
as they would give him pride "in the day of the Lord Jesus" (cf. 1 Cor 15:31; Phil 4:1;
1 Thess 2:19, 20).

Notes

12 In all three editions of the UBS, ἁπλότητι, (*haplotēti*, "integrity"), a Western and Byzantine
reading, is preferred over the Alexandrian reading ἁγιότητι (*hagiotēti*, "holiness," NIV), but
the editors give their preference a "D" rating, showing that "there is a very high degree of doubt
concerning the reading selected for the text."

2. *Charge of fickleness answered*

1:15–22

> ¹⁵Because I was confident of this, I planned to visit you first so that you might
> benefit twice. ¹⁶I planned to visit you on my way to Macedonia and to come back
> to you from Macedonia, and then to have you send me on my way to Judea.

¹⁷When I planned this, did I do it lightly? Or do I make my plans in a worldly manner so that in the same breath I say, "Yes, yes" and "No, no"?

¹⁸But as surely as God is faithful, our message to you is not "Yes" and "No." ¹⁹For the Son of God, Jesus Christ, who was preached among you by me and Silas and Timothy, was not "Yes" and "No," but in him it has always been "Yes." ²⁰For no matter how many promises God has made, they are "Yes" in Christ. And so through him the "Amen" is spoken by us to the glory of God. ²¹Now it is God who makes both us and you stand firm in Christ. He anointed us, ²²set his seal of ownership on us, and put his Spirit in our hearts as a deposit, guaranteeing what is to come.

15-17 In 1 Corinthians 16:2–8 and in these three verses are found the outlines of two different itineraries relating to Paul and Corinth. In the earlier Epistle, the plan (hereafter Plan A) was: Ephesus–Macedonia–Corinth–Jerusalem (possibly). But in 2 Corinthians 1, the route (Plan B) is: Ephesus–Corinth–Macedonia–Corinth–Judea (now definitely). If, as is probable, Plan A discloses Paul's original intention, Plan B, made after the writing of 1 Corinthians, introduces two modifications of that previous itinerary: Paul now planned to visit Corinth twice—before and after his activity in Macedonia; and his intention of traveling to Judea with the collection was now settled.

But not only did Paul have to explain these changes. His actual itinerary (see Introduction, 1.b) seems to have been: Ephesus–Corinth (= the "painful visit")–Ephesus (where the Demetrius riot occurred)–Troas (2:12, 13)–Macedonia (7:5—the place of writing). In other words, neither Plan A nor Plan B was carried out as intended. Plan A was nullified by Paul's crossing from Ephesus to Corinth on the "painful visit," and Plan B was annulled by his return to Ephesus after that visit. It may be said that after the "sorrowful visit" Paul reverted to Plan A (see Acts 20:1–3, 16). To Plan A Paul had seemed to say, "Yes–No–Yes"; to Plan B, "Yes–No." The apostle had apparently provided his opponents with a convenient handle for a charge of fickleness!

His detractors were shrewd enough to convert the charge into one of capricious vacillation, levity of character (*elaphria*, translated "lightly"). His arbitrary changing of travel plans, they urged, was motivated purely by self-interest, with no concern for broken promises or for needs at Corinth. He made his plans on mere impulse like a worldly man, according to the mood of the moment, so that he could say, "Yes, yes" one day and "No, no" the next day, or "Yes" at one moment and "No" immediately afterwards, with the result that he seemed to be saying both "Yes" and "No" in the same breath. That Paul is actually quoting the accusation of certain Corinthians seems indicated by his use of the definite article with *elaphria* ("fickleness") and with the twice-stated (cf. Matt 5:37) *nai* ("yes") and *ou* ("no") (v.17).

18 Paul is so distressed by this charge and so convinced of his innocence that he solemnly invokes the unquestionable trustworthiness of God (1 Cor 1:9; cf. 11:10) as guaranteeing and testifying to the consistency of his message to the Corinthians. Neither in proclaiming the good news to them nor in telling them of his travel plans was his language "an ambiguous blend of Yes and No" (NEB). How could the messenger of a faithful God vacillate between a reassuring "Yes" and a disconcerting "No" or deliver a message that was not an emphatic "Yes"?

19,20 Paul now elaborates this last point. The message originally proclaimed at Corinth (Acts 18:5) by the threefold testimony (cf. 13:1; Deut 19:15) of Paul, Silvanus, (= Silas) and Timothy centered in none other than God's Son in whom inconsistency and indecision had no place. So Paul draws a contrast between the humanity of the messengers and the divinity of the Person who was the essence of their message (the unusual position of *gar*, "for," emphasizes *tou theou*, "of God," v.19). Indeed, in and through him (*en autō*) the divine "Yes" has come into effect as a permanent reality (*gegonen*, perfect tense, v.19), because all God's promises (cf. 7:1; Rom 9:4; 15:8), whatever their number, find their fulfillment or affirmative in him (v.20a). "They are 'Yes' in Christ," since he forms the climax and summation of the divine self-revelation. That is why (*dio kai*), in their corporate worship offered to God through Christ, Christians joyfully utter the "Yes" or "Amen" of agreement and consecration (cf. Rev 1:7; 3:14; 22:20). Such a response enhances God's glory (v.20b).

The Corinthians' "Amen" to the gospel declaration itself validated the apostolic preaching (cf. 1 Cor 1:6; 2 Cor 3:2, 3; 13:5, 6). With his consistency confirmed here, was it likely that Paul would act in a worldly manner in relatively trivial affairs? How could they distrust the apostle who himself had taught them to affirm the trustworthiness of God by repeating the "Amen"? This is a potent *a fortiori* argument.

21,22 In defending himself against the charge of levity (v.17a), Paul has appealed to his making decisions as a man in Christ who acts *kata pneuma* ("by the Spirit" or "in a spiritual manner," a phrase implied in Paul's argument), not *kata sarka* ("in a worldly manner"—v.17b); the trustworthiness and faithfulness of God whose sure word he preaches (v.18); the unambiguous and positive nature of the message they proclaimed—Jesus Christ, the Son of God (v.19); and the validation of that sure proclamation in the Corinthian use of the liturgical response, "Amen" (v.20). Finally (vv.21, 22), Paul pointed to the constant activity of God in producing stability in Paul *and* the Corinthians!—those who have been brought into intimate and dynamic relation with Christ, who is God's secure and permanent "Yes."

Each of the four Greek participles in vv.21, 22 has God as its subject (*theos*, "God," being emphatic by position, v.21). The first (*bebaiōn*, present tense), a technical, legal term denoting a seller's guaranteeing of the validity of a purchase (see Deiss BS, 104–109), refers to God's continuous strengthening of believers in their faith in Christ and his progressive enriching of their knowledge of Christ. The other three participles are in the aorist tense, indicating what took place at the time of conversion and baptism. The phrase "he anointed (*chrisas*) us," which follows immediately after a reference to Christ (*Christos*, "the Anointed One"), shows that those to whom God now gives a firm standing, he once commissioned for his service by consecrating them as his "anointed ones" and imparting those gifts necessary for their task (see note). The last two participles are intimately related (see note). God "set his seal of ownership [*sphragisamenos*] on us" in that he "put [*dous*] his spirit in our hearts as a deposit, guaranteeing what is to come." Associated with the idea of sealing are the ideas of ownership, authentication, and security; the believer is "branded" as God's property, the reality of his faith is attested, and his status is guaranteed "against the day of redemption" (Eph 4:30).

Notes

15 Since an apostolic visit might be both a means of spiritual benefit (χάρις, *charis*; Rom 1:11; 15:29) and a source of personal pleasure (χαρά, *chara*; Phil 1:25), the sense is not materially altered whether χάριν (charin) or χαράν (charan) be read. The latter variant may have arisen from 1:24 or 2:3.

18 It is noteworthy that several of the crucial Gr. terms in vv.15–24 represent various forms of the Sem. root אמן ('-m-n): πιστός (pistos, v. 18) = נאמן (ne*mān), ναί (nai, vv.19, 20) or ἀμήν (amēn, v.20) = אמן ('āmēn), βεβαιῶν (bebaiōn, v.21) = מאמין (ma*mîn), πίστις (pistis, v.24) = אמונה (*mûnāh). It is possible that the train of Paul's thought was influenced by these word associations (a case of Sem. thoughts being clothed in Gr. words), though they would not have been recognized by the predominantly Gentile congregation at Corinth. See further W.C. van Unnik, "Reisepläne und Amen-sagen, Zusammenhang and Gedankenfolge in 2. Korinther 1:15–24," *Studia Paulina in honorem Johannis de Zwaan* (Haarlem: Bohn, 1953), pp. 215–234.

Ὁ λόγος ἡμῶν (ho logos hēmōn, "our message") probably refers to the preaching of the gospel as well as generally to Paul's written or spoken word. Thus "our message to you is (and was) not 'Yes' and 'No.'"

20 For the community use of "Amen" as a response indicating agreement and commitment, see Deut 27:15–26; 1 Chron 16:36; Neh 5:13; 8:6; Ps 106:48; 1 Cor 14:16; Rev 22:20.

21,22 Although σὺν ὑμῖν (syn hymin, lit. "with you") is not repeated with the last three participles, it is to be understood with each (Eph 1:13 and 4:30 use σφραγίζειν [sphragizein] in reference to all believers). Paul is not here thinking exclusively of the gift or office of apostleship.

The anarthrous participle δούς (dous, "having given"), which is linked to the articular participle σφραγισάμενος (sphragisamenos, "having sealed") by a virtually epexegetic καί (kai, "and"), is explicative. "Sealing" is God's giving of the Spirit as a "deposit" or "pledge" (ἀρραβών, arrhabōn) of inheritance (cf. Eph 1:14). For Paul the Spirit was thus the promise of fulfillment, as well as the fulfillment of promise (Gal 3:14; Eph 1:13).

---

3. *A cancelled painful visit*

1:23–2:4

> [23]I call God as my witness that it was in order to spare you that I did not return to Corinth. [24]Not that we lord it over your faith, but we work with you for your joy, because it is by faith you stand firm. [1]So I made up my mind that I would not make another painful visit to you. [2]For if I grieve you, who is left to make me glad but you whom I have grieved? [3]I wrote as I did so that when I came I should not be distressed by those who ought to make me rejoice. I had confidence in all of you, that you would all share my joy. [4]For I wrote you out of great distress and anguish of heart and with many tears, not to grieve you but to let you know the depth of my love for you.

Allied to the charge that Paul had arbitrarily altered his travel plans regarding Corinth according to the mood of the moment, there was in all probability the accusation that by doing so he had shown himself to be a spiritual dictator who tried to dominate his converts and their faith and did not hesitate to cause them pain.

1:23–2:1 In answering this charge, Paul solemnly invokes the God who is faithful (1:18) as Paul's own witness to the truth of statements like these: "The reason I postponed my intended visit to Corinth was to spare you a second painful visit (1:23b; 2:1). So far from being unstable in my desires, as some of you insist (cf. 1:17), I have the settled purpose of promoting your highest good and joy (1:24) and saving you unnecessary pain or sorrow."

The matter of Paul's planned and actual itinerary is complicated (see the discussion at 1:15–17, and Introduction, 1.b). It was to spare the Corinthians and himself further pain that he refrained from returning to Corinth from Ephesus after the so-called "painful visit." "I made up my mind" (2:1) refers to a decision Paul made at Ephesus after hearing of the insult hurled at him or one of his deputies at Corinth by "the wrongdoer" of 7:12 (see the commentary on 2:5–8). He resolved to pay the Corinthians an "epistolary visit" (2:3, 4; 7:8, 12) instead of another personal visit that might have proved mutually painful.

For Paul to speak of "sparing" the Corinthians (v.23) implied that he might have punished or pained them. He therefore proceeds in 1:24, which is parenthetical, to reject the inference—probably also an actual Corinthian charge—that he was some tyrannical overlord, seeking to intimidate and domineer in matters of faith and conduct. An apostle was obligated to serve his converts; he had no right to dominate them. It was his privilege to work with them to secure their "joy in the faith" (Phil 1:25), not to lord it over them by causing them unnecessary pain. Indeed, with regard to their faith, he could not be despotic nor had he any need to do so, because they had a firm standing of their own by their exercise of faith (or, "in the realm of faith," *tē...pistei*, 1:24).

2 Here Paul acknowledges that his decision not to revisit Corinth personally had been partially determined by his reflection that to inflict needless pain on the Corinthians at that time would have effectively dried up the only source of his own happiness. His joy was intimately connected with theirs (1:24). To cause them pain was to experience pain himself, a pain that could be relieved and then converted into gladness only by their repentance (see 7:8–10).

3,4 In place of a second painful visit to Corinth that would not have been advantageous in the situation, Paul wrote the Corinthians a letter that has come to be known as the "sorrowful [or, severe] letter" (see Introduction, 7.b). His aim in writing it was to avoid being pained by them when he finally did pay another personal visit (v.3a). It was incongruous to Paul that his converts, who ought to have been a constant source of joy to him (1 Thess 2:19, 20), could prove, and in fact had proved, to be a cause of distress to their spiritual father. Yet in writing the "severe letter" he had had the buoyant assurance that whatever made him glad would give all of them pleasure too, for they were all one in joy, as in sorrow (v.3b).

In v.4a Paul describes the origin (*ek*, "out of") and circumstances (*dia*, "with") of this sorrowful letter. It was born of anguish and produced with tears. While parts of 1 Corinthians may be said to have been written "out of deep affliction and spiritual anguish," this is hardly true of that Epistle regarded as a whole, especially if its beginning and ending are any indication of its general tone. Rather, the letter referred to here and in 7:8, 12 is to be identified with a letter, no longer extant, that Paul sent to Corinth after 1 Corinthians had been delivered and after his "painful visit" (see Introduction, 7.b. 3).

A second purpose (cf. v.3; 2:9; 7:12) behind the "tearful letter" is stated in v.4b. Although the letter arose from anguish and actually proved painful to its recipients (7:8), its aim was not vindictive or even vindicative. On the contrary, it sought to convince the Corinthians of the intensity of Paul's affectionate concern for them.

Notes

1:23 Ἐπὶ τὴν ἐμὴν ψυχήν (*epi tēn emēn psychēn* = Heb. נַפְשִׁי־עַל, *'al-napšî*), which is not represented in the tr., means "against myself" or "with my life as the forfeit." So sure is Paul of his own truthfulness at this point that he can say, "Let God destroy me if I am lying."

2:1 Since πάλιν (*palin*, "again," "another") precedes and qualifies ἐν λύπῃ (*en lypē*, "painful"), and not ἐλθεῖν (*elthein*, "visit"), there is the implication of an earlier painful visit (cf. 13:2). It is unlikely that this visit is to be equated either with 1 Corinthians, reckoned as a sorrowful visit (cf. 2:4), or with Paul's initial visit to Corinth (Acts 18:1-18), which, as far as the Corinthians were concerned, was anything but painful. The visit probably occurred between the sending of 1 Corinthians (where only the founding visit is referred to; see 1 Cor 2:1-3; 11:2; 15:3) and the dispatch of the "severe letter" (see the Introduction, 7.a).

2:2 There are eight uses of the λύπη (*lypē*) concept in vv.1-7 (cf. the eight uses in 7:8-11). This usage, which describes the feeling or creating of pain, can be consistently reflected in tr. by rendering λύπη (*lypē*) by "pain," λυπέω (*lypeō*) by "cause pain" or "pain," and ἐν λύπῃ (*en lypē*) by "painfully."

---

4. Forgiveness for the offender

2:5-11

5If anyone has caused grief, he has not so much grieved me as he has grieved all of you, to some extent—not to put it too severely. 6The punishment inflicted on him by the majority is sufficient for him. 7Now instead, you ought to forgive and comfort him, so that he will not be overwhelmed by excessive sorrow. 8I urge you, therefore, to reaffirm your love for him. 9The reason I wrote you was to see if you would stand the test and be obedient in everything. 10If you forgive anyone, I also forgive him. And what I have forgiven—if there was anything to forgive—I have forgiven in the sight of Christ for your sake, 11in order that Satan might not outwit us. For we are not unaware of his schemes.

In the preceding section (1:23-2:4) Paul has spoken about feeling pain, causing pain, and avoiding further pain. All three aspects recur in this paragraph with reference to a certain wrongdoer at Corinth. Particularly apparent here is Paul's sensitivity as a pastor: He avoids naming the culprit (vv.5-8); he recognizes that Christian discipline is not simply retributive but also remedial (vv.6, 7); he understands the feelings and psychological needs of the penitent wrongdoer (vv.6-8); he appeals to his own conduct as an example for the Corinthians to follow (v.10); and he is aware of the divisive operation of Satan within the Christian community (v.11).

5,6 Many older commentators found in vv.5-11 a further reference to the man guilty of incest (1 Cor 5). But most modern writers rightly reject this identification for a variety of reasons (see Introduction, 7.b.3]a; for a defense of the equation 1 Cor 5 = 2 Cor 2, see the commentary of P.E. Hughes, ad loc.).

Evidently, after Paul's painful visit an insult of some description had been directed against him or one of his representatives either by a visitor to Corinth (so C.K. Barrett) or by a Corinthian, who perhaps at that time headed the opposition to the apostle at Corinth and objected in particular to Paul's disciplinary methods such as those outlined in 1 Cor 5. Paul here discounts the sorrow caused him by the unfortunate episode. Verse 5 may be rendered, "If anyone has caused pain, he had caused pain not so much to me as to all of you—to some extent (*apo merous*), not to exaggerate the point" (see note).

On the basis of Titus's report about the Corinthian reaction to the "stern letter" (see 7:7–11), Paul counsels the church to terminate the discipline they had inflicted on "the individual in question" (*ho toioutos*, v.6; NIV, "him"). Whether a formal gathering of the church had been held and whether disciplinary measures (temporary suspension of church privileges?) had been decided on by general vote or consensus, it is impossible to say. The words rendered "the majority" (*hoi pleiones*) may simply mean "the main body," or "the whole group," referring generally to the membership (cf. the use of *hā-rabbîm*, "the many," by the Qumran community). But since "the majority" is certainly a possible rendering, the question remains: What was the view of the implied minority? In light of v.7a, it seems likely that they were a pro-Pauline clique, the "ultra-Paulinists," who regarded the penalty as insufficient.

7–9 Instead of continuing or increasing the punishment, the Corinthians ought to rescue the man from inordinate grief and complete his reformation by forgiving and encouraging him and by a public reaffirmation of their love for him. This would serve to assure the wrongdoer that God had, in fact, forgiven him. In this way, the community would in effect be remitting or loosing his sins (cf. Matt 16:19; 18:18; John 20:23) by declaring and confirming to him the reality of divine forgiveness.

A positive Corinthian response to this plea would afford Paul further evidence of the church's willingness to acknowledge his divinely given authority. By reproving the offender after hearing the "severe letter," they had stood the test and proved their obedience in all respects (cf. 7:11, 12). Now by ending the punishment, they would be doing the same. There was no inconsistency in first "binding" and then "loosing"; "if your brother sins, rebuke him, and if he repents, forgive him" (Luke 17:3). In each case they were proving their loyalty to the apostle.

10,11 Paul here aligns himself with the Corinthian decision to forgive the person in question—a decision he trusts they will make after receiving the present letter. "Your verdict of forgiveness is also mine," or as the NEB puts it: "Anyone who has your forgiveness has mine too." But he hastens to add that he has already forgiven the man—if, in fact, there was anything to forgive. Clearly it was Paul, not the Corinthians, who had taken the initiative in this matter of forgiveness.

Verse 10 affords perhaps the clearest evidence that the offense was basically a personal act of effrontery against Paul or possibly his acknowledged or delegated representative. There was need for Paul's personal forgiveness, although, in deference to the penitent offender's feelings, he discounts the personal pain he himself experienced (v.5) and deliberately understates the seriousness of the offense (v.10) lest anyone imagine that he considered himself virtuous in granting forgiveness so readily. All this would be inappropriate if he were describing a sin of incest (1 Cor 5).

The circumstances and purpose of Paul's forgiveness are then defined (vv.10b, 11). First, forgiveness was granted "in the sight of Christ," as Christ looked on as a witness and approved—Christ, who taught that willingness to forgive one's brother was a precondition for the receipt of divine forgiveness (Matt 5:12, 14, 15; 18:23–35). And in Colossians 3:13 (cf. Eph 4:32) Paul grounds the Christian obligation to forgive others on the Christian experience of God's forgiveness in Christ. Moreover, forgiveness was granted for the welfare of the Corinthians ("for your sake"), that is, to preserve unity and to relieve them of their patent embarrassment at not having acted against the offender before Paul wrote to them. They keenly felt their disloyalty to Paul (7:7, 11).

Verse 11 states an additional but related purpose. This was to avoid being outwitted by the master strategist, Satan, who was bent on creating discord within the church at Corinth, either between the church at large and a dissident minority or between the repentant wrongdoer and his fellow Christians. To withhold forgiveness when the man was repentant was to play into the hands of Satan, who already had gained one advantage when the man sinned. There is a point at which punishment can become purely vindictive (cf. v.6) and suffering a penalty can drive one to despair (v.7; Col 3:21). Christian discipline certainly includes punishment administered in love, but it is not simply retributive or punitive; it is also remedial or reformatory (cf. 1 Cor 5:5; 11:32; 2 Cor 7:9, 10; 13:10). It aims at reinstatement after repentance, through forgiveness and reconciliation.

Notes

5 Εἰ...τις (ei...tis, "if anyone") is conditional only in form; in sense it is equivalent to ὅς (hos, "the person who"; cf. 7:14, Gr.). Οὐκ ἐμέ (ouk eme, "not...me") should not be pressed to exclude Paul from the experience of pain. Sometimes he uses the negative, not with an absolute meaning ("not at all"), but in a relative sense ("not so much," NIV, or "not primarily" or "not only"; cf. 1 Cor 1:17; 2 Cor 7:12). If the verb ἐπιβαρέω (epibareō) is here used transitively, as it usually is, the meaning will be "not to be too severe [with him, or with anyone]"; if it is intransitive, "not to put it too severely" (NIV), or "not to labour the point" (NEB), or "not to exaggerate."

6 For a defense of the view that ἐπιτιμία (epitimia) should be rendered "reproof," not "punishment" or "penalty," see C.K. Barrett, in loc.

8 The verb κυρόω (kuroō) often means "ratify" or "validate," but here may carry the sense "decide in favor of (love for him)" (BAG, p. 462), perhaps implying a public reinstatement and readmission to fellowship following the earlier formal reproof or punishment. As a common legal term (see Gal 3:15 and MM, p. 366), its juxtaposition here with ἀγάπη (agapē, "love") is noteworthy.

11 Νοήματα (noēmata) here has the pejorative sense of "schemes," "designs," "plots," or "wiles" (= Gr. μεθοδεῖαι, methodeiai, Eph 6:11), but Paul uses it also with the neutral meaning of "minds" (3:14; 4:4; 11:3; Phil 4:7). His point in v.11 is that one of the Christian's defenses against the devil's stratagems is prior awareness of his purposes and methods, particularly his wish to turn good (the man's repentance) into evil (his downfall through excessive grief).

5. Restlessness at Troas

2:12,13

[12]Now when I went to Troas to preach the gospel of Christ and found that the Lord had opened a door for me, [13]I still had no peace of mind, because I did not find my brother Titus there. So I said good-by and went on to Macedonia.

12,13 This is the final section in Paul's explanation of his recent conduct. For a reconstruction of the events leading up to the sending of the "severe letter," see the Introduction (7.a.3). Titus was dispatched to Corinth with this "letter of tears" while Paul continued work in and around Ephesus (cf. Acts 19:22b, "he stayed in the province of Asia a little longer"), the city to which he had returned after his brief "painful visit" to Corinth. Paul's departure for Troas, mentioned in v.12 (by a coasting vessel? cf. Acts

20:13–15), probably was precipitated by the Demetrius riot (Acts 19:23–41). Evidently he had already planned to leave the city, for when he sent Titus to Corinth, he arranged to meet him at Troas, or, failing that, probably at Philippi.

We may safely assume that Paul actually preached in Troas, though v.12 speaks only of his intent. He would recognize that the "door" of opportunity was "open" (note Acts 16:6–10) only after he had grasped the evangelistic opportunities initially afforded by the Lord. But evangelism was curtailed (remarkable, in the light of 1 Cor 9:16!) owing to Paul's restless spirit (perhaps seen as a device used by Satan, cf. v.11). This disquiet (7:5, 6) was caused by several factors: (1) the disheartening opposition at Ephesus, which had caused his premature departure; (2) persistent uncertainty and fears concerning the situation at Corinth (7:5b), because of Titus's nonarrival; and (3) concern for the safety of Titus in travel (note 7:6b, 7a), particularly if he was carrying the completed Corinthian collection.

Notes

12 Because Alexandria Troas was frequently the point where land travel became sea travel (or vice-versa) or where a change of ship occurred, it was a suitable center and base for missionary activity (W.M. Ramsay. "Roads and Travel [in NT]." HDB, 5:389, 400).
13 That Paul was somewhat embarrassed by his premature departure from Troas may be indicated by his particular mention of the reluctant and solemn farewell, the verb ἀποταξάμενος (apotaxamenos, "said good-by") never being used elsewhere by Paul. Αὐτοῖς (autois), "[I said good-by] to them" (not in NIV), indicates that some converts were won in Troas (cf. Acts 20:6–12).

C. *Major Digression—the Apostolic Ministry Described* (2:14–7:4)

1. *Its grandeur and superiority* (2:14–4:6)

a. *The privilege of apostolic service*

2:14–17

14But thanks be to God, who always leads us in triumphal procession in Christ and through us spreads everywhere the fragrance of the knowledge of him. 15For we are to God the aroma of Christ among those who are being saved and those who are perishing. 16To the one we are the stench of death; to the other, the fragrance of life. And who is equal to such a task? 17Unlike so many, we do not peddle the word of God for profit. On the contrary, in Christ we speak before God with sincerity, like men sent from God.

14 Here begins the so-called "great digression," brought about by Paul's remembering his happy reunion with Titus in Macedonia, who brought encouraging news from Corinth that relieved Paul's fretful tension (7:5–16). In the favorable Corinthian reaction to the "letter of tears," reported by Titus, Paul saw God's vindication of his apostleship and a triumph of God's grace in the hearts of the Corinthians.

Paul likens the irresistible advance of the gospel, in spite of temporary frustration, to a Roman *triumphus* ("triumph") in which the victorious general, along with his proud soldiers, used to lead in triumphal procession the wretched prisoners of war who were thus exposed to public ridicule. Not all the details of this picture are to be pressed. The apostles, as well as Christians in general, may be either exultant soldiers who share in the benefits of Christ's victory (cf. Rom 8:37) or willing captives who count it a privilege to be part of God's "triumph" (cf. Rom 1:1; Col 4:10). The metaphor is certainly suggestive: Christ undertook a battle not rightly his; we share in a triumph not rightly ours.

In the following reference to the diffusion of fragrance, Paul may simply be developing the imagery, for sacrifices were offered when the procession reached the temple of Jupiter Capitolinus (Jos. *War* VII 5. 6) and perfumes may have been sprinkled or incense burned along the processional route. Through the apostles, God was spreading far and wide the fragrant knowledge of himself to be gained through knowing Christ (Col 2:2, 3).

15,16a Syntactically, v.15 is ambiguous so that several translations are possible: (1) "We are the sweet odor (of sacrifice) that ascends from Christ to God among those who are on the way to salvation and those who are on the way to destruction." (2) "I live for God as the fragrance of Christ breathed alike on those who are being saved and on those who are perishing" (Moffatt). (3) "We are to God the aroma of Christ among..." (NIV). This third option is to be preferred. As faithful preachers and followers of Christ, the apostles themselves formed a sweet savor of Christ rising up to God as a pleasing odor (cf. Lev 1:9, 13, 17; Num 15:7). To the extent that they diffused the fragrance of Christ, they were that fragrance or aroma. Irrespective of the human response to the gospel, its proclamation delights God's heart, because it centers on the Son whom he loves.

Behind Paul's thought in both these verses may be the rabbinic concept of the Law as simultaneously life-giving and death-dealing. "As the bee reserves her honey for her owner and her sting for others, so the words of the Torah are an elixir of life for Israel and a deadly poison to the nations of the world" (Deuteronomy Rabbah 1.5, cited by T.W. Manson; see notes). Just as the Torah had a beneficial effect upon those who received and obeyed it and a lethal effect upon those who rejected it, so the proclaimers of Christ are a "life-giving perfume" to those who believe the gospel and so are being saved and at the same time a "death-dealing drug" to those who repudiate it and so are perishing (vv.15b, 16a; cf. 1 Cor 1:18, 23, 24).

16b,17 To Paul's urgent question "Who is equal to such a task (of preaching the gospel of Christ or being the aroma of Christ)?" the answer may be either, "We apostles are, for we are not peddlers of an adulterated message," or "No one is, if he depends on his own resources." The latter reply is supported by 3:4-6; the former by 3:1.

By the phrase "unlike so many," Paul may be referring to the numerous wandering teachers and philosophers of the first century (see note on 11:8) who expected or demanded payment for what they claimed was "the word of God," or (and this is more likely; note the "some people" of 3:1) to the group of his Judaizing opponents at Corinth who converted preaching into a means of personal gain. In contrast, Paul appeals to the sincerity of his motives and the purity of the message. This was shown by his divine commission ("like men sent from God"; cf. Gal 1:1, 12, 15, 16), his sense of divine dependence and responsibility ("we speak before God") and his divine authority and power ("in Christ"). The principle is clear: As those who dispense the life-giving remedy for sin, preachers must avoid diluting or adulterating the medicine of life, the Word of God.

Notes

14 Θριαμβεύω (*thriambeuō*) means "lead [about] in triumphal procession," not "cause to triumph" (KJV). The only other NT use of the verb is in Col 2:15, where the despoiled powers and authorities are viewed as unwilling captives driven before the triumphal chariot of God or Christ. See further L. Williamson, Jr., "Led in Triumph. Paul's Use of *Thriambeuō*," INT, XXII (3, 1968), pp. 317–332.

Τὴν ὀσμὴν τῆς γνώσεως αὐτοῦ (*tēn osmēn tēs gnōseōs autou*) may mean "the fragrance that consists of [or results from] the knowledge of God" or "the fragrant knowledge of Christ [or God]."

16 Ὀσμή (*osmē*) may refer to either a pleasant odor ("fragrance"; John 12:3) or an unpleasant odor ("stench"; Tobit 8:3). Similarly, in Jewish literature סם (*sam*) is used of both a lethal drug ("poison") and a sweet-smelling perfume or spice. See the illuminating article by T.W. Manson, "2 Cor 2:14-17: Suggestions towards an Exegesis," in *Studia Paulina in honorem Johannis de Zwaan* (Haarlem: Bohn, 1953), pp. 155–162.

The twice-used ἐκ...εἰς (*ek...eis*, lit. "out of...into") combination defines nature or source (ἐκ) and effect (εἰς). Thus, "to the latter we are [or, the message is] an odor of death that brings death, to the former an odor of life that imparts life." C.K. Barrett renders the prepositional phrases as "issuing from...leading to...," whereas A. Plummer paraphrases them in this way: "exhaled from...and breathing...." Alternatively, the prepositions may point to a continual progression ("from...to") from bad to worse or from good to better, with death or life as the final outcome (M. Zerwick. *Analysis Philologica Novi Testamenti Graeci* [Rome: Pontifical Biblical Institute, 1966³], p. 395).

17 Some MSS (including the important p⁴⁶), versions, and Fathers read οἱ λοιποί (*hoi loipoi*, "the rest") in place of οἱ πολλοί (*hoi polloi*, "the many" or "the majority"). Either reading presents a remarkable accusation. On the term καπηλεύοντες (*kapēleuontes*, "hawking"; "peddle," NIV), see P.E. Hughes, in loc.

---

b. *The results of the ministry*

3:1-3

¹Are we beginning to commend ourselves again? Or do we need, like some people, letters of recommendation to you or from you? ²You yourselves are our letter, written on our hearts, known and read by everybody. ³You show that you are a letter from Christ, the result of our ministry, written not with ink but with the Spirit of the living God, not on tablets of stone but on tablets of human hearts.

1 Behind each of the two questions in this verse, both of which expect the answer "No!" stands an actual or expected charge against Paul. Since he had just spoken of the distinctive role of apostles (2:14-16) and of his divine commission and authority (2:17; note also 1:12 and 1 Cor 4:15, 16; 11:1; 14:18; 15:10), some might say, "Paul, once again you are indulging in your notorious habit of self-commendation." The second assertion, which Paul answers and which was made by some of "the many" who were making a profit out of preaching (2:17), might have run like this: "Since Jerusalem is the fount of Christianity, anyone working outside Jerusalem must be able to give proof of his commission by letters of recommendation. We brought you Corinthians commendatory letters from Jerusalem and you yourselves have supplied us with such when we have visited other places. Why should you regard Paul as an exception? Does not his unconcern about letters of recommendation prove he is an intruder and impostor?"

Paul is not here disparaging the use of letters of introduction. Their use had already become established within the Christian world (see Acts 18:27) and Paul himself had sought epistolary credentials from the high priest at Jerusalem before setting out for the synagogues of Damascus (Acts 9:2; 22:5). Also he himself gave what amounted to commendatory letters (Rom 16:1, 2; 1 Cor 16:3, 10, 11; 2 Cor 8:16–24).

His opponents apparently carried letters as their credentials, probably not from the three Jerusalem "pillars" (Gal 2:9) or the Twelve, but from the Pharisaic wing of the Jerusalem church, those Judaizers who regarded the scrupulous observance of the Mosaic law as essential for salvation (Acts 15:5) and were unable to distinguish between the law-abiding conduct of the Twelve and legalistic teaching.

2,3 The latter of the two questions posed in v.1 Paul now answers explicitly. He insists that for him to carry commendatory letters to Corinth would be completely superfluous. The most complimentary letter he could possibly possess had already been written (cf. 1 Cor 9:2). Their very lives as men and women "in Christ," the result of the grace of Christ operative in his ministry, were an eloquent letter all could read. To bring another letter would amount to a personal insult to the Corinthians; it certainly would ignore the past and present work of Christ in their hearts. They themselves were Paul's testimonial (see note), guaranteeing his apostolic status and authority.

It may have been Paul's immediate circumstances—dictating a letter to an amanuensis —that suggested the metaphor of letter writing. If Christ wrote the letter and the Spirit was the amanuensis who recorded it, Paul may have regarded himself either as the messenger who delivered it to its destination or as the person who published it. But the order of reference in v.3 (Christ–Paul–the Spirit) may suggest simply the twofold idea of author (Christ through the Spirit) and amanuensis (Paul).

Now the imagery is further developed and explained (v.3b). The letter was no human document recorded in ink on papyrus. Nor was it a divine composition, such as the Decalogue, engraved on inanimate tablets of stone (Exod 31:18; 32:15, 16). Rather the letter was of divine authorship, "written by the Spirit of the living God," and was indelibly inscribed on living tablets, sensitive human hearts (Jer 31:33; 32:38; Ezek 11:19; 36:26). Proof of Paul's genuineness was to be found not in written characters but in human characters.

So Paul delivers a powerful rebuttal to his opponents. His commendatory letter had been written before theirs; it was indelible; it was widely circulated, not confidential or unpublished; its author was Christ, not a partisan group within the Jerusalem church.

Notes

2 RSV prefers the reading ὑμῶν (hymōn, "your") (א 33) over ἡμῶν (hēmōn, "our"): "written on your hearts." This may be more in harmony with the context (7:3 could account for hēmōn), but the more difficult reading ("written on our hearts," NEB, NIV), which has the stronger MS support, is by no means impossible. Paul is saying, "Our own hearts [cf. 1:1, 19] testify that you are our credentials, and wherever we go and speak of your faith in Christ everyone else also can read your letter of recommendation about us."

c. Competence for service

3:4-6

> ⁴Such confidence as this is ours through Christ before God. ⁵Not that we are competent of ourselves to judge anything we do, but our competence comes from God. ⁶He has enabled us to be ministers of a new covenant—not of the letter but of the Spirit; for the letter kills, but the Spirit gives life.

4,5 Paul's confidence before God in claiming that the Corinthians were a letter written by Christ validating his apostolic credentials came through Christ (v.4). It was not the product of a pious wish or imagination. Still speaking of this confidence before God, he disowns any ability to form a competent judgment on the results of his own ministry or any personal right to lay claim to the results of what was in reality God's work. His qualification and source of competence for the work of the ministry, including the assessment of its success, were not natural ability or personal initiative but divine enabling. Paul's confidence came through Christ, his competence from God, and he says all this against the background of his opponents' claim to be self-sufficient.

6 Paul realized that to be divinely commissioned was to be divinely equipped. His equipment to be a minister of a new covenant was given at his Damascus call when he was named a "chosen instrument" of God and filled with his Spirit (Acts 9:15, 17-19).

There follows a contrast between two basic characteristics of the old and new covenants. The basis of the old covenant between Yahweh (Jehovah) and Israel was a lifeless, written code, "the book of the covenant" (Exod 24:7). The basis of the new covenant between God and the church is a dynamic, pervasive Spirit. The written code (or "letter") pronounced a sentence of death (Rom 7:9-11; Gal 3:10), but the Spirit brings a transformation of life (Rom 7:6; 8:3). Though the new covenant was ratified by the shedding of Christ's blood (Heb 13:20) and is symbolized in the communion cup (Luke 22:20; 1 Cor 11:25), it becomes operative only through the indwelling Spirit who imparts new life. Where "the letter" was powerless, the Spirit is powerful in producing holiness of life, in enabling a person fully to meet the righteous requirements of the law (Rom 8:4). This is what makes the new covenant "new" (see note) and the old covenant (3:14) "old" (see Heb 8:6-13). In themselves words cannot produce righteousness, even though they be divine oracles. There has to be a vitalizing Spirit to charge the words with transforming power.

Notes

6 It is difficult, if not impossible, always to maintain a distinction in the NT between καινός (*kainos*) and νέος (*neos*) or cognate terms. Compare, e.g., the use of these terms and their cognate verbs in Eph 4:23, 24 and Col 3:10. Sometimes, however, *neos* implies recency (newness in time or origin) and *kainos*, superiority (newness in nature or quality). See further J. Behm, TDNT, 3:447-454; 4:896-901.

d. The surpassing glory of the new covenant

3:7-11

> [7]Now if the ministry that brought death, which was engraved in letters on stone, came with glory, so that the Israelites could not look steadily at the face of Moses because of its glory, fading though it was, [8]will not the ministry of the Spirit be even more glorious? [9]If the ministry that condemns men is glorious, how much more glorious is the ministry that brings righteousness! [10]For what was glorious has no glory now in comparison with the surpassing glory. [11]And if what was fading away came with glory, how much greater is the glory of that which lasts!

Thus far in chapter three, Paul's thought has progressed from the idea of commendatory letters written on hearts by the Spirit to reflection on the new covenant promised by God through Jeremiah under which the law would be written on men's hearts (Jer 31:31–34). This now prompts him to compare the old and new economies. Each involved a distinctive ministry that was accompanied by glory, but so superior was the glory of the new covenant that the glory of the old faded into insignificance by comparison.

7–9 Not only in these three verses but also in the remainder of the chapter Paul provides a commentary on selected points of the narrative in Exodus 34:29–35. When Moses descended from Mount Sinai with the two tablets on which were written the Ten Commandments, his face shone so brightly that "the Israelites could not look steadily" at him. Well then, argues Paul, if such glory attended the giving of the law under the ministry or administration that brought death and condemns men, how much more glorious will be the ministry of the Spirit that brings righteousness! What was a distinctive and positive feature of the old order must also characterize the new economy, but in greater measure. The new covenant has surpassing glory inasmuch as it is a more adequate revelation of God's character.

10,11 The comparison between the covenants advances one step further. The new covenant is not simply characterized by greater glory. So pronounced is the contrast between the two economies or dispensations that what once was rightly considered resplendent now appears scarcely resplendent at all (v.10). "If the sun is up, the brightness of the moon is no longer bright" (M. Zerwick), or as J.A. Bengel long ago expressed it, "The greater light obscures the lesser." The old covenant suffers immeasurably from a comparison with the new. It belonged in fact to a vanishing order, an economy that began to fade immediately after its inception, as was typified by the divine glory reflected on Moses's face—a glory that began to fade as soon as he left the divine presence. On the other hand, a covenant destined to be permanent (cf. Heb 13:20) must be invested with a far greater glory.

Notes

9 The third ed. of the UBS text, unlike the first and second, prefers the reading τῇ διακονίᾳ (*tē diakonia*) on the basis of the strong external evidence (p^{46} ℵ A C D* G), and explains the nominative reading ἡ διακονία (*hē diakonia*) as resulting from scribal assimilation to the *diakonia* that precedes (and follows). The tr. will then run: "If there was glory in the ministry that condemns men...."

164

11 Τὸ καταργούμενον (to katargoumenon; cf. v.7) may mean "what was destined to pass away" or "what was in process of fading away."

---

e. *Veiling and unveiling*

3:12–18

> [12]Therefore, since we have such a hope, we are very bold. [13]We are not like Moses, who veiled his face to keep the Israelites from gazing at it while the radiance was fading away. [14]But their minds were made dull; for to this day the same veil remains when the old covenant is read. It has not been removed, because only in Christ is it taken away. [15]Even to this day when Moses is read, a veil covers their hearts. [16]But whenever anyone turns to the Lord, "the veil is taken away." [17]Now the Lord is the Spirit, and where the Spirit of the Lord is, there is freedom. [18]And we, who with unveiled faces all reflect the Lord's glory, are being transformed into his likeness with ever-increasing glory, which comes from the Lord, who is the Spirit.

12,13 As participants in the new covenant, Paul and his fellow apostles and fellow preachers had the sure hope that it was a permanent, irrevocable covenant, never to be superseded and never to be surpassed in splendor. This accounted for their boldness and confidence (see note on *parrhēsia*) in preaching. They had nothing to conceal but every reason for fearless candor (v.12).

This idea of openness prompts Paul to continue his *midrash* on Exodus 34:29–35. This OT passage suggested that after each encounter between Moses and Yahweh in the "tent of meeting," when Moses returned to the people of Israel to tell them what he had been commanded, they were dazzled by the radiance of his face. When he had finished speaking to them, he used to veil his face. "But whenever Moses went in before the Lord to speak with him, he took the veil off, until he came out"(Exod 34:34, RSV). Although the OT does not explicitly state that the radiance on the face of Moses gradually faded and then disappeared, Paul deduced that the reason for Moses's veiling or masking his face was not so much to prevent the Israelites from being dazzled by its brightness (cf. Exod 34:30, 31) as to prevent them from continuing to gaze in amazement till his face had totally lost the brilliance of the reflected glory (cf. v.7). He was attempting to teach them, Paul implies, that the newly established order was destined to be eclipsed and pass away.

P.E. Hughes (in loc.) argues that the purpose of Moses' veiling was to prevent the Israelites from looking "right on to the end" of what was transient. It was an acted parable condemning the people, showing them that their sins had made them unable and unworthy to behold even temporary glory without interruption. Others believe that Moses wished to avoid the personal embarrassment of having the people realize the splendor of his face was fading, or that he did not want to undermine their confidence in the present dispensation by letting them see it was transient (see note).

14,15 Moses' laudable attempt was however, unsuccessful; instead of recognizing the significance of the fading glory, the Israelites became dulled in their powers of perception. Paul finds evidence of this spiritual insensitivity in the fact that down to his own day, when the old covenant (= the OT) was read in the synagogue or the Torah studied, the ability of the Jews to recognize the impermanence of the Mosaic order was impaired. A "veil" covered their hearts comparable to the veil that covered Moses's face. Paul could call it the "same" veil, because in both cases a veil prevented vision, whether physical or spiritual, or because it was identical to the veil of ignorance about the transitory nature of the Mosaic economy covering the hearts of the contemporaries of Moses. This veil remained unlifted (see note) in the case of the unbelieving Jew, because only as he came to be "in Christ" was the veil set aside.

16 In LXX Exodus 34:34 reads, "But whenever Moses went in before the Lord to speak to him, he used to take off the veil until he went out." Only three Greek words remain the same, as Paul here alludes to this verse (see note for the significance of the change of verb tenses). The subject of the verb *epistrepsē* ("turns") is unexpressed. It may be "the heart [of a Jew]," from v.15b; "the Jew" or "Israel"; or "a person," Jew or Gentile. The last option may be preferable, but in the context Paul is thinking particularly of the Jew.

The verse restates and amplifies what is stated at the end of v.14, viz., that only in Christ is the veil set aside. Whenever a person turns to the Lord and finds in him the end or fulfillment of the law (Rom 10:4), the Lord completely removes the veil from his heart. No longer is his spiritual perception impaired (v.14). He recognizes that the dispensation of grace has superseded the dispensation of the law (cf. John 1:17). He is a "new creation" in Christ (5:17).

17 Out of its context, this verse might suggest that Paul is identifying the risen Christ with the Spirit (as W. Bousset and others have held). But v.17 explains v.16. "The Lord" referred to in the quotation from Exodus 34:34, to whom the Jew must now turn for the removal of the veil, is none other than the life-giving Spirit of the living God (cf. vv.3, 6, 8). This is an affirmation about the Spirit, not about Christ; it describes his function, not his identity (as though the Spirit were the Lord [= Yahweh] of v.16).

Another view finds here a functional equivalence between Christ and the Spirit: in v.14 it is Christ who removes the veil; in v.16 it is the Spirit. Again, some believe Christ (*ho Kyrios*) is being identified as "life-giving Spirit" (1 Cor 15:45; cf. 2 Cor 3:6).

Paul's point in v.17b is that though the Spirit is Lord, who has the right to exercise authority, his presence brings liberation, not bondage (Rom 8:15). Not only does he remove the veil; he also sets a person free from bondage to sin, to death, and to the law as a means of acquiring righteousness.

18 In vv.4–6 Paul was speaking primarily of the apostolic ministry. Now, as he draws his conclusion concerning the superiority of the new covenant against the background of his commentary on Exodus 34, he refers to Christian experience in general. Under the new covenant, not one man alone, but all Christians behold and then reflect (see note) the glory of the Lord. Moreover, unlike the Jews, who still read the law with veiled hearts, Christians, with unveiled faces, behold in the mirror of the gospel the glory of Yahweh, which is Christ. Again, the glory is displayed not outwardly on the face but inwardly in the character. Finally, so far from losing its intensity or luster, the glory experienced under the new covenant progressively increases until the Christian finally acquires a "glorious body" like that of the risen Christ (Phil 3:21).

Paul concludes by noting that the progressive transformation of the Christian's character is the work of the Lord who is the Spirit (cf. v.17a). After conversion to the Spirit (v.16), there is liberation through the Spirit (v.17b) and transformation by the Spirit (v.18).

Notes

12 Παρρησία (*parrhēsia*) originally meant "frankness or freedom in speaking" or "fearless candor" but came to denote "barefacedness," "boldness," or "confidence" or "openness" in action as well as word. See further W.C. van Unnik, "The Christian's Freedom of Speech in the New Testament." *Bulletin of the John Rylands Library*, XLIV (2, 1962), pp. 466–488; and " 'With Unveiled Face,' an Exegesis of 2 Corinthians iii 12–18." Nov Test VI (2–3, 1963), pp. 153–169.

13 Τοῦ καταργουμένου (*tou katargoumenou*, neuter) seems to refer, not precisely to the δόξα (*doxa*, feminine) but to the fading brightness of the old order or dispensation (note the neuters of vv.10, 11). Thus "Moses used to place [ἐτίθει, *etithei*] a veil over his face to prevent the Israelites from gazing at the end of the fading brightness." Significantly, in rabbinic tradition the glory of Moses's face was undiminished right up to the day of his death when he was 120 years old.

14 H. Seesemann (TDNT, 5:720, n.13) suggests that Paul may have coined the phrase "old covenant" to match Jeremiah's "new covenant" (Jer 31:31) and the eucharistic tradition of the cup as the "new covenant" in Christ's blood (1 Cor 11:25).

The Gr. of v.14c may be punctuated in two basic ways: (1) with a comma after μένει (*menei*, "remains"), reflected in NIV (also NEB); (2) with a comma after ἀνακαλυπτόμενον (*anakalyptomenon*, lit. "being unveiled"), either (a) "that same veil remains unlifted, because [ὅτι, *hoti*] only through Christ is it taken away" (RSV), or (b) "the same veil remaineth unlifted; which *veil* [reading ὅ τι, *ho ti*, as = ὅ, *ho*] is done away in Christ" (RV; also KJV).

16 In Exod 34:34 LXX has εἰσεπορεύετο (*eiseporeueto*) and περιῃρεῖτο (*periēreito*), both imperfects, whereas Paul has an aorist (ἐπιστρέψῃ, *epistrepsē*, "turns" [single act]) and a present (περιαιρεῖται, *periaireitai*, "is removed"). The change accords with his omission of the subject "Moses." He is thinking not of the habitual practice of one man (viz., Moses' entering of the "tent of meeting"), but of a single "turning" and "removal" in the case of many men.

Περιαιρεῖται (*periaireitai*) may be (1) middle (like its LXX equivalent, where Moses is the subject): "whenever anyone turns to the Lord, he *removes* the veil," where "he" may be the "anyone" or the "Lord"; or preferably (2) passive: "whenever anyone [or the Jew, or Israel, or their heart] turns to the Lord, the veil *is removed*" (as in NIV).

17 In Pauline usage ὁ Κύριος (*ho Kyrios*) generally means "Christ," and Κύριος (*Kyrios*) signifies Yahweh. In this verse ὁ κύριος refers to Yahweh, for the article is anaphoric, pointing back to the anarthrous κύριον (*kyrion* = Yahweh) in v.16. See M. Zerwick, *Biblical Greek* (Rome: Pontifical Biblical Institute, 1963), p. 54, paragraph 169; and the article by J.D.G. Dunn, "2 Corinthians III. 17—'The Lord is the Spirit.' " *Journal of Theological Studies*, XXI (2, 1970), pp. 309–320.

18 Three related meanings of κατοπτριζόμενοι (*katoptrizomenoi*) are possible: (1) "beholding as in a mirror" (cf. 1 Cor 13:12); (2) "reflecting like a mirror"; (3) "beholding" (Vul. *speculantes*), with no necessary reference to a mirror. Some (e.g., K. Prümm, J. Jervell) believe Paul used this ambiguous verb intentionally. See further J.-F. Collange. *Énigmes de la deuxième Épître de Paul aux Corinthiens* (Cambridge: Cambridge University Press, 1972), pp. 116–118, and P.E. Hughes, in loc.

---

f. The light brought by the gospel

4:1-6

¹Therefore, since through God's mercy we have this ministry, we do not lose heart. ²Rather, we have renounced secret and shameful ways; we do not use deception, nor do we distort the word of God. On the contrary, by setting forth the truth plainly we commend ourselves to every man's conscience in the sight of God. ³And even if our gospel is veiled, it is veiled to those who are perishing. ⁴The god

of this age has blinded the minds of unbelievers, so that they cannot see the light of the gospel of the glory of Christ, who is the image of God. [5]For we do not preach ourselves, but Jesus Christ as Lord, and ourselves as your servants for Jesus' sake. [6]For God who said, "Let light shine out of darkness," made his light shine in our hearts to give us the light of the knowledge of the glory of God in the face of Christ.

1 At 4:1 Paul resumes the theme of 3:6—divine appointment and provision to be a minister of a new covenant. He had no reason to lose heart (cf. Gal 6:9), for God in his mercy had granted him a privilege exceeding that of Moses (cf. 1 Tim 1:12–16). He had been called not to communicate the law but to dispense grace. A minister of the gospel has a higher calling than even the mediator of the law. Paul regarded this divine commission to serve under the new covenant as more than compensating for all the trials he endured for being true to his calling (vv.7–12, 17; cf. Rom 8:18), including the malicious charges of his Corinthian opponents (note v.2).

2 To this thought of refusing to grow disheartened Paul will return presently (v.16). Now he expands his brief self-defense of 2:17. Evidently he had been accused of deceitful behavior (cf. 7:2; 12:16). This he emphatically rejects. The openness marking the new covenant had always been reflected in his conduct. His tactics had never been secretive or deceptive, nor had he ever dishonestly manipulated the message of God entrusted to him. His not insisting on Gentile compliance with the Mosaic law had probably given rise to the charge that he willfully adulterated the gospel (cf. 2:17).

In any self-defense, self-commendation must play some part. But Paul's self-commendation was distinctive. He commended himself, not by self-vindication at every point, but simply by the open declaration of the truth (in particular, the gospel and its implications). His appeal was not directed to a partisan spirit or the prejudices of men but "to every man's conscience." His self-commendation was undertaken with God as onlooker.

3,4 Paul's gospel, some had claimed, was designed only for a spiritually minded élite. What he said was obscure, just as what he did was underhanded (v.2). For the sake of argument, Paul concedes his critics' point. Even if his gospel is veiled in the case of some people, it is not his doing, because he sets forth the truth plainly (v.2). The veiling, where it exists (cf. 3:14, 15), comes from the unbelief of "those who are perishing" (cf. 1 Cor 1:18; 2 Cor 2:15), whose minds have been blinded by the god of "the present evil age" (Gal 1:4), who wishes to prevent them from seeing the gospel-light that focuses on Christ's glory as the image of God.

"The god of this age" refers, of course, not to God the Father, but to Satan regarded as "the prince of this world" (John 12:31) or as the one whom this age has made its god. If dualism is found in Paul, it is an ethical and temporal dualism, not a material or metaphysical one. Satan is *not* the god of "the age to come."

When Paul calls Christ "the image of God," he is asserting that Christ is the visible and perfect representation of the invisible God (Col 1:15; cf. John 1:18), the precise expression of the unseen God. When used of the relation of Christ to God, *eikōn* (image) implies both personality and distinctiveness.

5 Though Paul might have been forced to commend himself to every man's conscience (v.2; cf. 1:12; 6:4), he never advertised or preached himself. The essence of his gospel was the proclamation of "Jesus Christ as Lord" (Rom 10:9; 1 Cor 12:3; Col 2:6, NIV), a

message faithfully delivered by him and eagerly embraced by the Corinthians (1:18–22). Paul saw himself related to his converts, not as a spiritual overlord (1:24) but as a willing servant as well as a concerned father (1 Cor 4:15). In this he followed in the footsteps of "the Lord of glory" (1 Cor 2:8), who himself had adopted the status and rôle of a servant (Phil 2:7; cf. Rom 15:8). Paul was both preacher (v.5a) and pastor (v.5b).

6 Paul now states the reason why he preached Christ and served the Corinthians. It was because God had dispelled his darkness by illuminating his heart and had given him a knowledge of Christ he wished to share (cf. Acts 9:15; 26:16, 18; Gal 1:15, 16). In the second creation, as in the first, darkness is dispersed and light is created by divine intervention, but in one case it was a personal word: "Let there be light" (Gen 1:3, which is expanded by Paul on the basis of Gen 1:2); in the other case it was a personal act: "God shone in our hearts" (cf. 1 Peter 2:9).

This is an unmistakable allusion to Paul's Damascus encounter with the risen Christ when God "saw fit to reveal his Son" to him (Gal 1:15, 16). Each of the three Lucan accounts of Paul's conversion mentions the noonday "light from heaven, brighter than the sun" (Acts 9:3, 8, 9; 22:6, 9, 11; 26:13) and emphasizes the personal and revelatory nature of the experience (Acts 9:4, 5; 22:7–10; 26:14–18). It was in the unveiled face (cf. 3:7, 13, 18) of Christ that Paul saw God's glory (see note).

Notes

2 Other possible meanings of τὰ κρυπτὰ τῆς αἰσχύνης (ta krypta tēs aischynēs) are (1) "the behaviour that shame hides" (C.K. Barrett) or "the things that one hides from a sense of shame" (BAG, p. 82), and (2) "the secrecy prompted by shame" (*Twentieth Century New Testament*).
4 The verb αὐγάζειν (augazein, lit. "to shine forth") is here used transitively: "so that they cannot [or, might not] *see* the light . . . ," not intransitively (as in many EV): "that the light . . . should not *dawn* [or, shine forth] upon them" (see ASV). This latter rendering requires αὐτοῖς (autois, "on them") (that is absent from the older MSS). See BAG, p. 120.
5 For a discussion of the significance of the early church's confession "Jesus is Lord," see the author's article on "Lord" in the revised ISBE.
6 The piling up of genitives is typical of Paul's Gr. style. Few studies are more rewarding for exegesis and theology than an examination of his use of the genitive. Here, "of the knowledge" may be an epexegetic genitive (the light consists of the knowledge), or better, a genitive of source (the illumination that springs from knowledge); "of the glory" is objective (Paul came to know the glory); "of God" and "of Christ" are possessive (the glory spoken of is God's, the countenance mentioned is Christ's).
Ἐν προσώπῳ (en prosōpō) here means "in the face of Christ" or "in the person of Christ," whereas in 2:10 it is not to be taken literally and means "in the presence of Christ" (the suggestion of C.F.D. Moule. *An Idiom Book of New Testament Greek* [Cambridge: Cambridge University Press, 1960²], p. 184).

2. *(The apostolic ministry) Its suffering and glory* (4:7–5:10)

a. *The trials and rewards of apostolic service*

4:7–15

> [7]But we have this treasure in jars of clay to show that this all-surpassing power is from God and not from us. [8]We are hard pressed on every side, but not crushed; perplexed, but not in despair; [9]persecuted, but not abandoned; struck down, but not destroyed. [10]We always carry around in our body the death of Jesus, so that the life of Jesus may also be revealed in our body. [11]For we who are alive are always being given over to death for Jesus' sake, so that his life may be revealed in our mortal body. [12]So then, death is at work in us, but life is at work in you.
>
> [13]It is written: "I believed; therefore I have spoken." With that same spirit of faith we also believe and therefore speak, [14]because we know that the one who raised the Lord Jesus from the dead will also raise us with Jesus and present us with you in his presence. [15]All this is for your benefit, so that the grace that is reaching more and more people may cause thanksgiving to overflow to the glory of God.

No person was ever more aware of the paradoxical nature of Christianity than Paul. And perhaps none of his Epistles contains more paradoxes than 2 Corinthians. With their numerous paradoxes, then, verses 7 to 12 are typical of this Epistle and of Paul's style.

7 Here is the first paradox—the difference between the indescribable value of the gospel treasure and the apparent worthlessness of the gospel's ministers. Verse 6 refers to the treasure in the "jars of clay" as "the illumination that comes from the knowledge of God's glory." In describing those to whom the gospel is entrusted (1 Thess 2:4) as "earthenware vessels," Paul is not disparaging the human body or implying that the body is simply the receptacle of the soul (see note). Rather, he is contrasting the relative insignificance and unattractiveness of the bearers of the light with the inestimable worth and beauty of the light itself. Behind this contrast Paul sees a divine purpose—that men may recognize that "this all-surpassing power" is God's alone. His power finds its full scope in human weakness (12:9).

8,9 There follows a series of four vivid antitheses that illustrate both the weakness of Paul in discharging his commission and the power of God in preserving his life and his spirit. Each metaphor may reflect gladiatorial or military combat. Paul was "hard pressed on every side," but not completely cornered or without room for movement, never driven to surrender. He was "bewildered ... [but] never at ... wits' end" (NEB), or (as an attempt to retain the word-play of the Greek) "at a loss, but never totally at a loss." He was hounded by the foe, but not left to his mercy. He was knocked to the ground, but not permanently "grounded."

10,11 Verse 10 summarizes the four preceding contrasts in the paradox: "always dying, yet never lifeless." In the phrase "the death [or, dying] of Jesus," Paul sums up the experience of being "hard pressed," "perplexed," "persecuted," and "struck down" during the course of his service for him. On the other hand, he uses the phrase "the life of Jesus" to express the Lord's saving him from being crushed, from despair, from abandonment, and from destruction, all of which prefigures the Christian's final deliverance from mortality at the resurrection. This idea of "life in the midst of death" is, of course, closely related to the theme of 2 Corinthians 1–7—"comfort in the midst of affliction" (see Introduction, 9).

But the meaning of the arresting phrase "the dying of Jesus" is also explained by what follows, since v.11a amplifies v.10a. "The dying of Jesus" that Paul "carried around" in his body (v.10a) was nothing other than his being always "given over to death for Jesus' sake" (v.11a). He faced perilous hazards every hour and death every day, as he says in 1 Corinthians 15:30, 31 (cf. 1 Cor 4:9). This contextual interpretation of the phrase seems preferable to understanding it as a reference to the Christian's once-for-all baptismal identification with Christ in his death (Rom 6:3–5), or his daily mortification of his sinful nature (Gal 5:24; cf. Luke 9:23), or the gradual weakening of his physical powers while serving Christ.

Both verses stress (through *hina kai*, "so that . . . also") the fact that the death and the life of Jesus were simultaneously evident in the apostle's experience (cf. 1:4, 5). It was not a matter of life after death, or even of life through death, but of life in the midst of death. Paul's repeated deliverances from death evidenced the resurrecting power of God (1:9, 10), just as his refusal to despair in the face of the danger of death and persistent opposition (4:1, 16; 5:6) displayed the resurrection-life of Jesus operative in his "mortal body" (cf. Phil 3:10).

12 With a bold stroke, Paul relates this theme of "life in death" to his earlier statements in chapter 1 about vicarious suffering (1:3–7). There he had said, "I suffer for Christ; God comforts me; I comfort you during your suffering." Here his thought seems to be "I suffer exposure to physical death for your sakes [cf. v.15a]; you enjoy more of the risen life of Christ as a consequence." He apparently saw not only a causal but also a proportional relation between his "death" and the "life" of the Corinthian believers. The deeper his experience of the trials and sufferings of the apostolic life, the richer their experience of the joys and privileges of Christian existence (cf. Col 1:24; 2 Tim 2:10). The "middle term" between his experience and theirs was the divine comfort that, having received, he could then dispense (cf. 1:4). This rich theology of suffering was forged on the anvil of his own experience of "the sufferings of Christ."

13,14 But what enabled Paul faithfully to discharge his ministry (3:6; 4:1, 5), even though it involved suffering? It was his sharing the psalmist's conviction that faith cannot remain silent and his own Christian conviction that Christ's resurrection guarantees the resurrection of believers.

The exact meaning of the Hebrew text of Psalm 116:10a is uncertain (see notes). In his quotation Paul follows the LXX (Ps 115:1) exactly: "I believed; therefore I have spoken," a translation of the Hebrew in accord with the spirit of the psalm, though not with its precise words. The psalmist recounts a divine deliverance from a desperate illness and its accompanying despondency (vv.1–11) and then considers how he might most fittingly render his devotion to the Lord (vv.12–19). In a real sense, then, the psalmist's expression of thanksgiving arose from his vindicated trust in God: "I held firm to my faith and was vindicated; therefore I have spoken." Paul, for his part, could not remain silent about the gospel he believed: "Woe to me if I do not preach the gospel" (1 Cor 9:16).

Another reason Paul proclaimed the good news with the utmost confidence (cf. 3:12) was his firm conviction of his personal resurrection and his being presented along with all believers before the presence of God or Christ (cf. 11:2; Eph 5:27; Col 1:22). Christians will be raised "with Jesus" (cf. 1 Thess 4:14) in the sense that the resurrected Christ forms the prototype and ground of their resurrection (1 Cor 15:23). In Christ's resurrection from the dead as the firstfruits of the Easter harvest, believers have the pledge of the full ingathering.

15 This verse concludes a section of Paul's thought, for in v.16 he repeats the phrase "we do not lose heart" from v.1. Rather movingly, the apostle reminds his converts that he endures all his afflictions with resilience, not to promote his own good but for their benefit (cf. 4:5), and ultimately for God's glory. As God's grace expanded in their hearts and through them reached ever-increasing numbers, so too, the volume of thanksgiving to God for the receipt of illumination (cf. 4:6) would increase and promote the glory of God.

Notes

7 For Paul the σκεῦος (skeuos, "jar") was no more the container in which was placed the "treasure" of a ψυχή (psychē, "life," "soul") than the "outer man" was a detachable outer garment clothing "the inner man." Σκεύη (skeuē) refers to whole persons, who, although insignificant and weak in themselves, become God's powerful instruments in communicating the treasure of the gospel. Paul's anthropology was basically monistic, not dualistic; see D.E.H. Whiteley, *The Theology of St. Paul* (Philadelphia: Fortress Press, 1964), pp. 31–44.

13 To facilitate understanding, the NIV breaks up one Gr. sentence into two and rearranges the word order. As it stands, v.13 reads, "But since we have the same spirit of faith as that reflected in the Scripture 'I believed and so I spoke,' we too believe and that is why we speak."

The Heb. of Ps 116:10a reads, האמנתי כי אדבר (heʾĕmantî, kî ʾᵃdabbēr), which could be translated, (1) "I believed, for I will speak"; (2) "I kept my faith, even when I said, ('I am greatly afflicted')" (RSV; similarly JB); or (3) "I believed, therefore I spoke" (LXX, followed here by Paul; Vul.; similarly KJV). In the first case, speaking is the proof of belief; in the third, belief is the ground for speaking. Some (e.g., H.L. Goudge) have suggested that Paul viewed not the psalmist but Christ himself as speaking in the psalm (vv.3, 4 are thought to portray Gethsemane; and vv.5–9, Easter). Paul's spirit would then be "the spirit" of Christ.

15 Another possible tr. might be: "All this is for your benefit, so that the expansion of grace may cause thanksgiving to abound through [the winning of] increasing numbers [of converts], to the glory of God."

b. Glory through suffering

4:16–18

> ¹⁶Therefore we do not lose heart. Though outwardly we are wasting away, yet inwardly we are being renewed day by day. ¹⁷For our light and momentary troubles are achieving for us an eternal glory that far outweighs them all. ¹⁸So we fix our eyes not on what is seen, but on what is unseen. For what is seen is temporary, but what is unseen is eternal.

16 "Therefore we do not lose heart" looks back to vv.14, 15 and v.1. Paul has now supplied several reasons for his refusal to grow discouraged in spite of seemingly overwhelming odds: (1) his divine commission as a minister of a new and superior covenant (4:1), (2) the prospect of sharing Christ's triumphant resurrection from the dead (4:14), and (3) his immediate task of promoting the Corinthians' spiritual welfare and the glory of God (4:15).

But Paul was realistic enough to recognize that his toil and suffering had taken their toll physically. For this, however, there was splendid compensation. Matching the progressive weakening of his physical powers was the daily renewal of his spiritual powers (see note). It was as though the more he expended himself for the gospel's sake (cf. 12:15), the greater his spiritual resilience (cf. Eph 3:16).

17 Here Paul supplies a surprising definition of daily spiritual renewal. It is a constant production of solid, lasting glory (literally "an eternal weight of glory") out of all proportion to the slight, present affliction that causes physical weakness (v.16); or, as the NIV renders it, this eternal glory "far outweighs" any "light and momentary troubles" that are being presently experienced (cf. Rom 8:18). Quite naturally Paul seems to speak of glory as though it were a substantial entity that could be progressively added to. In a similar way in Colossians 1:5 Paul views Christian hope as an inheritance "stored up" in heaven.

Again, as in vv.12, 16, the idea of proportion seems to be present. Since it is actually the "troubles" that produce or achieve the glory, the greater the affliction Paul suffered, the greater the glory produced for him.

18 But this production of glory was by no means automatic. It was only as attention was focused on what was unseen that suffering led to glory. The participle with which the verse begins may be translated "provided [or, since] we keep our eyes fixed...."

Behind the contrast between "what is seen" and "what is unseen" is the Pauline tension between the "already" and the "not yet" (cf. Rom 8:24, 25; 1 Cor 13:12), the contrast between what is now seen by mortals and what is as yet hidden from mortal gaze, rather than the Platonic antithesis of the real and the ideal or a philosophical distinction between the visible and the invisible (cf. Col 1:16). Paul is not repudiating any interest in the visible world. Rather, he is affirming that his affections are set "on things above" (Col 3:1, 2), on lasting realities as yet unseen, on the age to come that is present in promises and blessings still to be fully realized. The antithesis is temporal and eschatological, not essential and philosophical.

This preoccupation with the realm "where Christ is seated at the right hand of God" (Col 3:1) was not the result of an arbitrary choice; it was an informed decision. Paul was profoundly aware that the present age is transient (cf. 1 Cor 7:31), whereas the age to come is eternal in the sense of being "destined to last for ever," and that his afflictions were temporary but his reward eternal.

Notes

16 NIV appropriately renders the phrases "our outer man" and "our inner [man]" by "outwardly we..." and "inwardly we...." Paul is not thinking of two distinct entities, "the body" and "the soul," but is considering his total existence from two different viewpoints. His "outer man" is his whole person in his "creaturely mortality" (J. Behm, TDNT, 2:699), the man of this age; his "inner man" is his whole person as a "new creation" (5:17) or a "new man" (Col 3:9, 10), the man of the age to come. Pauline anthropology is aspectival not partitive, synthetic not analytic. See W.D. Stacey, *The Pauline View of Man* (New York: St. Martin's, 1956), especially pp. 211–214.

17 Paul's unique phrase "an eternal weight of glory" was doubtless suggested to him by the Heb. כָּבוֹד (*kābôd*) which may mean both "weight" and "glory."

---

c. Confidence in the face of death

5:1-10

> [1]Now we know that if the earthly tent we live in is destroyed, we have a building from God, an eternal house in heaven, not built by human hands. [2]Meanwhile we groan, longing to be clothed with our heavenly dwelling, [3]since when we are clothed, we will not be found naked. [4]For while we are in this tent, we groan and are burdened, because we do not wish to be unclothed but to be clothed with our heavenly dwelling, so that what is mortal may be swallowed up by life. [5]Now it is God who has made us for this very purpose and has given us the Spirit as a deposit, guaranteeing what is to come.
>
> [6]Therefore we are always confident and know that as long as we are at home in the body we are away from the Lord. [7]We live by faith, not by sight. [8]We are confident, I say, and would prefer to be away from the body and at home with the Lord. [9]So we make it our goal to please him, whether we are at home in the body or away from it. [10]For we must all appear before the judgment seat of Christ, that each one may receive what is due him for the things done while in the body, whether good or bad.

No passage in 2 Corinthians has prompted more discussion than this. As a consequence, the diversity of scholarly interpretation is rather bewildering.

What Paul says here is directly related to the latter part of chapter 4. There he pointed out that even in the midst of affliction, perplexity and persecution, there was, through divine consolation, the hope of glory (4:8, 9, 13, 14, 17). Even in the presence of the ravages of mortality and death, there was, through divine intervention, the operation of life (4:10–12, 16; cf. 6:9). This twofold theme—life in the midst of death, glory after and through suffering—is continued in 5:1–10. Paul now specifies the sources of divine comfort afforded the believer who faces the possibility of imminent death. Basically, they are three: (1) certainty of the future possession of a spiritual body (v.1), (2) the present possession of the Spirit as the pledge of ultimate transformation (vv.4b, 5), and (3) knowledge that death begins a walk "in the realm of sight" (v.7) and involves departure to Christ's immediate presence where personal fellowship with him is enjoyed (v.8).

1 Apparently for the first time in his apostolic career Paul reckons seriously with the possibility—now a probability—of his death before the return of Christ. Previously, to judge by 1 Thessalonians 4:15, 17 and 1 Corinthians 15:51, he had expected to be among those Christians living when Christ returned. But now, as a result of his recent devastating encounter with death in Asia (1:8–11), he realized that he was likely to die before the Parousia, though he always entertained the hope of survival until the Advent (note Phil 3:20, 21).

As a Cilician "leatherworker" whose duties would include tentmaking, Paul naturally likened his present body to an earthly tent (cf. vv.2, 4) that might at any moment be dismantled or destroyed. This would simply mark the termination of the process of weakness and decay already at work in his body (4:16). But this possibility did not daunt him, for he was the assured recipient of a permanent heavenly house—the spiritual body provided by God (see notes).

2–4 These verses belong together, since v.4 expands v.2, while v.3 is parenthetical (cf. the similar structure of vv.6–8). One reason for Paul's assurance of his future acquisition of a resurrection body was the raising up of the temple of Christ's body (Mark 14:58; John 2:19, 21, 22) alluded to by the phrase "not built by human hands" in v.1. An additional reason was the experience of Spirit-inspired groaning (vv.2, 4; cf. Rom 8:23). Paul's sighing did not stem from a desire to become permanently disembodied but from an intense longing to take up residence in his "heavenly dwelling" ("we sigh, because we long . . . ," v.2 Wey.).

The passage does not define the precise nature of the "sighing" or "groaning," but the immediate context and Paul's thought elsewhere (Rom 8:19–23; Phil 3:20, 21) suggest it was his sense of frustration with the limitations and disabilities of mortal existence, knowing as he did that he was destined to possess a spiritual body perfectly adapted to the ecology of heaven. Paul sought liberation only from the imperfection of present embodiment, from "bondage to decay," not from any and every form of corporeality. After all, it is to Paul that Christian theology owes the doctrine of the "spiritual body" (1 Cor 15:35–49).

But not all at Corinth shared Paul's view of the Christian's destiny. There were some who taught that resurrection lay in the past, acccomplished spiritually and corporately for all believers at the resurrection of Christ or else personally experienced at the moment of baptism (cf. 2 Tim 2:17, 18). Having in mind these "proto-Gnostics" who denied any future, bodily resurrection but envisaged a disembodied immortality, Paul asserts, "We do not wish to be *un*clothed but to be *over*clothed with our heavenly dwelling."

This background also affords a satisfying interpretation of v.3. Perhaps Paul's opponents (1 Cor 15:12) had fastened on the apostle's innocent statement in 1 Cor 15:53, 54 about "putting on immortality" (see RSV and most EV) as the epitome of their own view. If so, Paul could be now repudiating this aberrant conception of the future: ". . . since when we are clothed, we will not be found naked" (as some of you would like to believe).

Of the many other interpretations of vv.2–4a, one may be sketched. Not a few commentators believe that Paul is expressing his own eager desire to avoid the unpleasantness or pain of a disembodied intermediate state by being preserved alive till the coming of Christ. He shrinks from the denudation of death ("we do not wish to be unclothed") and longs to put on his heavenly dwelling *over* his preserved earthly tent (see notes), though he is uncertain whether this will happen ("if, in fact, we shall be found clothed and not naked").

Verse 4b states the purpose and actual result of the receipt of the heavenly dwelling— the swallowing up of the mortal body by the revivifying action of the indwelling Spirit of life (Rom 8:2, 11; 2 Cor 3:6, 18). This transformation forms the climax of the incessant process of inward renewal (4:16b). In other words, 5:4b is related to 4:16b as 5:1a is related to 4:16a. For Paul, resurrection consummates rather than inaugurates the process of spiritual re-creation. From one point of view, the spiritual body was a future gift that came by outward investiture; from another, it was a present creation that finally came by inward transformation.

5 "This very purpose," for which God had "made" (better, "prepared") the believer is defined by v.4b as the transformation of the mortal body. Verse 5b indicates how the preparation took place. God has prepared the Christian believer for the resurrection-transformation by giving him the Spirit as the pledge of it (or "as a deposit, guaranteeing what is to come").

Undoubtedly the crucial word in the verse is *arrhabōn,* which had two basic meanings in commercial usage. It was (1) a pledge or guarantee, differing in kind from the final payment but rendering it obligatory or (2) a partial payment (first installment, down-payment, deposit) that required further payments but gave the payee a legal claim to the goods in question (see BAG, p. 109, for this second use). Clearly not all these elements apply to Paul's use of the word, for redemption is no process of reciprocal bargaining ratified by some contractually binding agreement but is the result of the grace of God, who bestows on believers his Spirit as an unsolicited gift. Certainly Paul did not regard the Spirit as a pledge to be returned (cf. Gen 38:17-20) or as an inferior part of the Christian's inheritance. Significantly, in Modern Greek *arrhabōna* means "engagement ring."

But how can the Spirit be God's pledge of the Christian's inheritance (Eph 1:13, 14; cf. 4:30)? No doubt through his empowering the Christian's daily re-creation (3:18; 4:16; Eph 3:16) and his future effecting of the Christian's resurrection transformation (Rom 8:11). His present work prefigures and guarantees his future completion of that work (cf. Phil 1:6).

6-8 With the assured hope of his acquisition of a glorified body (v.1) and having a pledge of his transformation in the presence and activity of the Spirit within him (v.5), Paul was always confident, even in the face of death. "But," he continues, "because we realize that we are absent from the Lord's presence as long as this body forms our residence, it is our preference to leave our home in this body and take up residence in the presence of the Lord" (a paraphrase of vv.6, 8).

Just as the repeated verb "we groan" shows vv.2 and 4 to be related, so "we are confident" relates vv.6 and 8, vv.3 and 7 being parenthetical in each case. But v.8 does not simply repeat v.6; it stands in antithetical parallelism to it. The corollary of "residence in the body = absence from the Lord" (v.6) is "absence from the body = residence with the Lord" (v.8). That is, what is implied in v.6 is stated positively in v.8: as soon as departure from mortal corporeality occurs (v.8a), residence in the Lord's presence begins (v.8b). This then means that the same moment of death that marks the destruction of the transitory earthly tent-dwelling (v.1) also marks the taking up of permanent residence "with the Lord" (v.8).

What did Paul understand to be involved in being "at home with the Lord"? To be sure, the Greek preposition *pros* (here meaning "with") in itself simply denotes location. Yet when it describes the interrelation of two persons, it necessarily implies a fellowship both active and reciprocal (cf. *pros* in Mark 6:3: "Are not his sisters here *with* us?"). In any case, since the phrase "at home with the Lord" depicts the Christian's eternal destiny (cf. 1 Thess 4:17; Phil 1:23), what is thus signified must supersede earthly experience where the believer "knows" the Lord (Phil 3:10). So being "at home with the Lord" is a higher form of the intimate fellowship with Christ that the believer experiences on earth.

In v.7 Paul corrects a possible misinterpretation of v.6. If the clause "we are away from the Lord" (v.6) is interpreted in an absolute sense, present fellowship with Christ would appear illusory and mortal embodiment would seem a hindrance to spirituality. Since both deductions would be totally false, Paul qualifies his statement by observing that "we do in fact still walk in the realm of faith, not of sight." To the believer the Lord is present, not to sight but to faith. Any "spatial" separation is temporary, not final.

9,10 Verse 9 follows vv.1-8 in much the same way as an ethical imperative frequently follows a doctrinal indicative in Paul's Epistles ("You are; therefore be!"). After stating profound doctrinal facts (vv.1–8) Paul shows their implications for behavior (v.9). His constant ambition to please Christ (v.9) was the direct outcome (*dio kai,* "that is why"; "so" in NIV) of his awareness that death would terminate his relative exile from Christ and inaugurate his "walking in the realm of sight in the presence of the Lord" (vv.6–8). To entertain the hope of person-to-person communion with Christ after death (v.8) naturally prompts the aspiration of gaining acceptance in his eyes before and after death (cf. Gal 1:10; Phil 1:20; Col 1:10; 1 Thess 4:1).

We should not try to draw any implication from v.9 regarding the possibility of performing actions during the "intermediate state" that may be pleasing to Christ. The recompense spoken of in v.10 rests exclusively on the basis of "the things done while in the body." Accordingly, "away from it" (the body) in v.9 probably alludes to the judgment.

In v.10 we find a second and secondary reason for Paul's eager striving to win Christ's approval. Not only was there his destiny with Christ (v.8), but there was also his accountability to Christ (v.10) requiring his compulsory attendance before the tribunal of Christ. From 1 Corinthians 4:5 we see that this involves not merely an "appearance" in the court of heaven (cf. Rom 14:10) but the divine illumination of what has been hidden by darkness and the divine exposure of secret aims and motives. The person thus scrutinized will then receive an equitable and full recompense ("what is due him").

Of whom is this attendance required? It is true that all men are accountable to God their maker and judge (Rom 2:1–11). In this context, however, Paul is thinking primarily, if not exclusively, of the Christian's obligation to "give an account of himself" (Rom 14:12). Appearance before Christ's tribunal is the privilege of Christians. It is concerned with the assessment of works and, indirectly, of character, not with the determination of destiny; with reward, not status. Judgment on the basis of works is not opposed to justification on the basis of faith. Delivered from "the works of the law" (Rom 3:28), the Christian is presently committed to "the work of faith," "action stemming from faith" (1 Thess 1:3), that will be assessed and rewarded at the *bēma* ("tribunal"). Yet not all verdicts will be comforting. The believer may "suffer loss" (1 Cor 3:15) by forfeiting Christ's praise or losing a reward that might have been his.

Notes

1–10 On this passage, consult the articles (listed in full in the bibliography, Introduction, 10) by R. Berry, E.E. Ellis, C.F.D. Moule, and the present writer.

1 Not all agree that the οἰκοδομή (*oikodomē,* "building") refers to the believer's resurrection body. Other proposed identifications are: heaven or a house in heaven (C. Hodge), the heavenly temple (H. Odeberg, G. Wagner), a celestial dwelling place (cf. John 14:2) (R.V.G. Tasker), a vestment of celestial glory (F. Prat), the heavenly mode of existence (F.W. Grosheide), the church as the body of Christ or as the new temple (J.A.T. Robinson, E.E. Ellis). Against these proposals, it may be observed that (1) the parallel in v.1b to the "earthly tent" of v.1a (clearly the physical body; cf. 4:10, 11, 16) is likely to be another type of personal embodiment and (2) the fourfold description of the *oikodomē* in v.1 (from God, permanent, heavenly, spiritual) matches Paul's description of the "spiritual body" in 1 Cor 15:38–54.

The present tense ἔχομεν (*echomen,* "we have") of the apodosis could refer to a present possession (though this would convert the condition ["if . . ."] into a concession ["even if . . .]),

177

but more probably it points to a future acquisition that is assured—viz., receipt of a spiritual body at the Parousia or at the moment of death.

2-4 Some commentators (e.g., H.A.W. Meyer, P.E. Hughes) emphasize the doubly compounded verb ἐπ-εν-δύσασθαι (ep-en-dysasthai) and translate it "to put [our heavenly dwelling] on *over* [the earthly tent we live in]," seeing here an allusion to Paul's desire to be alive at the Advent.

3 The UBS text (third ed.) expresses a slight preference ("D" rating) for ἐκδυσάμενοι (*ek-dysamenoi*, "being naked" over ἐνδυσάμενοι (*endysamenoi*, "being clothed") on the basis of internal evidence: "inasmuch as we, though unclothed, shall not be found naked." But B.M. Metzger rightly demurs (*A textual Commentary on the Greek New Testament* [New York: United Bible Societies, 1971], pp. 579, 580). External evidence (p⁴⁶ ℵ B C) supports *en-dysamenoi*, while *ekdysamenoi* (D F it) is an easier reading, an evident amendment to avoid the *prima facie* tautology of "clothed, not naked."

6-8 These verses are anacoluthic. Paul may have intended to write, "Therefore we are always confident, and because we know [εἰδότες, *eidotes*] that as long as we are at home in the body we are away from the Lord, we prefer to be away from the body and at home with the Lord." But the need to qualify his statement of v.6b prompted him to insert an explanatory parenthesis (v.7) that interrupted his flow of thought and caused him to recommence (with a resumptive δέ, *de*, "I say") in v.8 with his principal idea, "we are confident."

9 The NIV correctly supplies "in the body," where the Gr. has simply "whether at home or away." Others (e.g., E.B. Allo, J. Héring) supply "with the Lord" or its equivalent, producing the sense "whether at home with the Lord or absent from his presence."

---

3. (*The apostolic ministry*) *Its function and exercise* (5:11-6:10)

a. *Motivation for service*

5:11-15

> [11]Since, then, we know what it is to fear the Lord, we try to convince men. What we are is plain to God, and I hope it is also plain to your conscience. [12]We are not trying to commend ourselves to you again, but are giving you an opportunity to take pride in us, so that you can answer those who take pride in what is seen rather than in what is in the heart. [13]If we are out of our mind, it is for the sake of God; if we are in our right mind, it is for you. [14]For Christ's love compels us, because we are convinced that one died for all, and therefore all died. [15]And he died for all that those who live should no longer live for themselves, but for him who died for them and was raised again.

11 "The fear of the Lord" here is not personal piety nor the terror that the omnipotent Lord arouses in the hearts of men (e.g., Gen 35:5), but the reverential awe Paul had for Christ as his divine assessor and future judge (v.10). Aware of his personal accountability, Paul strove to persuade men. Of what did he "try to convince" them? Of the truth of the gospel, and the truth concerning himself; viz., that his motives were pure and sincere (cf. 1:12) and that his apostolic credentials and conduct were sound (cf. 3:1-6; 4:1-6). Notice that the open statement and defense of "the truth of the gospel" includes both exposition of the Scriptures about Jesus and the kingdom of God (Acts 17:2-4; 18:4; 19:8; 28:23) and disputation concerning the practical implications of the gospel (Gal 2:14).

Whether or not the persons to whom Paul addressed his appeal recognized his claims about the gospel or himself, God recognized him for what he was. "What we are is plain to God." Yet Paul realized it was necessary for the Corinthians to come to a proper understanding of his apostolic status and conduct. "I hope it is also plain to your conscience."

12 Paul insists that these assertions about himself in relation to God and men should not be interpreted as a further attempt (cf. 3:1) at self-commendation. But he wished his converts to have the necessary ammunition with which to defend his apostleship. They ought, he implies, to have had sufficient pride in him to have undertaken this defense on their own initiative (cf. 12:11) with the weapons to hand—viz., their personal experience of his legitimate apostolic authority, their own knowledge of his devoted service. However, he reluctantly supplies them with additional weaponry by reminding them of the testimony of their individual consciences.

Paul describes the opposition as those who prided themselves on outward appearances. No doubt they made superficial claims to superiority over him—such as their relation to the Jesus of history (5:16) and to Palestinian orthodoxy (11:22) or their greater number of visions and revelations (cf. 12:1-7). Paul was content to take his stand on what was not outwardly evident or fully provable, i.e., what was "in the heart"—transparency before God and men and the testimony of the conscience.

13 Whatever the background to this difficult verse, its general import seems clear. Paul disowns self-interest as a motive for any of his action; all is for God's glory (1 Cor 10:31; 2 Cor 4:15). Of this the Corinthians can be justly proud (v.12). This interpretation accords well with his following appeal (v.14) to Christ as "the man for others," and his definition of the purpose of Christ's death (v.15)—that believers should lead a life that is not centered on self but on Christ.

Verse 13a has been explained in several ways: (1) Paul's critics had accused him of being "out of his mind" (cf. Mark 3:21), perhaps because of his allegedly esoteric teaching (cf. Acts 26:24) or his ecstatic experiences or his indefatigable zeal and tireless work. To this charge he replies, "That is for God to judge." (2) Paul is referring to his experience of glossolalia or visions (cf. Acts 22:17-21), when to some he seemed "beside himself." "It is for God" (cf. 1 Cor 14:2) or "it is a matter between God and me," he answers. (3) On occasion the Corinthians had viewed Paul as having been carried away by excessive emotion. "It led to the glory to God," he affirms. (4) Paul had been criticized for his self-commendation, which appeared to be sheer lunacy. "It is in defense of God's cause," Paul replies. (5) In Jewish eyes, Paul's conversion was evidence of his madness.

14,15 Why was a life of self-pleasing impossible for Paul? Because of the supreme example of his Lord in dying for all. "The love Christ showed for us [see note] compels us to love and serve him and you [cf. v.13b], because when he died, sin's penalty was paid and we died to the self-life, while through his resurrection we live to please him [cf. v.9] by serving you." This, it seems, is the force of these verses in the context of Paul's argument. He has now isolated two motives for Christian service: knowledge of accountability to Christ (v.11) and awareness of Christ's example of self-sacrificing devotion (v.14); in other words, Christ as Savior and as Judge.

Ever since his conversion, Paul had felt "hemmed in" or without an option (*synechei*); he must expend himself in the service of others for Christ's sake (4:11, 12; 12:15). Also dating from his conversion he had two convictions about the death of Christ. The first was that since one man died on behalf of and in the place of all men, all had undergone death (v.14b). Which death? Either the death deservedly theirs because of sin (R.V.G. Tasker) or the death to sin and self that is involved in Christian living (C.K. Barrett). In neither case was the death a physical death like Christ's (notice the subsequent phrase "those who live"). In each case it was a potential, not an actual, "death" of "all men." Paul is not suggesting that, irrespective of their response and attitude, all men know forgiveness of sins or experience selfless living. There is universalism in the scope of redemption, since no man is excluded from God's offer of salvation; but there is a particularity in the application of redemption, since not all men appropriate the benefits afforded by this universally offered salvation.

Paul's second conviction was this: "Dying" with Christ should lead to "living for Christ" (v.15). Paul is not speaking of all men without exception but of "those who live" in union with the resurrected Christ. While all men died potentially when the Man who represented them all died, not all were raised when he rose. But for those who rose with Christ to walk "in newness of life" (Rom 6:4; Col 3:1, 2), slavery to sin and self has ended while devotion to Christ and his church has begun (cf. Rom 6:6, 11). The outcome of Christian self-denial is a Christ-centered life filled with concern for others.

Notes

11 Here Paul twice uses in the perfect tense, with the meaning of "is plain," the same verb (φανερόω, phanēroō) employed in v.10, where it is translated "appear." What Paul must be before Christ's tribunal he now seeks to be before God—"transparently open" (F.F. Bruce, in loc.).

13 As an aorist, ἐξέστημεν (exestēmen, "we are out of our mind"; cf. the parallel present tense, σωφρονοῦμεν, sōphronoumen, "we are in our right mind") may refer either to a single specific occasion when Paul was thought to be "out of his mind," or to habitual or intermittent conduct regarded as a unit.

The two datives θεῷ (theō) and ὑμῖν (hymin) are probably datives of advantage or interest (thus BDF, 101 par. 188 (2); RHG, p. 539): "for the sake of God" and "for you" (NIV).

14 In the context the genitive in the phrase ἡ ἀγάπη τοῦ Χριστοῦ (hē agapē tou Christou, lit. "the love of Christ") is less likely to be objective ("our love for Christ") than subjective ("the love Christ showed"), though some commentators (e.g., H. Lietzmann) and grammarians (e.g., M. Zerwick) believe that both senses are intended. Zerwick comments (Biblical Greek [Rome: Pontifical Biblical Institute, 1963], p. 13): "In interpreting the sacred text . . . we must beware lest we sacrifice to clarity of meaning part of the fulness of the meaning." It is certainly true that the Christian's love for Christ motivates his action (i.e., love of Christ rather than love of money, love of position, etc.), but Paul here is concentrating on an earlier stage of motivation.

b. The message of reconciliation

5:16–6:2

16So from now on we regard no one from a worldly point of view. Though we once regarded Christ in this way, we do so no longer. 17Therefore, if anyone is in Christ, he is a new creation; the old has gone, the new has come! 18All this is from God, who reconciled us to himself through Christ and gave us the ministry of reconciliation: 19that God was reconciling the world to himself in Christ, not counting men's sins against them. And he has committed to us the message of reconciliation. 20We are therefore Christ's ambassadors, as though God were making his appeal through us. We implore you on Christ's behalf: Be reconciled to God.

²¹God made him who had no sin to be sin for us, so that in him we might become the righteousness of God.

¹As God's fellow workers we urge you not to receive God's grace in vain. ²For he says,

> "At the time of my favor I heard you,
> and on the day of salvation I helped you."

I tell you, now is the time of God's favor, now is the day of salvation.

16 With the conjunction *hōste* ("so"; "therefore" in v.17a) Paul introduces the first of two (vv.16, 17) consequences of Christ's death and his own living for Christ. Since his conversion ("from now on"), when he gained the twofold conviction about his own "death" (v.14) and life (v.15), Paul had ceased to make superficial personal judgments (= regarding men "from a worldly point of view") based on external appearances (v.12). It was now his custom to view men, not primarily in terms of nationality but in terms of spiritual status. The Jew-Gentile division was less important for him than the Christian-unbeliever distinction (Rom 2:28, 29; 1 Cor 5:12, 13; Gal 3:28; 6:10; Eph 2:11–22; Col 3:11). Both men and events were seen in light of the new creation.

Similarly, his sincere yet superficial preconversion estimate of Jesus as a misguided messianic pretender whose followers must be extirpated (Acts 9:1, 2; 26:9–11) he now repudiated as being totally erroneous, for he had come to recognize him as the divinely appointed Messiah whose death had brought life (vv.14, 15). Paul's encounter with the risen Lord on the Damascus road effected the twofold change in attitude: Jesus was the Messiah and Lord; Gentile believers were his brothers "in Christ" while his unbelieving compatriots were "without Christ."

17 Paul next states the second outcome of the death and resurrection of Christ (vv. 14, 15). Whenever a person comes to be part of the body of Christ by faith, there is a new act of creation on God's part. One set of conditions or relationships has passed out of existence (*parēlthen*, aorist); another set has come to stay (*gegonen*, perfect). And v.16 indicates that the principal area of change is that of attitude toward Christ and other people. Knowledge "from a worldly point of view" has given place to knowledge in the light of the cross (cf. Gal 6:15). Clearly Paul emphasizes the discontinuity between the two orders and the "newness" of the person in Christ, but in other contexts he implies the coexistence of the present age and the age to come (e.g., 1 Cor 10:11; Gal 1:4) or speaks of the renewal or rebirth of the individual (Rom 12:2; Eph 4:23; Tit 3:5).

18,19 "All this is from God" looks back to the new attitudes of v.16 and the new creation of v.17. God is as surely the author of the second creation as he was of the first (cf. 4:6).

At this point Paul passes from the subjective to the objective aspects of the atonement as he states the fact of reconciliation. Elsewhere he shows that reconciliation is the divine act by which, on the basis of the death of Christ, God's holy displeasure against sinful man was appeased, the enmity between God and man was removed, and man was restored to proper relations with God. (See Rom 5:10, 11; Col 1:20–22, where the cosmic implications of reconciliation are expounded.) Reconciliation is not some polite ignoring or reduction of hostility but rather its total and objective removal.

These two verses make it clear that God was the reconciler, that it was mankind that God reconciled to himself (but cf. Col 1:20), although there is a sense in which this reconciliation was mutual; that Christ was God's agent in effecting reconciliation ("through Christ . . . in Christ"); that the reconciliation has been accomplished ("reconciled . . . was reconciling"); and that reconciliation involved the nonimputation of trespasses, i.e., forgiveness, which is complemented by the imputation of righteousness. In this passage those to whom God has committed the ministry or message of reconciliation (cf. 4:7) are primarily Paul and his fellow-ambassadors. Nevertheless, a reference to all believers cannot be excluded, particularly since not only apostles were reconciled to God (v.18a, "God . . . reconciled us").

20 As proclaimers of the "gospel of peace" (Eph 6:15), which was the good tidings about reconciliation, the apostles were acting on Christ's behalf as messengers and representatives duly appointed by him. Not only so. It was as if God were issuing a personal and direct invitation through them to their hearers to enter into the benefits of the reconciliation already achieved by Christ. "We implore you on Christ's behalf: Be reconciled to God" may be a summary of the "message of reconciliation" (there is no "you" in the Greek) or else specifically Paul's entreaty to the unregenerate at Corinth.

This appeal issued in Christ's name, this message of reconciliation, is the God-designed link between the objective work of reconciliation and its subjective appropriation by the sinner. From this viewpoint reconciliation is a continuing process as well as an accomplished fact. Yet there is a real sense in which reconciliation was effected before its results are subjectively felt. Paul speaks of *receiving* reconciliation (Rom 5:11), which would imply both an offer and something to offer.

21 Thus far Paul has been content to give the broadest outlines of the drama of reconciliation, stating merely the relationship between the principal actors, as it were. Now he explains, so far as human language and imagery permit, the "how" of reconciliation. The fifteen Greek words, carefully balanced, almost chiastic, defy final exegetical explanation, dealing as they do with the heart of the atonement.

There are three main ways of understanding the first section of the verse, particularly the second use of *hamartia*, "sin" (so L. Sabourin; see notes): (1) Treated as if he were a sinner, Christ became the object of God's wrath and bore the penalty and guilt of sin. (2) When Christ in his incarnation assumed human nature "in the likeness of sinful flesh" (Rom 8:3, RSV), God made him to be "sin." (3) In becoming a sacrifice for sin, Christ was made to be sin. The background to the first view is the idea of substitution; to the second, the notion of participation; to the third, the OT concept of sacrifice.

Although, as Sabourin observes, the Hebrew term *ḥaṭṭāʾṯ* (like *ʾāšām*) may mean both "sin" and "sacrifice for sin" (or "sin-offering"), it seems Paul's intent to say more than that Christ was made a sin-offering and yet less than that Christ became a sinner. So complete was the identification of the sinless Christ with the sin of the sinner, including its dire guilt and its dread consequence of separation from God, that Paul could say profoundly, "God made him . . . to be sin for us."

Paul's declaration of Christ's sinlessness may be compared with the statements of Peter (1 Peter 2:22, quoting Isa 53:9), John (1 John 3:5), and the author of Hebrews (Heb 4:15; 7:26). Just as "the righteousness of God" is extrinsic to us, so the sin with which Christ totally identified himself was extrinsic to him. He was without any acquaintance with sin that might have come through his ever having a sinful attitude or doing a sinful act. Both inwardly and outwardly he was inpeccable.

The glorious purpose of the Father's act in making Christ "to be sin" was that believers should "become the righteousness of God" in Christ. This is a bold restatement of the nature of justification. Not only does the believer receive from God a right standing before him on the basis of faith in Jesus (Phil 3:9), but here Paul says that "in Christ" the believer in some sense actually shares the righteousness that characterizes God himself (cf. 1 Cor 1:30).

6:1 If God made his appeal (*parakalountos*) to men through Paul (5:20), there was a sense in which Paul was a fellow worker with God (cf. 1 Cor 3:9, NIV). As such he was concerned to plead God's cause with unbeliever and believer alike. Hence this plea (*parakaloumen*), addressed to the whole body of Christians at Corinth, "not to receive God's grace in vain."

This latter phrase may mean one of two things: (1) The Corinthians were being exhorted not to show by their present lives that they had received God's grace to no purpose (cf. NEB: "You have received the grace of God; do not let it go for nothing"). Or (2) they were not now to spurn the grace of God, which was being perpetually offered to them (cf. Knox: "We entreat you not to offer God's grace an ineffectual welcome"). How would they fail, or show they had failed, to profit from that grace? By refusing to purify themselves from everything that contaminated body and spirit (7:1; 12:20, 21), or allowing a chasm to develop between faith and conduct, or embracing a different gospel (11:4)—one based on law keeping as the ground of acceptance before God.

2 To emphasize the seriousness and urgency of his appeal and to highlight the privilege of the present and the danger of procrastination, Paul quotes Isaiah 49:8 and then applies the passage to the age of grace.

In its original context the quotation belongs to a section of Isaiah 49 (vv.7–9) where Yahweh directly addresses his Servant who has been "deeply despised, abhorred by the nations" (Isa 49:7, RSV), promising him vindication before men in due time and calling on him to carry out the work of restoration after the return from exile. Paul uses the quotation to establish that the gospel era ("now") is "the day of salvation" when God's favor is shown to men. How unthinkable that such grace should be received in vain (v.1)!

Notes

16 Κατὰ σάρκα (*kata sarka*) in v.16b means "from a worldly point of view" (NIV, "in this way") and qualifies ἐγνώκαμεν (*egnōkamen*, "we regarded"), rather than meaning "after the flesh" (understood as = "physically") and qualifying Χριστόν (*Christon*). What Paul is rejecting is not knowledge of or interest in "Christ-after-the-flesh" (viz., the historical Jesus) but a κατὰ σάρκα outlook on Christ. His was a κατὰ πνεῦμα (*kata pneuma*, "after the spirit") or κατὰ σταυρόν (*kata stauron*, "after the cross") attitude. For a classification of views about this important verse, see J.W. Fraser, "Paul's Knowledge of Jesus: II Corinthians v.16 once more." NTS, XVII (3, 1971), pp. 293–313.

17 In the context the words καινὴ κτίσις (*kainē ktisis*) that form the verbless apodosis may mean either "he [the man in Christ] is a new creature [or creation, or being]" or "there is a new [act of] creation." Alternatively and with variant punctuation, it is possible to translate the verse: "So that if anyone is a new creature in Christ, the old order has passed ..." (thus J. Héring).

On the meaning and significance of the "in Christ" formula in Pauline thought, see R.N. Longenecker. *Paul, Apostle of Liberty* (New York: Harper and Row, 1964), pp. 160–170.

19 The NIV, following a number of EV and commentators, regards ἦν ... καταλλάσσων (*ēn ... katallassōn*) as a periphrastic imperfect, "[God] was reconciling." This makes ἐν Χριστῷ (*en*

Christō, "in Christ") in v.19 parallel to δια Χριστοῦ (*dia Christou,* "through Christ") in v.18. But it is equally possible to take the *ēn* as absolute and the *katallassōn* as adjectival; "God was in Christ, reconciling the world to himself" (thus KJV, E.B. Allo, H. Windisch). Some EV (e.g., RV, RSV, NEB) appear to reproduce the ambiguity of the Gr.: "God was in Christ reconciling. . . ." On the doctrine of reconciliation, see L. Morris, *The Apostolic Preaching of the Cross* (London: Tyndale, 1955), pp. 186–223.

21 "God made him who had no sin to be sin for us" does not, of course, imply any reluctance or resistance on Christ's part that was finally overcome. Ἐποίησεν (*epoiēsen,* "he made") points to God's ordaining that Christ be "made sin" (cf. Acts 2:23). The Father's set purpose not to spare his own Son but to give him up for us all (Rom 8:32) was matched by the Son's firm resolution to go to Jerusalem to suffer (Mark 8:31; Luke 9:51).

For a discussion of the three interpretations of v.21a outlined in the commentary and a defense of the view that ἁμαρτία (*hamartia*) here means "sacrifice for sin," see L. Sabourin, "Note sur 2 Cor. 5, 21: Le Christ fait 'péché'." *Sciences Ecclésiastiques,* XI (3, 1959), pp. 419–424; or (with S. Lyonnet) his *Sin, Redemption, and Sacrifice* [Rome: Pontifical Biblical Institute, 1970], pp. 185–296 (which includes a history of the interpretation of this verse), especially 250–253.

6:1 For a treatment of NT passages dealing with the doctrines of perseverance and apostasy, see I.H. Marshall, *Kept by the Power of God* (London: Epworth Press, 1969).

---

c. The hardships of apostolic service

6:3–10

3We put no stumbling block in anyone's path, so that our ministry will not be discredited. 4Rather, in every way we show ourselves to be servants of God: in great endurance; in troubles, hardships and distresses; 5in beatings, imprisonments and riots; in hard work, sleepless nights and hunger; 6in purity, understanding, patience and kindness; in the Holy Spirit and in sincere love; 7in truthful speech and in the power of God; with weapons of righteousness in the right hand and in the left; 8through glory and dishonor, praise and blame; genuine, yet regarded as impostors; 9known, yet regarded as unknown; dying, and yet we live on; beaten, and yet not killed; 10sorrowful, yet always rejoicing; poor, yet making many rich; having nothing, and yet possessing everything.

3 Since v.2 is grammatically a parenthesis, v.3 is closely connected to v.1 and 5:20. As was fitting for a fellow worker with God who was acting as an ambassador for Christ, Paul tried to put "no stumbling block in anyone's path" lest the ministry should incur discredit. (This interpretation takes *didontes* as a conative present.) That various accusations should have been leveled against Paul was inevitable, given the success of his ministry and the jealousy of men. His concern was that such charges should be totally without foundation, that no "minister of reconciliation" should be guilty of inconsistent or dishonest conduct, and that no handle be given adversaries who wished to ridicule or malign the gospel. The life of the Christian minister is the most eloquent advertisement for the gospel.

4,5 Paul proceeds to itemize his hardships (cf. 1 Cor 4:9–13; 2 Cor 4:8, 9; 11:23–29) as he seeks to commend and defend his ministry as a servant of God and provide the Corinthians with further material they might use in his defense (cf. 5:12). Paul's commendation was a matter of actions, not words.

After a reference to the great endurance that marked all his service and suffering (cf.

12:12), Paul lists nine afflictions, which fall into three groups. First are general trials. "Troubles" are oppressive experiences. "Hardships" refer to unrelieved adverse circumstances, while "distresses" are frustrating "tight corners" (cf. 4:8). In the second group are sufferings directly inflicted by men—"beatings, imprisonments, and riots." To the third category belong self-inflicted hardships. "Hard work" includes the arduous task of incessant preaching and the toil of manual labor (cf. 1 Thess 2:9; 2 Thess 3:7, 8). *Nēsteiai* probably refers to voluntary hunger, i.e., fastings (cf. 11:27, where involuntary hunger (*limos*) and fastings (*nēsteiai*) seem to be distinguished), just as *agrypniai* (cf. 11:27) means voluntary abstention from sleep (e.g., Acts 20:7-11, 31).

6,7 From mention of outward circumstances (vv.4b,5) Paul moves on to specify the inward qualities he sought to display (v.6) and the spiritual equipment he relied on (v.7) during the discharging of his apostolic commission.

"Purity" refers to both moral uprightness and singleness of purpose." "Understanding" is not simply pastoral insight but also knowledge of the Christian faith and sensitivity to God's will (cf. 1 Peter 3:7). By "patience" Paul means the endurance of insult or injury without anger or retaliation. "Kindness" is the generous and sympathetic disposition that acts in love. Because a reference to the person of the Holy Spirit seems out of place in the midst of a catalog of moral virtues, some scholars (quite legitimately) have translated the phrase *en pneumati hagiō* by "in a spirit that is holy" (A. Plummer) or "in holiness of spirit" or "by gifts of the Holy Spirit" (NEB). This last rendering rightly emphasizes that Paul is thinking of the Spirit as the source of all spiritual graces. By metonymy, then, "the Holy Spirit" probably denotes the gifts or graces of the Holy Spirit (so J. Calvin).

After a reference to his proclamation of the truth in the power of God (v.7a; cf. 1 Cor 2:1-5), Paul introduces a military metaphor (cf. Wisd Sol 5:17-22) that he had used earlier (1 Thess 5:8) and would develop later (Rom 6:13; Eph 6:11-17). "Weapons of righteousness" means either "weapons supplied by God (Eph 6:10, 11) as a result of justification" or "weapons that consist of personal integrity" (or, of the gospel as "the word of truth," v.7a, RV). Weapons "in the right hand and in the left" could signify "for attack and for defense" or may allude to "the sword of the Spirit" and "the shield of faith" that form part of the Christian's armor (Eph 6:16, 17).

8-10 Behind these verses, which can all too easily be dismissed simply as evidence of Paul's oriental hyperbole or rhetorical style, there probably lie a number of actual allegations his calumniators made against him (cf. Rom 3:8; 1 Cor 4:13). Though we should not always try to find an opponent lurking behind Paul's statements, in some quarters, Paul had probably become an object of disrepute and slander (v.8). He was thought a "nobody" who relied on deceit to become a "somebody" (vv.8b, 9a), an irresponsible person who, needlessly courting danger and death, suffered for his trouble (vv.9b, c), a morose individual lacking the power that wealth affords (v.10). Precision in this reconstruction is impossible, since the charges of Paul's opponents are being inferred from his supposed reply to them.

"Glory and dishonor, praise and blame" (v.8) may epitomize the two types of response to Paul's preaching, or contrast the opinion of men (dishonor, blame) with the reward of God (glory, praise). In the contrasts that follow (vv.8c-10) the paradoxical character of Paul's apostolic ministry is emphasized. If in fact various charges had been made against him, he takes the accusation, lets it stand or invests it with his own meaning, and supplies an opposing complement to form a series of antitheses that point to the vicissitudes and tension of living as a persecuted "ambassador for Christ" (5:20). From another viewpoint, as F.F. Bruce (in loc.) observes, the pairs of contrasts give the divine and the worldly assessment of apostolic life.

Notes

3 An alternative rendering of ἐν μηδενί (en mēdeni, tr. "in anyone's path" in NIV) would be "[we give no opportunity for scandal] in anything," taking μηδενί as neuter rather than masculine and as parallel to ἐν παντί (en panti, "in everything"; "in every way," NIV—v.4).

4 Verse 4a might be rendered more accurately: "Rather, as servants of God [note nom. διάκονοι, diakonoi, not acc. διακόνους, diakonous] we commend ourselves in every way"; see RHG, 454.

6–10 Just as there are three triplets in vv.4b, 5 prefaced by a general phrase ("in great endurance"), which applies to each triplet, so in vv.6–10 there is a discernible pattern: after four single nouns, each introduced by ἐν (en, "in") (v.6a), four pairs of words follow, each introduced by en (vv.6b, 7a). Then comes a triad of antitheses expressed by διά ... καί (dia ... kai, "through ... and") (vv.7b, 8), and finally seven antitheses couched in a ὡς ... καί (or δέ) (hōs ... kai [or de], "as ... and [or but]") contrast (vv.8c–10). This carefully balanced structure is well reflected in the fine paraphrase of A. Plummer, *A Critical and Exegetical Commentary on the Second Epistle of St. Paul to the Corinthians* (Edinburgh: T. and T. Clark, 1915), p. 166.

4. (*The apostolic ministry*) *Its openness and joy* (6:11–7:4)

a. *A plea for generous affection*

6:11–13

> [11]We have spoken freely to you, Corinthians, and opened wide our hearts to you. [12]We are not withholding our affection from you, but you are withholding yours from us. [13]As a fair exchange—I speak as to my children—open wide your hearts also.

11–13 It was not customary for Paul to address his readers by name. Only when his emotions had been deeply stirred—as at the bewitchment of the Galatians (Gal 3:1), at the generosity of the Philippians (Phil 4:15), or here, at the remarkable candor of his defense and the intensity of his affection for the Corinthians—did he depart from his custom. Behind his freedom of speech (cf. 3:12; 4:2) was a warmly receptive attitude of heart ("we have ... opened wide our hearts to you," v.11). "If there are any feelings of constriction or restraint in our relationship," he continues, "they are on your side, not mine. I appeal to you as my spiritual children [cf. 1 Cor 4:14, 15]: in fair exchange for my unrestricted affection, give me yours, too" (vv.12, 13 paraphrased). Although Paul's desire was for complete reciprocity in family relationships, he was acutely aware that affection could only be given, not taken.

b. *Minor digression—call to holiness*

6:14–7:1

> [14]Do not be yoked together with unbelievers. For what do righteousness and wickedness have in common? Or what fellowship can light have with darkness?

¹⁵What harmony is there between Christ and Belial? What does a believer have in common with an unbeliever? ¹⁶What agreement is there between the temple of God and idols? For we are the temple of the living God. As God has said:

"I will live with them and walk among them,
and I will be their God,
and they will be my people."
¹⁷"Therefore come out from them
and be separate,
                                        says the Lord.

Touch no unclean thing,
and I will receive you."
¹⁸"I will be a Father to you,
and you will be my sons and daughters,
                        says the Lord Almighty."

¹Since we have these promises, dear friends, let us purify ourselves from everything that contaminates body and spirit, and let us strive for perfection out of reverence for God.

For a brief discussion of the integrity of this section and for the suggestion that it forms a natural digression within Paul's argument, see the Introduction, 2.b.

14–16a Paul has just appealed to the Corinthians for mutual openness in affection as in speech. His own heart is open wide to them, but he knows and they know why they cannot reciprocate as fully as they ought. Some of them have an uneasy conscience about their continuing pagan associations they know Paul disapproves of. The apparent abruptness of v.14a after v.13 may be explained: (1) by this mutual knowledge; (2) by Paul's "coming to the point" immediately, as he sets forth the truth plainly (4:2) or speaks the truth in love (Eph 4:15); and (3) perhaps by a brief dictation pause.

Paul begins with a concise summary of his message in this brief digression (6:14–7:1), which repeats the main point of 1 Corinthians 10:1–22 where he warned the Corinthians of the danger of idolatry (note 1 Cor 10:14: "flee from idolatry").

"Do not be yoked together with unbelievers" (v.14a). Clearly this is not an injunction against all association with unbelievers (cf. 1 Cor 5:9, 10; 10:27). Paul actually encouraged the Christian partner in a mixed marriage to maintain the relationship as long as possible (1 Cor 7:12–16). Rather, this is a prohibition against forming close attachments with non-Christians. Paul's agricultural metaphor ("You must not get into double harness with unbelievers"—C.K. Barrett) is based on the command of Deuteronomy 22:10 that prohibited the yoking of an ox and an ass for ploughing, and also on Leviticus 19:19 where the crossbreeding of animals of different species is prohibited. Although precisely what might have constituted a "diverse yoke" or "double harness" for the Corinthians remains unstated, it clearly involved compromise with heathendom, such as contracting mixed marriages (cf. Deut 7:1–3) or initiating litigation before unbelievers in cases involving believers (1 Cor 6:1–8). Paul is content to state a general principle that needs specific application under the Spirit's guidance. In expanded form the principle might be expressed thus: "Do not form any relationship, whether temporary or permanent, with unbelievers that would lead to a compromise of Christian standards or jeopardize consistency of Christian witness. And why such separation? Because the unbeliever does not share the Christian's standards, sympathies, or goals."

Five rhetorical questions follow (vv.14b–16a), each of which presupposes a negative answer. They serve to stress the incompatibility of Christianity and heathenism, the incongruity of intimate relationships or fellowship between believers and unbelievers (cf. 1 Cor 10:21). After two comparisons of abstract nouns ("righteousness" and "light" with "wickedness" and "darkness"), there follow two personal comparisons—"Christ" and the "believer" with "Belial" (see note) and the "unbeliever." The final contrast (v.16a) climaxes the series and prompts what follows (vv.16b–18).

16b,c The chief reason why believers are not to enter any syncretistic or compromising relationship with unbelievers (v.14a) is that they belong exclusively to God. Corporately the Christian community forms "the temple [or sanctuary] of the living God" (cf. 1 Cor 3:16, 17; see also 6:19, which individualizes the truth); or, as Paul later expressed it, "a dwelling in which God lives by his Spirit" (Eph 2:22, NIV).

To establish this last point (v.16b) Paul quotes several OT passages. "I will live with them and walk among them" is based on Leviticus 26:11a, 12a, with possible allusions to Exodus 25:8; 29:45a; 1 Kings 6:13; Ezekiel 37:27a. God's promise to Israel in the wilderness, subsequently reiterated, becomes his promise to the church in the gospel era (cf. Rev 21:3). "I will be their God, and they will be my people" is a recurring promise of Yahweh to his covenant people (see Exod 6:7; Lev 26:12b; Jer 32:38; Ezek 37:27b).

17 In keeping with the promise of his presence and protection, God demands purity of life and separation from evil. " 'Therefore come out from them and be separate, says the Lord. Touch no unclean thing' " (v.17). Isaiah 52:11 is the source of Paul's citation; the differences may be explained by Paul's quoting from memory and applying the text to the Corinthian situation. In Isaiah, the call was for separation (= departure) from Babylon (autēs, "her," in LXX) with its pagan idolatry. In Paul, the call is for separation from unbelievers (autōn, "them," v.17 = apistoi, "unbelievers," v.14), with their pagan way of life. This verse, therefore, should not be used in defense of separation from believers on the ground of doctrinal differences.

"And [or then, kai] I will receive you" stems from Ezekiel 20:34, 41. God's acceptance and approval of his people is dependent on their obedience to his commands. Separation from the world leads to fellowship with God (cf. James 4:4).

18 The next mosaic of OT texts is composed of 2 Samuel 7:14a (with the necessary changes from singular to plural; cf. Hos 1:10) and 2 Samuel 7:27 (LXX, "Lord Almighty"), with the reference to "daughters" in 2 Corinthians 6:18 possibly coming from Isaiah 43:6. What God promised to Solomon through David and to Israel through Solomon (cf. Jer 31:9) finds its fulfillment in what God is to the community of believers through Christ (Gal 3:26; 4:6). If Christians corporately are the temple of the living God (v.16), individually they are the sons and daughters of the all-sovereign Lord (v.18).

7:1 In his chain of OT quotations Paul has stressed the privilege of being a dwelling place of God (v.16) and the benefits of compliance with the divine will (vv.17d, 18). So he continues, "Since we have promises such as these [tautas stands first for emphasis]. . ."—promises (vv.16, 17d, 18), not commands (v.17). As recipients of such promises of fellowship with God, all Christians ("let us," as in NIV; not "you must") are to avoid every source of possible defilement in any aspect of their lives. "Body and spirit" here denotes the Christian in his total personality, outwardly and inwardly, in his relations with other people and with God (cf. 1 Cor 7:34).

Paul is probably implying that the Corinthians had become defiled, perhaps by occasionally sharing meals at idol-shrines or by continuing to attend festivals or ceremonies in pagan temples (cf. 1 Cor 8:10; 10:14-22), or even by maintaining their membership in some local pagan cult. If they made a clean break (cf. *katharisōmen,* aorist) with pagan life in any and every form, they would be bringing their holiness nearer completion by this proof of their reverence for God. The Christian life involves separation (6:17), familial fellowship (6:18), and sanctification (7:1).

Notes

15 "Belial" (Heb. בְּלִיַּעַל, *beliyya'al*) may mean "worthlessness" or "the place from which there is no ascent" (= the abyss or Sheol); or, as here and in late Jewish literature, it may be used personally of the devil. See the full note of P.E. Hughes, in loc.
16 On the concept of the temple in biblical and extra-biblical literature, see R.J. McKelvey, *The New Temple: A Study of the Church* (New York: Oxford University Press, 1969).
17 On the Pauline formula λέγει κύριος (*legei kyrios,* "says the Lord") used in vv.17, 18, see E.E. Ellis, *Paul's Use of the Old Testament* (Edinburgh: Oliver and Boyd, 1957), pp. 107-113.
7:1 The end of the verse may be literally rendered: ". . . perfecting holiness (= becoming perfectly holy—BAG, p. 10) in the fear of God." The phrase ἐπιτελοῦντες ἁγιωσύνην (*epitelountes hagiōsynēn*) may indicate the result (". . . and thus make holiness perfect . . .") of the self-purification, viz., advance in holiness; if so, the emphasis on human responsibility in the process of sanctification is unmistakable. Or the phrase may denote the circumstances attendant on self-purification, being virtually a separate complementary injunction (so NIV). Ἐν φόβῳ θεοῦ (*en phobō theou*) may mean "in an atmosphere of reverential fear for God" (ἐν [*en,* "in"] denoting sphere or circumstances) or "by reverence for God" (instrumental ἐν).

c. Paul's pride and joy
7:2-4

²Make room for us in your hearts. We have wronged no one, we have corrupted no one, we have exploited no one. ³I do not say this to condemn you; I have said before that you have such a place in our hearts that we would live or die with you. ⁴I have great confidence in you; I take great pride in you. I am greatly encouraged; in all our troubles my joy knows no bounds.

2-4 After this brief digression (6:14-7:1) Paul renews his appeal (cf. 6:13) for the Corinthians' full affection. He knew of nothing in his past conduct or instruction that could cause them to doubt his sincerity or lose confidence in him. Paul had been accused of bringing about the moral and financial ruination of innocent victims at Corinth by callously exploiting them (v.2), and apparently some at Corinth were inclined, at least in part, to believe these charges. As before (cf. 1 Cor 4:4; 2 Cor 4:2; 5:11; 6:3), Paul can do no more in reply than appeal to his clear conscience and the Corinthians' knowledge of his conduct and insist that the charges are groundless.

But to mention the charges was not to imply that the Corinthians really believed them. "I do not say this to condemn you" (v.3a). Or Paul may mean that his effort to clear himself did not amount to blaming them. He reminds them (cf. 6:11) that they occupy a permanent and secure place in his love and concern. The leveling of charges, the arrival of death, the trials of life—none of these could divorce them from his affection (v.3b).

The situation at Corinth was not perfect and probably never would be. But Paul had grounds for great confidence and pride in his converts. In spite of all his frustrations and in the midst of all his affliction he was filled with comfort and overflowing with joy (v.4; cf. 6:10). The reason? The safe arrival of Titus in Macedonia with encouraging news about Corinth (vv.5-7). Quite naturally Paul has returned to his travel narrative that was suspended at 2:13.

Notes

4 Since παρρησία (*parrhēsia*) can mean "freedom of speech" as well as "confidence" (see note on 3:12), v.4a may also be rendered "I am perfectly frank with you" (NEB). And the following phrase can also be tr. thus: "I am always boasting about you" (*Twentieth Century New Testament*).

D. *Paul's Reconciliation With the Corinthians* (7:5-16)

1. *Comfort in Macedonia*

7:5-7

> 5For when we came into Macedonia, this body of ours had no rest, but we were harassed at every turn—conflicts on the outside, fears within. 6But God, who comforts the downcast, comforted us by the coming of Titus, 7and not only by his coming but also by the comfort you had given him. He told us about your affection, your deep sorrow, your ardent concern for me, so that my joy was greater than ever.

5 At this point Paul resumes the account of his movements broken off at 2:13. Although he expected to meet Titus when he (Paul) arrived in Macedonia, his hopes were frustrated just as they had been at Troas (2:12, 13). His body (*sarx*, "flesh") had no rest (*anesis*). In 2:13 he had said that his spirit (*pneuma*, NIV "mind") had experienced no rest (*anesis*) at Troas. If a distinction is to be drawn between the *pneuma* of 2:13 and the *sarx* of 7:5, terms often contrasted in Paul's writing (e.g., Gal 5:16-24), the former denotes Paul in his spiritual sensitivity; the latter, Paul in his physical suffering. But it is quite possible that the terms are here virtually synonymous, being used loosely of the whole person under the influence of popular, nontechnical usage.

"Fears within" alludes to Paul's persistent apprehension about Titus's reception at Corinth, his safety in travel, and the Corinthian response to the "severe letter." "Conflicts on the outside" may point to violent quarrelling that focused on Paul or to persistent opposition or persecution that beset him after his arrival in Macedonia.

6,7 It probably seemed to Paul that from the human point of view his whole future as apostle to the Gentiles was related to the Corinthians' reaction to his assertion of authority in the letter delivered by Titus. And now the nonarrival of Titus tended to confirm his worst fears (see the commentary at 2:12, 13).

God used three means to dispense comfort to the depressed or downhearted (*tapeinos* —BAG, p. 811) apostle: the actual arrival of Titus, doubtless including his personal ministrations to Paul (note the twofold reference to Titus's *parousia*, "coming"); Titus's positive experience at Corinth ("the comfort you have given him"); and the reassuring news he brought concerning the Corinthians' attitude toward Paul—their "affection" for him or longing (*epipothēsis*) to see him and be reconciled to him, their "deep sorrow" over their disloyal behavior, and their "ardent concern" to defend Paul's cause and to follow his directions in disciplining the guilty party. Titus's safe arrival from Corinth and the encouragement he had received there had brought Paul a joy that was increased by the favorable news Titus brought.

2. The severe letter and its effect

7:8–13a

> [8]Even if I caused you sorrow by my letter, I do not regret it. Though I did regret it—I see that my letter hurt you, but only for a little while—[9]yet now I am happy, not because you were made sorry, but because your sorrow led you to repentance. For you became sorrowful as God intended and so were not harmed in any way by us. [10]Godly sorrow brings repentance that leads to salvation and leaves no regret, but worldly sorrow brings death. [11]See what this godly sorrow has produced in you: what earnestness, what eagerness to clear yourselves, what indignation, what alarm, what affection, what concern, what readiness to see justice done. At every point you have proved yourselves to be innocent in this matter. [12]So even though I wrote to you, it was not on account of the one who did the wrong or of the injured party, but rather that before God you could see for yourselves how devoted to us you are. [13a]By all this we are encouraged.

On the purpose and identification of the "severe letter," see the Introduction, 7.b.

8–10 "My letter" refers not to 1 Corinthians or a letter embodying 2 Corinthians 10–13 but to a letter no longer extant that was written after 1 Corinthians and Paul's "sorrowful visit" and was delivered by Titus. From the report of Titus Paul had learned for the first time that his letter had caused the Corinthians considerable distress, at least for a period (v.8). As a spiritual father who disliked causing pain for whatever reason, his first reaction was to regret (*metemelomēn*) that he had written so stern a letter that the recipients were pained by it: "I did regret it—[for, *gar*, read by some MSS] I see that my letter hurt you" (v.8b). But at some later time, possibly after Titus had completed his report or after Paul had had time to reflect on the whole episode, his initial regret caused by a natural, spontaneous reaction had altogether disappeared before the joyful realization that out of the temporary pain suffered by the Corinthians had come sincere repentance. So at the time of writing Paul could say, "I do not [now] regret it [*ou metamelomai*] . . . now I am happy . . . because your sorrow led you to repentance" (vv.8, 9). Of what had the Corinthians repented? Probably their failure to defend Paul before his detractor ("the one who did the wrong," v.12). Because their sorrow was "as God intended" (i.e., it produced repentance, v.10a), Paul's letter that had caused temporary pain caused no permanent harm (v.9b). The inference is clear: the imposition of discipline or the suffering of pain that does not, under God, lead to repentance, can cause irreparable harm.

Verse 10 describes two ways of reacting to pain or sorrow. God's way ("godly sorrow" or sorrow "as God intended," *kata theon*, vv.9, 10, 11) invariably produces a change of heart and this repentance "leads to salvation" and therefore gives no cause for regret. Sorrow borne in a worldly way (*tou kosmou*), on the other hand, does not lead to repentance but has the deadly effect of producing resentment or bitterness. What makes suffering remedial is not the actual experience of it but the reaction to it; a "godly" or positive reaction brings blessing, a "worldly" or negative reaction causes harm.

11 A splendid example of the beneficial outcome of "godly sorrow" was the positive response of the Corinthians to Paul's letter that had for a time pained them. It might have compounded trouble at Corinth and caused widespread resentment against Paul had it not been received in a spirit of humility and with a willingness to follow God's will. As it was, it produced in them "earnestness" or seriousness of purpose, "eagerness" to clear themselves from blame, "indignation" at the scandalous action of the person who denigrated Paul, "alarm" over their behavior and its effects, "affection" for Paul or longing (*epipothēsis*) to see him in person, "concern" lest he should visit them "rod in hand" (1 Cor 4:21; cf. 2 Cor 7:15; 13:2), and a "readiness to see justice done" by the punishment of the offender (cf. 2:6).

The second sentence in this verse has been interpreted in two ways. By their favorable response to the "severe letter" the Corinthians had proved themselves "to be innocent," i.e., they had now put themselves in the right after earlier complicity in the affair (thus A. Plummer). Alternatively, the meaning may be this: By their response the Corinthians showed Titus that they had always been guiltless in the matter (thus C.K. Barrett). The former view seems more probable in light of the term *odyrmos* ("mourning"; "deep sorrow," NIV) in v.7.

12,13a Paul's principal aim in writing the "severe letter" was that the Corinthians should come to recognize "before God" how devoted to their spiritual father they really were (cf. 2:9). Such recognition "before God" or "in the sight of God" would ensure future loyalty to Paul. Since this aim was achieved and God prevented the letter from making the Corinthians resentful (v.9b), Paul was encouraged (v.13a).

It is likely that this statement of Paul's chief aim in writing was influenced by his knowledge of the letter's outcome: Paul was unsure of Corinthian loyalty when he wrote the "severe letter"; hence his restlessness while waiting for Titus (2:12, 13; 7:5).

As it is stated, this Corinthian recognition was the sole purpose of the letter. However, what is expressed as a stark contrast ("not this, nor this, but that") is actually simply a comparison ("not so much this or this as that"). Another example of this Semitic thought pattern is found at 2:5 (where see note). Subsidiary objectives for the letter, then, were twofold: the punishment of the guilty party ("the one who did the wrong") (cf. 2:6, 9) and the vindication of "the injured party." Who the offender was is impossible to say (assuming he was not the man guilty of incest; see the commentary at 2:5, 6, 10, 11). C.K. Barrett (in loc.) argues strongly for his not being a Corinthian but an "anti-Pauline intruder." Commentators who believe that 1 Corinthians 5 and 2 Corinthians 2 are referring to the same matter (the case of the man guilty of incest) identify "the injured party" as the man's father (1 Cor 5:1). This is very unlikely (see Introduction, 7.b.3]a). More probably, Paul himself was the nameless "injured party."

3. *The relief of Titus*

7:13b–16

13bIn addition to our own encouragement, we were especially delighted to see how happy Titus was, because all of you helped put his mind at ease. 14I had boasted to him about you, and you have not embarrassed me. But just as everything we said to you was true, so our boasting about you to Titus has proved to be true as well. 15And his affection for you is all the greater when he remembers that you were all obedient, receiving him with fear and trembling. 16I am glad I can have complete confidence in you.

13b,14 Through the "godly sorrow" of the Corinthians, Titus was as relieved and encouraged as Paul (v.13a). Apparently Titus had had little or no occasion before his visit to Corinth as bearer of the "severe letter" to form an independent judgment about the Corinthians; so he was dependent on Paul's glowing recommendation. This would suggest that this visit, on which he also began to organize the collection (8:6a), was his first. But it is not impossible that he had already paid a very brief visit shortly after 1 Corinthians was received at Corinth to initiate the collection by carrying out the directions of 1 Corinthians 16:2.

Whether it was his first or second visit, he seems to have ventured on it with some trepidation that was possibly based on a previous encounter with the Corinthians. But all the believers had "helped put his mind at ease" (v.13b). However, the phrase (*anapepautai to pneuma autou*) may also mean "his spirit has been refreshed." Perhaps both refreshment and relief had come to Titus.

Paul's relief stemmed from the fact that his generous assurances to Titus about the Corinthians had not proved unfounded and therefore embarrassing (v.14). On the contrary (*alla*), just as his own truthfulness had been vindicated at Corinth (cf. 1:18–20), so also his boasting about them had now proved fully justified.

15,16 The reception of Titus at Corinth had been given "with fear and trembling"; i.e., the Corinthian Christians were anxious to the point of nervousness, fearing (cf. v.11) that corporately they would fail to meet all their obligations toward an envoy from Paul (cf. the same phrase *meta phobou kai tromou* in Eph 6:5; Phil 2:12; see also 1 Cor 2:3). Moreover, they had all readily complied with some demand Titus had made of them. Whenever he recalled their obedience and respectful deference to him, his affection grew all the warmer (v.15). This gave Paul good reason for complete confidence in the Corinthians (v.16) and a secure base from which to propose the completion of the collection (chs. 8, 9).

II. The Collection for the Saints at Jerusalem (2 Cor 8–9)

For a summary of the historical background and theological significance of the collection, see Introduction (7.c), where there is also a brief discussion of the integrity of these two chapters (2.c).

This was not the first time the Corinthians had heard of the collection for the poor at Jerusalem, for in 1 Corinthians 16:1–4 Paul gave them certain information and directions about the project they had probably requested in their earlier letter. (The *peri de*, "now about ...," in 1 Corinthians 16:1 points to a topic discussed in the Corinthians' letter to the apostle.) They may have been first informed about the collection by Paul's "previous letter" (referred to in 1 Cor 5:9, 11 and written perhaps in A.D. 53 or 54) or by news from the Galatian churches (cf. 1 Cor 16:1). Certainly 1 Corinthians 16:1 introduces the theme of "the collection for God's people" so abruptly and with such evident unconcern for the Corinthians' motivation or for their knowledge of the collection's purpose and destination that their previous acquaintance with the idea seems presupposed. Indeed, they had doubtless indicated to Paul their willingness to contribute.

Whether the Corinthians acted on Paul's instructions in 16:1, 2 is uncertain. But in all probability progress on the collection was soon halted in spite of Paul's "intermediate visit," particularly as the result of (1) the unfortunate incident alluded to in 2 Corinthians 2:5–11; 7:12 and its aftermath and (2) the malevolent influence of the intruders from Palestine who at least for a period gained their support from some Corinthian sympathizers (cf. 11:7–12, 20; 12:13–16). But when Paul sent Titus to deliver and reinforce the effect of the "letter of tears," he probably enjoined him to attempt to revive the flagging collection if the church responded favorably to the letter (cf. 8:6a). Now, with firm evidence from Titus of the Corinthians' loyalty to him (7:6–16), Paul can discuss the project again and press for its early completion.

A. *The Need for Generosity* (8:1–15)

1. *The generosity of the Macedonians*

8:1–5

> [1]And now, brothers, we want you to know about the grace that God has given the Macedonian churches. [2]Out of the most severe trial, their overflowing joy and their extreme poverty welled up in rich generosity. [3]For I testify that they gave as much as they were able, and even beyond their ability. Entirely on their own, [4]they urgently pleaded with us for the privilege of sharing in this service to the saints. [5]And they did not do as we expected, but they gave themselves first to the Lord and then to us in keeping with God's will.

1,2 Tactfully, Paul begins with an example, not a plea. Although they were then facing a severe ordeal involving persecution (cf. 1 Thess 1:6; 2:14), the Macedonian churches, such as those at Philippi, Thessalonica, and Berea, had contributed generously. As Paul expresses it, their "rich generosity" was the overflow of "overflowing joy" and "extreme poverty" (v.2). Their poverty no more impeded their generosity than their tribulation diminished their joy. This liberal giving by destitute Christians to fellow believers not personally known to them Paul traces to the influence of God's grace (v.1; cf. 9:14). The apostle was not concerned about the actual size of the gift but about the attitude of the givers ("joy ... generosity"; cf. Rom 12:8) and the relation between the size of the gift and the resources of the givers (cf. Mark 12:41–44).

3–5 In describing the nature of the Macedonians' "rich generosity," Paul makes several observations. First, they gave far more generously than their slender means and adverse circumstances really permitted them (v.3). Not that their judgment was unbalanced, but their eagerness to contribute led them to surpass all expectations.

Second, acting on their own initiative, they "urgently pleaded" with Paul for the privilege of fellowship (*koinōnia;* see note) in the collection (vv.3c, 4). Perhaps the request was conveyed by the Macedonians Gaius and Aristarchus, whom Luke describes as Paul's "traveling companions" (Acts 19:29) (cf. J. Weiss's suggestion in *Earliest Christianity* [New York: Harper, 1959], 1:354). Since 1 Corinthians 16:1 mentions only "the Galatian churches," not the Macedonian churches, and since 1 Corinthians 16:5 makes no reference to the collection, it seems likely that the collection in Macedonia began after the spring of A.D. 55 (the suggested date of 1 Corinthians). One reason for Paul's sending Timothy and Erastus into Macedonia (Acts 19:22) may have been to introduce the collection project there. Yet v.4a implies Paul's reluctance to encourage the Macedonians to contribute, since he knew of their desperate poverty (v.2).

194

Third, the reason the Macedonians exceeded Paul's expectations ("they did not do as we expected," v.5a) was that they did not restrict their contribution to financial aid. On the contrary (alla), "in keeping with God's will" they dedicated themselves first and foremost (prōton) to Christ but also to Paul for the performance of any service in connection with the collection (v.5). They recognized that dedication to Christ involved dedication to his servants and that dedication to them was in reality service for Christ. All was part of God's will.

Notes

1 The significant word χάρις (charis), found ten times in 2 Cor 8–9, has been appropriately rendered by the NIV in a variety of ways: (1) "grace," referring either to the divine generosity lavishly displayed (8:9) or to divine enablement, especially enablement to participate worthily in the collection (8:1; 9:8, 14); (2) "privilege," used of the honor and opportunity of participating in the offering (8:4); (3) "act of grace" or "offering," denoting the collection itself as an expression and proof of goodwill (8:6, 19); (4) "grace of giving," referring to grace as a virtuous act of sharing or as gracious help (8:7); and (5) "thanks" ("I thank . . .") (8:16; 9:15).

4 "The privilege of sharing [or fellowship]" (τὴν χάριν καὶ τὴν κοινωνίαν, tēn charin kai tēn koinōnian, an instance of hendiadys) alludes both to a brotherhood of contributors and to a fellowship between donors and recipients. As contributors to the collection, the Macedonian churches were giving tangible evidence of their oneness with other contributing Gentile churches and with the parent body in Jerusalem (with whom they had an affinity, see 1 Thess 2:14). On the concept of κοινωνία (koinōnia, "sharing"), see R.P. Martin. "Communion." NBD, pp. 245, 246.

2. A plea for liberal giving

8:6–12

> 6So we urged Titus, since he had earlier made a beginning, to bring also to completion this act of grace on your part. 7But just as you excel in everything—in faith, in speech, in knowledge, in complete earnestness and in your love for us—see that you also excel in this grace of giving.
>
> 8I am not commanding you, but I want to test the sincerity of your love by comparing it with the earnestness of others. 9For you know the grace of our Lord Jesus Christ, that though he was rich, yet for your sakes he became poor, so that you through his poverty might become rich.
>
> 10And here is my advice about what is best for you in this matter: Last year you were the first not only to give but also to have the desire to do so. 11Now finish the work, so that your eager willingness to do it may be matched by your completion of it, according to your means. 12For if the willingness is there, the gift is acceptable according to what one has, not according to what he does not have.

6,7 The sterling example of the Macedonians (vv.1–5) encouraged Paul to make arrangements for the completion of the Corinthian offering. "So we urged Titus . . . to bring . . . to completion this act of grace on your part" (v.6). None of the sophisticated and sensitive Corinthians would have missed the implication of the eis to: "The result was that [we urged Titus . . .]." Unlike the Macedonians, they were not facing persecution, nor were they in desperate financial straits. How willingly they ought to contribute!

Titus "had earlier made a beginning" (v.6). From the context it is clear that it was "a beginning" on the collection and also at Corinth. When it occurred is less clear. It may have been when he delivered the "severe letter," or at an earlier time either after or conceivably before Paul sent 1 Corinthians.

The earlier "act of grace" (NIV) or "gracious work" (RSV) that Titus had brought to a successful completion (implied by the "also," translating the first *kai*) was his task as Paul's special envoy to Corinth to deliver the "painful letter" and carry out its measures. In Paul's judgment something more than the dispatch of another letter was needed to make sure the Corinthians completed their offering. Titus should pay a second or third visit. Apart from his work at Corinth, he had probably already shown himself a man of considerable financial acumen (Gal 2:1 = Acts 11:29, 30).

A special visit from Titus, however, would not in itself guarantee the success of the collection. So Paul appeals to the Corinthians' desire to exhibit every sign of spirituality (cf. 1 Cor 1:5, 7; 12:31; 14:37). By using the word *charis* ("grace") of the virtue of giving (NIV, "grace of giving," v.7c), he makes it clear that generosity stands alongside faith, speech, knowledge, and love as an expression of divine grace in man (v.7). Already excelling in Christian virtues and gifts of the Spirit, the Corinthians were to make sure they exhibited the grace of liberality as well.

8 Although vested with full apostolic authority (10:8; 13:10), Paul declined to issue directives, preferring rather to request, suggest (cf. v.10), encourage, or appeal (cf. 1 Cor 7:6; 2 Cor 8:6, 10, 17). Spontaneity and warmth would be absent from the Corinthians' giving if coercion were present. But he did see in the enthusiastic generosity of the Macedonian churches a convenient standard for assessing the genuineness of the Corinthians' professed love for him and for all believers, as well as a compelling incentive to arouse them to action.

9 In encouraging the Corinthians to bring their contribution to a satisfactory completion (v.6), Paul has thus far appealed to the example of the Macedonians (vv.1–5), to their own promising beginning (v.6), to their desire for spiritual excellence (v.7), and again to the earnestness of the Macedonians (v.8). Now he turns to the supreme example of Christ. The transition from v.8 to v.9 (denoted by *gar*, "for") is illuminating, because it suggests that Paul saw in Christ the finest example of one who showed eagerness and generosity in giving as a demonstration of his love. If the sacrificial giving of the Macedonians did not stimulate emulation, the example of Christ's selflessness certainly would. Such doctrinal buttressing of ethical injunctions is typical of Paul (e.g., Rom 15:2, 3; Eph 5:2; Col 3:9, 10).

Christ "became poor" (*eptōcheusen*, an ingressive aorist) by the act of incarnation that followed his preincarnate renunciation of heavenly glory (cf. Phil 2:6–8). From wealth to "poverty"! Paul depicts the glory of heavenly existence as wealth, in comparison with which the lowliness of earthly existence amounts to "poverty." Thus it is not possible, from this verse alone, to deduce that Christ's life on earth was one of indigence. In the context the stress is on his voluntary surrender of glory contrasted with the spiritual wealth derived by others (Eph 1:3) through his gracious act of giving. Unlike the Macedonians, who gave when they were extremely poor (v.2), Christ gave when he was incalculably rich. In their present circumstances the Corinthians fitted somewhere between these extremes. Like the Macedonians (v.5), Christ gave himself. The Corinthians would do well to emulate these examples.

10,11 Again Paul emphasizes that he is not giving orders but offering advice (cf. v.8a), though an imperative follows in v.11! It is clear from 1 Corinthians 7:25, 40, however, that such a considered opinion came from one who regarded himself as worthy of trust. The apostle hints at several reasons why it was "best" (or "expedient") for the Corinthians to bring their contribution to a completion quickly: (1) A considerable time (cf. "last year," v.10) had elapsed since they had expressed an "eager willingness" to help. (2) Since their enthusiastic intention had already been partially translated into action (v.10b), it was incumbent on them, having put their hands to the plough, not to look back but to bring the project to a successful completion. "Completion" needed to match intention (v.11; cf. Phil 1:6). (3) They enjoyed a twofold precedence over the Macedonians. In beginning a collection and even before that in deciding to contribute, they were earlier ("the first," v.10b). But now the Macedonians themselves had completed their offering! (4) The Macedonians had contributed "even beyond their ability" (v.3); now the Corinthians were being asked to contribute "according to . . . (their) means" (v.11).

12 The phrase "according to your means" at the end of v.11 is now explained. Provided a gift is willingly given, its acceptability is determined solely on the basis of what a person might possess, not on the basis of what he does not own. God assesses the "value" of a monetary gift not in terms of the actual amount given, but by comparing what is given with the total financial resources of the giver. This is the lesson of Mark 12:41–44 (the widow's offering). No one is expected to give "according to what he does not have."

Notes

7 The NIV translates the reading ἐξ ὑμῶν ἐν ἡμῖν (ex hymōn en hēmin, "your [love] for us"), which suits the context and has wide geographical support (Alexandrian, Western, and Byzantine families), but the three editions of the UBS give a slight preference (a "D" rating) to the alternative reading, ἐξ ἡμῶν ἐν ὑμῖν (ex hēmōn en hymin, "our [love] for you"), which is supported by important witnesses (such as p[46] B 1739). However, the latter reading is awkward in the context unless it is taken to mean "[the love] that is in you which I inspired."

9 In the phrase τῇ ἐκείνου πτωχείᾳ (tē ekeinou ptōcheia, "through his poverty") the dative probably means "as a consequence of" rather than "by means of." Christians are enriched not exactly or solely by Christ's poverty (=incarnation) but by his death as the climax of his entire incarnate life of obedient service. Paul would have been the first to insist on the centrality of the cross (e.g., see Rom 5:8–10; Col 1:20, 22) and to observe that Calvary complements Bethlehem. The incarnation became a saving event through the crucifixion. However, if ptōcheia ("poverty") here sums up the total ministry and passion of Christ, the difficulty disappears.

10 The phrase ἀπὸ πέρυσι (apo perusi, 8:10, 9:2) is notoriously ambiguous, for it may mean "last year" (NIV, and see MM, p. 510) or "a year ago" (RSV), and it is uncertain which calendar Paul was following (see the possibilities mentioned in the Introduction, 4.3). Some period under two years is demanded. Moreover, the Corinthians' desire to contribute may date from their first hearing of the project in Paul's "previous letter" or from the Galatian believers, or from their written enquiry about the collection (answered in 1 Cor 16:1–4).

3. The aim of equality

8:13-15

¹³Our desire is not that others might be relieved while you are hard pressed, but that there might be equality. ¹⁴At the present time your plenty will supply what they need, so that in turn their plenty will supply what you need. Then there will be equality, ¹⁵as it is written:

"He that gathered much did not have too much,
and he that gathered little did not have
too little."

13,14 Perhaps one reason the collection project had been languishing at Corinth was that there was some such objection as this to it: "As if we had no financial problems of our own, Paul is imposing fresh burdens on us so that others can become free of burdens." On the other hand, Paul may simply be anticipating an objection of this type. Christian giving, he insists, does not aim at an exchange of financial burdens but rather at an equal sharing of them and an equal supply of the necessities of life. The rich are not called upon to give so lavishly that they become poor and the poor become rich. That would simply prolong inequality. But those who enjoy a greater share of material benefits are called upon to make certain that those who have a smaller share through no fault of their own are not in want. Where the Christian poor give to the poor, as in the case of the extremely poor Macedonians, who gave "even beyond their ability" (8:2, 3), this is a notable demonstration of God's grace (8:1).

If v.13 alludes to an equal sharing of burdens that will lead to equality of supply, then v.14 speaks of mutual sacrifice that will maintain equality. Paul here is not predicting economic plenty in Jerusalem and an economic dearth in Corinth that would reverse present roles. But he saw that with the uncertainty of economic conditions in the first century it was not inconceivable for the Jerusalem Christians some day to become the donors of financial aid and the Corinthian Christians the recipients. Admittedly, the chronic poverty in Jerusalem would have made it appear unlikely that the Jerusalem church would ever come to have a surplus, even were the Corinthians to have a deficiency. This has led some scholars (e.g., E.B. Allo, K.F. Nickle) to suggest that Paul is not envisaging repayment in kind. What the Jerusalem believers would dispense was nothing other than what they had already supplied to Gentile churches—namely, the spiritual blessings of the gospel (cf. Rom 15:27).

15 Paul now illustrates this principle of equality of supply from the account of God's provision of manna to the Israelites in the wilderness (Exod 16:13–36). Although some gathered more than others and some less, the needs of all were met. Miraculously there was equal provision, with neither surplus nor deficiency. "He that gathered much had nothing over, and he that gathered little had no lack" (Exod 16:18 RSV). Any imbalance that might have been caused by hoarding was ruled out, for on the second day manna that had not been used putrefied (Exod 16:20). But Paul's illustration also points to a contrast. The equality the Israelites miraculously experienced in the wilderness was enforced; the equality Christians are themselves to create in the church and the world is voluntary.

Notes

13,14 A variant punctuation of the Gr. text (placing a stop after θλῖψις [*thlipsis,* "distress"] and reading the following three words with v.14), favored by the UBS, produces this rendering: "Our desire is not that others might be relieved while you are hard pressed, but that, as a matter of equality [ἐξ ἰσότητος, *ex isotētos*], at the present time. . . ."

B. The Mission of Titus and His Companions (8:16–9:5)

1. The delegates and their credentials

8:16–24

[16]I thank God, who put into the heart of Titus the same concern I have for you. [17]For Titus not only welcomed our appeal, but he is coming to you with much enthusiasm and on his own initiative. [18]And we are sending along with him the brother who is praised by all the churches for his service to the gospel. [19]What is more, he was chosen by the churches to accompany us as we carry the offering, which we administer in order to honor the Lord himself and to show our eagerness to help. [20]We want to avoid any criticism of the way we administer this liberal gift. [21]For we are taking pains to do what is right, not only in the eyes of the Lord but also in the eyes of men.

[22]In addition, we are sending with them our brother who has often proved to us in many ways that he is zealous, and now even more so because of his great confidence in you. [23]As for Titus, he is my partner and fellow worker among you; as for our brothers, they are representatives of the churches and an honor to Christ. [24]Therefore, show these men the proof of your love and the reason for our pride in you, so that all the churches can see it.

This section amounts to a "letter of commendation" (cf. 3:1) from Paul to the church at Corinth, giving the credentials of the three appointed delegates and encouraging the Corinthians to welcome them warmly.

16,17 Although Titus's affection for the Corinthians naturally developed as a result of his positive interaction with them (7:13–15), Paul could trace Titus's keen interest in their welfare to the providential working of God (v.16). Nothing could be more reassuring to the Corinthians than to know that the devotion and concern for them shared by Paul and Titus were simply a reflection of God's own affection for them. And it was concern for them, not for their money. As Paul later (12:14) comments, "What I want is not your possessions but you."

Paul proceeds (v.17) to describe the intensity of Titus's concern. It was true that Paul had "urged" him to arrange for the collection to be completed (v.6), but this invitation had merely confirmed Titus's eager willingness. Although technically he might be responding to an appeal he had "welcomed" (contrast with this 1 Corinthians 16:12), in reality he was going "on his own initiative" (*authairetos*). This word may contain a hint that Titus often worked independently of Paul's mission.

18,19 The unidentified Christian brother that Paul was sending with Titus had a double qualification. He was well known and highly praised in all the (Macedonian?) churches "for his service to the gospel" (v.18)—perhaps as an administrator (cf. 1 Cor 12:28) as well as an evangelist or teacher. Also, he had been selected and commissioned by an unspecified number of churches (in Macedonia?—see note on 8:23) to travel with Paul in administering the collection (v.19). Originally the verb *cheirotoneō* indicated election by "stretching out the hand" (i.e., voting), but this meaning cannot be pressed in NT usage where the term simply denotes appointment (e.g., Acts 14:23) with no implication of the "laying on of hands."

Paul adds a phrase explaining why he personally was supervising the administration of the collection. He sought to promote not his own glory but the Lord's and to prove his "eagerness to help" (v.19b; cf. Gal 2:10).

20,21 Experience had taught Paul that he must anticipate the suspicions or accusations of his detractors and take the necessary precautions (e.g., 11:9, 12). As the prime mover behind the Jerusalem collection that he expected to be sizable ("this liberal gift," v.20), he was particularly susceptible to malicious charges that the whole project was designed to bribe the Jerusalem church to fully support his ministry or that he was quietly retaining a commission for his services as administrator of the gift. This explains, for example, his original uncertainty as to whether he would accompany the churches' delegates to Jerusalem (1 Cor 16:3, 4; but cf. 2 Cor 1:16; Rom 15:25), his insistence that the Corinthians appoint their own accredited representatives (1 Cor 16:3), and his sending to Corinth (before he arrived!) two delegates along with his personal representative, Titus (vv.18, 19, 22, 23).

Paul was not one who sought the praise of men (Gal 1:10), but he recognized that the progress of the gospel was hindered if its ministers for any reason acquired a reputation for dishonest dealings (cf. 1 Cor 9:12; 2 Cor 4:2; 6:3). Verse 21 is virtually a quotation of Proverbs 3:4 in LXX: "And aim at what is honorable before the Lord and men."

22 The second anonymous representative who would travel to Corinth with Titus is identified simply as "our brother." As in v.18 ("the brother"), the relationship indicated is spiritual, not physical (see commentary on 1:1). On many occasions and "in many ways" Paul had proved his zeal, which in the present matter was all the greater "because of his great confidence" that this mission to Corinth would prove successful and that the Corinthians would fulfill his high hopes for a "liberal gift" (v.20).

Why are both the "brothers" who would accompany Titus mentioned without identification? Either because both would be personally introduced by Titus when the present letter was first read at Corinth, or because both delegates, as renowned appointees of the Macedonian churches, were already well known at Corinth, whether or not they had visited the city.

Why were three delegates chosen? Would not one have sufficed? Evidently Paul was more susceptible to misrepresentation at Corinth than in most of the other churches he had founded. Added precautions were necessary. To have sent one personal representative would have been to lay himself open to slanderous gossip (cf. 12:16–18). Two independent envoys would be able to testify to his honest intentions and conduct. Second, it is not impossible that Paul wished to exert some subtle yet legitimate pressure on the Corinthians (cf. 9:4), knowing as he did the somewhat erratic progress of the collection at Corinth thus far, the propensity of the Corinthians for disorderliness (cf. 1 Cor 14:33, 40), and the disturbing effect of the parasitical intruders from Palestine.

23 As he sums up the credentials of the three delegates, Paul draws a distinction between Titus, his "partner" or colleague and personally appointed representative, and the two "representatives of the churches." Titus, like Timothy (Rom 16:21), is described as Paul's "fellow worker," though the partnership seems to be restricted by the phrase "among you," another possible indication of Titus's relative independence of Paul before this association. If any one should raise questions about Titus's two companions, says Paul, three facts are relevant: they are "brothers" in Christ; they are the appointees and envoys (*apostoloi*) of the Macedonian churches; by life and service they are a credit (*doxa*) to Christ (though *doxa* here may indicate that they are a worthy reflection of the glory of Christ).

In light of the reference to "the Macedonian churches" in v.1, "[all] the churches" mentioned in vv.18, 19, 23, 24 are probably Macedonian and therefore the two delegates sent with Titus were probably from this province. Significantly, it was the Macedonians in general who had placed themselves at the disposal of Paul for service relating to the collection. But some writers (e.g., J.H. Bernard, P.E. Hughes, K.F. Nickle) object to this identification on the ground that Paul's appeal to the possible embarrassment of "any Macedonians" (9:4) at finding the Corinthians unprepared would have little point if Titus's companions were Macedonian. It should be observed, however, that the two colleagues of Titus did not expect to find the collection at Corinth complete.

24 Paul's short "letter of commendation" (vv.16–24) concludes with a warm appeal. The Corinthians were to give evidence of their love for Christ and for the members of his Body (cf. v.8) by extending to the three delegates warm hospitality and by cooperating with their efforts to supervise the final arrangements for the collection. Also, they were to show the reason for Paul's pride in them or to vindicate his proud, confident boasting about them (cf. 7:14) by contributing eagerly, promptly, and generously (cf. vv.7, 20). All was to be done "so that all the churches [of Macedonia, or, churches that are contributing to the collection] can see it"; or "[as though you were] in the presence and under the gaze of the churches from which the delegates have come."

Notes

17 The aorist ἐξῆλθεν (*exēlthen*, "he is coming"), like the aorists συνεπέμψαμεν (*synepempsamen*, "we are sending along," vv.18, 22) and ἔπεμψα (*epempsa*, "I am sending," 9:3), is probably epistolary (thus RSV, NEB, NIV, and most commentators). But it is not impossible that Titus and the two brothers had left after 2 Corinthians 1–7 was written and that all these aorists are preterite (thus E.B. Allo).

18 For a discussion of the possible identifications of the Christian brother mentioned in this verse, see the special note of P.E. Hughes, in loc.

23 Εἴτε ὑπέρ...εἴτε... (*eite hyper...eite...*) is elliptical and means "if anyone enquires about...if anyone enquires about..." (cf. KJV, which rightly catches the sense).

2. *The need for readiness*

9:1–5

¹There is no need for me to write to you about this service to the saints. ²For I know your eagerness to help, and I have been boasting about it to the Macedonians, telling them that since last year you in Achaia were ready to give; and your enthusiasm has stirred most of them to action. ³But I am sending the brothers in

order that our boasting about you in this matter should not prove hollow, but that you may be ready, as I said you would be. ⁴For if any Macedonians come with me and find you unprepared, we—not to say anything about you—would be ashamed of having been so confident. ⁵So I thought it necessary to urge the brothers to visit you in advance and finish the arrangements for the generous gift you had promised. Then it will be ready as a generous gift, not as one grudgingly given.

1 As rendered in some English versions, this verse suggests that Paul is introducing a new subject. An alternative translation, however, highlights the close connection between chapters eight and nine: "For to begin with [*men gar*], it is superfluous for me to be writing as I am [*to graphein*] about this [*tēs*] service to the saints, since I know your eagerness to help...." Translated thus, vv.1, 2a are clearly resumptive and state the reason why Paul was convinced that his pride in the Corinthians and his boasting about them (8:24) would not prove to have been misguided.

2 In 8:10 (cf. 8:6) Paul dated the beginning of the collection at Corinth as "last year" (*apo perusi*). Here, using the same Greek phrase, he speaks of his current boast to the Macedonians—"since last year you in Achaia [certainly including the Corinthians] were ready to give" ("to give" has been rightly supplied from the context).

On the basis of this apparent discrepancy, some have concluded that chapters eight and nine cannot belong together within a single letter, chapter nine clearly being later than chapter eight. Others claim that Paul cannot be acquitted of duplicity: just as he exaggerated Macedonian poverty and generosity in exhorting the Corinthians to complete their offering (8:2-6), so here he unwittingly indicates that he was grossly overstating the extent of the Corinthians' "readiness" in his effort to have the Macedonians contribute quickly and liberally.

We must draw a careful distinction between the Corinthians' ready desire to give and the actual readiness of having completed the collection. In this verse, "eagerness to help," readiness "to give," and "enthusiasm" are all parallel expressions (cf. "eager willingness to do" the work, 8:11) and are virtually synonymous. From vv.3-5 it is clear that the Corinthians were not yet ready or prepared. The relation, then, between chapters eight and nine seems to be this: The Corinthian readiness of intention and eagerness in initiating the collection (cf. 8:10, 11) were appealed to by Paul as an example worthy of emulation when he was encouraging the Macedonians to make their contribution (9:2). Thus it was the Corinthians' "enthusiasm" to participate in the collection, not their "completion" of it (8:11), that had "stirred most of them [the Macedonians] to action" (9:2). On the other hand, because the Macedonians had successfully completed (8:1-5) what they had enthusiastically commenced under the stimulus of the Corinthian example, their exemplary action formed one ground of Paul's appeal to the Corinthians to complete their contribution (8:6, 10, 11).

3,4 Although Paul knew that the Corinthians were so eager to help that further written reminders about the collection were superfluous (vv.1, 2), he was sending (*epempsa*, epistolary aorist; see note on 8:17) a "personal" reminder in the form of the "brothers." This seems the sense of the *men...de* contrast between v.1 and v.3. Probably all three delegates mentioned in 8:16-24 are referred to. Without the discussion of chapter 8 immediately preceding, the allusive reference to "the brothers" in vv.3, 5 would be scarcely explicable; this argues for the unity of these two chapters.

There were two situations Paul wished to avoid. One was that his repeated and confident boast to the Macedonians about the Corinthians' "eagerness to help" (v.2) and their expected "readiness" on his arrival should turn out to be without foundation (v.3). The other was that when the delegates of the Macedonian churches (not to be confused with the two companions of Titus) arrived at Corinth with Paul on his forthcoming visit (12:14; 13:1, 2), the Corinthians would be still unprepared and this would lead to his acute embarrassment—not to mention that of the Corinthians themselves (v.4).

5 To make certain that neither of these predicaments arose, Paul "thought it necessary to urge the brothers" to prepare for his coming to Corinth by supervising final arrangements for the collection there. He reminds the Corinthians of their earlier commitment ("the generous gift you had promised"). By a prompt response when the brothers arrived, they would be fulfilling an obligation they had voluntarily assumed and would be ensuring that the gift was not "grudgingly given" (see note).

Twice in this verse the Corinthian contribution is called a *eulogia* ("generous gift"). In classical Greek the word was generally used of "fine speaking" (in a good or a bad sense) or of "praise" (cf. English "eulogy"). But in biblical Greek it commonly refers to the actual "act of blessing" or consecration whether by God or man, or to "a blessing" as some concrete benefit given by God or man (see BAG, p. 323). Here it may bear the latter sense, as "a benefit bestowed" by the Corinthian believers on the Jerusalem saints. But other ideas are suggested by the word. First, the Corinthian contribution would be "an act that produced blessing" (i.e., thanksgiving to God) (cf. vv.11–13). Second, Paul hoped that the collection (*logia*, 1 Cor 16:1) at Corinth would be a "first-rate collection" (*eu-logia*). Third, since blessing implies generosity, the word may denote "a generous (or bountiful) gift" (NIV).

Notes

1 Διακονία (*diakonia*, "service") here is virtually a technical term for the raising and administering of charitable financial relief (cf. Acts 6:1; 11:29; 12:25; Rom 15:31; 2 Cor 8:4; 9:12, 13).
2 The present tense καυχῶμαι (*kauchōmai*, "I have been boasting" [NIV]) indicates that 2 Cor was not written immediately after Paul's arrival in Macedonia. (See Introduction, 1.b. 6–9.)
5 The words μὴ ὡς πλεονεξίαν (*mē hōs pleonexian*) may mean (1) "not as a matter of avarice [or covetousness]," i.e., the Corinthians were not to give grudgingly as a result of a desire to get or keep rather than give; or (2) "not as a matter of extortion," i.e., neither Paul nor the envoys would forcibly or subtly extract a contribution from the Corinthians. The contrast with εὐλογίαν (*eulogian*, "generous gift") in v.5 and the use of φειδομένως (*pheidomenōs*, "sparingly") in antithesis to ἐπ' εὐλογίαις (*ep' eulogiais*, "generously") in v.6 support the former meaning (preferred by BAG, p. 673, and reflected in NIV). Two attitudes to giving (generously—grudgingly) are being contrasted, not two ways of securing a gift (by voluntary act—by extortion).

C. *The Results of Generosity* (9:6–15)

1. *The enrichment of the giver*

9:6–11

⁶Remember this: Whoever sows sparingly will also reap sparingly, and whoever sows generously will also reap generously. ⁷Each man should give what he has

decided in his heart to give, not reluctantly or under compulsion, for God loves a cheerful giver. [8]And God is able to make all grace abound to you, so that in all things at all times, having all that you need, you will abound in every good work. [9]As it is written:

> "He has scattered abroad his gifts to the poor;
> his righteousness endures for ever."

[10]Now he who supplies seed to the sower and bread for food will also supply and increase your store of seed and will enlarge the harvest of your righteousness. [11]You will be made rich in every way so that you can be generous on every occasion, and through us your generosity will result in thanksgiving to God.

6,7 To emphasize the rewards of generous giving (v.5), Paul cites what appears to be a proverb (v.6): "scanty sowing, scanty harvest; plentiful sowing, plentiful harvest" (*Twentieth Century New Testament*). No exact parallel to this maxim is extant, but a similar sentiment is expressed in several places in Proverbs (e.g., 11:24, 25; 19:17; 22:8, 9), in Luke 6:38 (where Jesus says, "Give, and it will be given to you. ... For with the measure you use, it will be measured to you," NIV), and in Galatians 6:7 ("A man reaps what he sows," NIV).

The image of the harvest naturally suggests the freedom of the sower to plant as much seed as he chooses—whether "sparingly" or "generously." Similarly, each man is responsible first to decide "in his heart" what he should give (cf. Acts 11:29; 1 Cor 16:2) and then to give what he has decided (v.7). Giving should result from inward resolve, not from impulsive or casual decision. Once the amount to be given has been determined, says Paul, the gift should be given cheerfully (since the cheerful giver always receives God's approval—*agapa*, gnomic present; cf. Prov 22:8, LXX), "not reluctantly [as though all giving were painful; cf. Tobit 4:7] or under compulsion" (because there seems to be no alternative or because pressure has been exerted).

8,9 One way God's approval of the cheerful giver (v.7b) finds expression is in the provision of both spiritual grace and material prosperity ("all grace") that will enable him constantly and generously to dispense spiritual and material benefits ("you will abound in every good work," v.8). As regularly as the resources of the cheerful giver are taxed by his generous giving, they are replenished by divine grace. This gives him a "complete self-sufficiency" (*pasan autarkeian;* "all that you need," NIV) born of dependence on an all-sufficient God. In the writings of the Cynics and Stoics, on the other hand, this same term (*autarkeia*) denoted an intrinsic self-sufficiency that made a man independent of external circumstance.

But *autarkeia* may also mean "contentment," as in 1 Timothy 6:6 ("godliness with contentment is great gain"). Some commentators therefore interpret v.8 to mean that God supplies the generous person with multiplied material blessings, so that, content as he himself is in every circumstance (cf. Phil 4:11), he may be able to shower multiplied benefits of every kind on the needy. But to restrict "all grace" to temporal benefits seems unnecessary.

At this point Paul quotes Psalm 112 to illustrate the generosity of "the man who fears the Lord" (112:1) and the positive results of his prodigal giving. From "the wealth and riches ... in his house" (112:3a), the God-fearing man freely distributes his gifts to the poor (112:9a). As a result, his benevolent acts of piety ("his righteousness") will never be forgotten but rather will have permanent beneficial effects in this life, as well as gaining him an eternal reward in the life to come (112:9b).

10,11 In v.6 Paul observed that the person who sows sparingly will reap a meager harvest. Now he develops the imagery of sowing and reaping to reinforce the point that generosity pays handsome dividends. He argues from God's bounty in nature to his even greater liberality in grace. The crops of the generous person are always full and his harvests rich. If God supplies man with the seed needed to produce a harvest of grain, and thus food (cf. Isa 55:10), he certainly will supply and multiply all the resources ("your store of seed") needed to produce a full harvest of good deeds ("your righteousness"; cf. Hos 10:12, LXX).

Verse 11a restates v.8, though this is not to say, as some do, that vv.9, 10 are parenthetical. God continues to enrich the benevolent person so that he can go on enriching others by his generosity (cf. 1:4). The greater the giving, the greater the enrichment. The greater the enrichment, the greater the resources to give. Paul then adds a statement (v.11b) that he will develop in vv.12–15. The Jerusalem saints, as the grateful recipients of the Corinthians' liberal gift administered by Paul and his colleagues, would express their thanks to God, the source of all good gifts (cf. James 1:17). Liberality is thus seen to be truly a *eulogia* (v.8), a gracious act that prompts thanksgiving to God.

Notes

9 The two aorists (ἐσκόρπισεν, *eskorpisen*, and ἔδωκεν, *edōken*) in the quotation from Ps 112:9 are probably gnomic: "he distributes freely, he gives. . . ." For a discussion of the various possible meanings of "his righteousness endures for ever," see A. Plummer (ICC), in loc. Both the psalmist and Paul are speaking about a particular type of man, not about God.

11 The participle πλουτιζόμενοι (*ploutizomenoi*, "being made rich") has been construed as (1) in apposition to ἔχοντες (*echontes*, "having," v.8) and therefore dependent on ἵνα...περισσεύητε (*hina...perisseuēte*, "so that...you will abound"), vv.9, 10 being parenthetical; (2) standing for a finite verb, with either ἐστέ (*este*, "you are"), ἔστε (*este*, "be!") or ἔσεσθε (*esesthe*, "you will be") to be supplied with the participle; or (3) anacoluthic, being in agreement with the ὑμεῖς (*hymeis*) to be supplied from v.10.

2. The offering of thanks to God

9:12–15

> [12] This service that you perform is not only supplying the needs of God's people but is also overflowing in many expressions of thanks to God. [13] Because of the service by which you have proved yourselves, men will praise God for the obedience that accompanies your confession of the gospel of Christ, and for your generosity in sharing with them and with everyone else. [14] And in their prayers for you their hearts will go out to you, because of the surpassing grace God has given you. [15] Thanks be to God for his indescribable gift!

12,13 The believers at Corinth are now reminded (vv.12–15) of the encouraging results that will stem from their generous gift. Not only does the service (*leitourgia*; see note) of giving enrich the donor (vv.6–11) and help supply the needs of the recipients (v.12a), but above all, it promotes the glory of God by prompting "many expressions of thanks" to him. The overflow of almsgiving is praise offered to God.

Having stated the bare fact that Corinthian liberality would prompt thanksgiving to God (vv.11b, 12b), Paul gives the reason for such thanksgiving (v.13a) and its content (v.13b,c).

The saints at Jerusalem, as well as other Christians who heard of the collection, would praise God because this act of Christian service had proved the reality and vigor of the Corinthians' faith (v.13a), which may have come under suspicion at Jerusalem through reports of certain irregularities in the Corinthian church. Then there would be two items for thanksgiving (vv.13b,c). One was the Corinthians' obedience to the dictates of the gospel that accompanied their "confession of the gospel of Christ," a gospel that called for "contributing to the needs of the saints" (Rom 12:13). The other was the Corinthians' sacrificial liberality (haplotēs, "generosity") demonstrated in sharing material benefits with the Jerusalem church and therefore in one sense with all Christians (cf. 1 Cor 12:26). Notice that praise is offered less for the gift itself than for the spiritual virtues of the donors expressed in the gift.

14 There are still other results of generosity. Paul is convinced the giving will be reciprocal. The Jerusalem believers will receive material benefits and in return will dispense the spiritual blessing of intercession for the Corinthians. (This, however, is not the clue to the interpretation of 8:14.) As they pray, they will recall "the surpassing grace" imparted to the Corinthians by God (cf. 8:1) and evident in their sacrificial liberality; as a result, their hearts will be warmed towards those at Corinth and they will long to see them and enjoy a closer relation with them.

15 This doxology is a final appeal to the lofty grandeur of divine giving (cf. 8:9; 9:8, 10, 11). Since the gift is said to be given by God ("his. . .gift") and beyond adequate human description ("indescribable"), it could hardly be the Corinthian contribution or even the boon of Jewish-Gentile reconciliation in Christ alluded to in v.14a, but must refer secondarily to the surpassing grace that God imparts (v.14b) and primarily to the Father's gift of the Son (cf. Rom 8:32).

Were Paul's appeals to the Corinthians in these two chapters successful? The apostle paid his third visit to Corinth as planned (12:14; 13:1), spending three months (the winter of A.D. 56–57) in Greece (Acts 20:2, 3), during which he wrote Romans (see Rom 16:23; 1 Cor 1:14). In Romans 15:26, 27 he writes, "For Macedonia and Achaia have been pleased to make some contribution (koinōnian tina; see note) for the poor among the saints at Jerusalem; they were pleased to do it. . ." (RSV). Evidently in the five or so months between the writing of 2 Corinthians and Romans, the believers at Corinth had responded to Paul's appeals. Why then does Acts 20:4 make no reference to a delegate or delegates from Achaia? It is unlikely that Paul himself was their appointed delegate, but it is possible that Titus was, and for some reason Titus is nowhere mentioned in Acts.

Notes

12 In extra-biblical usage λειτουργία (leitourgia, "service") denotes personal, civic, or priestly service often performed voluntarily (see MM, p. 373 and H. Strathmann, TDNT, 4:215–219).

Its use here may imply that Paul regarded the collection as a voluntary act of service to God as well as a means of promoting the welfare of the Christian community at Jerusalem.

13 The subject of δοξάζοντες (*doxazontes*, "praising") is unexpressed. The RSV (and UBS, by making v.12 a parenthesis) takes it to be the Corinthians ("you will glorify God"), while the NIV assumes an indefinite subject (doubtless with special reference to the Jerusalem Christians = οἱ ἄγιοι, *hoi hagioi*, "the saints"; NIV, "God's people," in v.12): "men will praise God" (similarly NEB). It is highly improbable that "unbelievers in Judea" (Rom 15:31) are included or that Paul envisaged that the conversion of Israel would result from the successful delivery of the collection and the witness of the Gentile delegates (for these views, see K.F. Nickle. *The Collection* [Naperville: Allenson, 1966], pp. 129–143). It is, however, fair to observe that Paul's optimism (reflected in vv.12–14) about the results of the collection did not blind him to the real uncertainties concerning the Jewish reaction to the project (see Rom 15:30, 31).

15 The indefinite adjective τινά (*tina*, "some") in Romans 15:26 should not be interpreted as a derogatory reference to the size of the contribution from Macedonia and Achaia. It simply refers to an indefinite yet not therefore insignificant quantity (see BAG, p. 828).

III. Paul's Vindication of His Apostolic Authority (2 Cor 10–13)

A. *The Exercise of Apostolic Rights and Authority* (10:1–11:15)

1. *The potency of apostolic authority*

10:1–11

¹By the meekness and gentleness of Christ, I appeal to you—I, Paul, who am "timid" when face to face with you, but "bold" when away! ²I beg you that when I come I may not have to be as bold as I expect to be toward some people who think that we live by the standards of this world. ³For though we live in the world, we do not wage war as the world does. ⁴The weapons we fight with are not the weapons of the world. On the contrary, they have divine power to tear down strongholds. ⁵We demolish arguments and every pretension that sets itself up against the knowledge of God, and we take captive every thought to make it obedient to Christ. ⁶And we will be ready to punish every act of disobedience, once your obedience is complete.

⁷You are looking only on the surface of things. If anyone is confident that he belongs to Christ, he should consider again that we belong to Christ just as much as he. ⁸For even if I boast somewhat freely about the authority the Lord gave us for building you up rather than pulling you down, I will not be ashamed of it. ⁹I do not want to seem to be trying to frighten you with my letters. ¹⁰For some say, "His letters are weighty and forceful, but in person he is unimpressive and his speaking amounts to nothing." ¹¹Such people should realize that what we are in our letters when we are absent, we will be in our actions when we are present.

No commentator denies that there is an abrupt change of tone at this point in the letter. Defenders of the unity of the Epistle explain the change in various ways, some of which are more convincing than others: a pause in dictation (E. Stange, W. Michaelis), coupled with the arrival of disturbing news; like chapters 1–7, chapters 10–13 are tempered polemic, with not a few tender expressions of affection (e.g., 11:2, 3; 12:14, 15a); Paul intentionally reserves his criticism until after his commendation (A. Jülicher); after consolidating his apostolic authority (1–7), Paul then exercises it (10–13); the contrast between 1–9 and 10–13 has been overdrawn—all 2 Corinthians is polemical in tone, 10:1 marking an intensification of degree, not a variation of kind (W. Ellis); a change of audience—in 1–9 Paul addresses the whole church, in 10–13 the intruders and their partisans (A. Wikenhauser); uncertainty in Paul's mind concerning the sincerity of the Corinthians' repentance; the awkward transition at 10:1 reflects a previous suppression of deep feelings (A. Menzies, A. Robertson); the vagaries of Paul's temperament (W. Sanday, H.L. Goudge)—abrupt changes of mood are reflected elsewhere in Paul's letters (e.g., at 1 Cor 4:8). Some of these scholars give more than one of the above explanations.

1,2 There is no evidence that Paul now addresses only a sector of the Corinthian church—those favorably disposed toward his adversaries from Palestine. On the contrary, regularly throughout these next four chapters (as here in v.2) Paul identifies the views of certain unnamed people (e.g., 10:7, 10–12; 11:4, 12, 13, 15, 20–23; 13:2)—whether Paul's rivals or their partisans at Corinth—who formed a recognizable subversive element at Corinth. He does this in an effort to alert the entire church (cf. 12:19; 13:11–13) to the danger of becoming spiritually infected.

Paul had been accused of being courageous and bold at a distance, shooting his epistolary arrows, such as the "severe letter," but subservient and weak-kneed when personally present, feebly voicing his demands (cf. v.10 and 1 Cor 2:3). This charge Paul ironically repeats in v.1b as a prelude to an appeal ("I beg you") to all the Corinthians regarding a vocal minority ("some people") who persisted in thinking that worldly standards and motives governed all his conduct and that he relied on human powers and methods in his ministry (cf. 1:17; 2:17; 3:5; 4:2; 7:2).

What Paul wished to avoid on his forthcoming visit was a display of boldness—boldness when present not absent! Yet he indicates his total readiness to exercise his apostolic authority, whatever the outcome, if the Corinthians do not repudiate his calumniators and mend their ways (cf. 12:20, 21; 13:11). His "meekness and gentleness" as a true servant of Christ (cf. Matt 11:29) should not be confused with timidity (cf. 13:10). It was his preference to come to Corinth "with love in a spirit of gentleness" (also prautēs) but if necessary he was ready "to come rod in hand" (1 Cor 4:21).

3,4 A clear distinction is drawn between existence "in the world" and worldly conduct and techniques. Paul does not deny his human weakness, yet he affirms that a spiritual warfare demands spiritual weapons (vv.3, 4a; cf. Eph 6:11–17). A successful campaign can be waged in the spiritual realm only as worldly weapons are abandoned and total reliance is placed on the spiritual weaponry, which is divinely potent (see note) for demolishing apparently impregnable fortresses where evil is entrenched and from which the gospel is attacked (v.4b).

5 What are these fortified positions that crumble before the weapons of the Spirit? Fanciful human sophistry and intellectual pretensions, or as Paul expresses it in 1 Corinthians 3:19, "the wisdom of this world." The phrase pan hypsōma (translated "every pretension") refers to any human act or attitude that forms an obstacle to the emancipating knowledge of God contained in the gospel of Christ crucified and therefore keeps men in oppressive bondage to sin. Closely related is the expression pan noēma ("every thought"). By this Paul probably means every human machination or foul design that temporarily frustrates the divine plan (cf. "every act of disobedience," v.6) and so needs forcibly to be reduced to obedience to Christ. It is not a case of the Christian's effort to force all his thoughts to be pleasing to Christ. Rather the picture seems to be that of a military operation in enemy territory that seeks to thwart every single hostile plan of battle, so that there will be universal allegiance to Christ.

6 If circumstances forced Paul to turn from "meekness and gentleness" to a stern assertion of his authority, from appeal to discipline, his plan of action was in two stages. First, there was the need to bring the Corinthians' obedience to completion (cf. 2:9; 7:15). This would be achieved when they dissociated themselves from the interlopers, fully recognized Paul's apostolic authority, and made a total break with idolatry (6:14–7:1). Second, there was the punishment of "every act of disobedience" performed by his adversaries from Palestine or by any Corinthians who remained insubordinate. Precisely what form the punishment would take cannot be known.

Only after securing a firm base in the Corinthian church would Paul risk a face-to-face confrontation with those who still opposed him. Unless a church as a whole is willing to recognize and support spiritual discipline, that discipline will remain largely ineffective. Another important principle emerges when vv.5 and 6 are compared. Obedience to Christ entails submission to his appointed representatives.

7 Paul's opponents were not unaware that the most successful way to undermine his effectiveness was to cast doubt on the genuineness of his apostleship. If his converts could be persuaded that he lacked apostolic credentials, they would cease to believe his teaching.

In response, Paul does not discourage the testing of credentials (cf. 13:2, 3) but casts doubt on the adequacy of the criteria the Corinthians were using. They were impressed by externals or outward appearances (cf. 5:12). They were "looking only on the surface of things"—the confident claim to "belong to Christ" as his authorized apostle (see note), the commendatory letter (3:1), the authoritarian manner (11:20), the spectacular vision, the remarkable ecstatic experience (cf. 12:1–7), rhetorical skill (11:6), and "pure" Jewishness (11:22).

Here Paul argues that the right to make a subjective claim based on personal conviction cannot fairly be granted his opponents and yet denied him. Later he will mention more objective criteria for testing apostolic credentials (see 10:8; 11:23–28; 12:9, 10, 12–15; 13:5, 6). In all this, his motive was not personal vindication but the desire to defend the Corinthian church from the danger of apostasy (cf. 11:2, 3).

8 If the need for self-defense in the face of calumny compelled Paul to boast "somewhat freely" about his apostolic authority, he was confident that he would not be embarrassed by a charge of exaggeration or deception, for the facts themselves spoke eloquently in his favor. Everyone knew that the result of his service at Corinth had been the upbuilding of the Corinthian church in faith and in harmony, while the presence of the false apostles had produced friction and division ("pulling down") (cf. 1 Cor 3:17). In Galatians (1:1, 11, 12, 15, 16) Paul had emphasized against his opponents the divine origin of his call and gospel. Here he stresses the divine origin of his authority (cf. 3:5, 6; 13:10) and its employment for the common good (1 Cor 12:7).

9–11 However legitimately Paul may have boasted about his God-given authority, he decides to refrain from expanding his simple claim in v.8 lest he appear to be frightening the Corinthians into submission by "weighty and forceful" letters (vv.9, 10a). He had no desire to give substance to the charge that he was bold and impressive only when absent (cf. v.1). Those who compared unfavorably what they believed to be his epistolary boldness, "unimpressive" presence, or "contemptible" rhetoric (v.10) are reminded that when present with them he would act in precise accord with his letters (v.11; cf. 13:2, 10).

It is not difficult to understand the origin of the malicious accusation against Paul reported in v.10. His earlier letters to Corinth (the "previous letter," 1 Corinthians, and the "severe letter") had each been "forceful." In fact, to judge by their contents, actual or probable, they seemed to be growing more forceful each time! And 1 Corinthians was certainly a "weighty" or impressive letter (cf. 2 Peter 3:16). Moreover, unlike his opponents (11:20), Paul avoided self-assertiveness and admitted the inferiority of his rhetorical skills (1 Cor 1:17; 2:1–5; 2 Cor 11:6). What he firmly resists, however, is the inference drawn from the claim about his personal bearing and his manner of speaking—namely, that he was " 'timid' when face to face" (v.1).

Notes

4 The dative τῷ θεῷ (tō theō) after δυνατά (dynata) may be (1) instrumental, "made powerful by God" (cf. KJV); (2) a dative of respect or an ethic dative, "in the eyes of God" (cf. RV); (3) a dative of advantage or interest, "for God," "for God's service;" or (4) a Hebraism (cf. Jonah 3:3, LXX; Acts 7:20), with the sense of an elative superlative, "divinely [= extremely, supernaturally] powerful" (cf. Moff, NEB, NASB).

7 The form βλέπετε (blepete) may be (1) an indicative, thus NIV text ("You are looking"); (2) an imperative, thus NIV footnote ("Look at the obvious facts") and most EV; or (3) an indicative with an interrogative sense: "Do you see what is in front of you?" (similarly KJV).

In this context "belonging to Christ" does not mean being a Christian (cf. 1 Cor 15:23) or being a member of the Christ-party (1 Cor 1:12), but being a genuine apostle and servant of Christ (cf. 11:13, 23). Yet it is possible that, as a result of their denial of his claim to apostleship, Paul's rivals questioned his status as a Christian; a false apostle hardly "belonged to Christ."

2. Legitimate spheres of activity and boasting

10:12–18

¹²We do not dare to classify or compare ourselves with some who commend themselves. When they measure themselves by themselves and compare themselves with themselves, they are not wise. ¹³We, however, will not boast beyond proper limits, but will confine our boasting to the field God has assigned to us, a field that reaches even to you. ¹⁴We are not going too far in our boasting, as would be the case if we had not come to you, for we did get as far as you with the gospel of Christ. ¹⁵Neither do we go beyond our limits by boasting of work done by others. Our hope is that, as your faith continues to grow, our area of activity among you will greatly expand, ¹⁶so that we can preach the gospel in the regions beyond you. For we do not want to boast about work already done in another man's territory. ¹⁷But, "Let him who boasts, boast in the Lord." ¹⁸For it is not the man who commends himself who is approved, but the man whom the Lord commends.

Behind Paul's continuing self-defense in this section lies an indirect attack on the intruders from Palestine. From his firm denials ("we do not," vv.12, 16; "we. . .will not," v.13; "we are not," v.14; "neither do we," v.15; "it is not," v.18) we may deduce the content of his charges against his rivals, not in this case, as so often elsewhere, the content of accusations made against him. Only in v.12b does Paul make a direct charge. It is twofold: First, the false apostles had trespassed on his legitimate "sphere of authority" or "province" at Corinth in defiance of the agreement of Galatians 2:1–10. Second, in their unrestrained self-commendation (v.12) his opponents were laying a false claim to credit for work he had done in his own "territory" in Corinth.

12 In one aspect of his conduct, Paul admits his "timidity" (cf. v.1). He lacked the boldness and temerity to align or compare himself with those who indulged in self-praise, "those who write their own testimonials" (Phillips)! Writing ironically, he asserts that in their folly his opponents were establishing their own conduct as normative and then finding great satisfaction in always measuring up to the standard. The implication is clear. If the Corinthians tried to assess Paul's credentials against the artificial and subjective criteria established by his detractors, they would be just as foolish.

13,14 Unlike his adversaries, Paul refused to boast of what had occurred beyond the limits of his own ministry as the apostle to the Gentiles (Acts 9:15; Gal 2:9). In boasting about his "field" at Corinth and appealing by implication to the very existence of the Corinthian church as a vindication of his apostleship (cf. 3:2, 3), he was "not going too far" or overstepping his limits, since historically his God-ordained field had included Corinth. In fact, he had been "the first to come all the way" (see note) to the Corinthians with the gospel of Christ (v.14b, RSV; cf. 1 Cor 3:6, 10). God's formation of a Christian community at Corinth as a result of Paul's pioneer evangelism established Corinth as his legitimate "province" or "sphere of influence" (*kanōn*). But in no sense was the territory of Achaia assigned exclusively to Paul before his actual ministry there.

The activity of the false apostles at Corinth encroached on Paul's legitimate "province" because it violated the concordat of Galatians 2:1-10. Whether or not this episode described in Galatians 2 is related to Acts 11:29, 30 (A.D. 46) or Acts 15:1-21 (A.D. 49), it predated the arrival at Corinth of these Palestinian intruders (perhaps late in A.D. 55). Even if these interlopers had no relationship with the Jerusalem church (see the Introduction, 7.d. 2), they must have been aware of the agreement of Galatians 2 and in particular the fact that the Jerusalem apostles recognized Paul as having been entrusted with special responsibility for the propagation of the gospel among the Gentiles or uncircumcised (Gal 2:7-9). True, their presence at Corinth was not technically an infringement on any precisely defined apostolic "treaty," but it amounted at least to a repudiation of the spirit of this agreement concerning apostolic "division of labor," for they were not in Corinth to aid Paul (as Apollos had been, 1 Cor 3:5, 6) but to supplant him.

This illegitimate invasion of Paul's rightful mission field may well have constituted one of those "acts of disobedience" (v.6) Paul planned to punish on his next visit.

15,16 Twice here (vv.15a, 16b) Paul indirectly chides his opponents for priding themselves on work already done by others. They probably boasted that the spiritual vitality of the Corinthians was directly attributable to them and had come in spite of Paul's influence. And not a few Corinthians were acknowledging their proud claim to spiritual jurisdiction (11:22). Paul, however, so far from "boasting of work done by others" (v.15), made it his policy to avoid preaching the gospel where Christ had already been named lest he build on another man's foundation (Rom 15:18-21), though he welcomed another's watering what he himself had planted (1 Cor 3:6, 10).

As their one spiritual father (1 Cor 4:15), Paul hoped that the enlargement of his influence among the Corinthians and the improvement of their estimation of him would accompany or even result from the growth of their faith. Then and only then would he contemplate fulfilling his eager desire to visit the Christians at Rome (Acts 19:21; Rom

1:11; 15:24) and to advance westward to Spain (Rom 15:24, 28). How could he prosecute pioneer evangelism in the western Mediterranean when his converts in the eastern Mediterranean were unsettled and in danger of apostasy (11:3)?

In one sense, Paul's future was in the Corinthians' hands. His evangelistic outreach would be the joyful outcome or the overflow (*eis perisseian*, "in overflowing measure;" NIV, "greatly") of his total acceptance at Corinth. The principle illustrated here is this: A task undertaken at the direction of God or in fulfillment of a divine commission should not be left unfulfilled simply for the sake of grasping new opportunities; consolidation precedes advance. The call to begin is the call to complete (cf. Phil 1:6).

17,18 As in 1 Corinthians 1:31, Paul cites Jeremiah 9:24. Boasting is illegitimate, whether it be of one's own accomplishments or status (1 Cor 1:31), or of another person's achievements as though they were one's own (v.16). For the Christian, only boasting "in the Lord" is legitimate—that is, boasting of what Jesus Christ has done for him (Gal 6:14) or through him (Rom 15:18; cf. Acts 14:27), or can do through him. (Here Paul is confident the Lord will make his work in Rome and Spain fruitful.)

So far from being an evidence or guarantee of divine approval, self-commendation (such as Paul's adversaries practiced) is a disqualification (v.18). Only the person who boasts in the Lord and so gives God his due glory enjoys the Lord's commendation, which is real approval. To gain Christ's approval during life and after death at Christ's tribunal was Paul's goal (5:9).

Notes

12,13 Some commentators (e.g., H. Windisch, J. Héring) prefer the shorter Western reading (D* G it) that omits the four words οὐ συνιᾶσιν. ἡμεῖς δέ (*ou syniasin. hēmeis de,* "they are not wise. We, however"). The sense will then be (reading the participles of v.12b as first person, not third person): "When we measure ourselves by ourselves and compare ourselves with ourselves (i.e., in terms of our God-given commission and self-imposed ideals), we will not be boasting beyond proper limits but in keeping with the limits determined by the sphere God has allotted to us." This Western text, however, probably arose through a transcriptional error (the scribe passing from οὐ [*ou*] to οὐκ [*ouk*]) or through an effort to remove the harsh οὐ συνιᾶσιν (*ou syniasin,* "they are senseless").

14 Although ἐφθάσαμεν (*ephthasamen*) could mean simply "we reached" (NIV, "we did get"), it may also be tr. "we were the first to reach" (NEB) (cf. 1 Thess 4:15), reflecting Paul's understanding of his apostolic commission as that of pioneer evangelism among the Gentiles.

15 If ἐν ὑμῖν (*en hymin,* v.15) here means "through you," "with your help" (BV), rather than "among you" (NIV), then the enlargement of Paul's sphere of activity is not at Corinth but "in the regions beyond" (v.16), viz., the western Mediterranean.

3. Paul's jealousy for the Corinthians

11:1–6

¹I hope you will put up with a little of my foolishness; but you are already doing that. ²I am jealous for you with a godly jealousy. I promised you to one husband, to Christ, so that I might present you as a pure virgin to him. ³But I am afraid that just as Eve was deceived by the serpent's cunning, your minds may somehow be

led astray from your sincere and pure devotion to Christ. ⁴For if someone comes to you and preaches a Jesus other than the Jesus we preached, or if you receive a different spirit from the one you received, or a different gospel from the one you accepted, you put up with it easily enough. ⁵But I do not think I am in the least inferior to those "super-apostles." ⁶I may not be a trained speaker, but I do have knowledge. We have made this perfectly clear to you in every way.

1 Paul has firmly stated that self-praise is inadmissible and worthless (3:1; 5:12; 10:12), but he realizes that the present situation demands it if his converts at Corinth are to be preserved intact for Christ (v.2). His antagonists were indulging in self-praise (5:12; 10:7, 12–18) and the Corinthians were evidently to a large extent sympathetic. Consequently his hand was forced (12:11); he must indulge in foolish boasting in order to win the Corinthians' attention and gain a fair hearing. Reluctantly, he decides to employ his opponents' methods; unlike theirs, his motive is not personal gain but the Corinthians' welfare (v.2). He would be boasting "in the Lord" (10:17). So he ironically requests the Corinthians' indulgence, knowing they had already been humoring "a little of. . .[his] foolishness" (see 6:3–10; 10:13–17).

2 As R. Bultmann has rightly observed, Paul supplies three grounds (each introduced by *gar*, "for") for his appeal to the Corinthians to bear with him: (1) his divine jealousy for the Corinthians especially when they were endangered (vv.2, 3); (2) their willingness to put up with rivals who presented an adulterated message (v.4); and (3) his claim not to be in the least inferior to the "super-apostles" (v.5).

With a jealousy that sprang from God and was like God's own jealousy for his people (e.g., Hos 2:19, 20; 4:12; 6:4; 11:8), Paul was jealous for his converts' undivided loyalty to Christ in the interval between their conversion (=betrothal to Christ) and their glorification (=presentation to Christ). He pictures himself as the father of the bride (cf. 1 Cor 4:15; 2 Cor 12:14), whose ultimate purpose in betrothing "the church of God in Corinth" (1:1) to her heavenly bridegroom Jesus Christ, was to present her as a virgin to her husband at his appearance (cf. 4:14; Eph 5:27; 1 John 3:2, 3).

Human jealousy is a vice, but to share divine jealousy is a virtue. It is the motive and object of the jealousy that is all-important. There is a place for a spiritual father's passionate concern for the exclusive and pure devotion to Christ of his spiritual children, and also a place for anger at potential violators of that purity (11:29).

3 Prompting Paul's jealousy for Corinthian fidelity was his fear, based on disturbing evidence (v.4), that their minds and affections might be corrupted so that they would lose their single-minded faithfulness to Christ. He recognized the false apostles as Satan's agents (v.15), capable of repeating at Corinth what Satan had successfully achieved in the garden of Eden (Gen 3:13; 1 Tim 2:14)—complete deception (*exēpatēsen*) by cunning. The danger was not moral corruption but intellectual deception (see v.4) leading to spiritual apostasy.

4 Paul's fear had a foundation in fact. The "if" does not introduce some hypothetical condition ("if someone were to come") but an actual situation ("if, as has happened, someone comes"). In justification of his plea for the Corinthians' tolerance of his enforced boasting (v.1), Paul ironically appeals to the ready welcome they gave visitors who came proclaiming a message other than the gospel that they had embraced and that had

brought them salvation. Surely they ought to show their father in the faith the same degree of tolerance they showed a newcomer preaching a different faith!

It is impossible to reconstruct the precise content of the message of these false apostles, and it is uncertain whether Paul is here alluding to the Holy Spirit or to a spirit of fear and slavery (Rom 8:15; 2 Tim 1:7) as opposed to a spirit of peace and freedom (Rom 14:17; 2 Cor 3:17). What seems clear, however, is that the willingness of the Corinthian believers to entertain the eloquent preacher of an adulterated gospel (cf. Gal 1:6–9) that added human merit to divine grace and gave an interpretation of the earthly ministry of Jesus and the function of the Spirit radically different from Paul's illustrated their tendency to look "only on the surface of things" (10:7) and their preoccupation with manner rather than matter (1 Cor 1:17; 2:1, 4, 5; 13:1; 2 Cor 10:10; 11:6).

5 The third justification for the request of v.1a now appears (see commentary on v.2). Still engaging in his "senseless" but pardonable self-praise, Paul expresses his opinion that he is in no way inferior to the "super-apostles." It seems unlikely that he is referring to the false apostles themselves (alluded to in v.4 as visitors). Even writing ironically, Paul would scarcely claim to be on a par with those he describes in v.13 as "deceitful workmen" and in v.15 as servants of Satan. On the other hand, the "super-apostles" are not to be equated exactly with the Jerusalem apostles or the three "pillars" of the Jerusalem church (Gal 2:9). The expression is either the description of the Twelve used by Paul's opponents and here (as in 12:11, where see commentary) quoted by Paul, or, more probably, the apostle's ironical description of the exalted view of the Twelve held by the "false apostles" (see Introduction, 7.d.2). In this verse, then, Paul claims to be in no respect inferior to the original apostles (see 1 Cor 9:1; 15:5–8, 10) with whom he was being unfavorably compared and whose authority his adversaries illegitimately invoked in support of their Judaizing program at Corinth. If the Corinthians bore with intruders (v.4) and their exalted claims concerning the Twelve (v.5), they ought also to bear with Paul in his foolishness (v.1; cf. v.16).

6 This is not an explanation of the truth of v.5; to admit an exception ("I may not be a trained speaker") immediately after the bold assertion, "I am in no way inferior" (v.5), would be intolerable. Rather, Paul is rating himself by the criteria used by the Corinthians to assess the credentials of apostles or visiting missionaries (thus C.K. Barrett).

With regard to his lack of professional training and skill in rhetoric, Paul is quite willing to admit his deficiency (cf. 10:10) and perhaps even his inferiority to the "false apostles." But in his judgment his expertise in knowledge, which he had made perfectly clear to the Corinthians, more than compensated for this deficiency. Matter was more significant than manner (cf. v.4 and 1 Cor 2:13, NIV).

Notes

1 The NIV takes ἀνέχεσθε (anechesthe) in v.1b as an indicative. It may also be an imperative, giving v.1b the sense, "Yes, please do put up with me!" or "Please try... !" (PH).

3 In Jewish tradition Eve was thought to have been sexually seduced by the serpent (see C.K. Barrett, in loc.). Although the verb Paul uses (ἐξαπατάω, exapataō, "deceive") could refer to such seduction, here it probably simply denotes Satanic perversion of human intellectual or spiritual sensibilities (like the verb φθείρω, phtheirō, "lead astray," which follows). Paul here seems to view Christ as the last Adam and the Church as the last Eve in danger of infidelity.

6 On the theme "Paul's Boasting in Relation to Contemporary Professional Practice," see E.A. Judge, *Australian Biblical Review*, XVI (1–4, 1968), pp. 37–50.

---

4. Financial dependence and independence

11:7–12

> 7Was it a sin for me to lower myself in order to elevate you by preaching the gospel of God to you free of charge? 8I robbed other churches by receiving support from them so as to serve you. 9And when I was with you and needed something, I was not a burden to anyone, for the brothers who came from Macedonia supplied what I needed. I have kept myself from being a burden to you in any way, and will continue to do so: 10As surely as the truth of Christ is in me, nobody in the regions of Achaia will stop this boasting of mine. 11Why? Because I do not love you? God knows I do! 12And I will keep on doing what I am doing in order to cut the ground from under those who want an opportunity to be considered equal with us in the things they boast about.

7,8 In spite of what Paul had written in 1 Corinthians 9:3–18 about the matter, the believers at Corinth had been influenced by the pseudo-apostles into thinking that the acceptance of remuneration for teaching was another criterion of true apostolicity. Their thought seemed to be: "If it is the apostles' right to refrain from working for a living and to get their living by the gospel [1 Cor 9:6, 14], why has Paul always refused to accept our gifts and yet receives support from other churches?" No doubt Paul's rivals interpreted his refusal as evidence of his being a false apostle.

In his defense, notable for its powerful irony, Paul makes two points. He committed no offense, surely, simply by waiving his apostolic right to support (1 Cor 9:12, 15, 18) so that no one could charge him with peddling God's word for profit (2:17). Second, his purpose in "humbling" himself in the Corinthians' eyes to undertake manual labor while ministering to them (see Acts 18:3) was to "elevate" them above their inherited idolatry and vicious past (v.7; cf. 4:12; 8:9), just as his "robbing" other churches of money they could not really spare was motivated solely by his desire to serve the Corinthians gratuitously and more effectively (v.8). It was Paul's policy not to accept financial support from churches in which he was currently ministering (see note).

9 During his initial visit to Corinth (Fall A.D. 50–Spring A.D. 52), Paul had at first supported himself by plying his trade as a "leather-worker" (*skēnopoios*, Acts 18:3), but on the arrival of Silas and Timothy from Macedonia, "he began to devote himself entirely to preaching" (*syneicheto tō logō*, Acts 18:5). It is a fair inference from the present verse that the reason for this alteration in Paul's daily schedule was that the "brothers who came from Macedonia" brought monetary gifts from Philippi (Phil 4:15) and possibly Thessalonica (cf. 1 Thess 3:6). Providentially the gift arrived just when his resources had failed and he had begun to feel need (*hysterētheis*). Even in this extremity he had not been a burden to anyone. Financial independence would continue to be his policy with regard to Corinth.

10–12 This policy, which enabled Paul to boast that he was preaching the gospel free of charge (v.7; cf. 1 Cor 9:18), he resolutely refused to abandon (cf. 1 Cor 9:15). It was Christ's truth he was speaking when he affirmed that he would not bow to pressure from his opponents anywhere in Achaia regarding this issue (v.10).

As to the motive for Paul's inflexible policy, two conflicting explanations are mentioned. Some had malevolently asserted that it was evidence of his lack of affection for the Corinthians. Paul dismisses this by appealing to God's knowledge of his heart (v.11). His own explanation is given in v.12.

Like the wandering preachers of the day (see note on v.8), the intruders at Corinth had apparently received some remuneration for their instruction. Regarding themselves as in some sense apostles, they probably felt fully within their rights in accepting or even demanding appropriate wages; this validated their apostleship. But Paul's stance was an acute embarrassment to them, for they could not boast as he did about preaching a message gratuitously. This, then, was Paul's motive for persisting in his longstanding policy—to deprive his opponents of the opportunity they longed for so they might boast that they were working at Corinth on precisely the same terms he had been. He hoped his financial independence would highlight his rivals' financial dependence and cause the Corinthians to rethink their attitude toward him.

Notes

8 The itinerant philosophers or teachers of the Hellenistic age commonly gained their financial support by charging a fee for their instruction, though the less scrupulous charlatans would rely on begging. Traveling teachers who were concerned about their reputation would often work at a trade. Under the influence of the example set by Jesus in the missions of the Twelve and the Seventy (Luke 9:3, 4; 10:4, 7), early Christianity came to recognize another legitimate method of support in addition to manual labor. An itinerant missionary might receive hospitality and even gifts from the community to which he was ministering (1 Cor 9:6, 11, 14; 3 John 5-8 and cf. Didache 11:4-6). In Christian usage the verb προπέμπω (propempō, "send forth," "escort") often had the technical sense of supplying a visitor with food, money, or companions for travel and so "helping him on his way" (see Acts 15:3; Rom 15:24; 1 Cor 16:6, 11; 2 Cor 1:16; Titus 3:13; 3 John 6).

12 "The things they [Paul's opponents] boast about" may refer to the legitimacy of their Corinthian ministry, their claimed apostleship, or, preferably, their acceptance of support as proof of their apostleship.

5. False apostles

11:13-15

13For such men are false apostles, deceitful workmen, masquerading as apostles of Christ. 14And no wonder, for Satan himself masquerades as an angel of light. 15It is not surprising, then, if his servants masquerade as servants of righteousness. Their end will be what their actions deserve.

13-15 Paul does not even contest the right of his adversaries to support but rather lays against them a single all-embracing charge. Those who vaunted their apostleship and vainly sought equality with him were in fact "false apostles," apostolic pretenders who passed themselves off as "righteous servants" of Christ (cf. 11:23) while in reality they were agents of Satan. Like their principal, the arch-deceiver (John 8:44) whose habit was to masquerade "as a shining angel," they relied on disguise and deceit in carrying out their nefarious schemes such as the corruption of the intellect and the diversion of the affections from Christ (vv.3, 4). What was false was not simply their claim to apostleship but also their message. Behind both were Satanic designs upon the Corinthians—designs Paul was well aware of (2:11). The destiny of these men would accord with the actual deeds they performed (cf. 5:10; Phil 3:19), not the outward appearance they adopted (cf. 5:12). As preachers of "a different gospel" (v.4), they stood under the anathema of Galatians 1:8, 9.

When referring to the "super-apostles" (11:5; 12:11), Paul shows remarkable restraint; he is not their inferior in any respect. But he does not hesitate to attack ruthlessly the Judaizing intruders from Jerusalem. In one case Paul is defensive and mildly ironical; in the other case he is polemical and intensely serious. The solution to the problem of the Palestinian interlopers was not excommunication, since it was not a case of professing believers whose conduct gave the lie to their profession. Part of the Pauline solution was outright condemnation, since the intruders were minions of Satan who sought to impose certain elements of Jewish teaching and practice on Gentile Christians as prerequisites for salvation (see Introduction, 7.d. 1, 3).

B. Boasting "As a Fool" (11:16–12:13)

1. Justification for foolish boasting

11:16–21a

> [16]I repeat: Let no one take me for a fool. But if you do, then receive me just as you would a fool, so that I may do a little boasting. [17]In this self-confident boasting I am not talking as the Lord would, but as a fool. [18]Since many are boasting in the way the world does, I too will boast. [19]You gladly put up with fools since you are so wise! [20]In fact, you even put up with anyone who enslaves you or exploits you or takes advantage of you or pushes himself forward or slaps you in the face. [21a]To my shame I admit that we were too weak for that!

16 Paul now resumes from vv.1–6 the theme of foolish boasting, after he has digressed to defend his policy regarding financial support (vv.7–12) and to describe the true identity of his opponents (vv. 13–15). He has decided to boast as his opponents do, because he knows the Corinthians' determination to compare him with his rivals and their vulnerability to those who commend themselves. From 11:16 to 12:13 he engages in *ad hominem* argumentation, boasting about things that are not "boastworthy" and answering fools according to their folly (Prov 26:5). There was a danger, however, that some Corinthians might not see or wish to see that Paul was simply playing a part. But even if they thought he was actually a fool and not just a play-actor, he solicits their indulgence as he does "a little boasting."

17,18 The RSV is probably right in interpreting these two verses as a parenthesis, since "for [*gar*] you gladly bear with fools" (v.19a, RSV) looks back to "receive me just as you would a fool" (v.16). Under normal circumstances, Paul is saying (in vv.17, 18), his conduct and words as a servant of Christ and of the Corinthians (4:5; 11:23) would have been marked by "the meekness and gentleness of Christ" (10:1), not the "self-confident boasting" of the fool (v.17). It was not the example of Christ, but the need to follow the example of his opponents (note the *kagō*, "I too" in vv.16, 18) in order to win over the Corinthians, that had driven him to this desperate measure of self-exaltation.

As hesitant as Paul is to talk "as a fool," his reluctance is partially overcome when he recalls that his converts have grown accustomed to self-advertisement. Many (*polloi*, as in 2:17) at Corinth, as generally elsewhere, were bragging "in the way the world does," i.e., boasting of personal privileges and achievements (as Paul himself does, beginning at v.22).

19–21a Probably no verses in the epistle are more scathingly ironical than these. Not only do the Corinthians humor fools; they do so "gladly," because the folly of the fool serves to highlight the wisdom of "the wise" (*phronimoi*, as in 1 Cor 4:10).

Their tolerance apparently had no limits. They put up not only with the speech of fools but also with the despotism of tyrants. The intruding aliens had "reduced them to slavery" by robbing them of their liberty in Christ and seeking to reimpose the Mosaic law (cf. Gal 2:4; 5:1). They had exploited them by greedily devouring any and all maintenance offered them (cf. Mark 12:40). They had entrapped them with tantalizing bait (cf. Luke 5:5); they had put on airs of superiority and had gravely insulted and humiliated them.

None of Paul's readers or hearers would have failed to catch his message with its indictment of their inconsistency. Claiming to be followers of a meek, gentle Christ (10:1; cf. Matt 11:29), they were impressed by and willingly submitted to the aggressiveness and authoritarianism of teachers masquerading as apostles of Christ (v.13); yet they were unimpressed by Paul's "weak" considerateness as a genuine "apostle of Christ Jesus" (1:1; 10:1, 10). Paul has to confess with shame (but really with biting irony) that his character had been too weak and his disposition too mild to use the tactics of the opposition (v.21a)!

2. Paul's heritage and trials

11:21b–29

> 21bWhat anyone else dares to boast about—I am speaking as a fool—I also dare to boast about. 22Are they Hebrews? So am I. Are they Israelites? So am I. Are they Abraham's descendants? So am I. 23Are they servants of Christ? (I am out of my mind to talk like this.) I am more. I have worked much harder, been in prison more frequently, been flogged more severely, and been exposed to death again and again. 24Five times I received from the Jews the forty lashes minus one. 25Three times I was beaten with rods, once I was stoned, three times I was shipwrecked, I spent a night and a day in the open sea, 26I have been constantly on the move. I have been in danger from rivers, in danger from bandits, in danger from my own countrymen, in danger from Gentiles; in danger in the city, in danger in the country, in danger at sea; and in danger from false brothers. 27I have labored and toiled and have often gone without sleep; I have known hunger and thirst and have often gone without food; I have been cold and naked. 28Besides everything else, I face daily the pressure of my concern for all the churches. 29Who is weak, and I do not feel weak? Who is led into sin, and I do not inwardly burn?

21b,22 Already Paul has made several efforts to begin sustained boasting (see 10:8; 11:1, 6, 16). Now he finally brings himself to this distasteful task. No bold claim made by his rivals will go unmatched (v.21b). So to the first three claims mentioned, he responds with the simple, disarming word *kagō*, "so am I."

By "Hebrews" is meant Jews of Palestinian descent, especially those whose native tongue was Aramaic or Hebrew and whose intellectual and cultural heritage was within Palestinian rather than Diaspora Judaism. If this is an accurate description of "Hebrews," then "Hellenists" would be Jews living in Palestine (Acts 6:1) or the Diaspora for whom Greek was the first or only language and whose outlook owed more to Diaspora Judaism than to Palestinian Judaism, though this distinction within Judaism should not be pressed. Whether he was brought up in Tarsus or in Jerusalem (see note), Paul was a Hebrew of Hebrew parentage (Phil 3:5). As an "Israelite" Paul was a member of God's people and kingdom, Israel. As a descendant of Abraham who had been "circumcised on the eighth day" (Phil 3:5), Paul was an heir to the covenants based on God's promise (Eph 2:12). All in all, with regard to descent, citizenship, and heritage, he was the equal of his rivals.

23-25 When Paul turns from the matter of nationality (v.22) to that of achievement (vv.23–29), he lays claim to superiority over his rivals, not simply equality with them, and begins to speak as a madman (v.23), not simply as a fool (vv.16, 17, 21). Although he compares himself with both the "super-apostles" and the "false apostles," in the former case the comparison is negative ("I am not in the least inferior," 11:5; 12:11), in the latter case it is positive ("...more...much harder...more frequently...more severely," v.23).

In the light of v.13, where the false apostles are called "deceitful workmen, masquerading as apostles of Christ," it might seem unlikely that Paul, by implication, would here concede his opponents to be "servants of Christ." But note that "Are they...?" means "Do they claim to be...?" and that in v.13 is found Paul's estimate of them, in v.23 their estimate of themselves, which Paul concedes for the sake of the comparison that follows.

At v.23 Paul's list of "accomplishments" begins, but unlike the imperial *res gestae* Paul's list recounts not triumphs but apparent defeats and relates not to strengths but "weaknesses" (11:30; 12:5, 9, 10). This accords with his view that lowliness and weakness as seen in Christian service provide the only incontestable vindication of apostleship.

If we compare this list of Paul's sufferings (cf. 1 Cor 4:9–13; 2 Cor 4:8–12; 6:4, 5) with the account of his experiences given in Acts, it immediately becomes clear how fragmentary, but not how unreliable, Luke's record is. Since the writing of 2 Corinthians fits into Luke's account at Acts 20:2a, only the events recorded before this verse relate to the comparison. To be sure, Luke gives ample proof of Paul's hard work (v.23) and records his stoning at Lystra (v.25; Acts 14:19). But he mentions only one imprisonment (cf. v.23) before Acts 20—that at Philippi (Acts 16:23–40)—and only one of his three (Roman?) beatings with rods (v.25), also at Philippi (Acts 16:22, 23). From Acts we know nothing of other imprisonments (v.23; cf. 1 Clement 5:6). Those at Jerusalem, Caesarea, and Rome occurred later. Nor do we know about the five whippings in Jewish synagogical courts (v.24), about the other two beatings at the hands of Gentiles (v.25, but note 2 Tim 3:11), or about the three shipwrecks and the night and day in the open sea, probably clinging to wreckage while awaiting rescue (cf. the later shipwreck, Acts 27:13–44). (Verse 24 shows Paul's reluctance to surrender his Jewish status or associations—C.K. Barrett, in loc.) Paul's life was even more colorful than Acts would lead the reader to believe!

26,27 From specific hardships (vv.24, 25) Paul turns to the dangers he confronted (v.26) and the privations he endured (v.27; cf. 6:5). In speaking of "danger from rivers" and "danger from bandits" he would be thinking especially of crossing the Taurus range between Perga in Pamphylia and Antioch in Phrygia near Pisidia (Acts 13:14; 14:24), a journey made hazardous by the mountain torrents and the predatory Pisidian highlanders. Acts records several examples of Jewish plots against Paul's life before this time (e.g.,

Acts 9:23, 29; 14:19; 18:12) but only two incidents involving "danger from Gentiles" (at Philippi, Acts 16:16–40; and at Ephesus, Acts 19:23–41). "Danger from false brothers" may point to Paul's being betrayed to local authorities by counterfeit Christians and the resulting reprisals (similarly J. Héring).

Paul's "sleepless nights" (*agrypniai*, as in 6:5) could refer to insomnia because of physical discomfort or illness, but more probably the phrase alludes to voluntary sleeplessness from pressure of work. As C.K. Barrett (in loc.) suggests, Paul may have undertaken some of his voluntary fasts ("I...have often gone without food"; cf. 6:5) because of his determination not to accept support from the Corinthians (1 Cor 9:12, 15, 18; 2 Cor 11:7–12).

28,29 None of the afflictions mentioned in vv.23–27 was a continuous experience. Paul's crowning trial and privilege was, however, incessant—the daily pressure of his anxious concern (*merimna*) for all the churches (cf. Acts 20:18–21, 28–31). If his trials at Corinth were any indication, the total burden he always bore must have been well-nigh oppressive.

Yet Paul did not violate the teaching of Jesus about anxiety (cf. Matt 6:25–34, where the verbal form of *merimna* occurs frequently). His concern arose from seeking first the kingdom of God; he was grappling realistically with present, not future problems; and he had no anxiety about the relatively trivial matters of food and clothing (as v.27 shows). But as a faithful "under-shepherd," he shared the constant burden of the chief shepherd with regard to all the sheep.

This total identification of shepherd with sheep, or of spiritual father with children in the faith, is now illustrated (v.29). Paul was at one with all his converts (cf. 1 Cor 12:26), sympathizing with their weakness in faith, conduct or conscience (cf. 1 Cor 8:7–13; 9:22). It is difficult to know what Paul means when he says, "I inwardly burn" (29b). The following suggestions have been made: He was fired with indignation at the person who caused another to sin (cf. Matt 18:6; 1 Cor 8:10–13; Gal 5:12, and the present situation with the false apostles); his heart burned with shame when a Christian brother fell or when someone dishonored the name of Christ; or he was so ablaze with compassion for the person who was "led into sin" that he shared his remorse. Perhaps all three were involved, though the last view best suits the context.

Notes

---

22 On the terms "Hebrew" and 'Israelite" in NT usage, see W. Gutbrod, TDNT, 3:375–391. That Jerusalem was the city of Paul's boyhood and upbringing (cf. Acts 22:3; 26:4) has been argued by W.C. van Unnik in his book *Tarsus or Jerusalem: the City of Paul's Youth* (Epworth: London, 1962).
28 The phrase χωρὶς τῶν παρεκτός (*chōris tōn parektos*) means either "apart from external trials" (cf. KJV, RV, NEB; C.K. Barrett) or "apart from the things left unmentioned" (cf. RSV, Am. Trans., Wey, JB, NIV; A. Plummer, P.E. Hughes). Moff. takes the phrase with what precedes: "...and all the rest of it."

 The noun ἐπίστασις (*epistasis*) probably means "pressure" (being defined by the phrase that follows), but other possibilities include "attention," "superintendence," "conspiring," "hindrance"; see BAG, p. 300, and the footnote in P.E. Hughes, in loc.

---

3. Escape from Damascus

11:30-33

> [30]If I must boast, I will boast of the things that show my weakness. [31]The God and Father of the Lord Jesus, who is to be praised forever, knows that I am not lying. [32]In Damascus the governor under King Aretas had the city of the Damascenes guarded in order to arrest me. [33]But I was lowered in a basket from a window in the wall and slipped through his hand.

30,31 For a moment Paul pauses and reflects on the paragraph he has just dictated to his stunned amanuensis. Both he and his opponents might boast, but *his* boasting was distinctive, since, paradoxically, he prided himself on evidences of his weakness that became evidences of God's surpassing power in supporting and delivering him (cf. 1:8-10; 3:5; 4:7, 10, 11; 12:5, 9, 10).

Because he had been so precise in describing his afflictions and perils (see especially vv.24, 25), he realized that the record sounded not only incredible but also out of keeping for an apostle and that his rivals might easily dismiss it as gross exaggeration. Hence his appeal to the divine omniscience (cf. 1:18; 11:10, 11 and Rom 9:1; Gal 1:20; 1 Tim 2:7). Such an invocation of God as a witness or testimony to his truthfulness (v.31) was not, of course, a repudiation of Christ's ban on unnecessary or frivolous swearing (Matt 5:33-37; James 5:12). The trustworthiness of Paul's word had been impugned (cf. 1:17, 18).

32,33 After the solemn invocation of v.31, the account of a nocturnal escape from Damascus might seem trivial and out of place. Perhaps Paul mentions the episode because it had shattered the residual pride of Saul the Pharisee (cf. Acts 9:1, 2) and had become the supreme example of the humiliation and weakness he was boasting about (v.30). Or he may be referring to it because his detractors had used it to ridicule him and prove his cowardice (cf. 10:1, 10). Or again, he may be speaking of it because it was probably the first attempt on his life and such a significant reversal of roles (Acts 9:1, 2!) that it had been indelibly impressed on his memory. Whatever the reason for its inclusion here, the episode forms a suitable backdrop for what follows: an embarrassing descent to escape the hands of men and then an exhilarating ascent into the presence of God (12:2-4).

Aretas IV, the father-in-law of Herod Antipas, ruled over the kingdom of the Nabataean Arabs from c. 9 B.C. to A.D. 40. Nabataea (= the "Arabia" of Gal 1:17) stretched east and south of the river Jordan. Why did Aretas or his governor (*ethnarchēs*) want to arrest Paul? Probably because the king had been offended by Paul's evangelistic activity in his kingdom (Gal 1:17). It is unlikely that Paul's sojourn in Arabia was simply a "spiritual retreat," for Luke is careful to note that *immediately* after his conversion Paul began to dispute in the synagogues of Damascus (Acts 9:20; see also Gal 1:22, 23).

Luke's account of Paul's escape (Acts 9:23-25) reveals that the Jews were watching the gates in order to kill Paul; here in 2 Corinthians 11 we are told that the governor under King Aretas had the city guarded in order to arrest Paul. What was the relation between the Jews and the governor? It is uncertain whether Damascus was under Nabataean rule, Roman rule, or joint sovereignty at the time (c. A.D. 35). From 63 B.C. until A.D. 34 Damascus was Roman. But since no Roman coins dating from A.D. 34-62 have been found in Damascus, some scholars hold that during that time (including the reigns of Caligula and Claudius, A.D. 37-41 and A.D. 41-54) the city was under Nabataean rule, the governor being a deputy of King Aretas who lived at Petra. P.E. Hughes (in loc.) proposes that the ethnarch himself was a Jew, responsible for Damascene Jews, so that the guard he appointed was composed entirely of Jews.

However, the gap in the numismatic record is negative and therefore indecisive as evidence. Damascus was probably still under Roman rule and the ethnarch may have been the head of a semi-autonomous colony of Nabataeans in Damascus (so F.F. Bruce, in loc., following E. Meyer). According to this view there was a coalition of Jews (thus Luke) and Nabataeans (thus Paul), acting through the Nabataean ethnarch to arrest and kill Paul. This is more probable than the suggestion that the Jews were watching for Paul inside the walls and the Nabataeans outside.

Whatever the solution to these historical questions, the fact of Paul's providential deliverance through the ingenuity of "his disciples" (Acts 9:25a) remains secure. He "slipped through the governor's hands."

4. A vision and its aftermath

12:1-10

> [1]I must go on boasting. Although there is nothing to be gained, I will go on to visions and revelations from the Lord. [2]I know a man in Christ who fourteen years ago was caught up to the third heaven. Whether it was in the body or out of the body I do not know—God knows. [3]And I know that this man—whether in the body or apart from the body I do not know, but God knows—[4]was caught up to Paradise. He heard inexpressible things, things that man is not permitted to tell. [5]I will boast about a man like that, but I will not boast about myself, except about my weaknesses. [6]Even if I should choose to boast, I would not be a fool, because I would be speaking the truth. But I refrain, so no one will think more of me than is warranted by what I do or say.
>
> [7]To keep me from becoming conceited because of these surpassingly great revelations, there was given me a thorn in my flesh, a messenger of Satan, to torment me. [8]Three times I pleaded with the Lord to take it away from me. [9]But he said to me, "My grace is sufficient for you, for my power is made perfect in weakness." Therefore, I will boast all the more gladly about my weaknesses, so that Christ's power may rest on me. [10]That is why, for Christ's sake, I delight in weaknesses, in insults, in hardships, in persecutions, in difficulties. For when I am weak, then I am strong.

1 Again Paul stresses that in this matter of boasting he has had no choice. By insisting that their teachers display their "credentials" ("one must boast," *kauchasthai dei* [v.1; 11:30], they said), the Corinthians were forcing him to break a fourteen-year silence (v.2) and boast about a vision the Lord gave him (see note) (cf. 1 Cor 4:7b). To do so would not edify the church or be a personal gain, though the Corinthians would see that he was not outmatched by his rivals in one important area of their boasting.

It should not be overlooked that Paul's mention of his ecstatic rapture was a necessary introduction to what he says about his "thorn in his flesh" (vv.7–10), another evidence of his weakness.

If Paul intended to distinguish between "visions" and "revelations," then the difference is that a vision is always seen, whereas a revelation may be either seen or perceived in some other way; all visions are also revelations, but not all revelations come through visions. From Acts it is clear that, apart from his Damascus vision of Christ (Acts 9:3–9; 26:19; Gal 1:16), Paul not infrequently had visions (Acts 9:12; 16:9, 10; 18:9, 10; 22:17–21; 23:11; 27:23, 24).

2-4 None of the visions recorded in Acts can be identified with the vision or revelation related here, since it occurred fourteen years before the time of writing (A.D. 56)—that is, c. A.D. 43 by inclusive reckoning, during the ten so-called "silent years" (A.D. 35-45) that Paul spent in Syria and Cilicia (Gal 1:21) and that Acts says nothing about. (But note Acts 9:30; 11:25.)

Is Paul recounting his own experience when he writes enigmatically, "I know a man in Christ . . . he heard . . ."? Undoubtedly so, for several reasons: (1) He knew the exact time the revelation took place (v.2) and that its content was beyond words even if it were permissible to try to communicate it (v.4). (2) The revelation was directly related to the receipt of a "thorn," which was given, says Paul, "to me" (v.7). (3) The reference to a lack of awareness whether he was in the body or not (vv.2, 3) points to a personal experience. (4) Paul would be unlikely to feel embarrassment (cf. v.1) about boasting on another person's behalf (cf. v.5a). (5) For Paul to relate a remarkable experience that happened to some Christian unknown to the Corinthians but known to Paul would scarcely fit the context.

The scene of the vision was the "hidden Paradise" of Jewish thought (see note), the abode of the righteous dead that is here located within the third heaven (literally, ". . . as far as [heōs] the third heaven . . . into [eis] Paradise," vv.2b, 4a; cf. 2 Enoch 8:1). If Paul was quite certain of the location of the vision, he was equally *uncertain* about whether the experience happened to him in his body or apart from it, (vv.2b, 3b). Consciousness of God totally eclipsed any awareness of the physical world of space and time, removing any consciousness of embodiment. The suddenness of Paul's loss of any sense of physical orientation is suggested by the verb *harpazein* (vv.2, 4), that denotes a sudden rapture, not a gradual ascent (cf. its use in Acts 8:39 of Philip, and in 1 Thess 4:17 of believers at the Parousia).

What Paul heard (and saw?), human words were inadequate to relate (v.4b). What is more, he was not permitted to try to share the content of the revelation, perhaps because it had been designed for him alone, to fortify him for future service and sufferings (Acts 9:16; Rom 8:18). Glimpses the NT does give of the coming glory are aimed at strengthening faith and promoting holiness (cf. 2 Peter 3:10-14; 1 John 3:2, 3), not at satisfying curiosity.

5,6 The remarkable distinction between Paul and the certain "man in Christ" (v.2) or "man involved" (*ho toioutos*, v.3) comes into even sharper relief in v.5 and naturally prompts the question, If Paul is speaking of himself in vv.2-4, why does he objectify his experience? There are several reasons. First, he was clearly embarrassed at needing to boast at all (v.1)—an activity that in itself did not contribute to the common good (cf. 1 Cor 12:7). Second, he wished to avoid suggesting that he was in any sense a special kind of Christian. The revelation was given him as "a man in Christ"; the initiative had been not his but God's. Verse 5 suggests a third reason: Although Paul recognized the honor involved in being the recipient of a vision ("I will boast about a man like that," v.5a), he wanted to dispel any idea that it added to his personal status or importance.

Concerning himself as a man in Christ who had received a special revelation, Paul was prepared to boast if circumstances demanded it. But concerning himself as a man of action and accomplishment, he refused to boast under any circumstances. Only experiences that showed his weakness were suitable material for any enforced boasting (v.5). But in case some should assert that he had done nothing worth boasting about anyway, he adds a word of defense (v.6). If he were to boast of his strengths or things that were not inexpressible, or if he chose to divulge further details about his vision or describe other visions the Lord had given him, he would not be shown up as some fool who had prided himself on imagined glories only to be exposed for his false claims. And why would he not be exposed? Because he would be speaking truth, not falsehood or fiction. He had good reason to boast if that was what he wished to do. But he refrains because he wanted the Corinthians' estimate of him to be based on their recollection of his personal credentials (cf. 5:11b; 12:12). All this suggests that his rivals may have been boasting about imaginary visions or about exploits they claimed to have done before their arrival at Corinth.

7 Others might be tempted, "because of these surpassingly great revelations" (v.7) accorded to Paul, to form an estimate of him that outstripped the evidence (v.6b). But he himself was in no such danger. To keep him from becoming conceited (see note) there was given him a thorn in his flesh. Two inferences are fair. (1) The agent implied by *edothē* ("there was given"; cf. the "theological passives" in vv.2, 4) is God. This is confirmed by the fact that the "thorn" (*skolops*, see note) was given to achieve a beneficial purpose—the prevention of spiritual conceit—and that Paul requested the Lord for the departure of the messenger (v.8). (2) The "thorn" was given immediately or shortly after the vision described in vv.2–4.

It is significant that in vv.7–10 Paul speaks of himself in the first person (cf. vv.2–5); his reputation was in no danger of being illegitimately enhanced (cf. v.6) by describing the outcome of the vision!

The efforts that have been made to identify Paul's "thorn" are legion. Among the recurring suggestions are Jewish persecution, carnal temptation, epilepsy, chronic ophthalmia, a speech impediment, and a recurrent malady (such as malaria or Malta fever). But paucity of information and the obscurity of Paul's language have frustrated all attempts to solve this enigmatic problem. In fact, had Paul revealed what his *skolops* was, Christians of succeeding generations who lacked his particular affliction or disability would have tended to find his experience (vv.8–10) irrelevant. As it is, countless believers have been helped by his reference to his "thorn."

It is remarkable that Paul could regard his affliction as given by God and yet as "a messenger of Satan." This may support the view that the affliction was some type of physical malady, because in 1 Corinthians 5:5 (cf. 1 Cor 11:30; 1 Tim 1:20) Satan appears as God's agent for the infliction of disciplinary illness (cf. Job 2:1–10). Certainly a recurrent and tormenting illness could be considered "a messenger of Satan," for it might bring Paul within the shadow of death (cf. 2 Cor 1:8, 9) or hinder the advance of the gospel either by arousing the contempt of his hearers (cf. Gal 4:13, 14) or by frustrating his travel plans. Be that as it may, behind any and every machination of Satan, Paul could discern the overarching providence of a God who perpetually created good out of evil.

8 The "thorn" proved so tormenting to Paul that on three separate occasions (*tris;* cf. Mark 14:32–42) he "pleaded with the Lord [*ton kyrion*] to take it away" from him. In Paul *ho kyrios* refers to Jesus and *kyrios* to Yahweh (Jehovah). His prayer, then, was addressed to Jesus. In the NT, formal or liturgical prayer was customarily offered through Christ to the Father in the Spirit (Eph 2:18), but on occasion an individual (Acts 7:59) or a group (Acts 1:24) seems to have invoked the Lord Jesus directly.

9,10 The answer to Paul's prayer did not take the form he had expected. The thorn remained, but so too did his recollection of the divine reply (*eirēken*, "he has said," v.9a). In the distressing weakness inflicted at various times by his ailment, he would never lack

224

sufficient grace to be more than a conqueror (cf. Rom 8:35-37). This grace of Christ (13:14) was adequate for Paul, weak as he was, precisely because (gar, "for") divine power finds its full scope and strength only in human weakness—the greater the Christian's acknowledged weakness, the more evident Christ's enabling strength (cf. Eph 3:16; Phil 4:13). But it is not simply that weakness is a prerequisite for power. Both weakness and power existed simultaneously in Paul's life (note vv.9b, 10b), as they did in Christ's ministry and death. Indeed, the cross of Christ forms the supreme example of "power-in-weakness."

With this spiritual lesson well learned, Paul would gladly boast about things that exposed his weakness ("insults ... hardships ... persecutions ... difficulties," v.10) rather than pray for the removal of the "thorn" and its attendant weakness. It was not, however, in the weaknesses themselves that Paul took delight but in the opportunity sufferings endured "for Christ's sake" afforded him for Christ's power to reside and be effective in his life (v.9b).

Notes

1 NIV is right in taking κυρίου (kyriou) as a subjective genitive ("from the Lord") rather than an objective genitive ("of the Lord," in the sense that he was seen and revealed). This interpretation is confirmed by v.4 where Paul stresses what he heard rather than what he saw, and by the use of the "theological passives" ("was caught up," vv.2, 4; cf. "was given," v.7) where the unexpressed agent is clearly the Lord Jesus Christ or God the Father.

4 The eschatology of late Judaism drew a conceptual distinction among the first paradise (Gen 2 and 3), the last or eschatological paradise (cf. Rev 2:7), and the hidden paradise of the intervening period (cf. Luke 23:43; 2 Cor 12:4). See J. Jeremias, TDNT, 5:765-773.

7 In a wide variety of witnesses (including p[46] B ψ 1739 syr cop) the words ἵνα μὴ ὑπεραίρωμαι (hina mē hyperairōmai) are repeated at the end of v.7 (in the 3rd. ed. of UBS this reading is given a "C" rating). The effect of this repeated telic clause is to emphasize the divine purpose in the bestowal of the "thorn."

In the punctuation of UBS, the words translated "[and] because of these surpassingly great revelations" are construed with v.6. This would produce the sense "But I refrain, so no one will think more of me than is warranted by what I do or say [and] because of...."

In classical Greek σκόλοψ (skolops) commonly meant "stake" (Latin sudis), or, in the plural (σκόλοπες, skolopes), "stockade." In Septuagintal usage, however, as in the papyri (MM, pp. 578, 579), the word means "splinter" or "thorn" (e.g., Num 33:55; Ezek 28:24; Hos 2:6; Ecclus 43:19).

The dative τῇ σαρκί (tē sarki) may be either (1) locatival, "embedded in [or, driven into] my body," with σάρξ (sarx) being used in a neutral sense, or (2) a dative of "disadvantage," "to pierce my flesh" (Twentieth Century New Testament), with σάρξ referring either to the physical body or to the sensual nature.

8 Literally rendered, the verse runs: "With regard to this [angel] I begged the Lord three times that he [the angel] might depart from me." If τούτου (toutou, "this"; NIV, "it") is masculine, the antecedent could be either σκόλοψ (skolops, "thorn") or ἄγγελος (angelos, "messenger"); if neuter, the meaning will be "about this matter" or "because of that."

5. *Proof of apostleship*

12:11-13

[11]I have made a fool of myself, but you drove me to it. I ought to have been

commended by you, for I am not in the least inferior to the "super-apostles," even though I am nothing. ¹²The things that mark an apostle—signs, wonders and miracles—were done among you with great perseverance. ¹³How were you inferior to the other churches, except that I was never a burden to you? Forgive me this wrong!

11 His "boasting as a fool" now virtually over, Paul reiterates that it had been by coercion. It was not really the foolish boasting of his opponents that had driven him to boast but the folly of the Corinthians in heeding it and their failure to rally to his defense. If any Christian community was qualified to write Paul's testimonial, it was the Corinthian church. They had remained silent, forcing Paul to speak up. His action had been excusable, but not theirs. Commendation was what he deserved and they owed.

Nor was it that they lacked good reason to commend him, for, as they well knew, he was "not in the least inferior to the 'super-apostles' " at Jerusalem whom his rivals invoked so readily in support of their claims (see comments on 11:5). "Even though I am nothing" may be an ironical citation of his opponents' opinion of him or a serious disavowal of any personal merit that might have made him worthy of apostleship (cf. 1 Cor 15:8–10).

12 Here Paul gently reminds his converts of certain characteristics of his ministry at Corinth that proved he was a genuine apostle worth commending and in no way inferior to the Twelve. "Signs, wonders and miracles" (*dynameis*, "mighty deeds") do not describe three types of miracles but miracles in general considered from three aspects— their ability to authenticate the message ("signs"), evoke awe ("wonders") and display divine power ("mighty deeds"). These, of course, were not the only marks of apostleship (see note). There was also faithfulness to the apostolic message (11:4) and conduct that was consonant with the example of Christ (10:1; 13:14). To the latter category belongs "great perseverance" in the face of opposition, such as that shown by Paul at Corinth (Acts 18:6, 9, 10, 12–16). It was this characteristic of fortitude that distinguished him from the false apostles, who also claimed to have worked "signs and wonders." Significant, too, is Paul's use of the passive voice in this verse ("the things that mark an apostle . . . were done among you"); he disowns any credit for the supernatural signs accompanying his ministry and marking it as apostolic.

13 Again indulging in gentle irony, Paul observes that the only respect in which the marks of a true apostle were not evident in the apostolic church of Corinth was that of support. He never was a financial burden to them—an injustice for which he playfully pleads forgiveness! As in 1 Corinthians 9:1–18 and 2 Corinthians 11:5–12 (see the discussion there), Paul has moved naturally from a consideration of apostleship (vv.11, 12) to the issue of apostolic rights. He is distinguishing between certain signs of apostleship (perseverance, signs, wonders, mighty deeds) and a particular right of apostleship— namely, support from the church or churches being served. A church in which the signs of apostleship were displayed was no less apostolic because this optional right of an apostle had been waived by him. Nor was insistence on every legitimate personal right a mark of a genuine apostle (as the Corinthians were inclined to believe).

Notes

12 An alternative tr. of this verse would be: "At least [μέν, *men*], the marks [σημεῖα, *sēmeia*] of an apostle were produced in your midst with great fortitude, and were accompanied by signs [σημείοις, *sēmeiois*], portents and mighty deeds." In this case the "marks" are distinguishable from the "signs, portents and mighty deeds" (contrast NIV) and may refer to the transformed lives of the Corinthians and the Christlike character of Paul (so P.E. Hughes, in loc.).

C. *The Planned Third Visit* (12:14–13:10)

1. *A promise not to be burdensome*

12:14-18

> ¹⁴Now I am ready to visit you for the third time, and I will not be a burden to you, because what I want is not your possessions but you. After all, children should not have to save up for their parents, but parents for their children. ¹⁵So I will very gladly spend for you everything I have and expend myself as well. If I love you more, will you love me less? ¹⁶Be that as it may, I have not been a burden to you. Yet, crafty fellow that I am, I caught you by trickery! ¹⁷Did I exploit you through any of the men I sent you? ¹⁸I urged Titus to go to you and I sent our brother with him. Titus did not exploit you, did he? Did we not act in the same spirit and follow the same course?

14,15 The apostle announces that his third visit to Corinth is imminent (see note) and that his policy regarding support will not be altered. He is determined always to be financially independent of the Corinthians (cf. 1 Cor 9:15; 2 Cor 11:9, 12). They will have to continue bearing the "injury" he is inflicting on them (cf. v.13)! His affections were set on the Corinthians themselves (cf. 6:11, 12; 7:2, 3), not on what they owned and could share with him. He craved their reciprocated love (6:13; 12:15b), their Christian maturity (cf. 1 Cor 3:1–4; Col 1:28, 29), and their exclusive devotion to Christ (11:2, 3).

In defense of this refusal to accept support, he appeals to the self-evident truth that it is no part of children's obligation to save up and provide for their parents, but only parents for children. The principle, however, is not universally applicable. Paul defended the right of apostles to be supported by their spiritual children (1 Cor 9:3–14) and later asserted, "If anyone does not provide for his relatives, and especially for his immediate family, he has denied the faith and is worse than an unbeliever" (1 Tim 5:8, NIV).

Far from coveting the Corinthians' property, Paul planned to use all his own resources to achieve their highest good; neither property nor energies would be spared in his efforts to win their affection for Christ (cf. Acts 20:24). Yet he looked for "a fair exchange" (cf. 6:13): "Am I to be loved the less because I love you the more [i.e., so intensely]?" There may be an actual comparison here. If Paul's love for the Corinthians exceeded the love of a father for his children, how could they love him less than children love their father? In other words, Paul is seeking a response of filial love to his paternal affection (cf. 11:11).

16-18 Whether or not the Corinthians loved Paul the less for his intense love for them

("Be that as it may"), all were agreed that he himself (note *egō*) had not proved a financial strain on the church. Yet the rumor had circulated at Corinth that because Paul was unscrupulous by nature (*hyparchōn panourgos*, v.16), he had exploited the church's generosity and had gained surreptitiously through his agents what he had declined to accept personally. The collection for the poor at Jerusalem was simply a convenient way to fulfull his covert wish to live at the church's expense. There is no explicit reference in these verses to a charge of financial fraud, but the context renders this interpretation likely. The alternative would be to regard the exploitation (*pleonekteō*, vv.17, 18; cf. 2:11; 7:2) as the psychological pressure to which Paul allegedly subjected the Corinthians by refusing to exercise his personal right to remuneration and yet requesting generous contributions to the collection he was organizing.

Since Paul knew the charge had been maliciously made and was couched in general terms, he refutes it first by indirectly appealing to the Corinthians to adduce specific evidence (v.17) and then by referring to a particular occasion on which his chief agent had been sent to Corinth on a mission involving finance (v.18a). If Titus was guiltless, so too was Paul, for all their conduct had been governed by the same principles (v.18b).

Which visit of Titus does Paul refer to? Either the visit alluded to in 8:6a when he commenced the collection or the visit mentioned in 8:16–24 when he completed the collection. On either view, the mention of "our brother" in 12:18 requires explanation. Scholars who place 2 Corinthians 10–13 before 2 Corinthians 1–9 as a part of the "severe letter" and the defenders of the epistle's integrity generally prefer the first view. Those who regard chapters 10–13 as written some time later than chapters 1–9 tend to favor the second proposal.

Notes

---

14 Considered in the light of 13:1, 2, the statement "I am ready to visit you for the third time" cannot refer to two prior occasions on which Paul, though willing to visit Corinth or having prepared or decided to do so, had failed to carry through his purpose. If he had here appealed to his unfulfilled good intentions, he would have been liable to a just charge of fickleness (cf. 1:17). Nor were the previous visits implied in 12:14 simply "epistolary" visits (i.e., the "previous letter" and 1 Corinthians) or one actual and one "epistolary" visit. Paul had made two personal visits to Corinth before writing this letter—his founding visit (Acts 18:1–18) and the "painful visit" (see Introduction, 7.a). What would have been a third visit he had earlier cancelled lest it prove to be a second painful visit (1:23; 2:1).

---

2. *Fears about the unrepentant*

12:19–21

> [19]Have you been thinking all along that we have been defending ourselves to you? We have been speaking in the sight of God as those in Christ; and everything we do, dear friends, is for your strengthening. [20]For I am afraid that when I come I may not find you as I want you to be, and you may not find me as you want me to be. I fear that there may be quarreling, jealousy, outbursts of anger, factions, slander, gossip, arrogance and disorder. [21]I am afraid that when I come again my God will humble me before you, and I will be grieved over many who have sinned earlier and have not repented of the impurity, sexual sin and debauchery in which they have indulged.

19 Paul repudiates the suggestion, which might readily have occurred to any Corinthian, that he had all along been seeking to defend his conduct and reputation before a panel of Corinthian judges. It was to God or to Christ, not to the Corinthians, that Paul was ultimately accountable (cf. Rom 14:10; 1 Cor 4:3–5; 2 Cor 5:10), so that self-defense before men was never his primary concern. He had been speaking as a man in Christ whose words and motives were open before God (cf. 2:17; 5:11). His aim in all his relations with the Corinthians—especially his correspondence—was not personal vindication but their edification.

20,21 As the NIV rightly recognizes, Paul expresses here a threefold fear, though the verb *phoboumai*, "I am afraid" (v.20) occurs only once. Defined in general terms in the light of v.19, this fear was his apprehension that the present letter might not be wholly successful and that the Corinthians by harboring Judaizing intruders and persisting in sin would contribute to weakening, not consolidating, their church fellowship.

The first object of Paul's deep concern was the outcome of his impending visit to the Corinthians (v.20a). Would they be mutually disappointed and embarrassed—Paul, by the church's questioning of his apostleship and their refusal to break with sins of the spirit (v.20b) and of the flesh (v.21b), and the Corinthians, by Paul's vigorous exercise of church discipline (cf. 1 Cor 4:21; 5:3–5)? Second, the apostle is fearful that the sins that seemed endemic to Corinth (cf. 1 Cor 1:11, 12, 31; 3:3; 4:6; 5:2, 11; 8:1; 11:18; 14:33, 40) should still be rife as a consequence of the unrest and disorder created by the Palestinian intruders (v.20b).

Third, Paul fears a repetition of humiliation under God's hand (see note) that he had experienced on his second visit (2:1) as a result of certain unrepentant Corinthians (v.21). Any future humiliation would stem from his acute disappointment at the Corinthians' preference for domineering false apostles (11:20) and their supercilious attitude towards him (cf. 1 Cor 4:18, 19), as well as from his grief (*pentheō*, cf. 1 Cor 5:2) over those who had consistently rejected his call to holiness and were continuing unrepentant in their earlier gross sexual sins. These Corinthian libertines may have asserted that since " 'food [was] for the stomach and the stomach for food' " (1 Cor 6:13a, NIV), it followed as a natural corollary that the satisfaction of other physical appetites was equally inevitable and desirable—"the body is meant for immorality" (cf. 1 Cor 6:13b).

Notes

21 Πάλιν (*palin*, "again") probably should be construed with the entire clause that follows ("I fear lest again when I come my God should humiliate me in your presence") rather than simply with ταπεινώσῃ (*tapeinōsē*, "will humble") or ἐλθόντος (*elthontos*). In this humiliation (caused by Corinthian disloyalty and sin) God would be the agent only in the sense that he permitted it and would use it to remind Paul of his personal impotence and the all-surpassing divine power (cf. 4:7, 10, 11).

3. *Warning of impending discipline*
13:1-4

¹This will be my third visit to you. "Every matter must be established by the testimony of two or three witnesses." ²I already gave you a warning when I was

with you the second time. I now repeat it while absent: On my return I will not spare those who sinned earlier or any of the others, [3]since you are demanding proof that Christ is speaking through me. He is not weak in dealing with you, but is powerful among you. [4]For to be sure, he was crucified in weakness, yet he lives by God's power. Likewise, we are weak in him, yet by God's power we will live with him to serve you.

1,2 After expressing his personal forebodings about the forthcoming third visit (12:20, 21), Paul issues two direct warnings on the basis of those fears: "Every matter must be established by the testimony of two or three witnesses" (v.1) and "On my return I will not spare those who sinned earlier or any of the others" (v.2).

What are the "two or three witnesses"? Some believe Paul is referring to the legal strictness that would apply to the judicial investigation he or the assembled church (cf. Matt 18:15-20; 1 Cor 5:3-5) would conduct at Corinth: unsubstantiated accusations against Paul or any Corinthian would be ruled out of court. Others find a reference to Paul's three comings to Corinth (two actual, one promised) as three separate witnesses at whose testimony justice would certainly fall on the dissidents at Corinth on the imminent third visit. A third view sees in the "three witnesses" the threefold testimony or warning that Paul would not spare the Corinthians: (1) either 1 Corinthians 4:21 or the warning given on the second (= painful) visit; (2) the present warning in v.2b; and (3) either the third visit or Paul himself absent in Macedonia. On a fourth but improbable interpretation, the witnesses are not visits or warnings but people—i.e., Timothy, Titus, and Paul. Whether the second or third view is preferred, the general import is clear: "Sufficient warning has been given; punishment is imminent."

"Those who sinned earlier" are the immoral persons of 12:21b who did not repent during Paul's "painful visit" and were evidently still indulging in their sexual sins. "All the rest" ("any of the others," NIV) are probably those Corinthians who had been adversely influenced by the false apostles and were arrogantly fomenting unrest within the church (12:20b). Both groups here receive their final warning. If they remained unrepentant, he would be harsh in his use of authority (cf. v.10; 1 Cor 4:21), perhaps handing the wrongdoers over to Satan "for the destruction of the flesh" (= illness leading to death, unless there was repentance, 1 Cor 5:5; cf. 11:30).

3 It would seem that in their immaturity the Corinthians were unimpressed by Christ-like gentleness and meekness (10:1) but were overawed by arbitrary displays of power (11:20). In their misguided judgment, Paul's gentle demeanor, so unlike the temperament of the intruding false apostles, raised doubts about his claim to apostolic authority. He needed to give them some proof that Christ in his resurrection power was speaking through him. His reply was that, though he had previously been "weak" in the Corinthian estimation (10:1, 10), his impending severity would afford the proof they demanded that he was a spokesman of Christ—Christ, who was not weak in dealing with them but was powerful among them. The Corinthians had in effect challenged Christ (cf. 1:1), who would not disappoint them as he exhibited his resurrection power through his apostle.

4 The relationship between Christ and Paul with regard to weakness and power is now clarified. Jesus Christ was crucified "because of [ek; see note] weakness." This weakness was not, of course, physical frailty or moral impotence, but rather the "weakness" of nonretaliation or nonaggressiveness before men and the "weakness" of obedience to God. Christ's "weakness" in assuming the poverty of earthly existence (8:9) and in humbling himself and becoming obedient even to the point of death on a cross (Phil 2:8), was, however, the most perfect evidence of strength. The person who is "weak" in man's estimation because he seeks to do God's will is in fact supremely strong. But that "weakness" of Christ is past. Now he lives a resurrection life sustained by God's power, "the Spirit of holiness" (Rom 1:4).

As a result of being in Christ (*en autō*, "in him"), Paul shared in the weakness of his crucified Master. As a result of his fellowship with Christ (*sun autō*, "with him"), he shared in the mighty power of his risen Lord, a power imparted by God. From a human standpoint, the nonretaliation and nonassertiveness that had marked Paul's conduct on his second visit to Corinth (cf. 10:1, 10) were simply weakness. But on his forthcoming visit, God's power would be vigorously displayed through him in his dealings with the Corinthians (*eis hymas*; NIV renders this "to serve you").

Notes

4 The preposition ἐκ (*ek*, lit. "out of") in the phrase ἐξ ἀσθενείας (*ex astheneias*, "in weakness") indicates cause; see RHG, p. 598, BAG, p. 234 s.v. ἐκ 3f., and N. Turner, *A Grammar of New Testament Greek* by J.H. Moulton. vol. 3. Syntax (T. & T. Clark: Edinburgh, 1963), pp. 259, 260.

4. A plea for self-examination

13:5-10

> ⁵Examine yourselves to see whether you are in the faith; test yourselves. Do you not realize that Christ Jesus is in you—unless, of course, you fail the test? ⁶And I trust that you will discover that we have not failed the test. ⁷Now we pray to God that you will not do anything wrong. Not that people will see that we have stood the test but that you will do what is right even though we may seem to have failed. ⁸For we cannot do anything against the truth, but only for the truth. ⁹We are glad whenever we are weak but you are strong; and our prayer is for your perfection. ¹⁰This is why I write these things when I am absent, that when I come I may not have to be harsh in my use of authority—the authority the Lord gave me for building you up, not for tearing you down.

5,6 Rather than demanding proof (*dokimē*) that Christ was speaking through Paul (v.3), the Corinthians ought to be examining and testing (*dokimazō*) their own selves. The repeated *heautous* ("yourselves") is in each case emphatic by position. Paul continues like this: "Don't you know yourselves [*heautous*] sufficiently well to recognize that Christ Jesus lives within each of you [cf. Rom 8:9] and that therefore you are in the faith?" Although for the sake of emphasis he adds "unless, of course, you fail the test [*adokimoi*]," he does not believe the Corinthians are counterfeit and knows that no Corinthian is likely to form such a conclusion about himself.

As v.6 implies, the Corinthians' belief in the genuineness of their faith carried with it the proof of the genuineness of Paul's apostleship and gospel, for he had become their father in Christ Jesus through the gospel (1 Cor 4:15). They themselves as men and women in Christ formed the verification of his credentials (cf. 3:2, 3). Only if they doubted their own salvation should they doubt Paul's claim to be a true "apostle of Christ Jesus" (1:1). If they did not fail the test, neither did he (v.6).

7 Again, as in 3:1; 5:12; 12:19, Paul anticipates and answers the objection that he had been commending or defending himself. His chief desire and his prayer to God were not for his vindication (though he was concerned about this, v.6) but for their avoidance of wrongdoing, both for the sake of their life in Christ and so that they would not need to see his severity (vv.2, 10). The wrong they might do would certainly include a refusal to repent of sin (12:20, 21) and to repudiate the visitors from Palestine. It would be better that the Corinthians did what they knew to be good and right, even if this were to place Paul seemingly in the wrong, than that they should do something wrong. Paul did not expect to be shown up as counterfeit (*adokimoi*), but even such a price would be worth paying if it guaranteed that the Corinthians would do good. Not dissimilar is the sentiment expressed in Romans 9:3.

8 This verse, which has the appearance of being proverbial, may in this context bear one of two meanings. (1) Paul's concern was that truth, especially the truth of the gospel (cf. 4:2; 6:7), should prevail at all costs—even if it involved his exposure as a false apostle and counterfeit Christian (vv.6, 7). He would never be able to bring himself to hinder the advance of the truth or to propagate falsehood, such as a "different gospel" (11:4), without first changing his identity as an apostle. (2) Paul did not need to exercise his apostolic authority where "truth" already existed, but was able and willing, if necessary, to act decisively to establish "truth," i.e., to restore the Corinthians to wholeness (v.9b).

9,10 Paul's sole concern was to further and consolidate the truth of the gospel (cf. 1 Cor 9:16). So he was happy whenever his converts gave evidence of robust and mature Christian character. If the Corinthians were strong in Christ, there would be no occasion for him to use his apostolic authority harshly. He would be able to come to them in the "weakness" of a "gentle spirit" (1 Cor 4:21). Such "weakness" on his part as a result of "strength" on their part would make him rejoice. In fact, his prayer was precisely for the restoration of the Corinthians to spiritual strength and wholeness (*katartisis*; cf. v.11; 1 Cor 1:10; Gal 6:1).

If 12:20, 21 expresses Paul's fears about what he would find at Corinth on his arrival, 13:10 indicates his hope in this respect. But even here a veiled warning is registered. While the Lord had not invested Paul with apostolic authority primarily for the negative work of tearing down, if destruction proved to be a necessary prelude to the positive task of construction, it would be reluctantly undertaken—and with the same authority (cf. 10:8).

Was Paul's final visit to Corinth actually an unpleasant one? Though direct evidence is lacking, we have several indications that it was not unsuccessful. First, during the visit (which lasted three months according to Acts 20:2, 3, probably in the winter of A.D. 56–57) he wrote the Epistle to the Romans. This letter seems to betray some apprehension for the future (Rom 15:30, 31) but none for the present. Second, Paul would hardly have planned to visit Rome and then do pioneer evangelism in the west (Rom 15:24, 28), if the church in the city he was writing from was in a state of disorder and disloyalty. Third, it is clear from Romans 15:26, 27 that the Corinthians heeded Paul's appeal in 2 Corinthians 8–9 and completed their collection for the saints at Jerusalem. Twice Paul notes that they "were pleased" to contribute, scarcely an appropriate description unless the church in Corinth was in harmony with the promoter of the collection. Fourth, the very preservation of 2 Corinthians (presumably at Corinth) argues in favor of the success of the visit promised in it.

D. *Conclusion*

13:11-13

11Finally, brothers, good-by. Aim for perfection, listen to my appeal, be of one mind, live in peace. And the God of love and peace will be with you.
12Greet one another with a holy kiss. All the saints send their greetings.
13May the grace of the Lord Jesus Christ, and the love of God, and the fellowship of the Holy Spirit be with you all.

11 In closing, Paul issues a final appeal couched in general terms. The Corinthian believers were to strive to achieve that perfection or restored strength for which Paul himself was praying (v.9b). They were to heed his call for a break with all idolatry (6:14-7:1), for warm hospitality to be shown the three delegates, for a generous and prompt contribution to the Jerusalem relief fund (chapters 8, 9), and for a changed attitude toward him (chapters 10-13). They were also to agree in the Lord (cf. 1 Cor 1:10; Phil 4:2) and so live in peace without divided loyalties (11:2, 3; 12:20).

If in the concluding promise Paul is stressing love and peace as characteristics of God (cf. Rom 5:8; 1 Cor 14:33), the meaning will be: "[If you] aim for perfection. . ., then [*kai*] the God of love and peace will be with you." But if love and peace are here viewed as God's gifts ("the God who imparts love and peace"), Paul is indicating the divine resources that will enable the Corinthians to follow his injunctions.

12 Evidently the early church invested the kiss, a common form of salutation in the Orient, with a special and sacred significance (cf. Rom 16:16; 1 Cor 16:20; 1 Thess 5:26; 1 Peter 5:14). It expressed union and fellowship within the one family of God, and perhaps also was a sign of mutual forgiveness and reconciliation that was exchanged before the Lord's Supper was celebrated (cf. Matt 5:23, 24; 1 Cor 16:20b, 22).

The "saints" referred to may well be the Philippians, but they could be the Thessalonians or Bereans, depending on the place where this Epistle was written (see Introduction, 5). Like the "holy kiss," this epistolary greeting was an expression of unity within the one body of Christ.

13 Paul grounds his pastoral appeal for unity of spirit and for the rejection of discord (vv.11, 12) in the theological doctrine of the Trinity. The grace of Christ banishes self-assertiveness and self-seeking, the love of God puts jealousy and anger to flight, while the fellowship created by the Spirit (see note) leaves no room for quarreling and factions (cf. 12:21).

This embryonic Trinitarian formulation is noteworthy for the unusual "economic" order of Son, Father, Spirit. It is through the grace shown by Christ (8:9) in living and dying for men that God demonstrates his love (Rom 5:8) and the Spirit creates fellowship (Eph 4:3). This order also reflects Christian experience.

Notes

11 If παρακαλεῖσθε (*parakaleisthe*) is construed as a middle (rather than a passive, "be exhorted" = "listen to my appeal," NIV), it will mean "exhort (or, comfort) one another."

13 Since the first two genitives (τοῦ κυρίου Ἰησοῦ Χριστοῦ, *tou kyriou Iēsou Christou*, and τοῦ θεοῦ, *tou theou*) are clearly subjective ("the grace shown by the Lord Jesus Christ," "the love displayed by God"), it is more likely that the third genitive (τοῦ ἁγίου πνεύματος, *tou hagiou pneumatos*) is also subjective ("the fellowship engendered by the Holy Spirit"; cf. Eph 4:3) than that it is objective ("participation in the Holy Spirit"). But in defense of the latter view, see C.K. Barrett, *in loc.*

Printed in the United States
3421